BARRON'S

PRACTICE EXERCISES
FOR THE
TOEFL® TEST

BARRON'S

PRACTICE EXERCISES FOR THE TOEFL® TEST

Third Edition

by
Pamela J. Sharpe, Ph.D.
Associate Professor of
English as a Second Language
and Bilingual Education
Northern Arizona University—Yuma

BARRON'S

All inquiries should be addressed to:
Barron's Educational Series, Inc.
250 Wireless Boulevard
Hauppauge, New York 11788

Library of Congress Catalog Card No. 94-39249

International Standard Book No. 0-8120-3398-1

Library of Congress Cataloging-in-Publication Data
Sharpe, Pamela J.
  Practice exercises for the test of English as a foreign language,
    TOEFL / by Pamela Sharpe.—3rd ed.
    p.   cm.
  Rev. ed. of: Barron's practice exercises for the test of English
    as a foreign language, TOEFL. 2nd ed. © 1989.
  ISBN 0-8120-3398-1
  1. Test of English as a Foreign Language—Study guides.
2. English language—Textbooks for foreign speakers.   3. English
language—Examinations—Study guides.   I. Sharpe, Pamela J.
Barron's practice exercises for the test of English as a
foreign language, TOEFL.   II. Title.
PE1128.S524   1995
428'.0076—dc20

94-39249
CIP

PRINTED IN UNITED STATES OF AMERICA
678 100 98765

Contents

CORRECTING

Acknowledgments

I gratefully acknowledge those who have contributed to the third edition of *Barron's Practice Exercises for the TOEFL® Test:* My students, past and present, in classes and through correspondence, for asking the thoughtful questions that inspired the book and improved this edition; Robert and Lillie Sharpe for patiently researching the updates for all the practice exercises; and Liza Burby, Project Editor at Barron's Educational Series, for skillfully managing the production of the third edition.

UNIT ONE

PLANNING AND PREVIEWING

STUDY PLAN FOR THE TOEFL

Many students do not prepare for the TOEFL. They do not even read the *Bulletin of Information* that they receive from Educational Testing Service along with their application forms. You have an advantage. You have a study plan.

Barron's TOEFL Series

There are three books in the Barron's TOEFL series to help you prepare for the Test of English as a Foreign Language. Each book has a different purpose.

Barron's Practice Exercises for the TOEFL® Test

A book for intermediate learners who need preview and practice for the TOEFL. It includes a general preview of the TOEFL examination, a preview of the most frequently tested problems, and more than 1,000 items. Separate cassette tapes are available to give you practice in listening comprehension. This is the book that you are using now.

Barron's How to Prepare for the TOEFL

A book for high intermediate and advanced learners who need review and practice for the TOEFL. It includes questions and answers about the TOEFL examination, a detailed review of each section of the examination, practice exercises, and eight model tests similar to the actual TOEFL examination. Separate cassette tapes are available to give you practice in listening comprehension. It is a book that you can use after *Barron's Practice Exercises for the TOEFL® Test* if you need more detailed preparation before taking the TOEFL.

Barron's Pass Key to the TOEFL

A pocket-sized edition of *Barron's How to Prepare for the TOEFL*. It is for high intermediate and advanced learners who need review and practice for the TOEFL and want to be able to carry a smaller book with them. It includes questions and answers about the TOEFL examination, basic tips on how to prepare for the TOEFL, and five model tests from *Barron's How to Prepare for the TOEFL*. Separate tapes are available to give you practice in listening comprehension.

More About This Book

In preparing to take the TOEFL or any other examination, it is very important to preview the test and to have an opportunity to practice before you take it.

Previewing will help you become familiar with the test directions and will help you identify the types of problems that are frequently tested. Research has proven that when people know what to expect in an examination, they achieve higher scores.

Practicing will help you improve your skills in listening and reading and will help you increase your knowledge of structure and written expression.

The purpose of this book is to provide you with both preview and practice for a carefully selected series of problems. These are the problems that are most frequently tested on English proficiency examinations like the TOEFL.

By studying this book, you should know what to expect and you should improve your skills and increase your knowledge.

Planning to Take the TOEFL

Some learners take the TOEFL after they have finished studying this book, but others prefer to continue their preparation before taking it.

Study Plan I

This plan is for intermediate learners.
• First, use this book, *Barron's Practice Exercises for the TOEFL® Test*.
• Then, use *Barron's How to Prepare for the TOEFL*.

Study Plan II

This plan is for high intermediate learners.
• Use this book, *Barron's Practice Exercises for the TOEFL® Test*.

A Ten-Week Calendar for This Book

Week One

On Monday and Thursday, listen to Chapter 3, Exercises 1, 2, and 3.
On Tuesday and Friday, study Chapter 4, Exercises 1, 2, and 3.
On Wednesday and Saturday, read Chapter 5, Exercise 1.
On Sunday, review all the exercises that you have studied during the week and refer to the Answer Key in Chapter 7 and the Explanatory Answers in Chapter 8.

Week Two

On Monday and Thursday, listen to Chapter 3, Exercises 4, 5, and 6.
On Tuesday and Friday, study Chapter 4, Exercises 4 and 5.
On Wednesday and Saturday, read Chapter 5, Exercise 2.
On Sunday, review all the exercises that you have studied during the week and refer to the Answer Key in Chapter 7 and the Explanatory Answers in Chapter 8.

Week Three

On Monday and Thursday, listen to Chapter 3, Exercises 7, 8, and 9.
On Tuesday and Friday, study Chapter 4, Exercises 6 and 7.
On Wednesday and Saturday, read Chapter 5, Exercise 3.
On Sunday, review all the exercises that you have studied during the week and refer to the Answer Key in Chapter 7 and the Explanatory Answers in Chapter 8.

Week Four

On Monday and Thursday, listen to Chapter 3, Exercises 10 and 11.
On Tuesday and Friday, study Chapter 4, Exercises 8 and 9.
On Wednesday and Saturday, read Chapter 5, Exercise 4.
On Sunday, review all the exercises that you have studied during the week and refer to the Answer Key in Chapter 7 and the Explanatory Answers in Chapter 8.

Week Five

On Monday and Thursday, listen to Chapter 3, Exercises 12 and 13.
On Tuesday and Friday, study Chapter 4, Exercises 10 and 11.
On Wednesday and Saturday, read Chapter 5, Exercise 5.
On Sunday, review all the exercises that you have studied during the week and refer to the Answer Key in Chapter 7 and the Explanatory Answers in Chapter 8.

Week Six

On Monday and Thursday, listen to Chapter 3, Exercises 14, 15, and 16.
On Tuesday and Friday, study Chapter 4, Exercises 12 and 13.
On Wednesday and Saturday, read Chapter 5, Exercise 6.
On Sunday, review all the exercises that you have studied during the week and refer to the Answer Key in Chapter 7 and the Explanatory Answers in Chapter 8.

Week Seven

On Monday and Thursday, listen to Chapter 3, Exercise 17.
On Tuesday and Friday, study Chapter 4, Exercises 14 and 15.
On Wednesday and Saturday, read Chapter 5, Exercise 7.
On Sunday, review all the exercises that you have studied during the week and refer to the Answer Key in Chapter 7 and the Explanatory Answers in Chapter 8.

Week Eight

On Monday and Thursday, listen to Chapter 3, Exercises 18, 19, and 20.
On Tuesday and Friday, study Chapter 4, Exercises 16 and 17.
On Wednesday and Saturday, read Chapter 5, Exercise 8.
On Sunday, review all the exercises that you have studied during the week and refer to the Answer Key in Chapter 7 and the Explanatory Answers in Chapter 8.

Week Nine

On Monday and Thursday, listen to Chapter 3, Exercises 21, 22, and 23.
On Tuesday and Friday, study Chapter 4, Exercise 18.
On Wednesday and Saturday, read Chapter 5, Exercise 9.
On Sunday, review all the exercises that you have studied during the week and refer to the Answer Key in Chapter 7 and the Explanatory Answers in Chapter 8.

Week Ten

On Monday and Thursday, listen to Chapter 3, Exercise 24.
On Tuesday and Friday, study Chapter 4, Exercises 19 and 20.
On Wednesday and Saturday, read Chapter 5, Exercise 10.
On Sunday, review all the exercises that you have studied during the week and refer to the Answer Key in Chapter 7 and the Explanatory Answers in Chapter 8.

Adjusting the Calendar

Ideally, you will have ten weeks to prepare for the TOEFL. But if you have a shorter time to prepare, follow the plan in the same order, adjusting the time to meet your needs.

If you have taken the TOEFL before, you already know which section or sections are difficult for you. Even if you have not taken the TOEFL, you probably know your strong and weak points. If you are weak in listening comprehension, then you should spend more time preparing for Section 1. If you are weak in structure or reading, then you should spend more time preparing for Section 2 or 3.

If you are participating in a TOEFL administration that includes the Test of Written English (TWE), you should practice by completing one or two of the TWE essay questions in Chapter 6 every week.

Suggestions for Preparation

To improve your scores most, follow three suggestions. First, concentrate on listening, structure, writing ability, and reading. Your scores will improve because when you are engaged in listening and reading, you are practicing skills that you can apply during the examination regardless of the content of the material. When you are reviewing structure, you are studying a system that is smaller and, like the skills of listening and reading, has the potential for application on the TOEFL that you take. Many of the structures that you study should appear on the examination. But when you review lists of vocabulary, even very good lists, you may study hundreds of words but not find any of them on the examination. This is so because thousands of possible words may be tested.

Second, spend time preparing every day for at least an hour instead of sitting down to review once a week for seven hours. Even though you are studying for the same amount of time, research shows that shorter sessions every day produce better results on the test.

Finally, do not try to memorize questions from this or any other book. The questions on the test that you take will be very similar to the questions in this book, but they will not be exactly the same.

What you should try to do as you use this and your other books is to learn how to apply your knowledge. Do not hurry through the Practice Exercises. While you are checking your answers with the Answer Key, think about the correct answer. Why is it correct? Is it like other questions that you have seen before? Can you explain the answer to yourself before you check the Explanatory Answer?

Suggestions for Additional Preparation

Although this book should provide you with enough preview and practice material, some of you will want to do more to prepare for the TOEFL. Some of you will want to review and test yourselves by using Barron's How to Prepare for the TOEFL, which is written at a slightly higher level than this book.

Suggestions for Success

Your attitude will influence your success on the TOEFL examination. You must develop patterns of positive thinking. To help you, memorize the following sentences and bring them to mind after each study session. Bring them to mind when you begin to have negative thoughts, also.

I know more today than I did yesterday.
I am preparing.
I will succeed.
Remember, some tension is normal and good. Accept it. Use it constructively. It will motivate you to study. But don't panic or worry. Panic will cause loss of concentration and poor performance. Avoid people who panic or worry. Don't listen to them. They will encourage negative thoughts.

You know more today than you did yesterday.
You are preparing.
You will succeed.

PREVIEW OF THE TOEFL*

Section 1:   Listening Comprehension

In this section of the test, you will have an opportunity to demonstrate your ability to understand conversations and talks in English. There are three parts to this section. Answer all the questions on the basis of what is stated or implied by the speakers you hear. Do <u>not</u> take notes or write in your test book at any time. Do not turn the pages until you are told to do so.

Part A

Directions: In Part A you will hear short conversations between two people. After each conversation, you will hear a question about the conversation. The conversations and questions will not be repeated. After you hear a question, read the four possible answers in your test book and choose the best answer. Then, on your answer sheet, find the number of the question and fill in the space that corresponds to the letter of the answer you have chosen.

Here is an example.   **Sample Answer***
  On the recording, you will hear:
    (woman)   *I don't like this painting very much.*   ● Ⓑ Ⓒ Ⓓ
    (man)   *Neither do I.*
    (narrator)   *What does the name mean?*
  In your test book, you will read:

      (A) He doesn't like the painting either.
      (B) He doesn't know how to paint.
      (C) He doesn't have any paintings.
      (D) He doesn't know what to do.

You learn from the conversation that neither the man nor the woman likes the painting. The best answer to the question, "What does the man mean?" (A) "He doesn't like the painting either." Therefore, the correct choice is (A).

Part B

Directions: In this part of the test you will hear longer conversations. After each conversation you will hear several questions. The conversations and questions will not be repeated.

After you hear a question, read the four possible answers in your test book and choose the best answer. Then, on your answer sheet, find the number of the question and fill in the space that corresponds to the letter of the answer you have chosen.

Here is an example.
  On the recording, you will hear:
    (narrator)   *Questions 1 and 2. Listen to the conversation in a college bookstore.*
    (man)   *Excuse me. You can't take your books inside the bookstore. You have to leave them here in one of the lockers.*
    (woman)   *But I want to sell these books back. They are from last semester.*
    (man)   *Oh. Let me put a sticker on them then.*
    (woman)   *Thanks. And where do I take them for resale?*
    (man)   *See that sign? The one above the window at the back of the store? Right there! The one that says "Used Books." Just take them back there and give them to the manager.*

                                               Sample Answer
  You will hear: Ⓐ Ⓑ ● Ⓓ
    (narrator)   *Why did the man start a conversation with the woman?*
  In your test book, you will read:

      (A) To give her directions to the bookstore.
      (B) To help her open her locker.
      (C) To warn her not to take books into the bookstore.
      (D) To buy her book from last semester.

*Answers for the examples have been printed only in the horizontal format.

You learn from the conversation that the man will not let the woman take her books inside the bookstore. The best answer to the question, "Why did the man start a conversation with the woman?" is (C) "To warn her not to take books into the bookstore." Therefore, the correct choice is (C).

Here is another example.
You will hear:

Sample Answer
Ⓐ Ⓑ ● Ⓓ

(narrator) *What will the woman probably do next?*
In your test book, you will read:

      (A) Put her books in a locker.
      (B) Buy some used books for this semester.
      (C) Go to the window at the back of the store.
      (D) Put a sticker on the man's books.

The best answer to the question, "What will the woman probably do next?" is (C). "Go to the window at the back of the store." Therefore, the correct choice is (C).

Part C

Directions: In this part of the test you will hear several talks. After each talk, you will hear some questions. The talks and questions will not be repeated.

After you hear a question, read the four possible answers in your test book and choose the best answer. Then, on your answer sheet, find the number of the question and fill in the space that corresponds to the letter of the answer you have chosen.

Here is an example.
On the recording, you will hear:

(narrator) *Listen to an instructor talk to his class about a television program.*
   (man) *I'd like to tell you about an interesting TV program that'll be shown this coming Thursday. It'll be on from 9 to 10 pm on Channel 4. It's part of a series called "Mysteries of Human Biology." The subject of the program is the human brain—how it functions and how it can malfunction. Topics that will be covered are dreams, memory, and depression. These topics are illustrated with outstanding computer animation that makes the explanations easy to follow. Make an effort to see this show. Since we've been studying the nervous system in class, I know you'll find it very helpful.*

Sample Answer.
Ⓐ Ⓑ ● Ⓓ

You will hear:
   (narrator) *What is the main purpose of the program?*
In your test book, you will read:

      (A) To demonstrate the latest use of computer graphics
      (B) To discuss the possibility of an economic depression.
      (C) To explain the workings of the brain.
      (D) To dramatize a famous mystery story.

The best answer to the question, "What is the main purpose of the program?" is (C), "To explain the workings of the brain." Therefore, the correct choice is (C).

Here is another example.
You will hear:

Sample Answer
Ⓐ Ⓑ Ⓒ ●

(narrator) *Why does the speaker recommend watching the program?*
In your test book, you will read:

      (A) It is required of all science majors.
      (B) I will never be shown again.
      (C) It can help viewers improve their memory skills.
      (D) It will help with course work.

The best answer to the question, "Why does the speaker recommend watching the program?" is (D), "It will help with course work." Therefore, the correct choice is (D).

Remember, you are *not* allowed to take notes or write in your test book.

Section 2:   Structure and Written Expression

This section is designed to measure your ability to recognize language that is appropriate for standard written English. There are two types of questions in this section, with special directions for each type.

Structure

Directions: Questions 1–15 are incomplete sentences. Beneath each sentence you will see four words or phrases, marked (A), (B), (C), and (D). Choose the <u>one</u> word or phrase that best completes the sentence. Then, on your answer sheet, find the number of the question and fill in the space that corresponds to the letter of the answer you have chosen. Fill in the space so that the letter inside the oval cannot be seen.

Example I

Geysers have often been compared to volcanoes_____they both emit hot liquids from below the earth's surface.

Sample Answer

Ⓐ ● Ⓒ Ⓓ

        (A) due to
        (B) because
        (C) in spite of
        (D) regardless of

The sentence should read, "Geysers have often been compared to volcanoes because they both emit hot liquids from below the Earth's surface." Therefore, you should choose answer (B).

Example II

During the early period of ocean navigation,_____any need for sophisticated instruments and techniques.

Sample Answer

Ⓐ Ⓑ Ⓒ ●

        (A) so that hardly
        (B) where there hardly was
        (C) hardly was
        (D) there was hardly

The sentence should read, "During the early period of ocean navigation, there was hardly any need for sophisticated instruments and techniques." Therefore, you should choose answer (D).

Written Expression

Directions: In questions 1–25, each sentence has four underlined words or phrases. The four underlined parts of the sentence are marked (A), (B), (C), and (D). Identify the <u>one</u> underlined word or phrase that must be changed in order for the sentence to be correct. Then, on your answer sheet, find the number of the question and fill in the space that corresponds to the letter of the answer you have chosen.

Look at the following examples.

Example I

Sample Answer

● Ⓑ Ⓒ Ⓓ

Guppies are sometimes <u>call</u> rainbow <u>fish</u> <u>because</u> of the males' <u>bright</u> colors.
               (A)   (B) (C)   (D)

The sentence should read, "Guppies are sometimes called rainbow fish because of the males' bright colors." Therefore, you should choose answer (A).

Example II

Serving several term in Congress, Shirley Chisholm became an important United States politician.
  (A)   (B)   (C)   (D)

The sentence should read, "Serving several terms in Congress, Shirley Chisholm became an important United States politician." Therefore, you should choose answer (B).

Section 3: Reading Comprehension

This section is designed to measure your ability to read and understand short passages similar in topic and style to those that students are likely to encounter in North American universities and colleges. This section contains reading passages and questions about the passages.

Written Expression

Directions: In the Reading Comprehension section you will read several passages. Each one is followed by a number of questions about it. You are to choose the one best answer, (A), (B), (C), or (D), to each question. Then, on your answer sheet, find the number of the question and fill in the space that corresponds to the letter of the answer you have chosen.

Answer all questions about the information in a passage on the basis of what is stated or implied in the passage.

Here is an example.

        Read the following passage:

          The railroad was not the first institution to impose regularity on society, or to draw attention to the importance of precise timekeeping. For as long as merchants have set out their wares at daybreak and communal festivities have been celebrated, people have been in rough agreement
Line with their neighbors as to the time of day. The value of this tradition is today more apparent
(5) than ever. Were it not for public acceptance of a single yardstick of time, social life would be unbearably chaotic: the massive daily transfers of goods, services, and information would proceed in fits and starts; the very fabric of modern society would begin to unravel.

Example I

What is the main idea of the passage?

    (A) In modern society we must make more time for our neighbors.
    (B) The traditions of society are timeless.
    (C) An accepted way of measuring time is essential for the smooth functioning of society.
    (D) Society judges people by the times at which they conduct certain activities.

The main idea of the passage is that societies need to agree about how time is measured in order to function smoothly. Therefore, you should choose answer (C).

Example II

In line 4, the phrase "this tradition" refers to

    (A) the practice of starting the business day at dawn
    (B) friendly relations between neighbors
    (C) the railroad's reliance on time schedules
    (D) people's agreement on the measurement of time

The phrase "this tradition" refers to the preceding clause, "people have been in rough agreement with their neighbors as to the time of day." Therefore, you should choose answer (D).

UNIT TWO

PRACTICING

LISTENING COMPREHENSION

In this chapter, you will have an opportunity to practice your ability to understand spoken English. There are three different types of Practice Exercises, with special directions for each type. *Note:* Practice Exercises 1 to 24 are available on cassette tapes. To order these cassettes, use the order form on page 353. *Note also:* The Transcript for *all* the Listening Comprehension Practice Exercises can be found on page 305.

Listening Comprehension

Part A—Short Conversations

Directions: In Part A you will hear short conversations between two people. After each conversation, you will hear a question about the conversation. The conversations and questions will not be repeated. After you hear a question, read the four possible answers in your test book and choose the best answer. Then, on your answer sheet, find the number of the question and fill in the space that corresponds to the letter of the answer you have chosen.

EXERCISE 1:   Remembering Details From Direct Information

In some short conversations in Part A of the Listening Comprehension Section, you will be asked to remember details that are directly stated.

1. (A) He is tired.
   (B) He is drunk.
   (C) He is thirsty.
   (D) He is busy.

2. (A) She wants to pay by check.
   (B) She prefers to use a credit card.
   (C) She has cash.
   (D) She will need a loan.

3. (A) He was too short.
   (B) She didn't know him very well.
   (C) The expensive gift made her uncomfortable.
   (D) The man never gave her gifts.

4. (A) He thought she was a thief.
   (B) He wanted to secure it for her.
   (C) His job was to check everyone's belongings.
   (D) He was looking for a standard size.

5. (A) Study with her.
   (B) Help her on the test.
   (C) Take a break.
   (D) Lend her his notebook.

6. (A) Steve's girlfriend.
   (B) Steve's sister.
   (C) Steve.
   (D) Mary Anne.

7. (A) The door is locked.
   (B) The woman doesn't have the right key.
   (C) The door is stuck.
   (D) The doorknob is broken.

8. (A) Check the calculators.
   (B) Use a calculator to do his test.
   (C) Purchase a calculator.
   (D) Borrow a calculator.

9. (A) She thinks the man should pay the bills.
   (B) She thinks the man should ask his family for help.
   (C) She thinks the man should contact his roommate's family for money.
   (D) She thinks the man should leave.

10. (A) By filling out forms.
    (B) By filing his taxes.
    (C) By advising him about student loans.
    (D) By completing his application.

EXERCISE 2:   Selecting From Similar Alternatives

In some short conversations in Part A of the Listening Comprehension Section, you will be asked to select the correct detail from among several similar alternatives, all of which have been mentioned in different contexts in the conversation.

1. (A) They are brothers.
   (B) They are good friends.
   (C) They are cousins.
   (D) They are classmates.

2. (A) That the man live with Frank and Geoff.
   (B) That the man ask Geoff to be his roommate.
   (C) That the man and Steve be roommates.
   (D) That the man share a room with Frank.

3. (A) She earned an *A*.
   (B) She received a *B*.
   (C) Her grade was *C*.
   (D) She got a *D* or *F*.

4. (A) To buy the computer at a discount store.
   (B) To put an ad in the newspaper for a computer.
   (C) To go to a computer store to buy the computer.
   (D) To buy the computer at the university as part of a special offer.

5. (A) She didn't pay her fees.
   (B) She didn't register for the class.
   (C) She didn't attend the class.
   (D) She didn't have her name on the roster.

6. (A) The man will probably bring her a size 5½.
   (B) He will probably bring her a size 6.
   (C) He will probably bring her a size 7.
   (D) He will probably bring her a size 7½.

7. (A) That the woman needs new glasses.
   (B) That the woman has high blood pressure.
   (C) That the woman has very serious headaches.
   (D) That the woman is suffering from stress.

8. (A) She must begin writing a paper for her history class.
   (B) She must start writing up her laboratory assignments for her chemistry class.
   (C) She must begin studying for her English examination.
   (D) She must begin studying for her French examination.

9. (A) In New York.
   (B) In Boston.
   (C) In Michigan.
   (D) In Washington.

10. (A) First gear.
    (B) Second gear.
    (C) Reverse.
    (D) Drive.

EXERCISE 3: Understanding Changes of Opinion

In some short conversations in Part A of the Listening Comprehension Section, you will be asked to identify the speaker's final choice or decision after a change of opinion.

1. (A) She will get a ride with the man.
   (B) She will ride the airport shuttle.
   (C) She will drive her car.
   (D) She will rent a car.

2. (A) She would like eggs and potatoes.
   (B) She wants eggs and pancakes.
   (C) She wants to eat potato pancakes.
   (D) Pancakes is what she would like to eat.

3. (A) The man bought one box of cookies.
   (B) The man ordered four boxes of cookies.
   (C) He purchased five boxes of cookies.
   (D) He did not order any cookies this year.

4. (A) The number is 6-9-1.
   (B) The area code is 1-9-6.
   (C) 9-1-6 is the area code.
   (D) 6-1-9 is the correct number.

5. (A) She will pay five cents per page.
   (B) The price is ten cents a copy.
   (C) She owes fifteen cents per copy.
   (D) Twenty cents per page is the price.

6. (A) One dollar a minute.
   (B) One dollar a page.
   (C) Two dollars and fifty cents a minute.
   (D) Two dollars and fifty cents a page.

7. (A) See a documentary.
   (B) Change the channel.
   (C) Watch television.
   (D) Go to a movie.

8. (A) He wants all twenty-dollar bills.
   (B) He wants all fifty-dollar bills.
   (C) He wants all large bills.
   (D) He wants some twenty- and some fifty-dollar bills.

9. (A) The Country Kitchen.
   (B) The Country Home.
   (C) The Old House.
   (D) The Old Kitchen.

10. (A) He will be home at six o'clock.
    (B) He will not be home late.
    (C) He will be home a little after seven o'clock.
    (D) He will be home earlier than usual.

EXERCISE 4:   Recognizing the Meaning of Idioms

In some short conversations in Part A of the Listening Comprehension Section, you will be asked to paraphrase idiomatic expressions.

1. (A) She does not think that the man is serious.
    (B) She thinks that the man is going to take her to Florida.
    (C) She thinks that the man has a good idea.
    (D) She thinks that the man does not have any money.

2. (A) That she needs one more semester.
    (B) That she needs a hundred dollars.
    (C) That the increase will be difficult for her.
    (D) That the paper is not dependable.

3. (A) He has left the lecture.
    (B) He has used his last piece of paper.
    (C) He has said goodbye to the woman.
    (D) He has finished giving the lecture.

4. (A) He feels that the test was fair.
    (B) He agrees with the woman about the test.
    (C) He does not want the woman to tease him about the test.
    (D) He is not worried about the test.

5. (A) That the man does not pay attention.
    (B) That the man is very honest.
    (C) That the man has gone away.
    (D) That the man needs to repeat.

6. (A) That the sign has Mickey Mouse on it.
    (B) That they do not believe the sign.
    (C) That the course is very easy.
    (D) That they did not register for the course.

7. (A) She does not want the man to come for her.
    (B) She thinks that the man is a bother.
    (C) She does not want to go to class.
    (D) She accepts the man's offer.

8. (A) The man likes ice cream.
    (B) The man will tell the woman later whether he wants ice cream.
    (C) The man does not want to say whether he likes ice cream.
    (D) The man will get some ice cream for the woman.

9. (A) That she is glad Joan is moving.
    (B) That she does not believe that Joan will move.
    (C) That she saw Joan move.
    (D) That she believes Joan is moving because she saw her.

10. (A) He is angry with the woman.
    (B) He wants to talk with the woman.
    (C) It was a bad day for the man.
    (D) He does not know what day it is.

EXERCISE 5:   Solving Computations in Conversations

In some short conversations in Part A of the Listening Comprehension Section, you will be asked to perform simple mathematical computations like adding, subtracting, multiplying, or dividing. In other conversations, you will only need to listen for the answer.

1. (A) The man's mileage is half that of the woman.
    (B) The woman's mileage is the same as that of the man.
    (C) The woman's mileage is twice that of the man.
    (D) The man's mileage is twice that of the woman.

2. (A) At 10:00.
    (B) At 9:00.
    (C) At 9:15.
    (D) At 9:30.

3. (A) The man will pay ten dollars.
    (B) The man will pay twenty dollars.
    (C) The man will pay thirty dollars.
    (D) The man will pay forty dollars.

4. (A) Twenty dollars.
    (B) Twenty-five dollars.
    (C) Forty dollars.
    (D) Fifty dollars.

5. (A) He will pay $65.
    (B) He will pay $10.00.
    (C) He will pay $9.55.
    (D) He will not pay for the call.

6. (A) He did not have time to talk to the woman.
    (B) He was not wearing his watch.
    (C) It is exactly 1:15.
    (D) It is a little before 1:15.

7. (A) He may write a check for ten dollars.
    (B) He may not pay by check.
    (C) He may write a check for the amount of purchase.
    (D) He may write a check for twenty-five dollars.

8. (A) $5.45.
    (B) $1.00.
    (C) $ .95.
    (D) $2.05.

9. (A) They cost $13.
    (B) They cost $3.15.
    (C) They cost $18.
    (D) They cost $8.

10. (A) At nine o'clock.
    (B) At eleven o'clock.
    (C) At twelve o'clock.
    (D) At four o'clock.

EXERCISE 6: Drawing Conclusions About the Place

In some short conversations in Part A of the Listening Comprehension Section, you will be asked to draw conclusions about where the conversation is taking place. Words and phrases in the conversation will provide information for your conclusions.

1. (A) In a bakery.
    (B) In a restaurant.
    (C) In a bank.
    (D) On a farm.

2. (A) In a dentist's office.
    (B) In a drugstore.
    (C) In a dress shop.
    (D) In a restaurant.

3. (A) At a wedding.
    (B) On a honeymoon.
    (C) In Florida.
    (D) At an airport.

4. (A) In a laundry.
    (B) In an elevator.
    (C) In a library.
    (D) In a bakery.

5. (A) At a hospital.
    (B) At a political convention.
    (C) At a graduation.
    (D) At a funeral.

6. (A) In a bakery.
    (B) In a taxi.
    (C) In France.
    (D) In a post office.

7. (A) At a church.
    (B) At a library.
    (C) In England.
    (D) At a theater.

8. (A) In a doctor's office.
    (B) In a professor's office.
    (C) In a lawyer's office.
    (D) In a businessman's office.

9. (A) At a bookstore.
    (B) At a bank.
    (C) At a club.
    (D) At a grocery store.

10. (A) On an Indian reservation.
    (B) At a party.
    (C) At a restaurant.
    (D) On the telephone.

EXERCISE 7:   Drawing Conclusions About Feelings and Emotions

In some short conversations in Part A of the Listening Comprehension Section, you will be asked to draw conclusions about the feelings or emotions expressed by the speakers. Words and phrases as well as the tone of voice of speakers in the conversation will provide information for your conclusions.

1. (A) He is worried.
   (B) He is happy.
   (C) He feels confident.
   (D) He feels tired.

2. (A) He thought it was a very unrealistic movie.
   (B) He was impressed with the movie.
   (C) He agreed with the woman about the movie.
   (D) He liked the movie because it was a fairy tale.

3. (A) She does not know whether she did well.
   (B) She thinks that she improved her score.
   (C) She believes that she scored about 490.
   (D) She is concerned about the reading comprehension section.

4. (A) She believes that he is having a bad day.
   (B) She does not like the man.
   (C) She thinks that he never pays attention.
   (D) She likes to help the man every day.

5. (A) He forgot who he was.
   (B) He thinks that Rick and Lucy will forget to come.
   (C) He likes Rick, but not Lucy.
   (D) He does not want to invite them.

6. (A) He is surprised.
   (B) He is confused.
   (C) He does not agree.
   (D) He does not want to know.

7. (A) He does not care.
   (B) He does not like the lab assistant.
   (C) He does not like the grading system.
   (D) He does not agree with the woman.

8. (A) He feels protective of Terry.
   (B) The man is supportive.
   (C) He has his doubts about Terry.
   (D) He feels hostile toward Terry.

9. (A) He wants to go, but he won't.
   (B) He does not want to go, but he will.
   (C) He wants to go, and he will.
   (D) He does not want to go, and he won't.

10. (A) He thinks Janine would be difficult to live with.
    (B) He thinks Janine and the woman will like living together.
    (C) He thinks it would be better to live with Janine than with Carol.
    (D) He thinks that Janine and Carol should live together.

EXERCISE 8:   Making Predictions About the Future

In some short conversations in Part A of the Listening Comprehension Section, you will be asked to make predictions about the future activities of the speakers. Your prediction should be based on evidence in the conversation from which you can draw a logical conclusion.

1. (A) He will probably leave.
    (B) He will probably order the size orange juice they have.
    (C) He will probably not have any orange juice.
    (D) He will probably have orange juice instead of hot tea.

2. (A) Go to the kitchen to study.
    (B) Go to her chemistry class.
    (C) Go to the library to look for her book.
    (D) Go to the table to eat.

3. (A) Call London about the charges.
    (B) Accept the charges for the call.
    (C) Refuse the call from London.
    (D) Charge the call to someone in London.

4. (A) Ask the woman to make a copy for him.
    (B) Go across the street to make a copy.
    (C) Ask the woman for directions to the building.
    (D) Take his copies to the other building.

5. (A) Join the club.
    (B) Pay five dollars for a video.
    (C) Rent ten videos.
    (D) Go to the video store.

6. (A) Get directions.
    (B) Make a call.
    (C) Make a reservation.
    (D) Talk to the woman.

7. (A) Walk to the mall.
    (B) Get on the bus.
    (C) Cross the street to wait for the bus.
    (D) Take a taxi to the mall.

8. (A) Leave at once.
    (B) Call the highway patrol.
    (C) Go home with the man.
    (D) Drive carefully.

9. (A) Take the delivery to the university.
    (B) Refuse to make the delivery to the woman.
    (C) Make the delivery to the woman if she is close to the university.
    (D) Deliver to a main location three miles from the university where the woman can pick it up.

10. (A) Wait twenty minutes to be seated.
    (B) Wait five minutes to be seated.
    (C) Go right in to be seated.
    (D) Smoke while he waits to be seated.

EXERCISE 9:   Drawing Conclusions From Implied Information

In some short conversations in Part A of the Listening Comprehension Section, you will be asked to draw general conclusions about the speakers or the situation. Words and phrases and the tone of voice of speakers in the conversation will provide information for your conclusions.

1. (A) That he will not use the book.
   (B) That he will use the book in the library for two hours.
   (C) That he will check the book out before closing.
   (D) That he will reserve the book.

2. (A) That the woman cannot get a soda.
   (B) That he will go downstairs to get the woman a soda.
   (C) That the woman should go downstairs to get a soda.
   (D) That he does not know where to get a soda.

3. (A) She thought she had applied to the right school.
   (B) She attends an American university now.
   (C) She does not have to take the TOEFL.
   (D) She graduated from an American high school.

4. (A) That the woman was in line for a long time.
   (B) That the man was in line longer than the woman.
   (C) That the man registered quickly.
   (D) That the woman did not register.

5. (A) He prefers staying at home because he doesn't like to travel.
   (B) He prefers taking a plane because the bus is too slow.
   (C) He prefers taking a bus because the plane makes him nervous.
   (D) He prefers traveling with the woman.

6. (A) She will probably pay twenty-six dollars for the gloves.
   (B) She will probably buy the leather gloves.
   (C) She will probably buy both pairs of gloves.
   (D) She will probably buy the vinyl gloves.

7. (A) That Sally is serious about Bob.
   (B) That Bob is serious about Sally.
   (C) That Sally is not serious about Bob.
   (D) That Bob is not serious about Sally.

8. (A) Weights and measurements.
   (B) Political systems.
   (C) Employment.
   (D) Money.

9. (A) That she will go away.
   (B) That she will be sorry.
   (C) That she will not quit her job.
   (D) That she will not buy him a present.

10. (A) That she does not like plays.
    (B) That she went to see the play with the man and woman.
    (C) That she had not planned to attend the play.
    (D) That she was not at the play.

CUMULATIVE REVIEW FOR LISTENING COMPREHENSION
Part A—Short Conversations

EXERCISE 10: Part 1

In each problem in Part A of the Listening Comprehension Section, you will be asked to respond to a question about a short conversation. These cumulative exercises include a variety of short conversations.

1. (A) She wants to be a mathematician.
   (B) She wants to be an engineer.
   (C) She wants to teach in a college.
   (D) She wants to go into business.

2. (A) Twelve hundred dollars.
   (B) Eleven hundred dollars.
   (C) Fifteen hundred dollars.
   (D) Sixteen hundred dollars.

3. (A) Seven o'clock.
   (B) Seven-fifteen.
   (C) Seven-thirty.
   (D) Seven-fifty.

4. (A) Because he wanted to make an appointment with someone in the chemistry department.
   (B) Because the psychology department and the chemistry department have the same number.
   (C) Because he did not know the number of the psychology department.
   (D) Because the number he was trying to call was similar to that of the psychology department.

5. (A) One o'clock this afternoon.
   (B) One-forty-five this afternoon.
   (C) In twenty minutes.
   (D) In thirty minutes.

6. (A) A few minutes before two o'clock.
   (B) Exactly closing time.
   (C) A few minutes after two o'clock.
   (D) Two minutes after closing time.

7. (A) At a grocery store.
   (B) At a restaurant.
   (C) At a fast-food drive-through.
   (D) At a cafeteria.

8. (A) That the man does not know the woman.
   (B) That the woman wants to meet the man.
   (C) That the woman is late.
   (D) That the woman is not a student.

9. (A) Leave a message on her answering machine after nine o'clock.
   (B) Call her at home before nine o'clock.
   (C) Call Jack back at nine o'clock.
   (D) Call 674-9521 before nine o'clock.

10. (A) That they go to the cafeteria to eat.
    (B) That the man go home to get his lunch.
    (C) That they go to her house for lunch.
    (D) That they skip lunch.

EXERCISE 11: Part 2

1. (A) At the bookstore.
   (B) At a Christmas store.
   (C) At a pizza place.
   (D) At a dormitory.

2. (A) August 25.
   (B) August 20.
   (C) August 15.
   (D) August 5.

3. (A) Hawaii.
   (B) Los Angeles.
   (C) St. Louis.
   (D) Atlanta.

4. (A) That she is a dean.
   (B) That she works in the dean's office.
   (C) That she is a good student.
   (D) That she was not in school last semester.

5. (A) At a photographer's studio.
   (B) In a classroom.
   (C) At an optometrist's office.
   (D) At the Bureau of Motor Vehicles.

6. (A) On Circle Drive.
   (B) Just inside the entrance to the university.
   (C) At the first stop light.
   (D) One block away.

7. (A) She wants to find the college.
   (B) She wants to locate a bank close to campus.
   (C) She wants to apply for a grant at the college.
   (D) She wants to get to First Street.

8. (A) He does not drink.
   (B) He is not pleased.
   (C) He does not want to cause more work for the woman.
   (D) He does not want the woman to bother him.

9. (A) She likes him better than she likes Randy.
   (B) She does not know him.
   (C) She is not interested in him.
   (D) She does not know where he is.

10. (A) That the man was not going with them.
    (B) That the man had changed his mind.
    (C) That the trip had been canceled.
    (D) That the man was going to meet them after they returned.

Listening Comprehension

Part B—Extended Conversations

Directions: In this part of the test, you will hear longer conversations. After each conversation, you will be asked several questions. The conversations and questions will not be repeated.

After you hear a question, read the four possible answers in your test book and choose the best answer. Then, on your answer sheet, find the number of the question and fill in the space that corresponds to the letter of the answer you have chosen.

EXERCISE 12: Understanding and Interpreting Conversations Between Friends

In some extended conversations in Part B of the Listening Comprehension Section, you will be asked to recall information exchanged in conversations on different topics among friends in a variety of settings.

Conversation One

1. (A) The man's graduation.
   (B) The couple's engagement.
   (C) The man's smoking.
   (D) The man's stress.

2. (A) That the man rethink their plans.
   (B) That the man see a family doctor.
   (C) That the man see a psychiatrist.
   (D) That the man concentrate on his studies.

3. (A) Patient.
   (B) Surprised.
   (C) Worried.
   (D) Irritated.

4. (A) That she has stopped smoking.
   (B) That she does not want to get married.
   (C) That she has asked the man to quit smoking many times.
   (D) That she is not in love with the man.

Conversation Two

1. (A) The use of photographs in painting.
   (B) The TV program about Norman Rockwell.
   (C) *The Saturday Evening Post* magazine.
   (D) Exhibits of art on magazine covers.

2. (A) He imagined them.
   (B) He used magazine covers.
   (C) He hired models.
   (D) He read stories.

3. (A) He was a prolific painter.
   (B) He was an eccentric person.
   (C) He was an avid reader.
   (D) He was a good teacher.

4. (A) They will probably go to the exhibit.
   (B) They will probably see the special on television.
   (C) They will probably turn off the TV.
   (D) They will probably go to Miami.

Conversation Three

1. (A) The man is learning how to use a computer.
   (B) The woman is showing the man how to put page numbers on a document.
   (C) The man is printing a document.
   (D) The man is using his computer to do mathematical functions.

2. (A) He needs to press F-7 to return to the document before he prints it.
   (B) He has to print the document to see the page numbers.
   (C) The printer is not working correctly.
   (D) The numbers are on the screen but they don't print out.

3. (A) She wants the man to listen to the instructions and observe.
   (B) She wants the man to watch while she performs the operations.
   (C) She wants the man to ask questions so that she can help him.
   (D) She wants the man to try to do it while she gives him instructions.

4. (A) She is the man's girlfriend.
   (B) She works in a computer lab.
   (C) She does not want to help the man.
   (D) She does not know what to do.

Conversation Four

1. (A) Bill got hungry.
   (B) John noticed the time.
   (C) John had an exam.
   (D) John decided to go home.

2. (A) Because he has a test that night.
   (B) Because he plans to go home for the weekend.
   (C) Because he has not studied at all during the semester.
   (D) Because he is helping his friend.

3. (A) At six o'clock.
   (B) At six-thirty.
   (C) Over the weekend.
   (D) On Monday.

4. (A) Bill wants John to study with him.
   (B) Bill wants John to go home with him for the weekend.
   (C) Bill wants John to let him know if he orders a pizza.
   (D) Bill wants John to find out what is being served in the cafeteria.

EXERCISE 13: Understanding and Interpreting Conversations With Service Personnel

In some extended conversations in Part B of the Listening Comprehension Section, you will be asked to recall information exchanged in conversations with service personnel from stores, restaurants, airports, and other settings where services are performed.

Conversation One

1. (A) The man wants to obtain an international driver's license that he can use both in the U.S. and in his country.
    (B) The man wants to take a driver's test to get an Arizona driver's license.
    (C) The man wants to know whether he can use his international driver's license in Arizona.
    (D) The man wants to fill out an application for an Arizona driver's license.

2. (A) Show his student ID and pay ten dollars.
    (B) Use his international driver's license.
    (C) Take a driver's test and apply for a limited license.
    (D) Show proof of temporary residence.

3. (A) Less than one year.
    (B) Four years.
    (C) Five years.
    (D) Ten years.

4. (A) Fill out an application.
    (B) Go back to the university to get his ID.
    (C) Go to see his friend.
    (D) Take a written exam and an eye exam.

Conversation Two

1. (A) The man wants to place a classified ad in the newspaper.
    (B) The woman wants to find an apartment.
    (C) The man wants to pay for a newspaper subscription.
    (D) The woman wants to fill out an application for employment.

2. (A) Furniture.
    (B) Books.
    (C) Garden supplies.
    (D) An apartment.

3. (A) He will pay by check.
    (B) He will have the amount billed to his home address.
    (C) He will give the woman cash.
    (D) He will come back to pay when he is billed.

4. (A) To make it clearer to understand.
    (B) To make it longer to read.
    (C) To make it cheaper to print.
    (D) To make it easier to use.

Conversation Three

1. (A) To help the woman make a purchase.
   (B) To request the woman's identification.
   (C) To show the woman how to make out a check.
   (D) To register the woman for a course at City College.

2. (A) Money.
   (B) Money or credit cards.
   (C) Credit cards or checks.
   (D) Checks or money.

3. (A) She used her student ID card and a charge card.
   (B) She used her credit card.
   (C) She used her driver's license and her student ID card.
   (D) She used her telephone number and her student ID card.

4. (A) A clerk.
   (B) The woman's husband.
   (C) A police officer.
   (D) A bank teller.

Conversation Four

1. (A) In Pittsburgh.
   (B) At two o'clock.
   (C) At the bus station.
   (D) Because the woman needed a ticket.

2. (A) At 2:15 P.M.
   (B) At 11:00 A.M.
   (C) At 2:00 P.M.
   (D) At 1:45 P.M.

3. (A) One.
   (B) Two.
   (C) Three.
   (D) Four.

4. (A) That she has taken this trip before.
   (B) That she does not like to travel.
   (C) That she is traveling with a friend.
   (D) That she will take the bus again this month.

EXERCISE 14: Understanding and Interpreting Conversations With University Personnel

In some extended conversations in Part B of the Listening Comprehension Section, you will be asked to recall information exchanged in conversations with personnel in offices on a university campus.

Conversation One

1. (A) A sick friend.
   (B) A math class.
   (C) School policy.
   (D) The man's test.

2. (A) Because it is against the law.
   (B) Because the man is not a member of Terry's family.
   (C) Because the woman cannot find the test.
   (D) Because Terry was too sick to take the test.

3. (A) Young.
   (B) Purcell.
   (C) Raleigh.
   (D) Kelly.

4. (A) Call his friend.
   (B) Go to the office to get his test.
   (C) Send the woman a letter.
   (D) Take the test later.

Conversation Two

1. (A) A notice on the bulletin board.
   (B) A book for a class the man is taking.
   (C) A chemistry class that is being taught.
   (D) The library reserve desk.

2. (A) He is starting the course late.
   (B) The subject is difficult for him.
   (C) The professor is very reserved.
   (D) The book is difficult to read.

3. (A) Check out a chemistry book.
   (B) Make copies of all the pages in the book.
   (C) Put a notice on the bulletin board.
   (D) Look for a copy of the book on the reserve shelf.

4. (A) In the library.
   (B) In a bookstore.
   (C) In a clothing store.
   (D) In a dormitory.

Conversation Three

1. (A) The man wants to get authorization for a
        room change.
    (B) The man is worried about his friendship
        with his roommate.
    (C) The man needs a scholarship to continue
        living in the dormitory.
    (D) The man wants the head resident to talk to
        David for him.

2. (A) That David is not a serious student.
    (B) That David doesn't need to worry because
        he has a scholarship.
    (C) That David won't speak with him.
    (D) That David wants to move back to his
        home town.

3. (A) His roommate is noisy.
    (B) He isn't speaking to his roommate.
    (C) He does not like his roommate.
    (D) He doesn't know his roommate very well.

4. (A) Return on Monday.
    (B) Go home for a week.
    (C) Try to talk to David.
    (D) Speak with the head resident.

Conversation Four

1. (A) The work-study program.
    (B) Financial aid for international students.
    (C) The Williams Memorial Scholarship.
    (D) Part-time employment for foreigners on a
        student visa.

2. (A) The man.
    (B) The man's friend.
    (C) The woman.
    (D) The woman's friend.

3. (A) Because there is very little competition.
    (B) Because the student's grades are very high.
    (C) Because the scholarship is open to students
        from every country.
    (D) Because the student is from Chicago.

4. (A) Librarian.
    (B) Financial aid officer.
    (C) Engineer.
    (D) Secretary.

EXERCISE 15: Understanding and Interpreting Conversations With University Professors

In some extended conversations in Part B of the Listening Comprehension Section, you will be asked to recall information exchanged in conversations with university professors in their offices or classrooms.

Conversation One

1. (A) The man's last appointment.
   (B) Professor Irwin's office hours.
   (C) Student advisement during registration.
   (D) The man's health problems.

2. (A) Tuesday at two o'clock.
   (B) Thursday at two o'clock.
   (C) This afternoon at three o'clock.
   (D) Now.

3. (A) He should have made an appointment.
   (B) He should have called to cancel his appointment.
   (C) He should have come for his appointment.
   (D) He should have stayed at home until he was well.

4. (A) Uninterested.
   (B) Apologetic.
   (C) Sick.
   (D) Annoyed.

Conversation Two

1. (A) To take her final exam.
   (B) To apologize to the professor.
   (C) To change the date of her exam.
   (D) To schedule her flight.

2. (A) She is taking too many classes.
   (B) She lives too far from her family.
   (C) She made an error when she scheduled her trip.
   (D) She did not do well on her final exam.

3. (A) To allow the woman to repeat the exam.
   (B) To reschedule the woman's exam for another day.
   (C) To let the woman skip the final exam.
   (D) To give the woman a grade of incomplete.

4. (A) In March.
   (B) In May.
   (C) In November.
   (D) In December.

Conversation Three

1. (A) The woman's performance in her classes.
   (B) The woman's nomination for an award.
   (C) The professor's offer to help prepare the woman for an interview.
   (D) The results of the professor's meeting with the woman's other teachers.

2. (A) He did not see her.
   (B) He was busy answering his students' questions.
   (C) He was receiving an award.
   (D) He was collecting signatures from three other faculty members.

3. (A) A certificate signed by three professors.
   (B) A cash award and a certificate.
   (C) A medal worth five hundred dollars.
   (D) An opportunity to interview for an excellent position.

4. (A) Worried.
   (B) Surprised.
   (C) Flattered.
   (D) Confident.

Conversation Four

1. (A) To register the student for classes.
   (B) To register the student for placement tests.
   (C) To help the student change his major field of study.
   (D) To advise the student about the orientation to engineering program.

2. (A) Two.
   (B) Five.
   (C) Three.
   (D) Seventeen.

3. (A) A driver's license.
   (B) A permission slip.
   (C) A registration card.
   (D) Nothing.

4. (A) That he is majoring in mathematics.
   (B) That he has never taken a chemistry course.
   (C) That he is a freshman.
   (D) That he does not like his advisor.

EXERCISE 16: Understanding Class Discussions

In some conversations in Part B of the Listening Comprehension Section, you will be asked to understand class discussions similar to the conversations that might be heard in a college classroom. Be sure to listen for each person's opinion. It will help you to practice listening to movies and programs in English at the theater or on TV. Remember, it will help you even more if you don't watch the screen while you listen.

Conversation One

1. (A) To discuss the results of the lab experiment.
   (B) To answer Bob's question about the lab experiment.
   (C) To explain the method of collection by water displacement.
   (D) To prepare the students to do the lab experiment.

2. (A) Magnesium.
   (B) Limestone.
   (C) Carbon.
   (D) Water.

3. (A) The hydrochloric acid broke the carbon bonds in the carbon dioxide.
   (B) The magnesium oxide broke the carbon-oxygen bonds in the carbon dioxide.
   (C) The burning magnesium broke the carbon-oxygen bonds in the carbon dioxide.
   (D) The gas collection method broke the carbon-oxygen bonds in the carbon dioxide.

4. (A) That Bob does not get along with his lab partner.
   (B) That the students performed the experiment correctly.
   (C) That the students had problems, and could not complete the lab experiment.
   (D) That there was a fire in the lab during the experiment.

Conversation Two

1. (A) Admissions standards at the University of Michigan.
   (B) The use of standardized tests for college admissions.
   (C) The TOEFL (Test of English as a Foreign Language).
   (D) Evaluation without standardized tests.

2. (A) He believes that the tests are good.
   (B) He believes that the required test scores are too low.
   (C) He believes that they are more important than academic preparation.
   (D) He believes that the tests should not be used.

3. (A) That they don't always use the TOEFL and the Michigan Test scores correctly.
   (B) That they look at transcripts instead of scores.
   (C) That they should insist on a rigid cut-off score.
   (D) That they are looking for an appropriate alternative.

4. (A) In a college classroom.
   (B) At the Office of International Student Services.
   (C) In the cafeteria.
   (D) At a party.

Conversation Three

1. (A) The students did not understand the course requirements.
   (B) The students wanted to do a research paper instead of a final exam.
   (C) The professor changed the requirements for the course.
   (D) The professor offered to listen to the students' suggestions for the course.

2. (A) A report.
   (B) A book review.
   (C) An original study.
   (D) A five-page composition.

3. (A) An essay examination.
   (B) An objective examination.
   (C) An open-book examination.
   (D) A take-home examination.

4. (A) English 355.
   (B) Psychology 201.
   (C) Political Science 400.
   (D) Chemistry 370.

Conversation Four

1. (A) Making friends in a foreign country.
   (B) Spanish and French.
   (C) Foreign TV, radio, and other media.
   (D) Learning a foreign language.

2. (A) The language laboratory.
   (B) Travel.
   (C) Studying in high school.
   (D) Going to movies and watching TV.

3. (A) He believes that it is a good idea to do all of the things that Betty and Bill suggested.
   (B) He agrees with Betty.
   (C) He believes that going to class is the best way to learn.
   (D) He believes that it is ideal to live in a country where the language is spoken.

4. (A) He is not very knowledgeable.
   (B) He is respectful of his students.
   (C) He has a very formal manner in class.
   (D) He has traveled extensively.

CUMULATIVE REVIEW FOR LISTENING COMPREHENSION
Part B—Extended Conversations

EXERCISE 17

In each problem in Part B of the Listening Comprehension Section, you will be asked to respond to four questions about an extended conversation. These cumulative exercises include a variety of extended conversations.

Conversation One

1. (A) The man's test.
   (B) The woman's research paper.
   (C) Swimming.
   (D) Plans for the evening.

2. (A) Because she wants to study for a test.
   (B) Because she wants to go swimming at the student center.
   (C) Because she has to do research in the library.
   (D) Because she is not interested in the man.

3. (A) They will go to the Grill.
   (B) They will go to the library.
   (C) They will go swimming.
   (D) They will walk home.

4. (A) That he is not a student this semester.
   (B) That he is not a serious student.
   (C) That he is not very concerned about the woman.
   (D) That he is willing to compromise.

Conversation Two

1. (A) To schedule the woman for classes next semester.
   (B) To discuss a change of major.
   (C) To file for graduation.
   (D) To drop a class.

2. (A) Chemistry.
   (B) Engineering.
   (C) Business.
   (D) Accounting.

3. (A) That the woman must take more electives.
   (B) That the woman must take an extra semester in order to graduate.
   (C) That the woman should declare her major on an official form.
   (D) That the woman should finish her math courses first.

4. (A) She decides to change her major to business.
   (B) She decides not to do the extra work for the business degree.
   (C) She decides to take engineering courses next semester.
   (D) She decides to take eighteen hours this semester.

Conversation Three

1. (A) The man did not have transportation to school.
    (B) The man received a parking ticket.
    (C) The man went to the Student Union.
    (D) The man wanted to buy a parking permit.

2. (A) A student at the university.
    (B) The woman's cousin.
    (C) A police officer.
    (D) A visitor.

3. (A) Because he did not have a parking permit.
    (B) Because he parked in a visitor's lot.
    (C) Because he used a different car.
    (D) Because he was not a student at the university.

4. (A) Use his cousin's car.
    (B) Pay the parking fine.
    (C) Buy a parking permit.
    (D) Get a temporary permit.

Conversation Four

1. (A) The purchase of a ticket.
    (B) The Spring Symphony.
    (C) The Opera House.
    (D) The dates for the concert.

2. (A) A seat in the middle of the first balcony.
    (B) A seat on the side of the first balcony.
    (C) A seat in the back on the ground floor.
    (D) A seat in the front on the ground floor.

3. (A) A ten-dollar seat.
    (B) A twenty-dollar seat.
    (C) A fifty-dollar seat.
    (D) A season ticket.

4. (A) He does not have enough money for a ticket.
    (B) He plans to go to all of the concerts in the series.
    (C) He is going to attend the concert alone.
    (D) He knows the woman.

Part C—Mini Talks

<u>Directions:</u> In this part of the test, you will hear several talks. After each talk, you will hear some questions. The talks and questions will not be repeated.

After you hear a question, read the four possible answers in your test book and choose the best answer. Then, on your answer sheet, find the number of the question and fill in the space that corresponds to the letter of the answer you have chosen.

EXERCISE 18: Understanding Announcements and Advertisements

In some mini talks in Part C of the Listening Comprehension Section, you will be asked to understand announcements of services or events and advertisements of products or opinions. Be sure to listen for the topic, date, time, and sponsor of the announcement or advertisement. It will help you to practice listening to announcements and advertisements in English on radio and TV.

Mini Talk One

1. (A) To encourage correspondence by mail.
   (B) To persuade people to use Southern Telephone Company.
   (C) To help callers save money.
   (D) To inform the public about direct dialing.

2. (A) After five o'clock in the morning.
   (B) After eleven o'clock in the morning.
   (C) After five o'clock in the evening.
   (D) After eleven o'clock at night.

3. (A) $2.17.
   (B) $2.70.
   (C) $2.07.
   (D) $2.77.

4. (A) Dial the operator.
   (B) Check the phone book for the overseas operator's number so that he can help you.
   (C) Check the phone book for overseas area codes so that you can dial direct.
   (D) Call the Southern Telephone Company.

5. (A) Daytime calls do not require an operator.
   (B) Daytime calls have the most expensive rates.
   (C) It is not very common to make calls during the day.
   (D) Daytime calls are limited to ten minutes.

Mini Talk Two

1. (A) To inform the public about a new air service.
   (B) To advertise for Charlotte's finest restaurants.
   (C) To recommend large airplanes.
   (D) To encourage the use of travel agents.

2. (A) Appalachian Airlines is very large.
   (B) Appalachian Airlines is comfortable.
   (C) Appalachian Airlines is faster.
   (D) Appalachian Airlines is new.

3. (A) Only in the morning.
   (B) Only in the afternoon.
   (C) Only on Thursday.
   (D) Every morning and afternoon.

4. (A) 800-565-7000.
   (B) 800-575-7000.
   (C) 800-565-6000.
   (D) 800-575-6000.

5. (A) Travel agents in Atlanta.
   (B) Residents of the Charlotte area.
   (C) Employees of Appalachian Airlines.
   (D) Travelers to Florida.

Mini Talk Three

1. (A) If you drink, don't drive.
   (B) If you drink, drive carefully.
   (C) If you drink, don't invite your friends to ride with you.
   (D) If you drink, drive slowly.

2. (A) One thousand.
   (B) Fifty percent of all fatal accidents.
   (C) Approximately five hundred.
   (D) Two thousand.

3. (A) Three days in jail and a thirty-dollar fine.
   (B) Six days in jail and a thirty-dollar fine.
   (C) Thirty days in jail and a thirty-day suspension of one's driver's license.
   (D) Three days in jail and a thirty-day suspension of one's driver's license.

4. (A) Three days.
   (B) Thirty days.
   (C) Sixty days.
   (D) Six months.

5. (A) At a friend's party.
   (B) In a courtroom.
   (C) On a television station.
   (D) In a classroom.

Mini Talk Four

1. (A) To advertise a football game.
   (B) To sell tickets for a concert.
   (C) To provide a weather report.
   (D) To inform listeners about activities at the University.

2. (A) By calling Walter Murphy.
   (B) By going to the box office at the Student Union.
   (C) By mailing ten dollars to the Student Union.
   (D) By going to the ticket office at the sports arena.

3. (A) For early paintings.
   (B) For rocks and minerals.
   (C) For exhibits of American Indian art.
   (D) For collections of pottery.

4. (A) Poor–fair.
   (B) Fair–good.
   (C) Good–very good.
   (D) Very good–excellent.

5. (A) A student at the University of Colorado.
   (B) A radio announcer at WKID.
   (C) A meteorologist with the Colorado weather service.
   (D) A clerk at the ticket office at the Student Union.

EXERCISE 19:   Understanding News and Weather Reports

In some mini talks in Part C of the Listening Comprehension Section, you will be asked to understand news and weather reports. Be sure to listen for changes in topics. Three or four news stories may be reported. Listen for the weather report for today, and the weather prediction for the future, called the extended forecast. It will help you to practice listening to news and weather reports in English on radio and TV.

Mini Talk One

1. (A) The Miss U.S.A. Pageant.
   (B) The Miss State University Pageant.
   (C) The Miss Los Angeles Pageant.
   (D) The Miss California Pageant.

2. (A) She has brown hair and blue eyes.
   (B) She has blonde hair and blue eyes.
   (C) She has blonde hair and brown eyes.
   (D) She has brown hair and brown eyes.

3. (A) First.
   (B) Second.
   (C) Third.
   (D) Fourth.

4. (A) One thousand dollars.
   (B) Two thousand dollars.
   (C) Three thousand dollars.
   (D) Four thousand dollars.

5. (A) Return to State University.
   (B) Travel throughout California.
   (C) Give speeches about her experience.
   (D) Interview for a position in a theater group.

Mini Talk Two

1. (A) Increases in tuition and fees at American universities.
   (B) The cost of attending Ivy League schools.
   (C) The financial burden for out-of-state residents and foreign students at American universities.
   (D) The job market for recent graduates.

2. (A) Average tuition costs increased by 9 percent.
   (B) Average tuition costs increased by 20 percent.
   (C) Average tuition costs increased by 90 percent.
   (D) Average tuition costs increased by 200 percent.

3. (A) By $200.
   (B) By $5,300.
   (C) By $5,900.
   (D) By $11,200.

4. (A) That they must pay more than out-of-state students.
   (B) That only a few are accepted.
   (C) That they are not eligible for scholarships at state universities.
   (D) That their scholarships are very small.

5. (A) Critical.
   (B) Persuasive.
   (C) Informative.
   (D) Defensive.

Mini Talk Three

1. (A) To advise listeners to find shelter
       immediately.
   (B) To inform listeners that they should be
       alert for possible severe weather.
   (C) To cancel the warning from an earlier
       bulletin.
   (D) To warn people living in a five-county area
       that tornados have been sighted.

2. (A) Ten o'clock.
   (B) Two o'clock.
   (C) Twelve o'clock.
   (D) Five o'clock.

3. (A) The formation of a funnel cloud.
   (B) The sighting of a funnel cloud.
   (C) The bulletin issued by the National
       Weather Service.
   (D) The convergence of favorable conditions
       for a funnel cloud to form.

4. (A) None.
   (B) Three.
   (C) Five.
   (D) Ten.

5. (A) Turn the broadcast back on at ten o'clock.
   (B) Stay tuned to the broadcast until ten
       o'clock.
   (C) Call the National Weather Service for more
       information.
   (D) Take shelter until ten o'clock.

Mini Talk Four

1. (A) It is rainy and cool.
   (B) There are showers and thunderstorms.
   (C) It is cloudy and windy.
   (D) There are sunny skies and warm
       temperatures.

2. (A) Seventy degrees.
   (B) Eighty degrees.
   (C) Eighty-five degrees.
   (D) Ninety degrees.

3. (A) They were delayed until today.
   (B) They moved north of the area.
   (C) They ended overnight.
   (D) They moved south of the area.

4. (A) Today.
   (B) Tomorrow.
   (C) Thursday or Friday.
   (D) On the weekend.

5. (A) The broadcast probably occurred on
       Tuesday.
   (B) Thursday is the most likely day for the
       broadcast.
   (C) It is most probably broadcast on Friday.
   (D) This is probably the weekend broadcast.

EXERCISE 20: Understanding Informative Speeches

In some mini talks in Part C of the Listening Comprehension Section, you will be asked to understand informative speeches. Be sure to listen for the topic of the speech, the speaker's viewpoint, and the name or qualifications of the speaker as well as the details of the speech. It will help you to practice listening to editorials in English on radio and TV.

Mini Talk One

1. (A) To introduce the people who will participate in the program.
   (B) To explain the program to the people at the dinner.
   (C) To announce the winners of the annual international awards.
   (D) To welcome the people and thank those who participated in planning the dinner.

2. (A) The president of the International Student Association.
   (B) Jim Johnson of WQAD radio.
   (C) The director of the Office of International Student Affairs.
   (D) The chairperson of the program committee.

3. (A) They are drinking coffee and tea.
   (B) They are serving themselves dinner.
   (C) They are dancing.
   (D) They are arriving at the dinner.

4. (A) The students will go to a party at the International Office.
   (B) The students will go to a dance downtown.
   (C) The students will listen to the radio.
   (D) The students will dance in the dining room at State University.

5. (A) That there are many activities for students at State University.
   (B) That there are foreign students from many countries attending State University.
   (C) That the International Dinner is always well attended.
   (D) That the Office of International Student Affairs is not very active.

Mini Talk Two

1. (A) Federal regulations for urban development.
   (B) Trends in urban design.
   (C) Functional architecture.
   (D) Urban planning.

2. (A) From Yale University.
   (B) From Cornell University.
   (C) From Illinois University.
   (D) From Washington University.

3. (A) At Illinois University.
   (B) At the Twin Towers office building.
   (C) At the Department of Housing and Urban Development.
   (D) At a journal for architects.

4. (A) He does not want to introduce him.
   (B) He does not know him.
   (C) He respects him.
   (D) He does not believe that he is qualified.

5. (A) They will ask Dr. Taylor to sign his book.
   (B) They will ask questions of Dr. Taylor.
   (C) They will listen to Dr. Taylor's speech.
   (D) They will give Dr. Taylor an award.

Mini Talk Three

1. (A) The electric lamp.
    (B) The Community Book Club.
    (C) Great books of the Western world.
    (D) Thomas Alva Edison's love for books.

2. (A) Members of the Community Book Club.
    (B) A group of English teachers.
    (C) A club for historians.
    (D) A gathering of America's most celebrated inventors.

3. (A) Because Thomas Edison was a famous man.
    (B) Because Thomas Edison was a well-known literary figure.
    (C) Because Thomas Edison liked to read.
    (D) Because he chose to review a book about Thomas Edison.

4. (A) He used the money for travel.
    (B) He bought books and equipment for more experiments.
    (C) He donated the money to the public library.
    (D) He gave the money to his mother.

5. (A) He received most of his education from reading.
    (B) He never attended school.
    (C) He learned to read as a young man.
    (D) He read only science and technology books.

Mini Talk Four

1. (A) That everything at State University has changed in the past ten years.
    (B) That although the campus looks the same, some things have changed at State University.
    (C) That in spite of the changes on the campus, the commitments at State University are the same.
    (D) That everything has stayed the same at State University during the past ten years.

2. (A) A graduation.
    (B) A class reunion.
    (C) The dedication of a new building.
    (D) The groundbreaking ceremony for a pedestrian walkway on campus.

3. (A) The main campus looks the same.
    (B) The student population is the same.
    (C) The ideals are the same.
    (D) The Division of Continuing Education has the same programs.

4. (A) Because a bell tower was to be built on the site.
    (B) Because it was found to be unsafe.
    (C) Because a parking lot was to be constructed there.
    (D) Because no one wanted to preserve it.

5. (A) That they were able to purchase land to the Northwest of the campus.
    (B) That they were more interested in building parking lots than in preserving green areas.
    (C) That they did not consult with the community.
    (D) That they made efforts to preserve a sense of history in planning the new construction.

EXERCISE 21:   Understanding and Interpreting General Interest Topics

In some mini talks in Part C, you will be asked to understand general interest statements similar to feature stories reported on television news programs with a magazine format.

Mini Talk One

1. (A) Fast-food chains in America.
   (B) Healthy alternatives on the menus in fast-food restaurants.
   (C) The fat content of hamburgers at fast-food restaurants.
   (D) The charts at fast-food restaurants.

2. (A) Less than five teaspoons.
   (B) Five to ten teaspoons.
   (C) Ten to fifteen teaspoons.
   (D) More than fifteen teaspoons.

3. (A) About fifteen million dollars.
   (B) About fifty million dollars.
   (C) About fifteen billion dollars.
   (D) About fifty billion dollars.

4. (A) Fat, sodium, cholesterol and calorie counts for menu items.
   (B) Pictures of all the items on the menu.
   (C) The prices of all menu items.
   (D) A comparison of their menu items with those of other fast-food chains.

5. (A) That they are fat.
   (B) That they have started to eat less fast food.
   (C) That they are careful about the fat content of their food.
   (D) That they cannot eat at fast-food restaurants when they are dieting.

Mini Talk Two

1. (A) The effect of taxes on winning the lottery.
   (B) Tax rules set forth by the National Commission on Gambling.
   (C) Big winners in the lottery.
   (D) Federal taxes for millionaires.

2. (A) The first year.
   (B) The first three years.
   (C) The fifth year.
   (D) The last ten years.

3. (A) They tax them at very high rates.
   (B) They tax them at lower rates than does the United States.
   (C) They do not tax them at all.
   (D) They only tax them once, in a lump sum fee.

4. (A) None.
   (B) Only inheritance taxes.
   (C) Local, state, and federal.
   (D) Six kinds.

5. (A) That the government holds the most tickets.
   (B) That the government sells the tickets and keeps the revenue from sales.
   (C) That the government taxes the winners.
   (D) That the government collects the remainder of the installments when a winner dies.

Mini Talk Three

1. (A) The American eagle as a symbol on coins.
   (B) The history of gold coins in the United States.
   (C) The U.S. Mint.
   (D) The value to collectors of gold coins.

2. (A) Fifteen to one.
   (B) Fifteen and a quarter to one.
   (C) Fifteen and three quarters to one.
   (D) Fifteen to three.

3. (A) Five dollars.
   (B) Ten dollars.
   (C) Twenty dollars.
   (D) Fifty dollars.

4. (A) Gold coins may not be collected by individuals.
   (B) Gold coins may be collected but not exported.
   (C) There are no restrictions on the collection or sale of gold coins.
   (D) Only certain kinds of gold coins may be purchased and sold.

5. (A) Coin collecting is not restricted.
   (B) People try to sell their coins.
   (C) People do not have the funds to collect coins.
   (D) The interest in coin collecting increases.

Mini Talk Four

1. (A) To advertise sun screens.
   (B) To inform the public about overexposure to the sun.
   (C) To advocate outdoor sports.
   (D) To introduce Dr. Rigel from New York University.

2. (A) You injure your skin.
   (B) You produce enough melanin to protect you from the sun's rays.
   (C) You accelerate the body's immune system.
   (D) You get skin cancer.

3. (A) They should avoid outdoor activities.
   (B) They should use a high SPF formula sun screen.
   (C) They should be educated about sun exposure.
   (D) They should get a tan.

4. (A) To look healthy.
   (B) To tolerate more sun.
   (C) To enjoy outdoor activities.
   (D) To participate in sports.

5. (A) An SPF fifteen number is adequate for all people.
   (B) The higher the SPF number, the lower the sun screen.
   (C) An SPF fifteen number screens fifteen times the amount of sun that unprotected skin does.
   (D) A person with a dark complexion does not need a sun screen.

EXERCISE 22: Understanding and Interpreting Informal Academic Language

In some mini talks in Part C of the Listening Comprehension Section, you will be asked to understand informal academic statements similar to the announcements and explanations that might be heard at the beginning or end of a college class.

Mini Talk One

1. (A) A new way to take notes.
   (B) A short name for the survey reading method.
   (C) The five steps in the reading process.
   (D) Different ways to study for examinations.

2. (A) To take the first step.
   (B) To summarize.
   (C) To ask questions.
   (D) To look quickly.

3. (A) That one should think about the ideas while reading the words.
   (B) That one should always take notes.
   (C) That one should read only the titles and the important words, not the examples and details.
   (D) That one should read sequences of words.

4. (A) Read.
   (B) Recite.
   (C) Review.
   (D) Reread.

5. (A) In a freshman orientation course.
   (B) In a college dormitory.
   (C) In a test administration.
   (D) In a library.

Mini Talk Two

1. (A) To give an overview of the course.
   (B) To explain how to prepare for the test.
   (C) To cover the material from the textbooks.
   (D) To assist students with their lab assignments.

2. (A) Ten percent.
   (B) Twenty-five percent.
   (C) Forty percent.
   (D) Fifty percent.

3. (A) Ten percent.
   (B) Twenty-five percent.
   (C) Forty percent.
   (D) Fifty percent.

4. (A) That the students should not review their notes.
   (B) That there won't be any math problems on the test.
   (C) That there will be fifty math problems on the test.
   (D) That the math formulas will not be necessary for the test.

5. (A) An English class.
   (B) A history class.
   (C) A chemistry class.
   (D) A foreign language class.

Mini Talk Three

1. (A) The difference between plagiarism and legitimate writing strategies.
   (B) The penalties for plagiarism.
   (C) The use of quotations in term papers.
   (D) The requirement for a term paper on plagiarism.

2. (A) Using your own ideas.
   (B) Quoting someone's exact words and citing the source.
   (C) Enclosing someone's exact words in quotation marks.
   (D) Copying ideas without citing the source.

3. (A) Paraphrasing and plagiarizing.
   (B) Quoting and plagiarizing.
   (C) Paraphrasing and quoting.
   (D) Copying and paraphrasing.

4. (A) He will receive a lower grade.
   (B) He will be asked to repeat the course.
   (C) He will be asked to rewrite the paper.
   (D) He will fail the course.

5. (A) A writer.
   (B) A student.
   (C) A librarian.
   (D) A teacher.

Mini Talk Four

1. (A) To discuss incomplete grades.
   (B) To arrange for make-up exams.
   (C) To explain course policies and procedures.
   (D) To give an overview of the course content.

2. (A) He will allow the students one day after the due date before marking them down.
   (B) He will not accept late assignments.
   (C) He will subtract one letter from the grade for each day that the paper is late.
   (D) He will excuse students who are ill.

3. (A) He refuses to give them.
   (B) He gives the same exam.
   (C) He gives a more difficult exam.
   (D) He gives a multiple-choice exam.

4. (A) The student must submit a request form explaining why the incomplete is necessary.
   (B) The student must call the speaker to explain.
   (C) The student must arrange for the incomplete within one week of the final exam.
   (D) The student must register to take the course again.

5. (A) He is not very organized.
   (B) He does not like his students.
   (C) He does not mind if his students call him at home.
   (D) He does not give many exams.

EXERCISE 23:   Understanding Academic Statements

In some mini talks in Part C of the Listening Comprehension Section, you will be asked to understand formal academic statements similar to short lectures that might be heard in a college classroom. Be sure to listen for the topic of the lecture and the name or qualifications of the speaker as well as the details in the statement. It will help you to practice listening to lectures in English on educational radio and TV networks or in lecture halls.

<u>**Mini Talk One**</u>

1. (A) Heredity.
   (B) Environment.
   (C) Birth order.
   (D) Motivation.

2. (A) That birth order may influence personality.
   (B) That heredity and environment play a role in the development of the personality.
   (C) That there is research on birth order at the University of Texas at Arlington.
   (D) That firstborn children and only children have similar personalities.

3. (A) They are talkative.
   (B) They are ambitious.
   (C) They are truthful.
   (D) They are sociable.

4. (A) A man with younger sisters.
   (B) A man with older sisters.
   (C) A woman with younger sisters.
   (D) A woman with older sisters.

5. (A) An only child.
   (B) A first-born child.
   (C) A middle child.
   (D) A very young child.

<u>**Mini Talk Two**</u>

1. (A) To introduce the concept of inflation.
   (B) To discuss the causes of inflation.
   (C) To review yesterday's lecture on inflation.
   (D) To argue in favor of inflation.

2. (A) Rising prices.
   (B) Fixed income.
   (C) Real income.
   (D) Cost of living.

3. (A) Persons who have salaries agreed to in long-term contracts.
   (B) Persons who own businesses.
   (C) Persons with pensions.
   (D) Persons with slow-rising incomes.

4. (A) Inflation is controlled.
   (B) Real income decreases.
   (C) Purchasing power stays the same.
   (D) Dollar income increases.

5. (A) Discuss the questions.
   (B) Ask questions.
   (C) Give examples.
   (D) Begin the lecture.

Mini Talk Three

1. (A) The climax association.
   (B) Pioneer plants.
   (C) A forest fire.
   (D) A disturbance in the balance of nature.

2. (A) To demonstrate how man destroys his environment.
   (B) To show the process in establishing a climax association.
   (C) To prove that the balance of nature is not disturbed by local agitations.
   (D) To explain the "web of life."

3. (A) Because it prepares the environment for the forms that will replace it.
   (B) Because it is stable.
   (C) Because it assures that plants, animals, and minerals are replaced by exactly the same flora and fauna.
   (D) Because it is the only life that will ever be able to grow in areas where the balance of nature has been disturbed.

4. (A) That the association can continue to withstand competition for the area by other flora and fauna.
   (B) That the same kind of plants and animals are in evidence as were in the area prior to the disturbance.
   (C) That only one more stage of transition will follow it.
   (D) That the balance of nature is in a state of disturbance.

5. (A) In a geology class.
   (B) In a biology class.
   (C) In a history class.
   (D) In a political science class.

Mini Talk Four

1. (A) To propose a closer relationship between science and engineering.
   (B) To present a brief history of engineering.
   (C) To defend the popular distinctions between scientists and engineers.
   (D) To give examples that support the detachment of engineering from science.

2. (A) The scientist exploited the laws of nature.
   (B) The engineer was more practical.
   (C) The engineer was an intellectual.
   (D) The scientist was deeply involved in the practical application of his or her work.

3. (A) A French chemist and bacteriologist.
   (B) A Dutch astronomer, mathematician, and physicist.
   (C) A British mathematician and philosopher.
   (D) A Dutch chemist and philosopher.

4. (A) That it is detached from engineering.
   (B) That it is related to engineering.
   (C) That it is best explained by the historical distinctions made between science and engineering.
   (D) That it is a purely theoretical field.

5. (A) As examples of pure scientists.
   (B) As examples of scientists who represented the best of each century.
   (C) As examples of scientists who made practical as well as theoretical contributions.
   (D) As examples of engineers who knew something about pure science.

CUMULATIVE REVIEW FOR LISTENING COMPREHENSION
Part C—Mini Talks

EXERCISE 24

In each problem in Part C of the Listening Comprehension Section, you will be asked to respond to a question about a mini talk. These cumulative exercises include a variety of mini talks.

Mini Talk One

1. (A) Limestone formations.
   (B) Carlsbad Caverns.
   (C) The prehistory of North America.
   (D) Chemical reactions.

2. (A) Tourists.
   (B) Scholars.
   (C) Photographers.
   (D) Sports fans.

3. (A) They are sixty million years old.
   (B) They are as large as ten football fields.
   (C) They are the most spectacular caverns in North America.
   (D) They are made of a series of limestone formations.

4. (A) Limestone deposits developed.
   (B) Rainwater cracked the limestone.
   (C) The earth folded.
   (D) Stalactites formed.

5. (A) The speaker will take the group into the caverns.
   (B) The speaker will give the group a quiz.
   (C) The speaker will give a demonstration of how crystals are formed.
   (D) The speaker will say goodbye to the group.

Mini Talk Two

1. (A) It was the topic for a lecture in a class.
   (B) Some students in a class wanted clarification of the grading system.
   (C) The speaker was invited to give a paper about his new scoring system.
   (D) The teacher was required to defend holistic grading to a group of colleagues.

2. (A) It is a subjective score.
   (B) It is a nongraded system.
   (C) It is an evaluation based on a general impression.
   (D) It is a score for one of five criteria.

3. (A) That it is not one of the criteria for scoring.
   (B) That he ignores it as long as he can read it.
   (C) That it is one of the five criteria for evaluation.
   (D) That it is more important than any of the other criteria.

4. (A) Teacher-students.
   (B) Colleague-colleagues.
   (C) Writer-readers.
   (D) Teacher-supervisors.

5. (A) Defensive.
   (B) Informative.
   (C) Uncooperative.
   (D) Entertaining.

Mini Talk Three

1. (A) Migratory patterns of birds.
   (B) The habitat of waterfowl.
   (C) Life cycles of ducks.
   (D) Geese in the Northern Hemisphere.

2. (A) A male duck.
   (B) A male goose.
   (C) A female duck.
   (D) A female goose.

3. (A) The male and female mate for life.
   (B) Geese mate every three years.
   (C) The pair cares for a young bird until it is three years old.
   (D) Males attract females by displaying bright colors.

4. (A) To create a draft that makes flying easier for the birds behind the leader.
   (B) To make it possible for the leader to be seen.
   (C) To assure that each flock has only one leader.
   (D) To create a formation that assures the greatest safety for the young.

5. (A) That it took place in a physics class.
   (B) That it was part of a zoology lecture.
   (C) That it was a review of material from a previous class.
   (D) That the speaker is a student in the class.

Mini Talk Four

1. (A) Land grant colleges.
   (B) The cost of college tuition.
   (C) Congressman Justin Smith Morrill.
   (D) Bachelor's degrees.

2. (A) From taxes imposed by state governments.
   (B) From federal government grants.
   (C) From the sale of public land.
   (D) From fees paid by the first students.

3. (A) Because the first land grant college was established in Morrill.
   (B) Because Morrill College was the first land grant institution.
   (C) Because Congressman Morrill introduced the bill that created the land grant system.
   (D) Because Mr. Morrill donated the land for the first land grant college.

4. (A) Thirty percent of the total.
   (B) Forty percent of the total.
   (C) Forty-one percent of the total.
   (D) Seventy-five percent of the total.

5. (A) Because it is subsidized by state and federal governments.
   (B) Because the college is for middle-class families.
   (C) Because it is on public land.
   (D) Because the Congress oversees the administration.

STRUCTURE AND WRITTEN EXPRESSION

Structure and Written Expression

Part A—Structure Problems

<u>Directions:</u> Questions 1–15 are incomplete sentences. Beneath each sentence you will see four words or phrases, marked (A), (B), (C), and (D). Choose the <u>one</u> word or phrase that best completes the sentence. Then, on your answer sheet, find the number of the question and fill in the space that corresponds to the letter of the answer you have chosen. Fill in the space so that the letter inside the oval cannot be seen.

EXERCISE 1: Verbs (Part 1)

In some sentences in Part A of the Structure and Written Expression Section, you will be asked to identify the correct verb. In fact, most of the sentences in this part are verb problems. A verb is a word or phrase that expresses action or condition. A verb can be classified as transitive or intransitive according to whether it requires a complement; it can be classified further according to the kind of complement it requires, including not only nouns, pronouns, adjectives, and adverbs, but also -*ing* forms or infinitives.

1. Al's doctor insists _____ for a few days.
   (A) that he is resting
   (B) his resting
   (C) him to rest
   (D) that he rest

2. I don't like iced tea, and _____ .
   (A) she doesn't too
   (B) either doesn't she
   (C) neither does she
   (D) she doesn't neither

3. We wish that you _____ such a lot of work, because we know that you would have enjoyed the party.
   (A) hadn't had
   (B) hadn't
   (C) didn't have had
   (D) hadn't have

4. Since your roommate is visiting her family this weekend, _____ you like to have dinner with us tonight?
   (A) will
   (B) won't
   (C) do
   (D) wouldn't

5. Please _____ photocopies of documents.
   (A) not to submit
   (B) do not submit
   (C) no submit
   (D) not submit

6. I _____ bacon and eggs every morning.
   (A) am used to eat
   (B) used to eating
   (C) am used to eating
   (D) use to eat

7. The team really looks good tonight because the coach had them _____ every night this week.
   (A) practice
   (B) to practice
   (C) practiced
   (D) the practice

8. Would you mind _____, please?
   (A) to answer the telephone
   (B) answering the telephone
   (C) answer the telephone
   (D) to the telephone answering

9. You _____ your seats today if you want to go to the game.
   (A) had better to reserve
   (B) had to better reserve
   (C) had better reserve
   (D) had to reserve better

10. If it _____ so late, we could have coffee.
    (A) wasn't
    (B) isn't
    (C) weren't
    (D) not be

11. Your sister used to visit you quite often, _____?
    (A) didn't she
    (B) doesn't she
    (C) wouldn't she
    (D) hadn't she

12. If Bob _____ with us, he would have had a good time.
    (A) would come
    (B) would have come
    (C) had come
    (D) came

13. Frankly, I'd rather you _____ anything about it for the time being.
    (A) do
    (B) didn't do
    (C) don't
    (D) didn't

14. Since they aren't answering their telephone, they _____.
    (A) must have left
    (B) should have left
    (C) need have left
    (D) can have left

15. We were hurrying because we thought that the bell _____.
    (A) had already rang
    (B) has already rang
    (C) had already rung
    (D) have already ringing

EXERCISE 2: Verbs (Part 2)

1. I hadn't expected James to apologize, but I had hoped _____.
   - (A) him calling me
   - (B) that he would call me
   - (C) him to call me
   - (D) that he call me

2. My husband lived at home before we were married, and so _____.
   - (A) did I
   - (B) had I
   - (C) I had
   - (D) I did

3. Does your new secretary _____ shorthand?
   - (A) know to take
   - (B) know how to take
   - (C) know how take
   - (D) know how taking

4. Tommy had his big brother _____ his shoes for him.
   - (A) to tie
   - (B) tie
   - (C) tied
   - (D) tying

5. I wish that the weather _____ not so warm.
   - (A) was
   - (B) be
   - (C) were
   - (D) is

6. His English teacher recommends that he _____ a regular degree program.
   - (A) begin
   - (B) begins
   - (C) will begin
   - (D) is beginning

7. Let's go out for dinner, _____?
   - (A) will we
   - (B) don't we
   - (C) shall we
   - (D) are we

8. I'd _____ the operation unless it is absolutely necessary.
   - (A) rather not have
   - (B) not rather had
   - (C) rather not to have
   - (D) rather not having

9. Would you please _____ write on the test books?
   - (A) don't
   - (B) not to
   - (C) not
   - (D) to not

10. The old man asked her to move because he _____ in that chair.
    - (A) used to sit
    - (B) was used to sit
    - (C) used to sitting
    - (D) was used to sitting

11. After the way she treated you, if I _____ in your place, I wouldn't return the call.
    - (A) be
    - (B) am
    - (C) was
    - (D) were

12. If I _____ the flu I would have gone with you.
    - (A) hadn't
    - (B) hadn't had
    - (C) didn't have
    - (D) wouldn't have had

13. He's taken his medicine, _____?
    - (A) hasn't he
    - (B) didn't he
    - (C) doesn't he
    - (D) isn't he

14. Your mother and I are looking forward _____ you.
    - (A) of seeing
    - (B) for seeing
    - (C) to see
    - (D) to seeing

15. It is imperative that you _____ there in person.
    - (A) be
    - (B) will be
    - (C) will
    - (D) are

EXERCISE 3: Verbs (Part 3)

1. The brakes need _____.
   (A) adjusted
   (B) to adjustment
   (C) to adjust
   (D) adjusting

2. I wish that we _____ with my brother when he flies to England next week.
   (A) could go
   (B) had gone
   (C) will go
   (D) are going

3. Are you sure Miss Smith _____ use the new equipment?
   (A) knows to
   (B) knows the
   (C) knows how to
   (D) knows how

4. Mary and John _____ to the parties at the Student Union every Friday.
   (A) used to go
   (B) use to go
   (C) are used to go
   (D) were used to go

5. You _____ me, because I didn't say that.
   (A) must misunderstand
   (B) must be misunderstanding
   (C) must have misunderstood
   (D) had to misunderstand

6. _____ you rather sit by the window?
   (A) Don't
   (B) Will
   (C) Wouldn't
   (D) Won't

7. His government insisted that he _____ until he finished his degree.
   (A) should stay
   (B) shall stay
   (C) stayed
   (D) stay

8. After he had researched and _____ his paper, he found some additional material that he should have included.
   (A) wrote
   (B) written
   (C) writing
   (D) have written

9. The man who was driving the truck would not admit that he had been at fault, and _____.
   (A) neither the other driver
   (B) neither would the other driver
   (C) neither had the other driver
   (D) the other driver neither

10. If it _____ rain, we'll have the party outside.
    (A) wouldn't
    (B) doesn't
    (C) didn't
    (D) won't

11. Excuse me, but it is time to have your temperature _____.
    (A) taking
    (B) to take
    (C) take
    (D) taken

12. Almost everyone fails _____ the driver's test on the first try.
    (A) passing
    (B) to have passed
    (C) to pass
    (D) in passing

13. Mike had hoped _____ his letter.
    (A) her to answer
    (B) that she answer
    (C) that she would answer
    (D) her answering

14. I think that you had better _____ earlier so that you can get to class on time.
    (A) to start to get up
    (B) started getting up
    (C) start getting up
    (D) to get up

15. Today's weather isn't as cold as it was yesterday, _____?
    (A) wasn't it
    (B) was it
    (C) isn't it
    (D) is it

EXERCISE 4: Pronouns

In some sentences in Part A of the Structure and Written Expression Section, you will be asked to identify the correct pronoun. A pronoun is a word that can be used instead of a noun, usually to avoid repeating the noun. A pronoun may be singular or plural; masculine, feminine, or neuter; and first, second, or third person to agree with the noun to which it refers. A pronoun may be used as the subject of a sentence or a clause or as the object of a sentence, a clause, or a preposition. In English, pronouns are also used to express possessives and reflexives.

1. Tito was the only foreigner _____ I saw at the convention.
   (A) whom
   (B) which
   (C) who
   (D) what

2. They forgot about _____ them to join us for lunch.
   (A) us to ask
   (B) us asking
   (C) our asking
   (D) we asking

3. Our host family always invites my roommate and _____ to their house on Sundays.
   (A) me
   (B) my
   (C) I
   (D) mine

4. Because they usually receive the same score on standardized examinations, there is often disagreement as to _____ is the better student, Bob or Helen.
   (A) who
   (B) which
   (C) whom
   (D) whose

5. I really appreciate _____ to help me, but I am sure that I will be able to manage by myself
   (A) you to offer
   (B) your offering
   (C) that you offer
   (D) that you are offering

6. Do you know the woman _____ was hurt in the accident?
   (A) which
   (B) whom
   (C) who
   (D) whose

7. I would like to leave a message for _____ if I may.
   (A) they
   (B) them
   (C) their
   (D) theirs

8. A few of _____ are planning to drive to Florida during spring break.
   (A) we girls
   (B) us girls
   (C) girls we
   (D) girls

9. This is the woman _____ the artist said posed as a model for the painting.
   (A) who
   (B) whom
   (C) which
   (D) whose

10. Of those who took the exam with Jane and _____, I am the only one who studied for it.
    (A) he
    (B) his
    (C) him
    (D) himself

11. Let you and _____ agree to settle our differences without involving any of the other students.
    (A) I
    (B) myself
    (C) me
    (D) my

12. If you had told us earlier _____ he was, we could have introduced him at the meeting.
    (A) who
    (B) which
    (C) whom
    (D) whoever

13. I always ask my sister and _____ for advice.
    (A) her
    (B) she
    (C) hers
    (D) herself

14. Two of the notebooks _____ Tom had lost on the bus were returned to the main desk at his dormitory.
    (A) what
    (B) who
    (C) which
    (D) whose

15. He didn't seem to mind _____ TV while he was trying to study.
    (A) their watching
    (B) that they watch
    (C) them watching
    (D) them to watch

EXERCISE 5: Nouns

In some sentences in Part A of the Structure and Written Expression Section, you will be asked to identify the correct noun. A noun is a word that names persons, objects, and ideas. There are two basic classifications of nouns in English: count nouns and noncount nouns. Count nouns are those that can be made plural by *-s, -es,* or an irregular form. They are used in agreement with either singular or plural verbs. Noncount nouns are those that cannot be made plural in these ways. They are used in agreement with singular verbs. It is necessary to know whether a noun is count or noncount to maintain verb agreement and to choose correct adjective modifiers.

1. Please go to _____ to pick up your ID card.
   - (A) third window
   - (B) the window three
   - (C) window third
   - (D) the third window

2. May I have two _____ instead of beans, please?
   - (A) corn's ear
   - (B) ear of corns
   - (C) corn ears
   - (D) ears of corn

3. If you want to find good information about graduate programs in the United States, look in _____ of the *College Blue Books.*
   - (A) volume two
   - (B) volume second
   - (C) the volume two
   - (D) second volume

4. Let's buy our tickets while I still have _____ left.
   - (A) a few money
   - (B) a little moneys
   - (C) a few dollars
   - (D) a few dollar

5. The assignment for Monday was to read _____ in your textbooks.
   - (A) chapter tenth
   - (B) the chapter ten
   - (C) chapter the tenth
   - (D) the tenth chapter

6. I always put my best _____ in a safe-deposit box.
   - (A) jewelries
   - (B) jewelry's pieces
   - (C) pieces of jewelry
   - (D) piece of jewelries

7. It's a shame that you have _____ time in New York on the tour.
   - (A) so few
   - (B) so little
   - (C) a few
   - (D) a little

8. We haven't had _____ news from the disaster site since the earthquake.
   - (A) many
   - (B) quite a few
   - (C) much
   - (D) some

9. John F. Kennedy was _____ of the United States.
   - (A) the thirty-five president
   - (B) the thirty-fifth president
   - (C) the president thirty-fifth
   - (D) president the thirty-five

10. I'll have a cup of tea and _____.
    - (A) two toasts
    - (B) two piece of toasts
    - (C) two pieces of toast
    - (D) two pieces of toasts

11. The ticket agent said that the plane would be boarding at _____.
    - (A) the gate six
    - (B) sixth gate
    - (C) gate six
    - (D) the six gate

12. I will need _____ about the climate before I make a final decision.
    (A) a few informations
    (B) a few information
    (C) a little informations
    (D) a little information

13. Sending _____ "express mail" costs about ten times as much as sending it "regular delivery."
    (A) mails
    (B) a mail
    (C) a piece of mail
    (D) pieces of a mail

14. The Chicago bus is parked at _____.
    (A) the lane two
    (B) the two lane
    (C) lane two
    (D) lane the two

15. We don't have _____ tonight.
    (A) many homeworks
    (B) much homeworks
    (C) many homework
    (D) much homework

EXERCISE 6: Modifiers (Part 1)

In some sentences in Part A of the Structure and Written Expression Section, you will be asked to identify the correct modifier. A modifier can be an adjective or an adjectival phrase that describes a noun or an -*ing* form. A modifier can also be an adverb or an adverbial phrase that adds information about the verb, adjective, or another verb. Adjectives do not change form to agree with the nouns or -*ing* forms that they describe, but some adjectives are used only with count nouns and others are used only with noncount nouns.

1. She hasn't seen her family _____ three years ago.
   (A) since
   (B) for
   (C) from
   (D) before

2. Just put your coat in _____.
   (A) the hall closet
   (B) the closet of the hall
   (C) the hall's closet
   (D) hall closet

3. Bill came to work at the University thirty years _____ today.
   (A) since
   (B) before
   (C) from
   (D) ago

4. This drink tastes a little _____ to me.
   (A) strongly
   (B) so strong
   (C) strong
   (D) too much strong

5. I like these dishes, but _____ is a little too small.
   (A) the tea cup
   (B) the cup of tea
   (C) the tea's cup
   (D) the cup for the tea

6. My sister has a _____ baby.
   (A) two-months-old
   (B) two-month-olds
   (C) two-months-olds
   (D) two-month-old

7. The one in the window was _____ expensive that I couldn't afford it.
   (A) so
   (B) too
   (C) too much
   (D) very

8. We used to go skiing in Michigan every winter, but I haven't gone _____ the past five seasons.
   (A) from
   (B) for
   (C) to
   (D) since

9. It is _____ day that travel advisories have been issued for most of the major highways.
   (A) such snowy
   (B) so snowy
   (C) such a snowy
   (D) such snowy a

10. Our reservations are for _____.
    (A) sixth June
    (B) six June
    (C) the sixth of June
    (D) the six of June

11. They listened _____ while the examiner gave them the directions for Part I.
    (A) attentive
    (B) attentively
    (C) attentiveness
    (D) attention

12. The cookies that you sent over were _____ that I ate them all.
    (A) very good
    (B) too good
    (C) so good
    (D) good

13. Jacobson's is one of the most expensive
    _____ in the city.
    (A) department store
    (B) departments stores
    (C) departments store
    (D) department stores

14. I don't understand how John could have made
    _____ in judgment.
    (A) such big mistake
    (B) such a big mistake
    (C) so a big mistake
    (D) so big mistake

15. You can give me a receipt if you want to, but
    your word is _____ for me.
    (A) enough good
    (B) good as enough
    (C) good enough
    (D) good than enough

EXERCISE 7: Modifiers (Part 2)

1. Sam usually does his work very _____ and well, but today he seemed a little preoccupied.
   (A) careful
   (B) careful manner
   (C) carefully
   (D) care

2. Besides being expensive, the food in the cafeteria tastes _____.
   (A) badly
   (B) too badly
   (C) too much bad
   (D) bad

3. _____ here since 1976 when her parents moved from New York.
   (A) She's lived
   (B) She's living
   (C) She was living
   (D) She'd live

4. We'll get _____ by train if we leave tonight.
   (A) fast enough there
   (B) there fast enough
   (C) there enough fast
   (D) enough fast there

5. If the cab arrives _____, you will miss your flight.
   (A) lately
   (B) lateness
   (C) more later
   (D) late

6. It was _____ that we went camping in the mountains last weekend.
   (A) such nice weather
   (B) so nice a weather
   (C) too nice weather
   (D) nice weather so

7. The homecoming football game will be played on _____.
   (A) two September
   (B) the second of September
   (C) September two
   (D) the two of September

8. Mary overslept and was _____ late that she missed her bus.
   (A) so
   (B) too
   (C) much
   (D) very

9. Could you please tell me the _____ for Biology 457 and Chemistry 610?
   (A) rooms numbers
   (B) rooms number
   (C) room's number
   (D) room numbers

10. I think it's _____ to take a few more pictures.
    (A) enough light
    (B) light as enough
    (C) light enough
    (D) enough as light

11. Last Sunday was _____ that we took a drive in the country.
    (A) so beautiful day
    (B) such a beautiful a day
    (C) such a beautiful weather
    (D) so beautiful a day

12. The conference was organized for all of the _____ in the state.
    (A) mathematic teachers
    (B) mathematics teachers
    (C) mathematics teacher
    (D) mathematic's teachers

13. It is difficult to find a _____ in the Washington area for less than $1200 a month.
    (A) two-bedroom apartment
    (B) two-bedrooms apartment
    (C) two-bedrooms apartments
    (D) two-bedroom apartments

14. I am especially glad that Bob decided to come to the party because we hadn't seen him _____ several months.
    (A) since
    (B) until
    (C) before
    (D) for

15. John and I like to watch the games on TV because we can see more _____ than we could from a seat in the stadium.
    (A) clear
    (B) clearness
    (C) clearly
    (D) clearer

EXERCISE 8: Comparatives

In some sentences in Part A of the Structure and Written Expression Section, you will be asked to identify the correct comparative. A comparative can be a word or phrase that expresses similarity or difference. A comparative can also be a word ending like *-er* or *-est* that expresses a degree of comparison with adjectives and adverbs.

1. I will return your notes as soon as _____ copying them.
   (A) I will finish
   (B) I do finish
   (C) I finish
   (D) I be finished

2. _____ the worse I seem to feel.
   (A) When I take more medicine
   (B) The more medicine I take
   (C) Taking more of the medicine
   (D) More medicine taken

3. We will have to be careful not to get our suitcases mixed up because yours is almost the same _____ mine.
   (A) like
   (B) to
   (C) as
   (D) that

4. My new glasses cost me _____ the last pair that I bought.
   (A) times three
   (B) three times more
   (C) three times as much as
   (D) as much three times as

5. Although she is very popular, she is not _____ her sister.
   (A) pretty as
   (B) as pretty
   (C) prettier than
   (D) more pretty than

6. We are going to Florida as soon as _____ taking our final exams.
   (A) we're finish
   (B) we'll finish
   (C) we'd finish
   (D) we finish

7. This new soap is not much _____ the others that I have tried.
   (A) different
   (B) different than
   (C) different from
   (D) different that

8. Ms. Jones isn't as nice _____ Ms. Smith.
   (A) as
   (B) for
   (C) like
   (D) to

9. The rooms in Graduate Towers are _____ Patterson Hall.
   (A) larger than
   (B) larger than that of
   (C) larger than those in
   (D) larger than in

10. We'll be there as soon as we _____ a babysitter for our son.
    (A) will find
    (B) found
    (C) find
    (D) are finding

11. The final will be _____ the midterm.
    (A) alike
    (B) like
    (C) same
    (D) similar

12. They are _____ my other neighbors.
    (A) more friendlier than
    (B) friendly than
    (C) friendlier as
    (D) friendlier than

13. Tuition at an American university runs _____ six thousand dollars a semester.
    (A) so high as
    (B) as high to
    (C) as high as
    (D) as high than

14. _____ I get to know her, the more I like her.
    (A) For more
    (B) More
    (C) The more
    (D) The most

15. I would have paid _____ for my car if the salesman had insisted, because I really wanted it.
    (A) as much twice
    (B) much twice
    (C) twice as much
    (D) times two

EXERCISE 9: Connectors

In some sentences in Part A of the Structure and Written Expression Section, you will be asked to identify the correct connector. A connector is a word or phrase that joins words, phrases, or clauses. A connector expresses relationships between the words, phrases, and clauses that it joins. Some common relationships are cause and result, contradiction, substitution, addition, exception, example, and purpose.

1. We are considering buying a house in Gainesville, but we want to find out _____ there first.
   (A) what the taxes are
   (B) what are the taxes
   (C) the taxes what are
   (D) the taxes are

2. Betty moved from the dormitory _____ the noise.
   (A) because
   (B) cause
   (C) because of
   (D) caused from

3. I didn't hear _____ when he gave us the assignment.
   (A) what the professor says
   (B) that the professor said
   (C) what the professor said
   (D) which the professor says

4. He had to borrow a little money from his brother _____ he could finish his education without working.
   (A) so as
   (B) that
   (C) so that
   (D) in order so

5. I wonder where _____.
   (A) he did go
   (B) did he go
   (C) he went
   (D) went he

6. Both Mary and Ellen, _____ Jane, are studying nursing at New York University.
   (A) as well as
   (B) well
   (C) as well to
   (D) and well as

7. We had a disagreement _____ the bus was late.
   (A) because of
   (B) caused of
   (C) because
   (D) caused

8. _____ the light rain, the baseball game will not be cancelled unless the other team concedes.
   (A) Despite of
   (B) Despite in
   (C) In spite
   (D) Despite

9. I don't have any idea what _____ for graduation.
   (A) does she want
   (B) she wants
   (C) she want
   (D) is she wanting

10. We were both pleased _____ honored to be guests of the president.
    (A) also
    (B) and
    (C) alike
    (D) as

11. I wonder _____ on sale.
    (A) how much cost these shoes
    (B) how much do these shoes cost
    (C) how much these shoes cost
    (D) how much are these shoes cost

12. We moved to the front row _____ we could hear and see better.
    (A) so as
    (B) so that
    (C) such
    (D) such that

13. James plays not only on the basketball squad
    _____.
    (A) but on the baseball team
    (B) but on the baseball team also
    (C) also on the baseball team
    (D) but also on the baseball team

14. _____ his wealth, he is not spoiled.
    (A) Despite of
    (B) In despite
    (C) In spite of
    (D) In spite

15. Could you please tell me where _____?
    (A) is the nearest bus stop located
    (B) the nearest bus stop is located
    (C) is located the nearest bus stop
    (D) located is the nearest bus stop

CUMULATIVE REVIEW FOR STRUCTURE PROBLEMS
Part A—Structures

EXERCISE 10: Part 1

In the sentences in Part A of the Structure and Written Expression Section, you will be asked to identify the correct answer for a variety of structures. These cumulative exercises include a variety of structures.

1. The data on the winter migration patterns of the Monarch butterfly is very _____.
   - (A) interested
   - (B) interest
   - (C) interesting
   - (D) of interest

2. The cost of a thirty-second commercial on a network television station is $300,000, _____ for most businesses.
   - (A) so much
   - (B) much
   - (C) very much
   - (D) much too much

3. In the ocean, _____ more salt in the deeper water.
   - (A) is there
   - (B) it may be
   - (C) there is
   - (D) it is

4. Aluminum is used in construction because although it is light, it can hold up to ninety pounds of pressure per square inch without _____.
   - (A) it cracks
   - (B) to crack
   - (C) cracking
   - (D) it will crack

5. By the second year of production, the price of a new piece of technology _____ significantly.
   - (A) will decreased
   - (B) has decreased
   - (C) will have decreased
   - (D) will has decreased

6. In office longer than any other president, Franklin Delano Roosevelt was elected _____ four terms.
   - (A) while
   - (B) from
   - (C) of
   - (D) for

7. California, _____ more populous state than any of its Western neighbors, has greater representation in the House.
   - (A) a
   - (B) it is a
   - (C) that a
   - (D) is a

8. _____ pine trees bear cones.
   - (A) Virtually types
   - (B) All types virtually of
   - (C) Virtually all types of
   - (D) Types all virtually

9. How many musical notes of the 11,000 tones that the human ear can distinguish _____ in the musical scale?
   - (A) it is
   - (B) is it
   - (C) there are
   - (D) are there

10. The tendency to develop cancer, even in high-risk individuals, can be decreased _____ the amount of fruit and vegetables in the diet.
    - (A) to increase
    - (B) for increase
    - (C) for increasing
    - (D) by increasing

11. If endangered species _____ saved,
    rainforests must be protected.
    (A) are to be
    (B) be
    (C) can be
    (D) will be

12. A colony of ants is often observed _____ in
    cooperative activity.
    (A) engaging
    (B) to engages
    (C) engage
    (D) engages

13. It is not clear how much students learn _____
    television classes without supervision and
    monitoring.
    (A) for watching
    (B) from watching
    (C) by watch
    (D) to watch

14. In spite of the fact that 85 percent of all societies
    allow the men to take more than one wife,
    most prefer monogamy _____ polygamy.
    (A) than
    (B) to
    (C) for
    (D) that

15. The average spoken sentence in conversational
    English takes 2.5 seconds _____.
    (A) for to complete
    (B) completing
    (C) to complete
    (D) by completing

EXERCISE 11: Part 2

1. On the average, a healthy heart _____ to pump five tablespoons of blood with every beat.
   (A) must
   (B) ought
   (C) can
   (D) should

2. Only twenty years ago, most doctors agreed _____ truthful with their terminally ill patients, a trend that has reversed itself in modern medical practice.
   (A) don't to be
   (B) not to be
   (C) we shouldn't been
   (D) not to been

3. The New England states have had _____ serious earthquakes since the Ice Age.
   (A) none
   (B) not any
   (C) not
   (D) no

4. _____ orangutans live alone.
   (A) Near all
   (B) Almost all
   (C) The all
   (D) The most all

5. More murders are reported _____ December in the United States than during any other month.
   (A) on
   (B) in
   (C) at
   (D) for

6. William Torrey Harris was one of the first educators interested _____ a logical progression of topics in the school curriculum.
   (A) in establishing
   (B) for establishing
   (C) establishing
   (D) to establish

7. The Pilgrims _____ seven thousand dollars at 43 percent interest to make their journey in 1620.
   (A) lent
   (B) borrowing
   (C) to lend
   (D) borrowed

8. Stained glass becomes even more beautiful when it _____ because the corrosion diffuses light.
   (A) will age
   (B) ages
   (C) are aging
   (D) aged

9. All of the senses _____ smell must pass through intermediate gateways to be processed before they are registered in the brain.
   (A) until
   (B) but
   (C) to
   (D) for

10. Some hybrid flowers retain the fragrant scent of the nonhybrid, and _____ are bred without fragrance.
    (A) anothers
    (B) the other
    (C) some other
    (D) others

11. North American Indian tribes used sign language _____ with tribes that spoke a different language or dialect.
    (A) to communicating
    (B) for communicate
    (C) to communicate
    (D) for communicated

12. Adult eagles let their offspring _____ nests near their original nesting area.
    (A) build
    (B) builds
    (C) building
    (D) to build

13. Microwaves are used for cooking, telecommunications, _____.
    (A) and to diagnose medically
    (B) and medical diagnosing
    (C) and diagnosed medically
    (D) and medical diagnosis

14. Art tends to be _____ more after the death of the artist, but most literary works tend to decrease in value when the writer dies.
    (A) price
    (B) worthy
    (C) worth
    (D) value

15. A cure for juvenile diabetes _____ until more funds are allocated to basic research.
    (A) won't develop
    (B) aren't developing
    (C) don't develop
    (D) won't be developed

Part B—Written Expression

<u>Directions:</u> In questions 1–25, each sentence has four underlined words or phrases. The four underlined parts of the sentence are marked (A), (B), (C), and (D). Identify the <u>one</u> underlined word or phrase that must be changed in order for the sentence to be correct. Then, on your answer sheet, find the number of the question and fill in the space that corresponds to the letter of the answer you have chosen.

EXERCISE 12:   Point of View

In some sentences in Part B of the Structure and Written Expression Section, you will be asked to identify errors in point of view. Point of view is the relationship between the verb in the main clause of a sentence and other verbs, or between the verbs in a sentence and the adverbs that express time.

1. Although there are approximately 120 intensive language institutes in the United States in 1970, there are
   (A)   (B)   (C)
   more than three times as many now.
                (D)

2. Cartographers did not make an accurate map because the political situation in the area changes so rapidly
                                                                                       (A)   (B)

   that they were not able to draw the boundaries correctly.
                          (C)   (D)

3. This year designers are showing very bright colors and styles that were worn closer to the body than those
                                    (A)   (B)   (C)   (D)
   shown last year.

4. Everyone who saw *Star Wars* said that it is one of the best science fiction movies that had ever been
              (A)   (B)   (C)   (D)
   released.

5. If there were no alternative we will try to get enough people interested to charter a bus.
                (A)   (B)   (C)   (D)

6. Before he retired last April, Mr. Thompson is working as foreign student advisor for thirty years at
                     (A)   (B)   (C)   (D)
   Community College.

7. When he tried to make a reservation, he found that the hotel that he wants was completely filled because of a
              (A)   (B)   (C)   (D)
   convention.

8. The secretary thought that she will have to wait until tomorrow to send the letters because the mail had
                             (A)   (B)
   already gone, but her boss suggested that she take them to the post office instead.
           (C)   (D)

9. Although Emily Dickinson <u>publishes</u> <u>only</u> three of her verses before she died, today there <u>are</u> <u>more than</u> one
                                    (A)   (B)   (C) (D)
    thousand of her poems printed in many important collections.

10. Between <u>one thing and another</u>, Anna <u>does</u> not get through <u>with</u> her <u>term paper</u> last Friday.
                   (A)   (B)   (C)   (D)

11. Dew <u>usually</u> <u>disappeared</u> <u>by</u> seven o'clock <u>in the morning</u> when the sun comes up.
         (A)   (B)   (C)   (D)

12. She was among <u>the few</u> <u>who</u> <u>want</u> to quit <u>smoking</u> instead of cutting down.
                  (A)   (B) (C)   (D)

13. It is <u>an accepted custom</u> <u>for</u> guests <u>to take</u> their gifts to the wedding reception when the couple <u>invited them</u>
               (A)   (B)   (C)   (D)
    to attend.

14. I thought that they <u>are arriving</u> <u>at the airport</u> today, but so far no one from their embassy <u>has called</u>
                      (A)   (B)   (C)
    <u>to confirm</u> the time.
       (D)

15. <u>On</u> October 19, 1781, Cornwallis <u>surrenders</u> his army to General Washington, a gesture <u>that</u> signaled the end
    (A)   (B)   (C)   (D)
    of the Revolutionary War.

16. The price of coffee <u>is</u> low last month, but everyone <u>knows</u> that <u>it</u> is <u>going</u> to go up this month.
                          (A)   (B)   (C) (D)

17. Until the day she died, the old lady <u>who</u> <u>lives</u> <u>by</u> the University was working <u>part time</u> at the language lab.
                                    (A) (B) (C)   (D)

18. In a special report last year, Dan Rather said that the crime rate <u>is</u> increasing <u>in spite of</u> community and
                                                                       (A)   (B)
    government programs <u>aimed at</u> providing education and employment opportunities <u>for</u> first offenders.
                             (C)   (D)

19. In 1990, *Public Opinion Magazine* reported that 57 percent of all Americans strongly believe that mothers
                                                                              (A)   (B)

    with young children should not work outside of the home unless their families badly needed the extra
                          (C)   (D)

    income.

20. Last year the instructor told us that to remember details, it is important to take notes while listening to the
                                        (A)   (B)   (C)   (D)

    lecture, but the new instructor does not agree.

21. The fruit and vegetables at the Shop Mart are always very fresh because they were shipped in every day
        (A)   (B) (C)

    from the local farm markets.
                    (D)

22. The maid does not finish cleaning the rooms at College Dormitory yesterday because she had to help scrub
             (A)   (B)   (C)   (D)

    the floors in the kitchen and the cafeteria.

23. Since banks usually give gifts to customers who deposited large amounts to saving accounts, it is a good
                                                (A) (B)

    idea to ask the bank officials whether you are entitled to receive one.
         (C)   (D)

24. The race driver accelerated to 190 miles per hour and qualifies for the Indianapolis 500, America's
                                       (A)   (B)   (C)

    most celebrated auto racing competition.
        (D)

25. It is necessary to put a return address that included your name, street number, city, state, and zip code on all
                     (A)   (B)   (C)   (D)

    correspondence.

EXERCISE 13:   Agreement

In some sentences in Part B of the Structure and Written Expression Section, you will be asked to identify errors in agreement. Agreement is the relationship between a subject and verb or between a pronoun and noun, or between a pronoun and another pronoun. To agree, a subject and verb must both be singular or both be plural. To agree, a pronoun and the noun or pronoun to which it refers must both be singular or plural and both be masculine or feminine or neuter.

1. If one does not have respect for <u>himself</u>, <u>you</u> cannot expect <u>others</u> to respect <u>him</u>.
                                        (A)   (B)   (C)   (D)

2. What happened <u>at Kent State</u> <u>in 1970</u> <u>were</u> the result of the president's order <u>to invade</u> Cambodia.
                         (A)   (B)   (C)   (D)

3. The governor, with <u>his</u> wife and children, <u>are</u> at home <u>watching</u> the election returns <u>on television</u>.
                           (A)   (B)   (C)   (D)

4. Those of us <u>who</u> belong to the National Association for Foreign Student Affairs <u>should have</u> <u>their</u>
          (A)   (B)   (C)
    memberships renewed <u>in September</u>.
                         (D)

5. Both a term paper <u>and</u> a final exam <u>is</u> <u>required</u> <u>for</u> Chemistry 320.
                     (A)   (B) (C)   (D)

6. Neither my traveler's checks nor the money that my father <u>cabled</u> me <u>are</u> sufficient <u>to pay</u> <u>for the tickets</u>.
                                                   (A)   (B)   (C)   (D)

7. There <u>have been</u> <u>little</u> rain in the last <u>twenty-four-hour</u> period <u>because of</u> a high pressure area over most of
           (A)   (B)   (C)   (D)
    the state.

8. Everyone <u>who</u> <u>takes</u> the examination will receive <u>their</u> score reports <u>in six weeks</u>.
              (A) (B)   (C)   (D)

9. The popularity of soccer in the United States <u>were increased</u> <u>significantly</u> by <u>the playing</u> of the World Cup in
                                          (A)   (B)   (C)
    cities throughout the country <u>in 1994</u>.
                                (D)

10. Not one <u>in a hundred seeds</u> <u>develop</u> <u>into</u> a healthy plant, <u>even</u> under laboratory conditions.
                (A)   (B) (C)   (D)

11. Although the body <u>has been</u> reduced in size <u>by</u> eighteen inches, there <u>have been</u> <u>little</u> change in the engine
                        (A)   (B)   (C) (D)

    of the new models.

12. Benjamin Franklin <u>strongly</u> objected <u>to</u> the eagle's being chosen as the national bird <u>because of</u> <u>their</u>
                          (A)   (B)   (C)   (D)

    predatory nature.

13. In order to grow <u>well</u>, the Blue Spruce, <u>like</u> <u>other</u> pine trees, <u>require</u> a temperate climate.
                      (A)   (B) (C)   (D)

14. Few airports in the United States <u>is</u> as modern <u>as</u> <u>that</u> <u>of</u> Atlanta.
                                    (A)   (B)(C)(D)

15. Work <u>on improving</u> industrial disposal methods <u>were begun</u> in the early 1970s, <u>shortly</u> after the Clean Air
              (A)   (B)   (C)

    bill was passed <u>by Congress</u>.
                      (D)

16. The president, <u>with</u> his Secret Service staff and two White House aides, <u>are</u> en route <u>to</u> NBC studios <u>to tape</u>
              (A)   (B)   (C)   (D)

    a special press conference.

17. The officials of the Board of Elections asked that each voter <u>present</u> <u>their</u> registration card and a valid Texas
                                                      (A)   (B)

    driver's license before <u>receiving</u> a ballot.
    (C)   (D)

18. Those of us <u>who move</u> <u>during the semester</u> should have <u>their</u> addresses <u>changed</u> at the registrar's office.
                (A)   (B)   (C)   (D)

19. Neither of the two alternatives that <u>had been outlined</u> at <u>the</u> last meeting <u>were</u> acceptable <u>to</u> the executive
                                    (A)   (B)   (C)   (D)

    committee.

20. If one <u>had</u> considered the consequences <u>carefully</u>, <u>you</u> would not have agreed to sign a <u>two-year lease</u>.
      (A)   (B) (C)   (D)

21. Buenos Aires <u>is</u> one of the <u>world capitals</u> that <u>are</u> noted for <u>its</u> busy harbor.
                  (A)   (B)   (C)   (D)

22. In spite of <u>his being</u> a professor of chemical engineering, the one <u>who</u> <u>know</u> the most about theoretical
                   (A)   (B) (C)

    mathematics <u>is</u> Dr. Ayers.
               (D)

23. If one <u>has</u> a special medical condition such as diabetes, epilepsy, or allergy, it is advisable that <u>they carry</u>
           (A)   (B) (C)

    some kind of identification in order to avoid <u>being</u> given improper medication in an emergency.
                                                   (D)

24. It is surprising that there <u>were</u> not a serious objection to <u>their changing</u> the regulations for the chess
    (A)   (B)   (C)

    tournament without <u>consulting</u> the officials.
                       (D)

25. A large percentage of the federal employees at the Denver government center <u>are participating</u> in
                                                                    (A)

    an experimental <u>four-day</u> <u>work</u> week aimed at curbing gasoline consumption and pollution, two of
                          (B)   (C)

    <u>the most urgent problems</u> facing cities today.
               (D)

EXERCISE 14: Introductory Verbal Modifiers

In some sentences in Part B of the Structure and Written Expression Section, you will be asked to identify errors in introductory verbal modifiers and the subjects that they modify. Introductory verbal modifiers are -*ing* forms, participles, and infinitives. A phrase with an introductory verbal modifier occurs at the beginning of a sentence and is followed by a comma. The subject modified by an introductory verbal modifier must follow the comma. If the correct subject does not follow the comma, then the meaning of the sentence is changed. Often the changed meaning is not logical.

1. After finishing *Roots,* the one-hundred-year history of an African American family, the Nobel Prize
   (A)   (B)
   Committee awarded author Alex Haley a special citation for literary excellence.
              (C)   (D)

2. A competitive sport, gymnasts perform before officials who must use their judgment along with their
       (A)   (B)   (C)
   knowledge of the rules to determine the relative skill of each participant.
                          (D)

3. To remove stains from permanent press clothing, carefully soaking in cold water before washing with a
                     (A)   (B)   (C)   (D)
   regular detergent.

4. Found in Tanzania by Mary Leakey, some archeologists estimated that the three-million-year-old fossils
                    (A)   (B)
   were the oldest human remains to be discovered.
        (C)   (D)

5. After fighting the blaze for three days, the supertanker was hauled toward open seas by firefighters in an
        (A)   (B)
   effort to save the southern Caribbean from the worst oil spill in history.
           (C)   (D)

6. According to the conditions of their scholarships, after finishing their degrees, the University will employ
      (A)   (B)
   students for three years.
      (C)   (D)

7. Originally having been buried in Spain, and later moved to Santo Domingo in the Dominican Republic,
      (A)   (B)   (C)
   Columbus's final resting place is in Andalucia, Spain.
                             (D)

8. Written by Neil Simon, New York audiences received the new play enthusiastically at the world premiere
   (A)   (B)   (C)
   Saturday evening.
   (D)

9. By migrating to a warmer climate every fall, survival is assured for another year.
                   (A)   (B)   (C)   (D)

10. Saddened by the actor's sudden death, a memorial fund will be established so that family and friends
                (A)   (B)   (C)
    can make donations in his name to The American Cancer Society.
    (D)

11. To prevent cavities, dental floss should be used daily after brushing one's teeth.
                    (A)   (B)   (C) (D)

12. While researching the problem of violent crime, the Senate committee's discovery that handguns were used
                                    (A)   (B)
    to commit 64 percent of all murders in the United States.
    (C)   (D)

13. Trying to pay for a purchase with cash, salespersons often ask customers for credit cards instead.
          (A)   (B)   (C)   (D)

14. After reviewing the curriculum, several significant changes were made by the faculty in traditional business
          (A)   (B)   (C)   (D)
    programs at Harvard University.

15. Having hit more home runs than any other player in the history of baseball, Hank Aaron's record is famous.
        (A)   (B)   (C)   (D)

16. Banned in the U.S., the effect of fluorocarbons continues at a level that could eventually damage the ozone
        (A)   (B)   (C)
    layer, and bring about such serious results as high risk of skin cancer and global climate changes.
               (D)

17. To avoid jet lag, many doctors recommend that their patients <u>begin</u> adjusting one week before departure
     (A)   (B)
   time <u>by shifting</u> one hour each day toward the new <u>time schedule</u>.
           (C)   (D)

18. <u>After cooking in the microwave oven for five minutes</u>, one <u>should put</u> <u>most meat</u> dishes on a platter <u>to cool</u>.
                     (A)   (B)   (C)   (D)

19. <u>Traditionally</u> <u>named for women</u>, Bob <u>was chosen</u> as <u>the first</u> male name for a hurricane.
     (A)   (B)   (C)   (D)

20. Before testifying, <u>their answers</u> <u>were</u> sworn in <u>by</u> the <u>court</u>.
                     (A)   (B)   (C)   (D)

21. <u>By reading the instructions carefully</u>, mistakes <u>on the examination</u> <u>can</u> be <u>avoided</u>.
                (A)   (B)   (C)   (D)

22. <u>Having been divorced</u>, her credit could not <u>be</u> <u>established</u> <u>in spite of</u> her high income.
           (A)   (B)   (C)   (D)

23. <u>Attempting</u> to smuggle drugs into the country, customs officials <u>apprehended</u> the criminals and <u>took</u> them to
     (A)   (B)   (C)
   police headquarters <u>for questioning</u>.
                   (D)

24. While <u>trying</u> <u>to build</u> a tunnel <u>through</u> the Blue Ridge Mountains, coal <u>was discovered</u> by workmen at the
        (A)   (B)   (C)   (D)
   construction site.

25. <u>Founded in 1919</u>, students and teachers <u>who are</u> interested in spending several months abroad <u>may benefit</u>
       (A)   (B)   (C)
   from educational programs <u>administered by</u> the Institute for International Education.
                            (D)

EXERCISE 15:   Parallel Structure

In some sentences in Part B of the Structure and Written Expression Section, you will be asked to identify errors in parallel structure. Parallel structure is the use of the same grammatical structures for related ideas of equal importance. Related ideas of equal importance often occur in the form of a list. Sometimes related ideas of equal importance are connected by conjunctions, such as *and, but,* and *or.*

1. The committee decided to cancel its law suit, to approve the contract, and that it would adjourn the meeting.
                                          (A)   (B) (C)   (D)

2. Air travel is fast, safe, and it is convenient.
      (A)   (B)(C)   (D)

3. Rock music is not only popular in the United States but also abroad.
               (A)   (B)   (C)(D)

4. Every day the watchman would lock the doors, turning on the spot lights, and walk around the building.
            (A)   (B)   (C)   (D)

5. To control quality and making decisions about production are among the many responsibilities of an
                    (A)   (B)   (C) (D)
   industrial engineer.

6. I suggest that the instructor react to the situation by changing the textbook instead of to modify the
                              (A)   (B)   (C)
   objectives of the course.
        (D)

7. Dr. Johnson, the first woman elected president of the University, was intelligent, capable, and awareness of
                       (A)   (B)   (C)
   the problems to be solved.
         (D)

8. The insurance program used to include not only employees but their families.
                   (A)   (B) (C)   (D)

9. The six main parts of a business letter are the address, the inside address, the salutation, the body, the
         (A)   (B)   (C)
   closing, and signing your name.
            (D)

10. We solved the problem by using a computer rather <u>than</u> to do it all <u>by hand</u>.
                                                     (A) (B) (C)   (D)

11. To read literature and <u>being introduced to</u> a different culture <u>are</u> two excellent reasons <u>for studying</u> a foreign
                                (A)   (B)   (C)   (D)
    language.

12. The <u>proposed</u> increase in the utility rate <u>was</u> neither a fair request <u>and not</u> a practical <u>one</u>.
       (A)   (B)   (C)   (D)

13. Tom is <u>the best candidate</u> for the position <u>because</u> he understands the project, knows the University, and
                        (A)   (B)
    <u>who works very hard</u>.
    (C)   (D)

14. <u>Ice skating</u> and to go skiing <u>are</u> popular <u>winter sports</u> <u>in</u> the Northern United States.
      (A)   (B)   (C)   (D)

15. The surgeon examined <u>the</u> patient <u>quickly</u>, <u>and</u> then <u>the operation was begun</u>.
                           (A)   (B) (C)   (D)

16. Because we were not sure where <u>the house was</u>, and <u>because of the time</u>, we decided to <u>ask</u> <u>for</u> directions.
                                         (A)   (B)   (C) (D)

17. <u>To treat</u> minor diarrhea, drink plenty of liquids, especially tea, water, and carbonated beverages, <u>eat</u> soup,
    (A)   (B)
    yogurt, salty crackers, and bananas, and <u>avoiding</u> milk, butter, eggs, and meat <u>for</u> twenty-four hours.
                                          (C)   (D)

18. The new electric typewriters are equipped <u>not only</u> with an element for foreign languages but also <u>a key</u>
                                               (A)   (B)
    <u>for correcting</u> errors <u>automatically</u>.
      (C)   (D)

19. The examiner did not know whether to report the student for <u>cheating</u> <u>or</u> <u>warning</u> <u>him</u> first.
                                                     (A) (B) (C)   (D)

20. Jim had <u>spent</u> his vacation traveling in Arizona, <u>visiting</u> some of the <u>Indian reservations</u>, and <u>had finished</u>
         (A)   (B)   (C)   (D)
several paintings that he had begun last year.

21. The Smithsonian Institute is famous because it contains such interesting exhibits as the flag that <u>was raised</u>
                                                                                     (A)
over Fort McHenry <u>in 1812</u>, the airplane that the Wright brothers <u>built</u> for their first flight at Kitty Hawk,
                      (B)   (C)
and <u>there are</u> the gowns worn by every first lady since Martha Washington.
     (D)

22. Please send <u>me</u> <u>the</u> smallest, most <u>recently</u> published, and <u>less</u> expensive dictionary that you have available.
            (A)(B)   (C)   (D)

23. <u>In order</u> to become a law, a bill <u>must be passed</u> not <u>only</u> by the Senate but also <u>the House of Representatives.</u>
   (A)   (B)   (C)   (D)

24. The cloverleaf is a common engineering design for expressways that <u>permits</u> traffic <u>between</u> two
                                                           (A)   (B)
intersecting highways <u>to move</u> more safely, efficiently, and <u>with ease.</u>
                      (C)   (D)

25. A new product <u>should be judged</u> not by the promises made in commercials <u>and</u> advertisements, <u>but also</u> by
                   (A)   (B)   (C)
the results <u>demonstrated</u> in actual use.
          (D)

EXERCISE 16: Redundancy

In some sentences in Part B of the Structure and Written Expression Section, you will be asked to identify errors in redundancy. Redundancy is the unnecessary repetition of words and phrases.

1. Some international students <u>use</u> a cassette recorder <u>to make</u> tapes of their classes <u>so that</u> they can repeat the
                   (A)   (B)   (C)
lectures <u>again</u>.
       (D)

2. Blood plasma <u>it</u> is the transportation system for <u>all</u> of the <u>widely</u> separated organs in the <u>human body</u>.
            (A)   (B)   (C)   (D)

3. <u>It</u> is a good idea <u>to be</u> careful in <u>buying or purchasing</u> magazines from salespersons <u>who</u> may come to your
 (A)   (B)   (C)   (D)
door.

4. <u>Appointed</u> by the General Assembly <u>for</u> five years, the Secretary-General of the United Nations <u>must act</u>
     (A)   (B)   (C)
<u>in an impartial manner</u> toward all members.
       (D)

5. Since <u>there was not any clarity</u>, the <u>farm workers</u> refused <u>to sign</u> the new contract and voted to go on strike
             (A)   (B)   (C)
<u>instead</u>.
  (D)

6. Men <u>who</u> lived thousands of years <u>ago</u>, long before alphabets were devised, <u>they</u> used pictures to record
      (A)   (B)   (C)
events and <u>to communicate</u> ideas.
          (D)

7. If one does not pick up <u>his</u> drycleaning <u>within</u> thirty days, the management is not <u>obligated</u> to return it <u>back</u>.
                      (A)   (B)   (C)   (D)

8. Professor Baker is an authority <u>who knows a great deal</u> about the effects of a <u>rapid</u> <u>rise</u> in temperature <u>on</u>
                                (A)   (B) (C)   (D)
different metals and alloys.

9. Homestays in an American family add a great deal in terms of the experience that students have when they
                                          (A)   (B)   (C)
   are learning to speak English.
              (D)

10. Mr. Williams he told us that he was planning to get married next June.
             (A)   (B)   (C)   (D)

11. The Southern part of the United States has ideal conditions for raising cotton because the climate is
                                                            (A)
    sufficiently warm enough to allow a six-month growing period.
              (B)   (C)   (D)

12. A person who is competitive in nature is more likely to suffer from the effects of stress on his health.
           (A)   (B)   (C)   (D)

13. Charles Schulz he made the first drawing of the famous cartoon strip *Peanuts* thirty years ago.
            (A) (B)   (C)   (D)

14. Translations must be done in a careful manner so that the accuracy of the original manuscripts is preserved.
                (A)   (B)   (C)   (D)

15. International law is made up of the rules and customs that they deal with the relationships between different
                 (A)   (B) (C)   (D)
    nations and the citizens of different nations.

16. My mother she always says that if one burns himself in the kitchen, he should put an ice cube on the
              (A)   (B)   (C)
    affected area immediately.
             (D)

17. It was Isadora Duncan who was responsible for many of the new innovations that have made modern dance
    (A)   (B)   (C)
    different from classical ballet.
       (D)

18. This entry is <u>more perfect</u> <u>than</u> <u>that of</u> <u>the other</u> contestant.
                   (A)   (B)   (C)   (D)

19. *Little House on the Prairie,* a successful television program, was adapted from a <u>series</u> of books by a young
                                                                                               (A)

    pioneer woman <u>whose</u> life was similar to <u>that of</u> the character called <u>by name</u> Laura.
               (B)   (C)   (D)

20. <u>In recent years</u> great advances <u>forward</u> <u>have</u> been made in the field of <u>genetic research</u>.
      (A)   (B)   (C)   (D)

21. Today the United States <u>is</u> one of the few countries in the Western Hemisphere that <u>it</u> <u>has</u> laws <u>providing for</u>
                        (A)   (B)(C)   (D)

    the death penalty.

22. <u>According to</u> recent geological research, <u>the climate</u> of the states along the Canadian border <u>is</u> changing
      (A)   (B)   (C)

    with rapidity.
    (D)

23. My friend <u>she</u> had the admissions officer <u>send</u> me an I-20 <u>so that</u> I could <u>come</u> to the University.
            (A)   (B)   (C)   (D)

24. The South <u>is</u> mostly Democrat <u>in politics,</u> <u>while</u> the North has <u>both</u> Democrats and Republicans.
          (A)   (B)   (C)   (D)

25. World hunger <u>it</u> <u>is</u> one of the <u>most urgent</u> problems that <u>we face</u> today.
             (A)(B)   (C)   (D)

EXERCISE 17:   Word Choice

In some sentences in Part B of the Structure and Written Expression Section, you will be asked to identify errors in word choice. Word choice is the selection of words that express the exact meaning of an idea. Sometimes it is necessary to make a choice between words that are very similar in appearance but very different in meaning.

1. According to the Pythagorean theorem, the sum of the squares of the two sides of a triangle is equal as the
        (A)   (B) (C)   (D)
    square of the hypotenuse.

2. Although you must get off while the bus is being cleaned, you may leave your suitcases and other
                                         (A)   (B)   (C)
    belongings laying on your seats.
              (D)

3. The flag over the White House is risen at dawn every day by a color guard from the United States armed
             (A)   (B)   (C)   (D)
    forces.

4. Mr. Davis had to sell his business because he made some unwise investments and went broke.
            (A)   (B)   (C)   (D)

5. Commercials on the educational television network are generally shorter comparing those on other
                                          (A) (B)   (C)   (D)
    networks.

6. After trying without success to talk with them, Mr. Brown lost his patience and gave them their walking
                (A)   (B)   (C)   (D)
    papers.

7. The economy class on most airlines is similar as the first class, but there is usually less space assigned to
                   (A)   (B)   (C)   (D)
    each passenger.

8. Since everyone would like to find an apartment near to the University, there are very few vacancies in the
                          (A)   (B)   (C) (D)
    area.

9. The Food and Drug Administration has not declared the drug a carcinogen because it has not been proven
                                                                                   (A)

    conclusively that the effects in rats can be generalized for human beings.
       (B)   (C)   (D)

10. The carefulness with which she prepared the thesis was evident to the committee.
         (A)   (B)   (C)   (D)

11. Marian Anderson, recognized both in the U.S. and in Europe as a real great vocalist, was the first black
                                       (A)   (B)   (C) (D)

    singer to appear with the Metropolitan Opera Company.

12. Formally, when he lived in his country, he was a university professor, but now he is working toward a
      (A)   (B)   (C)   (D)

    higher degree at an American university.

13. In some states, the law allows drivers to turn right at a red light, but in other states, the law does not leave
                              (A)   (B)   (C)

    them do it.
     (D)

14. Bored of his job, he made an appointment to see an advisor at the counseling center.
      (A)   (B)   (C)   (D)

15. The effective of the project on the population will be difficult to measure unless we employ a statistician
        (A)   (B)   (C)

    to tabulate the variables.
      (D)

16. In spite of their differences, Jane has always been very considerable to her roommate.
     (A)   (B) (C)   (D)

17. He can't hardly remember the accident because he was only a four-year-old boy when it occurred.
       (A)   (B)   (C) (D)

18. If the water level had raised any higher, the dam would probably have broken.
        (A)   (B)   (C)   (D)

19. One should try to reconcile his views with those of his company when they are on conflict.
      　　　　　　(A)　　　　　　　　　(B)　　(C)　　　　　　　　　　　(D)

20. When a person is arrested, the cops must let him make one telephone call.
      　　　　　　　　　　　(A)　　　　　(B)(C)　　　　　　(D)

21. With regard of your letter dated May 1, I am canceling my subscription to *Time* magazine because I am
      　　　　　(A)　　　　　　　　　　　　　　　　　　　　　　　　　　　　　　(B)
    leaving the United States to return to my country.
      　　　　　　　　　(C)　　(D)

22. Most therapists agree that it is not a good idea for patients to lay in bed without exercising.
      　　　　　　　　　　　(A)　　　　　　　　　　　　　(B)　(C)　　　　(D)

23. Excepting for vending machines, there is no food service on campus during the ten-day spring break.
    (A)　　　　　　　　　　　　　(B)(C)　　　　　　　　　　　　　　(D)

24. When the owner of the disco suspicioned that their identification was not valid, he refused to serve them.
      　　　　　　　　　　　(A)　　　　　　　　　　　　(B)　　　　　　　　(C)　　(D)

25. The condition of menkind has been improved by recent technological advances.
      　　　　　　(A)　(B)　　　　　　　(C)　　　　　(D)

EXERCISE 18:   Structure

In some sentences in Part B of the Structure and Written Expression Section, you will be asked to identify errors in structure. Remember, structure is the correct use of verbs, pronouns, nouns, modifiers, comparatives, and connectors.

1. Of the two lectures, the first was by far the best, partly because the person who delivered it had such a
                  (A)   (B)   (C)   (D)
    dynamic style.

2. That modern science knows to assist women who are unable to give birth to babies by normal means is one
                        (A)   (B)   (C)   (D)
    of the miracles of the twentieth century.

3. After he had researched his paper and wrote it, he found some additional data that he should have included.
                               (A) (B)   (C)   (D)

4. Because of the light, the city seemed differently from the way that I had remembered it.
      (A)   (B)   (C)   (D)

5. The Federal Aviation Agency grounded all DC-10 aircraft ten years ago so they could be checked for
                             (A) (B)   (C)   (D)
    possible problems in the design of the under-wing jet systems, but no recent problems have required
    attention.

6. The colonel wanted to retreat, but the general insisted that he continue do everything necessary in order
                 (A)   (B)   (C)
    to win the battle.
    (D)

7. There are not many people which adapt to a new culture without feeling some disorientation at first.
       (A)   (B)   (C)   (D)

8. Bob wishes that his wife understands why he has not had time to write her lately.
                      (A)   (B)   (C) (D)

9. Because of the accident, the judge forbade Joe and me from driving for six months.
                                    (A) (B) (C) (D)

10. After he had <u>ran</u> the program through the computer, he <u>noticed</u> that he had forgotten <u>to do</u> the <u>last</u> operation.
               (A)   (B)   (C) (D)

11. <u>Most</u> small appliances have <u>ninety-days</u> guarantees that <u>entitle</u> the purchaser to free repair or replacement if
    (A)   (B)   (C)
    the item <u>breaks</u> before the expiration date.
          (D)

12. Although everyone in our group was pleased with <u>his</u> meal, Mrs. Brown insisted <u>on</u> <u>complaining</u> that the
                                       (A)   (B) (C)
    coffee <u>tasted badly</u>.
          (D)

13. <u>Let's you and I</u> agree <u>to cancel</u> the last shipment unless the company <u>meets</u> the conditions of <u>our</u> original
        (A)   (B)   (C)   (D)
    contract.

14. His recommendation that the Air Force <u>investigates</u> the UFO sighting <u>was</u> approved <u>by the commission</u> and
                                      (A)   (B)   (C)
    <u>referred to</u> the appropriate committee.
      (D)

15. Although she seems to be <u>very</u> mature, Ann is <u>much</u> younger <u>as</u> <u>the other girls</u> in her class.
                        (A)   (B)   (C)   (D)

16. Nuclear power plants are <u>still</u> supported <u>by</u> the Society of Professional Engineers <u>in spite</u> the unfortunate
                           (A)   (B)   (C)
    accident <u>at</u> Three Mile Island.
         (D)

17. Miss Smith returned home quite <u>lately</u> <u>that</u> night <u>to find</u> that someone had broken into her garage and <u>stolen</u>
                               (A) (B)   (C)   (D)
    her car.

18. If Mary <u>would have been</u> <u>more careful</u> in <u>proofreading</u> her dissertation, she would not have had to get <u>it</u>
           (A)   (B)   (C)   (D)
    typed again.

19. The more that she tried to remove the stain, the worst it looked.
            (A)   (B)   (C)   (D)

20. The national television networks have been criticized for not showing much good movies during prime time.
                                                (A)   (B)   (C)   (D)

21. This is the athlete whom everyone says will win the gold medal at the winter Olympic Games.
   (A)   (B)   (C)   (D)

22. If you would have checked your answer sheet more carefully, you would have corrected these errors
                  (A)   (B)   (C)

yourself.
 (D)

23. It was her who suggested that he go to New York in order to get a direct flight.
       (A) (B)   (C)   (D)

24. We veterans often fail taking advantage of the scholarship programs at the university level.
 (A)   (B)   (C)   (D)

25. It is necessary that the directors will sign all of the copies, not just the top one.
                          (A)   (B)   (C)   (D)

CUMULATIVE REVIEW FOR WRITTEN EXPRESSION
Part B—Style Problems

EXERCISE 19

In the sentences in Part B of the Structure and Written Expression Section, you will be asked to identify the incorrect answer from among four underlined alternatives. These cumulative exercises include a variety of style problems and structures.

1. That witches caused disasters and misfortunes it was widely believed among the colonists in Salem,
    (A)   (B)   (C)   (D)

    Massachusetts.

2. At the Hermitage, Andrew Jackson's home in Tennessee, even his glasses have been left exactly where he
                                                                          (A)   (B)

    lay them.
    (C) (D)

3. Ecology it teaches us that it is important to consider a variety of factors to make predictions about
           (A)   (B)   (C)

    the environment.
        (D)

4. School children in the same grade in American schools are usually the same old as their classmates.
                   (A)   (B) (C)   (D)

5. An understand of calculus is essential to the study of engineering.
       (A)   (B)   (C)   (D)

6. Although many higher structures have been build in New York City, none characterizes the skyline
              (A)   (B)   (C)

    better than the Empire State Building.
      (D)

7. The classify of plants begins with those having the simplest structure, and progresses to include the
        (A)   (B)

    most highly organized forms in four divisions called phylums.
          (C)   (D)

8. Alligators are about the same color than crocodiles, although the adults may be slightly darker with broader
                            (A)   (B)   (C)
   heads and blunter noses.
              (D)

9. Research in genetics and DNA having had a profound influence on the direction of treatment for
                                (A)   (B)   (C)
   a large number of diseases.
       (D)

10. Born in 1892, the Library of Congress is where Archibald MacLeish worked as a librarian
        (A)   (B)
    while he wrote both poems and plays.
        (C)   (D)

11. Laser disks provide images of best quality than those of either television signals or video tapes.
                 (A)   (B)   (C)   (D)

12. Most of the Cajun French who live in Louisiana can neither read nor writing the French variety that they
        (A)   (B)   (C)   (D)
    speak fluently.

13. A mature grove of aspen trees often have a single root system that supports numerous trunks.
                                (A)   (B)   (C)   (D)

14. Seven months before the stock market crashed in 1929, President Hoover said that the fruits of
                              (A)   (B)
    accomplishment in the nation are secure.
                            (C)   (D)

15. Snakes stick out their tongues, move them around, and also they retract them quickly to pick up odor
    (A)   (B)   (C)   (D)
    molecules that aid in detecting direction.

16. Some metals such gold, silver, copper, and tin occur naturally, and are easy to work.
    (A)   (B)   (C)   (D)

17. Refurbished as a <u>cruise</u> vessel, <u>tours</u> by the *S.S. Constitution* will sail from California to Hawaii, <u>stopping</u> at
               (A)   (B)   (C)
    <u>all of the major islands</u>.
          (D)

18. Bones <u>composed</u> <u>chiefly</u> of calcium, phosphorous, and a fibrous substance <u>known as</u> collagen.
     (A)   (B)   (C)   (D)

19. <u>Thought</u> by some to be the first <u>labor</u> party, the Workingman's Party struggled not only for better working
      (A)   (B)
    conditions <u>also</u> for public schools for <u>all children</u>.
           (C)   (D)

20. Although we once thought that Saturn <u>has</u> only seven rings, we now know that <u>it</u> has hundreds of rings
                                      (A)   (B)
    <u>extending</u> for thousands of <u>miles</u>.
       (C)   (D)

21. <u>One-cent</u> coins <u>issued</u> in the United States <u>since 1982</u> <u>is</u> 96 percent zinc.
      (A)   (B)   (C) (D)

22. <u>According to</u> a team <u>of</u> scientists, <u>there are</u> evidence that Mount Everest is still <u>rising</u>.
        (A)   (B)   (C)   (D)

23. <u>Most</u> archaeologists agree that humans <u>are living</u> in the area around Philadelphia for <u>about</u> twelve thousand
    (A)   (B)   (C) (D)
    years.

24. <u>The urinary system, including</u> both the bladder <u>and</u> the kidneys, <u>are contained</u> in the cavities of the trunk.
            (A)   (B)   (C)   (D)

25. The color of a star <u>depends</u> on the heat, and <u>how much energy</u> it <u>produces</u>.
      (A)   (B)   (C)   (D)

EXERCISE 20: Style (Part 2)

1. The cerebellum's <u>main functions</u> <u>are</u> <u>the maintenance</u> of posture and <u>move</u> the body.
                 (A)   (B)   (C)   (D)

2. <u>Because</u> the expense of traditional fuels and the concern that <u>they</u> <u>might run out</u>, we <u>have been investigating</u>
     (A)   (B)   (C)   (D)
   alternative sources of power.

3. The smallest <u>flying</u> dinosaurs <u>was</u> <u>about</u> <u>the</u> size of a robin.
            (A)   (B)   (C) (D)

4. In the Middle Ages, the word "masterpiece" referred to <u>a work</u> that <u>is completed</u> by a journeyman in order
                                               (A)   (B)   (C)
   to <u>qualify</u> as a master artisan.
      (D)

5. <u>At the core</u> of a star, temperatures and pressures are <u>so</u> great <u>as</u> particles collide and connect <u>in a process</u>
      (A)   (B)   (C)
   <u>called</u> fusion.
    (D)

6. <u>Porpoises</u> <u>swim</u> in circles when <u>they</u> <u>will sleep</u>.
      (A)   (B)   (C)   (D)

7. <u>In the 1920s</u>, art deco, <u>known for</u> plastic and <u>chrome-plated</u> objects, <u>were</u> very popular.
       (A)   (B)   (C)   (D)

8. Digital clocks, however precise, <u>they</u> cannot be <u>perfectly</u> accurate because <u>the earth's</u> rotation changes
                                        (A)   (B) (C)   (D)
   slightly over the year.

9. Before the 1800s, when William Young made <u>differently</u> shaped shoes for right and left feet, shoes <u>can</u>
                                                (A)   (B)
   be <u>worn</u> <u>on either foot</u>.
    (C)   (D)

10. The <u>average</u> temperature of rocks <u>on the surface</u> of the earth <u>are</u> 55 <u>degrees</u> F.
          (A)   (B)   (C)   (D)

11. According to the Congressional Record, almost one third of all new laws in 1991 are passed to celebrate
    (A)   (B)   (C)   (D)
    some day, week, or month for a special interest group's purposes, such as Music Week.

12. Scientists who study animal behavior thinks that only human beings get headaches.
                 (A)   (B)   (C)   (D)

13. Whereas a gas expands in a uniform manner in all directions, a vapor remains somewhat concentrated.
    (A)   (B)   (C)   (D)

14. Published by Penguin Press almost seventy years ago, Ernest Hemingway wrote A Farewell to Arms was the
              (A)   (B)   (C)   (D)
    first paperback book offered to the public.

15. Only seventeen on one hundred business calls get through to the correct person on the first attempt.
                  (A)   (B)   (C)   (D)

16. You can boost the sales of a product faster by increasing its advertising budget than to improve the product itself.
                                       (A)   (B)   (C)   (D)

17. The New York City subway system is the most longest underground railroad operating in the world.
                     (A)   (B)   (C)   (D)

18. With the develop of a cheap process for desalination, 97 percent of the earth's water will become available
            (A)   (B)   (C)   (D)
    for fresh-water purposes.

19. Nine of every ten people in the world lives in the country in which they were born.
           (A)   (B)   (C)   (D)

20. There are more potatoes cultivated than any the other vegetable crop worldwide.
    (A)   (B)   (C)   (D)

21. The fact that no fossilized remains of a plant or animal has been found on the floor of the Grand Canyon
                 (A)   (B)
    supports the claim that it existed before life on this planet.
    (C)   (D)

22. About one third <u>approximately</u> of all murder victims <u>are</u> <u>drunk</u> at the time they <u>are</u> assaulted.
                  (A)   (B) (C)   (D)

23. <u>Found</u> in and <u>near</u> the Mohave Desert, it is the Joshua Tree has a <u>limited</u> habitat.
     (A)   (B)   (C)   (D)

24. <u>During</u> the past decade, twenty million college graduates <u>spent</u> <u>more than</u> fifty billion dollars in <u>ten-year</u>
     (A)   (B)   (C)   (D)
    student loans.

25. As whole, mammals, <u>once</u> weaned, do not <u>routinely</u> drink <u>milk</u>.
     (A)   (B)   (C)   (D)

READING
COMPREHENSION

Reading Comprehension

Part A—General Interest

Directions: In the Reading Comprehension section you will read several passages. Each one is followed by a number of questions about it. You are to choose the <u>one</u> best answer, (A), (B), (C), or (D), to each question. Then, on your answer sheet, find the number of the question and fill in the space that corresponds to the letter of the answer you have chosen.

Answer all questions about the information in a passage on the basis of what is <u>stated</u> or <u>implied</u> in that passage.

EXERCISE 1: General Interest

In some passages, you will be asked to read general interest information on consumer-related topics, such as banking, driving, housing, and shopping. You will usually be reading this kind of information for details. First, read the passage quickly. Then, read the questions. After you have answered questions for the main idea, begin to answer the other questions by referring to the passage. Use key words in the questions to help you locate the place in the passage where the answer is found. It will help you to practice reading pamphlets, magazines, and tourist information written in English.

Passage One

After you decide what kind of car you want, which options you need, and how much you can afford to spend, you should shop at several dealerships. Buying a car is one of the few purchases that you will make in the United States that allows for negotiation. In the case of cars, new and used, the sticker price posted on the window is not fixed, and the car dealer will expect you to bargain. It has been estimated that fewer than
(5) 20 percent of all new car buyers end up paying an amount even close to the list price.

To save the most money, use the following strategies when you negotiate. In the first place, don't mention that you have a car to trade in until you have agreed on a price for the car you want to buy. If the salespersons know in advance, they may quote you a high price for the trade-in, but the price of the new car may be adjusted to include the added amount. In addition, buy a car that is already on the dealer's lot instead of ordering a car.
(10) The dealer has to pay insurance and finance charges for every car in the inventory and is usually willing to sell one for less money in order to reduce the overhead expenses. Furthermore, try to buy your new car at the end of the year, just before the next year's models arrive in the fall. Dealers are usually glad to move these cars off their lots to make room for the new models. If you can't wait until fall to buy your car, at least wait until the end of the month, when the dealer is trying to reach a set sales quota in order to earn a bonus from the manufacturer.
(15) Finally, don't mention to the car dealer that you intend to pay cash or use a bank for financing until the deal is closed. Some dealers will offer a lower price if they believe that they will have the opportunity to arrange the financing and collect a commission.

1. What is the author's main purpose in writing this passage?

   (A) To complain about car dealers
   (B) To offer advice to prospective car buyers
   (C) To sell new cars
   (D) To explain how to finance a car

2. According to the author, when should a buyer purchase a new car?

   (A) In December
   (B) In the fall
   (C) Near the first of the month
   (D) At the end of the week

3. The author recommends all of the following strategies for getting the best price on a new car EXCEPT

   (A) negotiating a lower price than the one that appears on the sticker
   (B) not telling the dealer that you have a car to trade in
   (C) financing the new car at the dealership
   (D) buying a car that is on the dealer's lot instead of ordering one

4. The word "inventory" in line 10 could best be replaced by

   (A) the cars that the dealer has to sell
   (B) the cars that the dealer has sold
   (C) the cars that the dealer must sell every month
   (D) the cars that the dealer will order

5. The word "one" in line 11 refers to

   (A) insurance
   (B) you
   (C) a car
   (D) the dealer

6. It can be inferred from the passage that

   (A) negotiating a price for most purchases is not common in the United States
   (B) car dealers in the United States are not honest
   (C) new cars are very expensive in the United States
   (D) most shoppers have a car to trade in.

Passage Two

CAUTION: Your signature on this legal document indicates that you have read and understood its contents and agree to abide by its conditions.

For apartment number <u>109</u> of University Park Apartments located at 600 University Park.

1. Security deposit. The amount of the security deposit is $250, at no time to be applied as rent, and to be refunded upon termination of agreement less any amount retained in payment of damages to the apartment. Should damages to the premises exceed the amount of the deposit, the resident agrees to
(5) reimburse the management for such excess.
2. Termination of agreement. The security deposit shall be refunded less any retained amount specified upon the termination of this agreement at the end of the original rental period if notice in writing of termination has been given thirty (30) days in advance of such termination, the keys have been returned to the management, and the premises are found upon inspection to be clean and
(10) undamaged.

1. This passage is

   (A) a rental agreement
   (B) a caution
   (C) a termination of agreement
   (D) a security deposit

2. Under what conditions could the manager refuse to return a security deposit?

   (A) If the keys were not returned 30 days before the resident planned to move
   (B) If the apartment were undamaged
   (C) If the resident did not give notice in writing
   (D) If the manager could not find another resident to take the apartment

3. The author mentions all of the following conditions in the document EXCEPT

   (A) terms for the security deposit
   (B) terms for payment of damages
   (C) terms for subleasing the apartment to another person
   (D) terms for returning the keys to the apartment

4. The word "premises" in line 11 most nearly means

   (A) furniture
   (B) floors
   (C) property
   (D) utilities

5. The word "its" in line 1 refers to

   (A) conditions
   (B) contents
   (C) document
   (D) signature

6. If a resident plans to move from University Park Apartments on June 15, when should he notify the manager?

   (A) On May 15
   (B) On June 1
   (C) On July 15
   (D) On June 15

Passage Three

General Appliance Company guarantees the product to be free from manufacturing defects for one year after the original date of purchase. If the product should become defective within the warranty period, General Appliance will repair or replace it free of charge, provided that damage to the product has not resulted from accident or misuse. Deliver the product to any one of the authorized service facilities whose
(5)   names and addresses are listed in the accompanying brochure. Direct any questions regarding the warranty to Consumer Service Division, General Appliance Company, 1621 Bergen Street, Newark, New Jersey 07102.

1. Which sentence below best summarizes this passage?

   (A) General Appliance Company is an honest manufacturer.
   (B) If a General Appliance product is damaged in an accident, the company will replace it.
   (C) If you have an accident while using a General Appliance product, the company will pay damages.
   (D) If a General Appliance product is defective when purchased, the company will repair or replace it.

2. Where should a defective product be taken for repair or replacement?

   (A) To the store where it was purchased
   (B) To the Consumer Service Division of General Appliance Company
   (C) To an authorized service facility
   (D) To the manufacturer that made the product

3. The author mentions all of the following procedures for customers to receive satisfaction from the company EXCEPT

   (A) take the defective product to an authorized facility
   (B) write to the Customer Service Division
   (C) consult the product brochure for names and addresses of service locations
   (D) wait for one year from the date of purchase for free replacement

4. Another word which is often used in place of "warranty" in line 2 is

   (A) purchase
   (B) manufacturing
   (C) product
   (D) guarantee

5. The word "it" in line 3 refers to

   (A) damage
   (B) the product
   (C) accident or misuse
   (D) the warranty period

6. We may assume that General Appliance Company would replace a product under which of the following circumstances?

   (A) When the purchase was made fourteen months ago
   (B) When the product was recently purchased on sale
   (C) When the product was dropped and damaged after purchase
   (D) When the replacement was paid for by the customer

Passage Four

In order to request telephone service in the United States, either call or visit your local telephone store. A sales representative will be glad to show you samples of the designs and colors available. Simply choose the design and color that you prefer, and leave your name, address, and employer's name with the sales representative. Students with scholarships should provide their sponsor's name instead of an employer's

(5) name. A fifty-dollar security deposit must be paid prior to telephone installation, and may be made by check, cash, Mastercard, or Visa. On the date that your telephone is to be installed, a responsible person, such as an apartment manager, must be at home to unlock the door for the serviceman.

1. The purpose of this passage is

   (A) to persuade
   (B) to correspond
   (C) to inform
   (D) to entertain

2. According to this passage, who will install your telephone?

   (A) A sales representative
   (B) A serviceman
   (C) A manager
   (D) An employer

3. The author mentions all of the following as steps for securing telephone service EXCEPT

   (A) Call or visit a telephone store.
   (B) Leave information with a sales representative.
   (C) Give the serviceman a key to your apartment.
   (D) Pay a fifty-dollar security deposit.

4. The word "samples" in line 2 most nearly means

   (A) prices
   (B) examples
   (C) pictures
   (D) catalog

5. The word "their" in line 4 refers to

   (A) scholarships
   (B) employers
   (C) sponsors
   (D) students

6. We can infer from this passage that

   (A) there is more than one kind of telephone
   (B) the person requesting telephone service must be at home when it is installed
   (C) students may not request telephone service
   (D) credit cards may not be used to pay for security deposits

Passage Five

Please follow these procedures in order to make a machine withdrawal from your City Bank checking or savings accounts:

1. Insert your card face up into the card slot on the machine teller.
2. Enter your four-digit identification number on the numbered buttons.

(5)
3. Press the withdrawal button for *checking* or the button for *savings*.
4. Enter the amount of withdrawal, either fifty or one hundred dollars, on the numbered buttons, and wait for your receipt to be printed.
5. Remove your card from the slot. The drawer will open with receipt and your cash withdrawal in fifty-dollar packets.

(10)   All customers are limited to two withdrawals in one twenty-four-hour period. If you attempt to withdraw more than the limited number of times, your card will be retained in the machine, and you will have to reclaim it in person at your main branch bank.

1. What is the main idea of this passage?

   (A) How to open an account at City Bank
   (B) How to use the City Bank machine teller
   (C) How to get a City Bank card
   (D) How to make deposits and withdrawals at City Bank

2. What happens when you remove your card from the machine?

   (A) Your identification number appears on a screen.
   (B) The drawer opens with your cash in it.
   (C) The process stops immediately.
   (D) Your receipt is printed.

3. All of the following steps must be performed in order to withdraw money from your accounts EXCEPT

   (A) The identification number must be entered.
   (B) Your card must be inserted in the machine.
   (C) The amount of the withdrawal must be entered.
   (D) The card must be reclaimed in person from a bank teller.

4. In line 8 "slot" is closest in meaning to

   (A) envelope
   (B) drawer
   (C) opening
   (D) box

5. The word "it" in line 12 refers to

   (A) machine
   (B) card
   (C) number
   (D) bank

6. It may be concluded from this passage that

   (A) a fifty-dollar withdrawal would be received in two packets
   (B) a typical identification number would be 10227
   (C) the maximum amount of money that may be withdrawn in one day is $200
   (D) withdrawals may be made from checking accounts only

Part B—Academic Information

Directions: In the Reading Comprehension section you will read several passages. Each one is followed by a number of questions about it. You are to choose the one best answer, (A), (B), (C), or (D), to each question. Then, on your answer sheet, find the number of the question and fill in the space that corresponds to the letter of the answer you have chosen.

Answer all questions about the information in a passage on the basis of what is stated or implied in that passage.

EXERCISE 2:   Academic Information

In some passages, you will be asked to read academic information, such as course descriptions and college regulations. You will usually be reading this kind of information for details. First, read the passage quickly. Then, read the questions. After you have answered questions for the main idea, begin to answer the other questions by referring to the passage. Use key words in the questions to help you locate the place in the passage where the answer is found. It will help you to practice reading catalogs and brochures distributed by American, Canadian, English, and Australian colleges and universities.

Passage One

In-state residents at State University pay one-fifth the amount in tuition fees that out-of-state residents are required to pay. This is true because State University is supported by state funds contributed in part by the taxpayers who reside in the state.

(5) The legal residence status of all students is determined at the time of their enrollment in State University and may not be changed unless the circumstances change. For example, a nonresident minor whose parents establish legal residence in the state or a nonresident adult who establishes legal residence in the state and maintains it for twelve months may petition for a change of status.

Personnel attached to military bases in the state are not eligible for legal residence status until they have lived in the state for one year. Foreign nationals who have entered the United States legally and hold green

(10) resident alien cards may be eligible for in-state status twelve months after the card has been issued provided that they have documenting evidence that they have lived in the state for twelve consecutive months. Acceptable evidence includes either a statement from the telephone company indicating that they have had a telephone in their name at the place of residence for one year or a statement from an employer that they have lived and worked in the state for one year. Purchase and ownership of property in the state or tax

(15) records indicating payment in the previous year will not be acceptable proof.

Students who have reason to believe that they have been classified incorrectly and are thus paying higher tuition fees may submit their cases in writing for review by the registrar.

1. With which of the following topics is the passage primarily concerned?

    (A) Residency requirements for students
    (B) Green cards for resident aliens
    (C) Acceptable evidence for resident status
    (D) Tuition restrictions for military personnel

2. Why do residents of other states pay higher tuition at State University?

    (A) Because they do not have green resident alien cards
    (B) Because they do not pay taxes in the state
    (C) Because they do not own homes in the state
    (D) Because they have not been classified correctly

3. The author mentions all of the following options as evidence of residence in state EXCEPT

    (A) a statement from the telephone company
    (B) a statement from an employer
    (C) documentation of twelve consecutive months in the state
    (D) a tax record

4. The word "consecutive" in line 11 is closest in meaning to

    (A) complete
    (B) continuous
    (C) acceptable
    (D) documented

5. The word "it" in line 7 refers to

    (A) residence
    (B) state
    (C) change
    (D) status

6. It can be inferred from the passage that an out-of-state resident pays

    (A) five times the amount that an in-state resident pays
    (B) twenty percent more than an in-state resident pays
    (C) one-fifth the amount that an in-state resident pays
    (D) twice as much as an in-state resident pays

Passage Two

To drop a course on the day of open registration, obtain a drop-add petition from your college office, complete it, and take it to your academic advisor for his or her signature. To add a course, go to the Student Union registration area, obtain a class card for the course you wish to add, and pay the additional fee at the registrar's desk.

(5)   To drop or add a course after the second day of classes, obtain a drop-add petition from your college office, complete it, and take it to the instructor of the course in question for his or her signature.

No drops or adds will be permitted after the first fifteen calendar days of each quarter without permission of the dean of your college.

1. This passage is a summary of how to

    (A) register for classes
    (B) drop a course
    (C) apply for admission to the University
    (D) change the classes on a student schedule

2. In order to add a course after the second day of classes, it is necessary to obtain the permission of

    (A) the dean of the college
    (B) the academic advisor
    (C) the instructor of the course
    (D) the registrar

3. The author mentions all of the following as requirements for dropping a course during open registration EXCEPT

    (A) get a drop-add petition at the college office
    (B) fill out the drop-add petition
    (C) have the academic advisor sign the drop-add petition
    (D) pay a fee at the registrar's office

4. The word "drop" in line 1 most nearly means

    (A) enroll in
    (B) withdraw from
    (C) pay for
    (D) stop offering

5. The word "it" in line 6 refers to

    (A) office
    (B) signature
    (C) petition
    (D) registration

6. It may be concluded from this passage that

    (A) everyone who wishes to add a course must do so during the first fifteen days of class
    (B) the University is on a semester system
    (C) all students are assigned to an academic advisor
    (D) registration is held in the college office

Passage Three

Candidates for the bachelor of business administration degree must complete 186 quarter hours of course work with a minimum of 372 quality points; that is, the equivalent of an average grade of C (2.0 on a 4.0 scale). Candidates must also maintain a cumulative grade point average of 2.0 or better in all required professional business courses, and must earn a minimum grade of C or better in each course in their area of
(5)   specialization. For example, students majoring in accounting must earn an average of C for all courses, including not only accounting courses but also history, English, math, and so on. They must earn a C or better in each accounting course. Accounting classes in which students have received a D, F, or Incomplete must be repeated.

1. Which sentence below best summarizes this passage?

   (A) Business majors must complete 186 hours with an average grade of C, and must earn a grade of C or better in each business course.
   (B) Business majors must repeat all accounting courses in which they receive a grade of less than C.
   (C) Business majors must earn at least 372 quality points in order to graduate.
   (D) Business majors must earn a grade of C or better in every class that they take, and must earn at least 186 quality points.

2. Which grade would be acceptable for a professional course?

   (A) I
   (B) C
   (C) D
   (D) F

3. The author mentions all of the following as requirements of candidates for the bachelor of business administration degree EXCEPT

   (A) an overall average grade of 2.0
   (B) 372 quarter hours of course work
   (C) a grade of C or better in each course in their specialization
   (D) a grade point average of 2.0 in all required professional courses

4. Another word which is often used in place of "specialization" in line 5 is

   (A) importance
   (B) degree
   (C) administration
   (D) major

5. The word "they" in line 6 refers to

   (A) candidates
   (B) courses
   (C) students
   (D) classes

6. We can infer that a student who had completed 170 quarter hours would be a

   (A) freshman
   (B) sophomore
   (C) junior
   (D) senior

Passage Four

A change in the federal regulations now requires that every international student admitted to the United States on an F-1 visa be assigned a social security number. The record will be marked to indicate that it is a nonwork number and may not be used for off-campus employment purposes. If the number is ever used in a job, the Social Security Office will notify the Immigration and Naturalization Service (INS). Unless prior
(5)   work permission has been granted by INS, the student may be asked to depart the country. Students who wish to work on campus may do so without notifying INS.

1. The title below that best expresses the ideas in this passage is

   (A) Invitation
   (B) Notice
   (C) Questionnaire
   (D) Application

2. Why are international students assigned social security numbers?

   (A) Because they need them in order to work off campus
   (B) Because they need them in order to depart the United States
   (C) Because they are required to have them in compliance with federal regulations
   (D) Because they need them in order to be granted F-1 status

3. All of the following are true concerning a social security number for international students EXCEPT

   (A) It is a nonwork number.
   (B) It may not be used for off-campus employment.
   (C) It is assigned only to students who want to work on campus.
   (D) It is used by students with F-1 visas.

4. In line 1, "regulations" is closest in meaning to

   (A) laws
   (B) government
   (C) employees
   (D) offices

5. The word "it" in line 2 refers to

   (A) number
   (B) employment
   (C) record
   (D) visa

6. Evidently, an international student can work without receiving permission from INS

   (A) at the Social Security Office
   (B) at State University library
   (C) nowhere
   (D) at the city airport

Passage Five

Accreditation is a system for setting national standards of quality in education. The United States is unique in the world because its accreditation system is not administered by the government, but rather by committees of educators and private agencies like the Middle States Association of Colleges and Secondary Schools and the Society of Engineers.

(5)   Before registering to study in any educational institution in the United States, a student should make certain that the institution is accredited in order to assure that the school has a recognized standard of organization, instruction, and financial support. Foreign students should be particularly careful to check an institution's accreditation because other governments or future employers may not recognize a degree earned from a school that has not received accreditation.

(10)   If a college is accredited, catalogs and brochures will usually indicate the accreditation status. If you are not sure about a certain school, don't hesitate to check its reputation with an education officer at the nearest U.S. embassy.

1. The title that best expresses the ideas in this passage is

    (A) Studying in the United States
    (B) Accreditation
    (C) How to Find the Best School
    (D) The Middle States Association of Colleges and Secondary Schools

2. What should students do in order to check the accreditation of a school that may interest them?

    (A) Write to the school.
    (B) Write to the U.S. Ministry of Education.
    (C) Register to study at the school.
    (D) Consult a U.S. embassy official.

3. According to the author, all of the following statements are true of the accreditation system in the United States EXCEPT

    (A) The accreditation status of a school will be listed in its catalogs and brochures.
    (B) Future employers will be influenced by the accreditation of a candidate's school.
    (C) Accreditation provides information about the standards of instruction and organization of a school.
    (D) The accreditation system is like that of many other countries.

4. The word "unique" in line 2 most nearly means

    (A) unusual
    (B) first
    (C) standard
    (D) large

5. The word "its" in line 11 refers to

    (A) school
    (B) status
    (C) embassy
    (D) reputation

6. From this passage, it may be concluded that an unaccredited school

    (A) does not offer a degree
    (B) may close because of financial disorganization
    (C) is administered by the government
    (D) is better than an accredited school

EXERCISE 3:   Textbooks/Biography

In most passages, you will be asked to read information contained in college textbooks, especially those used in courses like business, the natural sciences, the social sciences, and the arts.

The most frequently tested type of reading passage on the TOEFL is the textbook passage.

You will usually be reading this kind of information for details. First, read the passage quickly. Then, read the questions. After you have answered questions for the main idea, begin to answer the other questions by referring to the passage. Use key words in the questions to help you locate the place in the passage where the answer is found.

It will help you to practice reading textbooks written in English.

Passage One

William Lyon Mackenzie King was a Canadian statesman and leader of the Liberal Party who held the office of prime minister for a total of twenty-one years, longer than any public servant in the history of Canada. His father was a prominent judge, and his mother the daughter of William Lyon Mackenzie, leader of the rebellion of 1837 in Upper Canada. Greatly influenced by his famous grandfather, King was
(5) determined to serve his country in the role of reformer. After graduation from the University of Toronto with a degree in economics, he studied sociology and labor relations at Harvard and Chicago Universities. He served his fellow Canadians in many appointed and elected offices, including among them a seat in the parliament, before being elected prime minister in 1921. His three terms of office were marked by compromise, and he was often criticized for procrastination. Nevertheless, he earned the respect of most
(10) Canadians for his political astuteness and what one biographer, John Moir of the University of Toronto, has called his "essential Canadianness." According to Moir, King's methods may have been frustrating to some, but he was able to maintain unity and extend Canadian autonomy while acting within a difficult federal system.

1. What is the author's main point?

   (A) King made a valuable contribution to Canada.
   (B) King's methods were frustrating to many Canadians.
   (C) King came from a prominent Canadian family.
   (D) King held many positions in government.

2. According to biographer John Moir, why was King admired?

   (A) For his procrastination
   (B) For his willingness to compromise
   (C) For his ability to deal with frustration
   (D) For his Canadian persona

3. The author mentions all of the following universities as institutions where King studied EXCEPT

   (A) Harvard University
   (B) University of Upper Canada
   (C) Chicago University
   (D) University of Toronto

4. The word "autonomy" in line 12 could best be replaced by

   (A) independence
   (B) culture
   (C) friendship
   (D) conscientiousness

5. The word "them" in line 7 refers to

   (A) terms
   (B) Canadians
   (C) relations
   (D) offices

6. It can be inferred from the passage that William Lyon Mackenzie King was

   (A) proud of his family
   (B) not popular with the voters
   (C) not well educated
   (D) not willing to delay his judgment

Passage Two

Edwin Hubble was an American astronomer whose research led to discoveries about galaxies and the nature of the universe. He settled a long debate by demonstrating that the Andromeda nebula was located outside our galaxy, establishing the islands universe theory, which states that galaxies exist outside of our own. His study of the distribution of galaxies resulted in Hubble's Constant, a standard relationship between
(5)   a galaxy's distance from the earth and its speed of recession.

By 1925, Hubble had devised a classification system for the structure of galaxies and provided conclusive observational evidence for the expansion of the universe. His work pushed the one-hundred-inch Mount Wilson telescope beyond its capability and provided strong impetus for the construction of an instrument twice its size at Mount Palomar, which Hubble used during his last years of research. The
(10)   telescope that bears his name was launched on a space shuttle in 1990 and orbits the earth, collecting data about the size and age of the universe.

1. With what topic is the passage primarily concerned?

   (A) The Hubble telescope
   (B) The nature of the universe
   (C) Edwin Hubble's research
   (D) Hubble's classification system for the galaxies

2. Hubble's Constant states

   (A) that galaxies exist outside of ours
   (B) that there is a fixed relationship between the distance of a galaxy from the earth and its speed of recession
   (C) that the universe is expanding
   (D) that the Andromeda nebula is located outside our galaxy

3. The author mentions all of the following as accomplishments of Hubble EXCEPT

   (A) evidence for the expansion of the universe
   (B) a classification system for the structure of galaxies
   (C) the islands universe theory
   (D) a design for the space shuttle

4. The word "capability" in line 8 is closest in meaning to

   (A) confidence
   (B) capacity
   (C) quality
   (D) category

5. The word "its" in line 8 refers to

   (A) research
   (B) instrument
   (C) telescope
   (D) construction

6. The paragraph following the passage most probably discusses

   (A) Hubble's life
   (B) the telescope at Mount Palomar
   (C) recent information about the size and age of the universe
   (D) the space shuttle launch

Passage Three

According to legend, the first woman to join the Marine Corps was Lucy Brewer, who disguised herself as a man and served aboard the *U.S.S. Constitution* during the War of 1812. The first woman officially documented in Marine records, however, was Orpha Johnson. After working as a civilian clerk at Marine Corps headquarters, she entered the Marine Corps reserve in 1918. During World War I, women were
(5)   invited to join the Corps in order to meet the increased demand for personnel. By serving as typists and clerks, women freed thousands of male marines for overseas combat duty. At the end of the war, the women were transferred to inactive duty in Marine Corps Reserve units, and women did not resume an active role in the Marine Corps until World War II. During the Second World War, women were again asked to respond to the need for labor. Almost 20,000 women held positions in 200 specialties, including not only clerical and
(10) medical jobs but also technical and transportation services. After the war, many women were retained in the reserves, and then, beginning in 1948, women were permitted to enlist as regulars in the Marine Corps. By 1985, Gail Reals competed for and achieved the grade of Brigadier General, becoming the first woman to be so promoted. Today, women can be found in every branch and occupation of the United States Marine Corps.

1. With what topic is the passage primarily concerned?

   (A) The history of the Marine Corps
   (B) Women in the Marine Corps
   (C) The Marine Corps in World War II
   (D) Legends of the Marine Corps

2. Why is Gail Reals a significant figure in the history of the Marine Corps?

   (A) She was the first woman listed in the official Marine records.
   (B) She was the first woman to join the Marine Corps.
   (C) She was the first woman to be promoted to Brigadier General.
   (D) She was the first woman to enlist as a regular in the Marine Corps.

3. The author mentions all of the following as jobs performed by women in the Marine Corps EXCEPT

   (A) overseas combat duty
   (B) technical specialties
   (C) clerical work
   (D) medical professions

4. The word "enlist" in line 11 is closest in meaning to which of the following?

   (A) join
   (B) work
   (C) try
   (D) fight

5. The word "she" in line 4 refers to

   (A) personnel
   (B) Orpha Johnson
   (C) Lucy Brewer
   (D) the *U.S.S. Constitution*

6. The paragraph following the passage most probably discusses

   (A) other Marine Corps legends
   (B) Gail Reals' career
   (C) the role of women in today's Marine Corps
   (D) opposition to women in the Marine Corps

Passage Four

Ogden Nash was a poet, storyteller, humorist, and philosopher. Born in Rye, New York, and raised in Savannah, Georgia, he tried but failed to adapt himself to the academic and later the business world. After attending Harvard University briefly, he became a mail clerk on Wall Street, later advancing to bond salesman. His first job as a writer was to produce advertising copy for streetcar cards. Then, in 1925, he

(5) joined the advertising department of Doubleday Page and Company, one of the largest publishing houses in New York. Later, as a member of the editorial staff of *The New Yorker* magazine, he began writing short poems.

His verses are filled with humor and wry wit as well as the unexpected or improbable rhymes that have come to characterize them. One of his most famous poems is a two-line verse titled "Reflections on Ice-

(10) Breaking" in which he offers the following advice to young lovers: "Candy is dandy, but liquor is quicker." Beginning in 1931, and extending over the next four decades, Nash produced nineteen books of poetry. During the same time period, he was a favorite contributor to many leading magazines, and his name became a household word.

1. Which of the following would be the best title for the passage?

   (A) Poems in *The New Yorker*
   (B) Humor in Poetry
   (C) The Life and Work of Ogden Nash
   (D) Reflections on Ice-Breaking

2. Nash's first job was as a

   (A) mail clerk
   (B) bond salesman
   (C) writer of advertising copy
   (D) magazine writer

3. Nash is described as all of the following EXCEPT

   (A) a humorist
   (B) a popular poet
   (C) a prolific writer
   (D) an alcoholic

4. The word "leading" in line 12 could best be replaced by which of the following?

   (A) witty
   (B) contemporary
   (C) prominent
   (D) extravagant

5. The word "them" in line 9 refers to

   (A) rhymes
   (B) verses
   (C) editorial
   (D) publishing houses

6. In the second paragraph, what does Nash mean by "liquor is quicker"?

   (A) Young people should be warned against drinking alcohol.
   (B) It is quicker to make alcohol than it is to make candy.
   (C) Eating candy lasts longer than drinking alcohol.
   (D) Alcohol promotes romantic feelings faster than candy does.

Passage Five

Andrew Carnegie, known as the King of Steel, built the steel industry in the United States, and, in the process, became one of the wealthiest men in America. His success resulted in part from his ability to sell the product and in part from his policy of expanding during periods of economic decline, when most of his competitors were reducing their investments.

(5)   Carnegie believed that individuals should progress through hard work, but he also felt strongly that the wealthy should use their fortunes for the benefit of society. He opposed charity, preferring instead to provide educational opportunities that would allow others to help themselves. "He who dies rich, dies disgraced," he often said.

Among his more noteworthy contributions to society are those that bear his name, including the Carnegie
(10) Institute of Pittsburgh, which has a library, a museum of fine arts, and a museum of national history. He also founded a school of technology that is now part of Carnegie-Mellon University. Other philanthrophic gifts are the Carnegie Endowment for International Peace to promote understanding between nations, the Carnegie Institute of Washington to fund scientific research, and Carnegie Hall to provide a center for the arts.

(15)   Few Americans have been left untouched by Andrew Carnegie's generosity. His contributions of more than five million dollars established 2,500 libraries in small communities throughout the country and formed the nucleus of the public library system that we all enjoy today.

1. With which of the following topics is the passage primarily concerned?

   (A) The establishment of the public library system
   (B) The work of Carnegie-Mellon University
   (C) The building of the steel industry
   (D) The philanthropy of Andrew Carnegie

2. How many libraries did Carnegie establish for the public library system?

   (A) 25
   (B) 500
   (C) 2,500
   (D) Five million

3. The author mentions all of the following as recipients of philanthropic contributions by Carnegie EXCEPT

   (A) the arts
   (B) technology
   (C) economics
   (D) science

4. The word "fortunes" in line 6 could best be replaced by

   (A) assets
   (B) talents
   (C) influence
   (D) advice

5. The word "those" in line 9 refers to

   (A) opportunities
   (B) contributions
   (C) others
   (D) themselves

6. In the second paragraph, what does Carnegie mean when he says, "He who dies rich, dies disgraced"?

   (A) Rich people should be ashamed of their money.
   (B) Rich people should use their money for the benefit of society before they die.
   (C) Rich people often live disgraceful lives.
   (D) People should try to become rich before they die.

EXERCISE 4: Textbooks/History and Civics

Passage One

The first census of the American people in 1790 listed fewer than four million residents, most of whom had come from England. Ten years later, in 1800, although the English were still a majority, many Irish, Dutch, German, Swedish, Scottish, and French settlers had come to make their homes in the United States. Immigrants from all of these nations, along with an undocumented number of Africans who had been

(5) brought into the country as slaves, provided labor for the rapidly growing cities and the frontier farms. They built factories, roads, and canals, pushing West to settle towns on the edges of the American territory.

By 1880, large numbers of central and southern Europeans began to find their way to America. Italian, Greek, Russian, Austrian, Armenian, and Slavic immigrants settled in the cities where they supplied labor for hundreds of new industries. The census of 1910 listed almost one million immigrants.

(10) After the Civil War, many Asians began to arrive, primarily to work on the railroads in the West. Chinese laborers by the thousands led the way, followed by Korean and Japanese immigrants.

In more recent years, hundreds of thousands of refugees have come to the United States, the largest numbers from Hungary, Cuba, Lebanon, Syria, and the West Indies. With the close of the Vietnam War, thousands of Indochinese relocated in the United States.

(15) The United States is unique in the world because, with the notable exception of the Native Americans, all Americans are immigrants or the descendants of them.

1. Which of the following would be the best title for this passage?

   (A) A History of American Immigrants
   (B) A History of Immigration in the Nineteenth Century
   (C) A History of European Immigration to the United States
   (D) A History of Urban and Agricultural Development in the United States

2. When did many Italian immigrants enter the United States?

   (A) In 1790
   (B) In 1800
   (C) In 1880
   (D) In 1960

3. The author mentions all of the following as residents listed in the 1800 census EXCEPT

   (A) Germans
   (B) English
   (C) French
   (D) Italians

4. The word "majority" in line 2 is closest in meaning to

   (A) the largest number
   (B) the smallest number
   (C) the average number
   (D) the correct number

5. The word "them" in line 16 refers to

   (A) Native Americans
   (B) Americans
   (C) immigrants
   (D) descendants

6. It can be inferred from the passage that the author's attitude toward immigrants is

   (A) discourteous
   (B) respectful
   (C) prejudiced
   (D) disinterested

Passage Two

Federal policy toward the Native Americans has a long history of inconsistency, reversal, and failure. In the late 1700s, the United States government owned and operated factories, exchanging goods for furs with the hope that mutual satisfaction with trade would result in peace between Native Americans and the rush of settlers who were moving west. At the same time, the government supported missionary groups in their
(5)   efforts to build churches, schools, and model farms for those tribes that permitted them to live in their midst.

By the 1800s, federal negotiators were trying to convince many tribes to sell their land and move out of the line of frontier expansion, a policy that culminated in the forced expulsion of the major Southeastern tribes to the west. Over protests by Congress and the Supreme Court, President Andrew Jackson ordered the Native Americans to be removed to what is now Oklahoma. On the forced march, which the Cherokee
(10)   Nation refers to as the "Trail of Tears," many Native Americans died of disease, exposure, and hunger.

By the end of the 1800s, the government had discovered that some of the land allocated as permanent reservations for the Native Americans contained valuable resources. Congress passed the Dawes Severalty Act, and for the next forty years Indian agents and missionaries attempted to destroy the tribal system by separating the members. It was during this time that the government boarding schools were established to
(15)   educate Native American youth outside of the home environment.

Under the Indian Reorganization Act of 1934, scattered tribes were encouraged to reorganize their tribal governments. Anti-Indian sentiment resurfaced only ten years later, and by the 1950s relocation centers to move Native Americans from the reservations to urban areas were established.

Today, government policies are unclear. Many officials want to remove the federal government
(20)   completely from Native American governance. Others believe that the government should support Native American efforts to maintain their culture. Not surprisingly, the Native Americans themselves are ambivalent about the role of the federal government in their affairs.

1. What is the author's main point?

    (A) Government policies for Native Americans have not changed many times during the past three hundred years.
    (B) Today government officials are in agreement about their role in Native American affairs.
    (C) The federal government has been inconsistent and unclear in its policies for Native Americans.
    (D) The Indian Reorganization Act was a failure.

2. What was involved in "The Trail of Tears"?

    (A) Native American children were separated from their families and sent to boarding schools.
    (B) Native American families living in the Southeast were forced to move to Oklahoma.
    (C) Native American families were resettled on reservations.
    (D) Native Americans were moved from reservations to cities.

3. Native American policies are described as all of the following EXCEPT

    (A) inconsistent
    (B) destructive
    (C) permanent
    (D) unclear

4. The word "ambivalent" in line 22 refers to

    (A) exhibiting suspicion
    (B) experiencing contradictory feelings
    (C) expressing concern
    (D) demonstrating opposition

5. The word "them" in line 5 refers to

    (A) missionary groups
    (B) efforts
    (C) model farms
    (D) tribes

6. The paragraph following the passage most probably discusses

    (A) the Native American point of view regarding government policies today
    (B) the efforts by Native Americans to maintain their culture
    (C) the results of the reservation system
    (D) the intertribal councils that Native Americans have established

Passage Three

In the spring of 1934, storms swept across the Great Plains, but they were not rainstorms. They were the result of sun and drought and a terrible wind that blew millions of tons of topsoil from 300,000 square miles in Kansas, Texas, Oklahoma, Colorado, and New Mexico. This was the Dust Bowl. It buried fences, fields, and homes. It choked cattle and sickened the people who stayed. Three hundred and fifty thousand settlers
(5)   fled, many becoming part of a slow, sad caravan along Route 66 to California.

But wind and drought were not the only factors that combined to create the Dust Bowl. Only fifty years earlier, a carpet of buffalo grass had covered the Great Plains, protecting the soil and retaining the moisture in the ground. By the turn of the century, farmers had settled, homesteading in regions that had been used as range land. The increased demand for wheat during World War I encouraged farmers to plow and plant even
(10)   wider areas. Forty percent of the land that they plowed up had never been exposed to rain, wind, or sun before. When the drought and wind came, the land had been prepared for disaster.

1. With which of the following topics is the passage primarily concerned?

   (A) The Dust Bowl
   (B) The Great Plains
   (C) Homesteading
   (D) World War I

2. Where did many of the homesteaders go when they abandoned their farms?

   (A) To Kansas
   (B) To New Mexico
   (C) To Texas
   (D) To California

3. The author mentions all of the following as having contributed to the disaster EXCEPT

   (A) wind
   (B) drought
   (C) homesteading
   (D) rain

4. The word "fled" in line 5 is closest in meaning to which of the following phrases?

   (A) passed away
   (B) became ill
   (C) ran away
   (D) gave up

5. The word "It" in line 4 refers to

   (A) topsoil
   (B) the Dust Bowl
   (C) wind
   (D) result

6. It can be inferred from the passage that

   (A) ranchers caused the Dust Bowl by grazing too many buffalo on the grasslands
   (B) the Dust Bowl was brought to an end by rainstorms
   (C) the Great Plains is a wheat-producing region in the United States
   (D) all the homesteaders had to abandon their farms during the Dust Bowl

Passage Four

In his book *The Making of the President, 1960*, Theodore White made some insightful observations about the television debates between Kennedy and Nixon. He contended that the debates had to be analyzed within the context of the explosion in the field of communications. During the previous decade, Americans had purchased television sets at a phenomenal rate. By the evening of the debate, 88 percent of all American
(5) families owned a television set, and a very large percentage tuned into the debate.

The format was really less like a debate than like a press conference. Each candidate was allowed an opening statement of eight minutes, and then two and a half minutes to respond to each question proposed by a panel. There was no provision for dialogue between the candidates. As White observed, despite this format, Nixon proceeded as though he were in a personal debate with Kennedy, trying to score points from
(10) the reporters on the panel. In contrast, Kennedy spoke directly to the television viewers, concentrating on creating a dynamic and appealing image in order to influence them.

Later, Kennedy claimed that the debates were the single most important factor in the election. In White's view, the debates did change the direction of the campaign. From research studies, including the Gallup Poll, it appeared that Kennedy had gained at least 2 million votes as a result of the televised programs.
(15) When you consider that Kennedy won by a little more than 100,000 votes, the debates had to have made the difference. It has been clear to candidates since then that television debates are a very powerful tool.

1. What is the author's main point?

   (A) Television should be removed from politics.
   (B) The Gallup Poll was an accurate predictor of the 1960 election.
   (C) Kennedy's style in the TV debate affected the outcome of the election.
   (D) Eighty-eight percent of all Americans owned televisions in 1960.

2. How many votes did Kennedy gain as a result of the debates?

   (A) 88 percent
   (B) 100,000
   (C) 1,960,000
   (D) 2 million

3. The author mentions all the following as characteristics of the debate EXCEPT

   (A) a large television audience
   (B) a dialogue between the candidates
   (C) an opening statement by each candidate
   (D) questions by a panel of reporters

4. The word "dynamic" in line 11 is closest in meaning to

   (A) intelligent
   (B) energetic
   (C) attractive
   (D) conventional

5. The word "them" in line 11 refers to

   (A) candidates
   (B) reporters
   (C) viewers
   (D) points

6. The paragraph following the passage most probably discusses

   (A) the book by Theodore White
   (B) the history of television
   (C) the accuracy of the Gallup Poll
   (D) television debates by candidates after 1960

Passage Five

Canada is a constitutional monarchy with a parliamentary system of government modeled after that of Great Britain. The official head of state in Canada is Queen Elizabeth II of Britain, who is also Queen of Canada. The governor-general is the queen's personal representative in Canada and the official head of the Canadian parliament, although with very limited powers.

(5)   The federal parliament in Canada consists of the House of Commons and the Senate. The actual head of government is the prime minister, who is responsible for choosing a cabinet. The system is referred to as responsible government, which means that cabinet members sit in the parliament and are directly responsible to it, holding power only as long as a majority of the House of Commons shows confidence by voting with them.

(10)   The Canadian Senate has 102 members, appointed by the governor-general on the advice of the prime minister. Their actual function is advisory, although they may make minor changes in bills. The actual power resides in the House of Commons, the members of which are elected directly by the voters. General elections must be held at the end of every five years, but they may be held whenever issues require it, and most parliaments are dissolved before the end of the five-year term. When a government loses its majority

(15) support in a general election, a change of government occurs.

1. What does this passage mainly discuss?

   (A) The relationship between Canada and England
   (B) The Canadian election process
   (C) The Canadian system of government
   (D) The powers of parliament

2. When does a change of government occur in Canada?

   (A) When the governor-general decides to appoint a new government
   (B) When the voters do not return majority support for the government in a general election
   (C) When the prime minister advises the governor-general to appoint a new government
   (D) When the House of Commons votes for a new government

3. The governor-general is described as all of the following EXCEPT

   (A) the official head of parliament
   (B) the head of government
   (C) the queen's representative in Canada
   (D) the official who appoints the senate

4. The word "dissolved" in line 14 could best be replaced by

   (A) approved
   (B) evaluated
   (C) reorganized
   (D) dismissed

5. The word "it" in line 8 refers to

   (A) majority
   (B) parliament
   (C) cabinet
   (D) system

6. It can be inferred from the passage that the voters in Canada

   (A) choose the prime minister and the Cabinet
   (B) do not usually vote in general elections
   (C) allow their representatives in the House of Commons to vote in their behalf in general elections
   (D) determine when a change of government should occur

EXERCISE 5:   Textbooks/Social Sciences

Passage One

Although behavioral psychologists use many different kinds of equipment in operant conditioning experiments, one device that is frequently employed is the Skinner Box. The box, named for B. F. Skinner, the American psychologist who developed it, was used in Skinner's original operant conditioning experiment in 1932. The Skinner Box is a small, empty box except for a bar with a cup underneath it. In
(5)   Skinner's experiment, a rat that had been deprived of food for twenty-four hours was placed in the box. As the hungry animal began to explore its new environment, it accidentally hit the bar, and a food pellet dropped into the cup. The rat ate the pellet and continued exploring for more food. After hitting the bar three or four times with similar results, the animal learned that it could get food by pressing the bar. The food stimulus reinforced the bar pressing response. The rat had been conditioned.

1. What is the main idea in this passage?

    (A) That learning is often accidental
    (B) That B. F. Skinner is a behavioral
         psychologist
    (C) That a Skinner Box may be used for
         operant conditioning
    (D) That rats are able to learn simple tasks

2. How did the rat obtain more food?

    (A) By exploring
    (B) By hitting a bar
    (C) By making noise
    (D) By eating pellets

3. The author mentions all of the following as part
    of the Skinner box EXCEPT

    (A) a bar
    (B) a cup
    (C) food pellets
    (D) electric shock

4. The word "deprived" in line 5 is closest in
    meaning to

    (A) enticed
    (B) provided
    (C) denied
    (D) revealed

5. The word "it" in line 4 refers to

    (A) box
    (B) bar
    (C) cup
    (D) rat

6. It may be concluded that operant conditioning

    (A) always uses a Skinner Box
    (B) is no longer popular
    (C) involves a stimulus and a response
    (D) requires at least twenty-four hours

Passage Two

Persons sixty-five years and over already represent 13 percent of the total population in America, and by 2025 there will be 59 million elderly Americans, representing 21 percent of the population of the United States. Furthermore, the percentage of the population over age eighty-five will increase from about 1 percent currently to 5 percent in 2050. This population trend has been referred to as the graying of America.

(5) To explain this demographic change, we must look to three factors. Fertility, mortality, and immigration in large part influence all demographic trends. The large number of children born after World War II will increase the pool of elderly between 2010 and 2030. The "baby boom" will become the "senior boom" sixty-five years later. Although the birth rate is the most dramatic factor, the decline in the death rate is also significant. Medical advances have influenced life expectancy. For example, whereas only 40 percent of

(10) those Americans born in 1900 had a life expectancy of sixty-five, today 80 percent are expected to reach the classic retirement age. The average male life span, now 71.4 years, is expected to increase to 73.3 by 2005. Among females, the life span is projected to increase from the current 78.3 years to 81.3 years by 2005. In addition, immigration has contributed to the increasing number of elderly. After World War I, a massive immigration of young adults of child-bearing age occurred. Because the birth rates among this specialized

(15) population were very high, their children, now among the elderly, are a significant segment of the older population.

1. Which of the following would be the best title for the passage?

   (A) The Graying of America
   (B) Immigration Patterns in America
   (C) Trends in Life Expectancy
   (D) Baby Boomers

2. The average life expectancy for an American woman today is

   (A) 71.4 years
   (B) 73.3 years
   (C) 78.3 years
   (D) 81.3 years

3. The author mentions all of the following as factors that have influenced population trends EXCEPT

   (A) the "baby boom" after World War II
   (B) the immigration after World War I
   (C) the improvements in health care
   (D) the decline in the birth rate among young Americans

4. The word "pool" in line 7 refers to

   (A) a group of people
   (B) a general direction
   (C) a negative attitude
   (D) an increase in influence

5. The word "their" in line 15 refers to

   (A) females
   (B) elderly
   (C) young adults
   (D) birth rates

6. It can be inferred from the passage that the word "gray" is a reference to

   (A) the color hair typical of older people
   (B) the last name of the person who has studied the population trends
   (C) the diversity of colors in the population that mix to make gray
   (D) the dismal outlook for the future because of population trends

Passage Three

Whether one is awake or asleep, the brain emits electrical waves. During wakefulness, the waves are recorded at about ten small waves per second. With the onset of sleep, the waves become larger and slower. The largest, slowest waves occur during the first three hours of sleep. Mental activity slows down but does not stop. In fact, if awakened from slow-wave sleep, a person can often remember vague thoughts that
(5)   occurred during that period of sleep.

During sleep, intervals of small, fast waves also occur. These waves are similar to those experienced while awake. The eyes move rapidly, and it appears to the observer that the sleeper is watching some event. Sleepers who are awakened during this rapid-eye-movement sleep will often recall the details of dreams they have been having. Sleep of this kind is called dreaming sleep or rapid-eye-movement sleep, also known
(10) as REM sleep.

In a period of eight hours, most sleepers experience from three to five instances of REM sleep. Each instance lasts from five to thirty minutes with an interval of at least ninety minutes between each one. Later instances of REM sleep are usually of longer duration than are instances earlier in the eight-hour period.

People who suffer sleep deprivation experience fatigue, irritability, and loss of concentration. Sleep is
(15) essential because it regenerates the brain and the nervous system. Slow-wave sleep may be especially helpful in restoring muscle control, whereas REM sleep may be more important for mental activity. It appears that both kinds of sleep are necessary, and the recuperation of sleep of one kind will not compensate for a lack of the other kind of sleep.

1. What is the author's main purpose in the passage?

   (A) To describe REM sleep
   (B) To explain sleep deprivation
   (C) To discuss the two types of sleep
   (D) To recommend an increase in the number of hours of sleep

2. How many times per night do most sleepers experience REM sleep?

   (A) Eight
   (B) Three to five
   (C) Five to thirty
   (D) Ninety

3. The author mentions all the following as characteristics of REM sleep EXCEPT

   (A) vague thoughts
   (B) smaller brain waves
   (C) eye movements
   (D) dreams

4. The word "vague" in line 4 could best be replaced by

   (A) familiar
   (B) indefinite
   (C) unpleasant
   (D) detailed

5. The word "it" in line 15 refers to

   (A) deprivation
   (B) the brain
   (C) sleep
   (D) concentration

6. It can be inferred from the passage that students who are writing term papers

   (A) require slow wave sleep to increase mental activity
   (B) can stay up all night working and recover the sleep they need by sleeping for a few hours the next afternoon
   (C) need REM sleep to restore mental functioning
   (D) do not need as much sleep because of the heightened brain waves involved in creative activity

Passage Four

In the United States today there are more than half a million criminals serving time in prison. Most prisoners are male high-school dropouts between the ages of 18 and 29. Even more shocking is the fact that the number and rate of imprisonment has more than doubled over the past twenty years, and the recidivism—that is, the rate for rearrest—is more than 60 percent.

(5)   Although the stated goal of most prison systems, on both federal and state levels, is to rehabilitate the inmates and reintegrate them into society, the systems themselves do not support such a result. Prisons are usually geographically or psychologically isolated and terribly overcrowded. Even in the more enlightened prisons, only one-third of the inmates have vocational training opportunities or work release options.

If prisons are indeed to achieve the goal of rehabilitating offenders, then the prisons themselves will have
(10) to change. First, they will have to be smaller, housing no more than five hundred prisoners. Second, they will have to be built in or near population centers with community resources available for gradual reintegration into society. Finally, prison programs must be restructured to include work release and vocational and academic training that promises carry over into the inmate's life after release. Models for such collaborative efforts between the criminal justice system and the community already exist in several
(15) hundred half-way houses throughout the country.

1. What is the author's main point?

    (A) Prisons must be restructured if they are to accomplish the goal of rehabilitation.
    (B) Models for community collaboration have been successful.
    (C) Most of the criminals serving time in prison are high-school dropouts.
    (D) The criminal justice system must establish a better goal.

2. According to the author, how many prisoners are offered training or work release?

    (A) None
    (B) 33⅓ percent
    (C) 50 percent
    (D) 60 percent

3. The author mentions all the following as necessary to prison reform EXCEPT

    (A) newer buildings
    (B) smaller institutions
    (C) vocational training
    (D) collaboration with the community

4. The word "recidivism" in line 4 refers to

    (A) all people who are imprisoned
    (B) people who return to prison after release
    (C) people who drop out of high school
    (D) people who have been in prison for a long time

5. The word "them" in line 6 refers to

    (A) prison systems
    (B) inmates
    (C) goals
    (D) levels

6. The paragraph following this passage most probably discusses

    (A) the goals of most state and federal prisons
    (B) the cost of prison reform
    (C) examples of models for community collaboration
    (D) problems with the current criminal justice system

Passage Five

Standard usage includes those words and expressions understood, used, and accepted by a majority of the speakers of a language in any situation regardless of the level of formality. As such, these words and expressions are well defined and listed in standard dictionaries. Colloquialisms, on the other hand, are familiar words and idioms that are understood by almost all speakers of a language and used in informal
(5) speech or writing, but not considered appropriate for more formal situations. Almost all idiomatic expressions are colloquial language. Slang, however, refers to words and expressions understood by a large number of speakers but not accepted as good, formal usage by the majority. Colloquial expressions and even slang may be found in standard dictionaries but will be so identified. Both colloquial usage and slang are more common in speech than in writing.

(10) Colloquial speech often passes into standard speech. Some slang also passes into standard speech, but other slang expressions enjoy momentary popularity followed by obscurity. In some cases, the majority never accepts certain slang phrases but nevertheless retains them in their collective memories. Every generation seems to require its own set of words to describe familiar objects and events.

It has been pointed out by a number of linguists that three cultural conditions are necessary for the
(15) creation of a large body of slang expressions. First, the introduction and acceptance of new objects and situations in the society; second, a diverse population with a large number of subgroups; third, association among the subgroups and the majority population.

Finally, it is worth noting that the terms "standard," "colloquial," and "slang" exist only as abstract labels for scholars who study language. Only a tiny number of the speakers of any language will be aware that they
(20) are using colloquial or slang expressions. Most speakers of English will, during appropriate situations, select and use all three types of expressions.

1. With which of the following topics is the passage primarily concerned?

   (A) Standard speech
   (B) Idiomatic speech
   (C) Different types of speech
   (D) Dictionary usage

2. How is slang defined by the author?

   (A) Words and phrases accepted by the majority for formal usage
   (B) Words and phrases understood by the majority but not found in standard dictionaries
   (C) Words and phrases that are understood by a restricted group of speakers
   (D) Words and phrases understood by a large number of speakers but not accepted as formal usage

3. The author mentions all of the following as requirements for slang expressions to be created EXCEPT

   (A) new situations
   (B) a new generation
   (C) interaction among diverse groups
   (D) a number of linguists

4. The word "appropriate" in line 5 could best be replaced by

   (A) suitable
   (B) congenial
   (C) elegant
   (D) direct

5. The word "them" in line 12 refers to

   (A) words
   (B) slang phrases
   (C) memories
   (D) the majority

6. It can be inferred from the passage that the author

   (A) does not approve of either slang or colloquial speech in any situation
   (B) approves of colloquial speech in some situations, but not slang
   (C) approves of slang and colloquial speech in appropriate situations
   (D) does not approve of colloquial usage in writing

EXERCISE 6:   Literature

Passage One

Universally acclaimed as America's greatest playwright, Eugene O'Neill was born in 1888 in the heart of the theater district in New York City. As the son of an actor he had early exposure to the world of the theater. He attended Princeton University briefly in 1906, but returned to New York to work in a variety of jobs before joining the crew of a freighter as a seaman. Upon returning from voyages to South Africa and South
(5) America, he was hospitalized for six months to recuperate from tuberculosis. While he was recovering, he determined to write a play about his adventures on the sea. He went to Harvard, where he wrote the one-act *Bound East for Cardiff.* It was produced on Cape Cod by the Provincetown Players, an experimental theater group that was later to settle the famous Greenwich Village theater district in New York City. The Players produced several more of his one-acts in the years between 1916–1920. With the full-length play *Beyond the*
(10) *Horizon,* produced on Broadway in 1920, O'Neill's success was assured. The play won the Pulitzer prize for the best play of the year. O'Neill was to be awarded the prize again in 1922, 1928, and 1957 for *Anna Christie, Strange Interlude,* and *Long Day's Journey Into Night.* In 1936, he was awarded the Nobel prize for literature.

O'Neill's plays, forty-five in all, cover a wide range of dramatic subjects, but several themes emerge,
(15) including the ambivalence of family relationships, the struggle between the sexes, the conflict between spiritual and material desires, and the vision of modern man as a victim of uncontrollable circumstances. Most of O'Neill's characters are seeking for meaning in their lives. According to his biographers, most of the characters were portraits of himself and his family. In a sense, his work chronicled his life.

1. This passage is a summary of O'Neill's

   (A) work
   (B) life
   (C) work and life
   (D) family

2. How many times was O'Neill awarded the Pulitzer prize?

   (A) One
   (B) Three
   (C) Four
   (D) Five

3. The author mentions all of the following as themes for O'Neill's plays EXCEPT

   (A) life in college
   (B) adventures at sea
   (C) family life
   (D) relationships between men and women

4. The word "briefly" in line 3 is closest in meaning to

   (A) seriously
   (B) for a short time
   (C) on scholarship
   (D) without enthusiasm

5. The word "It" in line 7 refers to

   (A) Harvard
   (B) one-act play
   (C) theater group
   (D) theater district

6. We can infer from information in the passage that O'Neill's plays were not

   (A) controversial
   (B) autobiographical
   (C) optimistic
   (D) popular

Passage Two

At the age of sixty-five, Laura Ingalls Wilder began writing a series of novels for young people based on her early experiences on the American frontier. Born in the state of Wisconsin in 1867, she and her family were rugged pioneers. Seeking better farm land, they went by covered wagon to Missouri in 1869, then on to Kansas the next year, returning to Wisconsin in 1871, and traveling on to Minnesota and Iowa before
(5) settling permanently in South Dakota in 1879. Because of this constant moving, Wilder's early education took place sporadically in a succession of one-room schools. From age thirteen to sixteen, she attended school more regularly, although she never graduated.

At the age of eighteen, she married Almanzo James Wilder. They bought a small farm in the Ozarks, where they remained for the rest of their lives. Their only daughter, Rose, who had become a nationally
(10) known journalist, encouraged her mother to write. Serving as agent and editor, Rose negotiated with Harper's to publish her mother's first book, *Little House in the Big Woods*. Seven more books followed, each chronicling her early life on the plains. Written from the perspective of a child, they have remained popular with young readers from many nations. Twenty years after her death in 1957, more than 20 million copies had been sold, and they had been translated into fourteen languages. In 1974, a weekly television
(15) series, "Little House on the Prairie," was produced, based on the stories from the Wilder books.

1. What is the main topic of the passage?

   (A) American pioneer life
   (B) Children's literature
   (C) A weekly television series
   (D) Wilder's career

2. Laura Ingalls Wilder began writing novels

   (A) when she was a child on the frontier
   (B) right after she moved to the Ozarks
   (C) when she was a young mother
   (D) after her sixty-fifth birthday

3. The author mentions all of the following as events in the life of Laura Ingalls Wilder EXCEPT

   (A) She went west by covered wagon.
   (B) She graduated from a one-room school.
   (C) She married Almanzo Wilder.
   (D) She had one daughter.

4. The word "sporadically" in line 6 is closest in meaning to

   (A) with great success
   (B) for a long time
   (C) at irregular intervals
   (D) in a very efficient way

5. The word "they" in line 12 refers to

   (A) the plains
   (B) many nations
   (C) more books
   (D) young readers

6. It can be inferred from the passage that

   (A) Laura Ingalls Wilder wrote scripts for the television series
   (B) the Wilders were not happy living in the Ozarks
   (C) Wilder's daughter was not a successful writer
   (D) the Wilder books have a universal appeal

Passage Three

Edgar Allan Poe is today regarded as one of the premier authors of horror stories, but he received very little recognition and almost no money for his stories while he lived. Twenty-five of his greatest stories were published in a collection called *Tales of the Grotesque and Arabesque,* which appeared in 1840, but at the time little notice was taken of it. Three years later, another story, "The Gold Bug," was published, selling

(5) 300,000 copies, and by 1845 he had written twelve more stories, which he published in *Tales.* His best-known stories include "The Pit and the Pendulum" and "The Tell-Tale Heart." But it was a poem, "The Raven," that brought him his greatest recognition as a writer. The centerpiece of a collection of thirty poems published in a volume titled *The Raven and Other Poems,* it became quite popular. The theme of the poem is grief over the loss of an ideal love. The dramatic, almost theatrical tone, the intensity of the repetition, and

(10) the hypnotic rhythm reflect the narrator's despondent and desperate state of mind. When read aloud, it produces a powerful effect.

1. What is the author's main purpose in this passage?

   (A) To give examples of horror stories
   (B) To chronicle the work of Edgar Allan Poe
   (C) To compare Poe's stories with his poems
   (D) To suggest that "The Raven" be read aloud

2. According to the passage, which of the following tales sold 300,000 copies?

   (A) "The Tell-Tale Heart"
   (B) "The Gold Bug"
   (C) "The Raven"
   (D) "The Pit and the Pendulum"

3. The author mentions all of the following as features of "The Raven" EXCEPT

   (A) intense repetition
   (B) dramatic tone
   (C) cheerful mood
   (D) hypnotic rhythm

4. The word "recognition" in line 2 is closest in meaning to

   (A) criticism
   (B) opportunities
   (C) imitation
   (D) appreciation

5. The word "it" in line 4 refers to

   (A) a collection
   (B) the time
   (C) little notice
   (D) another story

6. It can be inferred from the passage that Edgar Allan Poe

   (A) lost his true love
   (B) lived in poverty
   (C) suffered a mental breakdown
   (D) died young

Passage Four

America's infatuation with the West was probably influenced in part by the appearance of tales of adventure in the dime novels of the 1860s. In these romantic stories, the cowboy was elevated to hero. One of the most popular and prolific authors of the dime novel was Ned Buntline, whose work laid the foundation for western fiction.

(5)   With the appearance in 1920 of *The Virginian* by Owen Wister, the western genre was established. By then, the cowboy was disappearing from the American scene, and the romantic figure was even more appealing. Wister also introduced several other memorable characters, including the villain, the gambler, and the love interest, a school marm. They became stock characters in the novels and the films that followed.

(10)   The next year, in *The Log of a Cowboy,* Andy Adams chronicled a trail drive from Mexico to Montana. Told simply and less dramatically, it was nonetheless popular and influential in the development of the new genre. Especially in his descriptions of places and real people like Bat Masterson and Wyatt Earp, Adams injected details that rang true.

     One interesting aspect of the development of the western genre is the fact that most of the authors were
(15) easterners. Ned Buntline wrote almost all of his novels before he ever went west. Owen Wister, a Philadelphian, was a Harvard graduate. Andy Adams, born in Indiana, was an easterner who went to Texas, became a ranch hand and, eventually, a trail driver. The western writer was an exception.

1. With what topic is the passage primarily concerned?

    (A) Eastern writers
    (B) Western genre
    (C) *The Virginian*
    (D) Dime novels

2. According to the passage, the event that marked the establishment of the western genre was

    (A) the publication of the dime novel
    (B) the appearance of *The Virginian*
    (C) the success of *Log of a Cowboy*
    (D) the descriptions of real people and places

3. The author mentions all of the following as easterners EXCEPT

    (A) Andy Adams
    (B) Ned Buntline
    (C) Bat Masterson
    (D) Owen Wister

4. The word "stock" in line 8 could best be replaced by

    (A) comic
    (B) vulgar
    (C) recurring
    (D) charming

5. The word "it" in line 11 refers to

    (A) the development
    (B) the next year
    (C) the new genre
    (D) The Log

6. The paragraph following the passage most probably discusses

    (A) westerners who wrote novels about the East
    (B) easterners who wrote novels about the West
    (C) trail drives in the old West
    (D) life in the East in the early 1900s

Passage Five

The Pearl by John Steinbeck is the retelling of a legend about a fisherman who finds a huge pearl, realizes that the discovery is destroying his life, and returns the pearl to the sea. It is told in a style so authentic that readers feel they are hearing the story from one of the villagers who knows all the characters. In spite of its apparent simplicity, however, there are several levels to appreciate in reading The Pearl.

(5)   Some critics have pointed out that the author was committed to ecology, and that this book was really his statement about the dangers of creating an imbalance in the natural environment. When the fisherman throws the pearl back into the sea, he is restoring the natural order. In fact, Steinbeck was a member of an expedition to explore marine life along the Gulf of California when he heard the legend of the "pearl of the world."

(10)   Other critics have suggested that Steinbeck's concern for the conditions of the working class was reflected in the relationships among the characters. The priest becomes interested in the poor fisherman's family after the pearl is found because he hopes to receive a donation that will enable him to improve his church. The doctor who has refused to treat the fisherman's baby in the past is solicitous when it becomes known that the fisherman has found a valuable pearl. An even more direct example of exploitation is the

(15) way that the pearl merchants take advantage of the fishermen in the village.

Finally, the work has been interpreted as an allegory of human desires, the vanity of material wealth, and the struggle between good and evil. Although the fisherman had dreamed of buying peace and happiness with the pearl, he realizes that these spiritual gifts are beyond price. They cannot be purchased.

Steinbeck himself writes in the introduction, "If this story is a parable, perhaps everyone takes his own

(20) meaning from it and reads his own life into it." Precisely this latitude for personal interpretation within the universal themes gives The Pearl such enduring appeal.

1. What is the author's main point?

    (A) Steinbeck retold a legend.
    (B) There are many levels to appreciate in The Pearl.
    (C) Spiritual gifts are beyond price.
    (D) The Pearl is a very simple story.

2. According to the passage, why has The Pearl remained so popular?

    (A) Because it allows the reader to interpret the story in a personal way
    (B) Because it is a beautiful story
    (C) Because it is a very easy story to read
    (D) Because the characters are realistic

3. The author mentions all of the following as reasons that Steinbeck may have written The Pearl EXCEPT

    (A) because he was making a statement about the exploitation of the poor
    (B) because he was expressing concern for the preservation of the environment
    (C) because he was trying to demonstrate the futility of materialism
    (D) because he wanted to create a legend that would last

4. The word "authentic" in line 3 could best be replaced by

    (A) spectacular
    (B) realistic
    (C) eloquent
    (D) sentimental

5. The word "it" in line 20 refers to

    (A) parable
    (B) introduction
    (C) meaning
    (D) life

6. It can be inferred from the passage that the author

    (A) does not agree with the critics
    (B) feels that The Pearl has one correct interpretation
    (C) does not appreciate Steinbeck's work
    (D) feels that reading The Pearl is a personal experience

EXERCISE 7:   Textbooks/Art and Entertainment

Passage One

The practice of signing and numbering individual prints was introduced by James Abbott McNeill Whistler, the nineteenth century artist best known for the painting of his mother, called "Arrangement in Grey and Black," but known to most of us as "Whistler's Mother." Whistler's brother-in-law, Sir Francis Seymour Haden, a less well-known artist, had speculated that collectors might find prints more attractive if
(5) they knew that there were only a limited number of copies produced. By signing the work in pencil, an artist could guarantee and personalize each print.

As soon as Whistler and Haden began signing and numbering their prints, their work began to increase in value. When other artists noticed that the signed prints encouraged higher prices, they began copying the practice.
(10) Although most prints are signed on the right-hand side in the margin below the image, the placement of the signature is a matter of personal choice. Indeed, prints have been signed within the image, in any of the margins, or even on the reverse side of the print. Wherever the artist elects to sign it, a signed print is still valued above an unsigned one, even in the same edition.

1. Which of the following would be the best title for the passage?

   (A) Whistler's Mother
   (B) Whistler's Greatest Works
   (C) The Practice of Signing Prints
   (D) Copying Limited Edition Prints

2. What made Whistler's work more valuable?

   (A) His fame as an artist
   (B) His painting of his mother
   (C) His signature on the prints
   (D) His brother-in-law's prints

3. The author mentions all of the following as reasons why a collector prefers a signed print EXCEPT

   (A) It guarantees the print's authenticity.
   (B) It makes the print more personal.
   (C) It encourages higher prices for the print.
   (D) It limits the number of copies of the print.

4. The word "speculated" in line 4 could best be replaced by

   (A) guessed
   (B) noticed
   (C) denied
   (D) announced

5. The word "it" in line 12 refers to

   (A) the same edition
   (B) the image
   (C) the reverse side
   (D) a print

6. It can be inferred from the passage that artists number their prints

   (A) as an accounting procedure
   (B) to guarantee a limited edition
   (C) when the buyer requests it
   (D) at the same place on each of the prints they produce

Passage Two

Jazz originated in the southern United States after the Civil War. It began as the musical expression of black people who had formerly been slaves, combining hymns, spirituals, and traditional work songs into a new form. The style was a blend of the rhythms brought to America by the Africans who were imported as slave labor and the popular music of the era that featured the ragtime piano. The term jazz itself is of

(5)   obscure, and possibly nonmusical origin, but it was first used to describe this particular kind of musical expression in about 1915.

Improvisation has always been one of the primary elements of jazz. While one instrument, often the trumpet, plays the melody, another instrument, usually the clarinet, embellishes and invents compatible melodies around the original theme. Such improvisation is the test of the jazz musician's skill.

(10)   A jazz band commonly includes four to twelve musicians with a relatively large proportion of the group in the rhythm section. There are a drummer, a bass player, and a pianist. Often there is also a banjo player or guitarist. In traditional jazz, the clarinet, trumpet, and trombone carry the melody, but in more modern jazz, the saxophone, violin, and flute may also be included in the melody section. Some jazz bands employ a blues singer.

(15)   Jazz first became popular outside the South in the 1920s, when jazz bands began to record, distribute, and even export their recordings to Europe. Since jazz is improvisational, it does not exist in the form of printed scores, and recorded performances were and still are the best way of preserving the music. A very basic library of recorded jazz would include work by such classic artists as Jelly Roll Morton, Louis Armstrong, Duke Ellington, Count Basie, and Billie Holiday. Theirs is probably America's most unique and most

(20)   important contribution to the musical world, although there are a few contemporary artists who are keeping the tradition alive.

1. With which of the following topics is the passage primarily concerned?

   (A) The History of Jazz
   (B) Jazz Musicians
   (C) Improvisation
   (D) Jazz Bands

2. The rhythms of jazz were first heard

   (A) in Europe
   (B) in Africa
   (C) in South America
   (D) in North America

3. The author mentions all of the following as characteristic of jazz EXCEPT

   (A) a large number of percussion instruments
   (B) a printed score for the music
   (C) a melody played by the trumpet
   (D) a ragtime piano

4. The word "blend" in line 3 is closest in meaning to

   (A) mixture
   (B) rejection
   (C) imitation
   (D) variety

5. The word "it" in line 5 refers to

   (A) era
   (B) kind
   (C) origin
   (D) term

6. The paragraph following the passage most probably discusses

   (A) recorded performances by jazz musicians
   (B) modern jazz musicians
   (C) famous blues singers
   (D) Louis Armstrong's contribution to jazz

Passage Three

Alfred Hitchcock's precut scripts are legendary. More than any other director, Hitchcock insisted on working from precise and detailed plans. He often used storyboarding, a series of framed drawings of his shots, especially for those sequences that would later require complex editing. Some of the scripts from which he worked included as many as six hundred sketches. Every camera shot was considered, and nothing
(5) extraneous was included.

By the time he had finished such a detailed plan, Hitchcock knew the script so well that he rarely had to refer to it. He then assumed his favorite role, and one that he compared to that of a conductor directing an orchestra without the score. It was at this point that his intuition served as his guide.

Because of the widespread popularity of suspense films, Hitchcock was always trying to avoid clichés by
(10) inventing new ways to present a similar plot. He was successful in part because he varied the mood from one film to another, and even introduced variation in the middle of a scene within the same film.

Hitchcock admitted that he was less interested in the story itself than in the telling of it. He was a master at using and creating techniques that infused the scene with strong emotions. Some of his most effective sequences are both terrifying and funny, providing the viewer with a juxtaposition of contradictory
(15) sensations.

1. What is the author's main purpose in the passage?

   (A) To describe Hitchcock's directing style
   (B) To explain how Hitchcock used storyboarding
   (C) To criticize Hitchcock's work
   (D) To compare Hitchcock with an orchestra conductor

2. What is storyboarding?

   (A) A detailed script of the story
   (B) An acting technique that requires using strong emotions
   (C) An effect produced by editing film
   (D) A sequence of drawings for the camera crew

3. Hitchcock's directing style is described as employing all of the following EXCEPT

   (A) focusing his attention on the story line
   (B) using many drawings of camera shots
   (C) seldom referring to the script while shooting a scene
   (D) relying on intuition while filming

4. The word "juxtaposition" in line 14 is closest in meaning to which of the following?

   (A) new idea
   (B) large number
   (C) close placement
   (D) difficult plan

5. The word "it" in line 7 refers to

   (A) shot
   (B) time
   (C) script
   (D) role

6. The paragraph following the passage most probably discusses

   (A) other directors of suspense films
   (B) examples of scenes in Hitchcock films that elicited contradictory emotions
   (C) the reason for Hitchcock's success
   (D) the importance of the story line to the suspense film

Passage Four

In order to establish photography as art, members of the Aesthetic Movement modeled their work on classical paintings. As the movement gained in popularity, photographers made a clear distinction between the artistic photography that conformed to the aesthetic standard used for paintings and the work of more realistic photographers that was beginning to appear. Since they were cloudy because of the gum bichromate

(5) plate that allowed for manual intervention, the aesthetic prints were easily distinguished from the more modern prints, which came to be called straightforward photographs. In contrast, the straightforward photographers produced images that were sharp and clear. The philosophy that surrounded the new photography rejected manipulation of either the subject matter or the print. The subjects included nature in its undisturbed state and people in everyday situations.

(10) A number of major exhibitions and the formation of photographic clubs during the late nineteenth century provided the impetus for the Photo-Secession Movement. Founded by Alfred Steiglitz in New York City in 1902, Photo-Secession had as its proposition the promotion of straightforward photography through exhibits and publications. One of the publications, *Camera Work,* has been recognized among the most beautiful journals ever produced. By the 1920s, the mechanical precision that had once been rejected as a

(15) defect by members of the Aesthetic Movement had become a hallmark of modern photography. Chiefly through the efforts of Steiglitz, modern photography had seceded from painting and emerged as a legitimate art form.

1. Which of the following would be the best title for the passage?

   (A) The Photo-Secession Movement
   (B) The Aesthetic Movement
   (C) Alfred Steiglitz
   (D) Photography as Art

2. How can earlier photographs be distinguished from more modern photographs?

   (A) They were not the same color.
   (B) They were not as clear.
   (C) They did not look like paintings.
   (D) They did not retouch them.

3. The Photo-Secession Movement is described as including all of the following EXCEPT

   (A) straightforward photographs
   (B) mechanical precision
   (C) sharp, clear images
   (D) manipulation of prints

4. The word "defect" in line 15 is closest in meaning to

   (A) disturbance
   (B) ideal
   (C) requirement
   (D) imperfection

5. The word "they" in line 4 refers to

   (A) paintings
   (B) aesthetic prints
   (C) modern prints
   (D) straightforward photographs

6. It can be inferred from the passage that the author

   (A) knew Alfred Steiglitz personally
   (B) was not interested in Alfred Steiglitz
   (C) disagreed with Alfred Steiglitz
   (D) admired Alfred Steiglitz

Passage Five

The Birds of America was a work conceived and executed on a grand scale. It was finally published by subscription in eighty-seven parts between 1826 and 1838 in huge double-elephant folios containing 435 life-sized hand-colored engravings. The engravings were executed after John James Audubon's original watercolors by master engraver Robert Havell.

(5)   The plates represent 1,065 American birds, identified as 489 different species. The text that accompanies the plates was printed in a separate five-volume edition entitled Ornithological Biography. Based on field notes by Audubon, it was edited by the respected naturalist William MacGillivray.

Although the entire double-elephant folio edition was never republished, more than 100 plates were printed in a separate five-volume edition in 1860 after Audubon's death. Plates from either of the editions

(10) are considered collector's items and may be purchased separately through galleries and other art dealers. All of them were well-received upon publication and remain popular today, but the "Wild Turkey Cock" is perhaps his most requested plate.

Although he was a watercolorist, Audubon made copies of some of his birds in oil either to give to friends or to raise funds for his publications. His reputation, however, rests on the original watercolors of the

(15) bird series, more than four hundred of which may be found in the New York Historical Society. They continue to be greatly admired because they are not only accurate in detail but also distinctive in composition and presentation.

Audubon enjoys a unique place in American art. A genius who concentrated his talent on the representation of a highly specialized subject, he really cannot be compared with any other artist. His name

(20) has become synonymous with ornithology as well as watercolor. More importantly, the work has withstood the test of time.

1. What does this passage mainly discuss?

    (A) The life of John James Audubon
    (B) The art of John James Audubon
    (C) Ornithology
    (D) American watercolorists

2. John James Audubon was best known for

    (A) his oil paintings
    (B) his watercolors
    (C) his ornithological field notes
    (D) his historical records

3. The Birds of America is described as all of the following EXCEPT

    (A) original
    (B) popular
    (C) accurate
    (D) unavailable

4. The word "specialized" in line 19 could best be replaced by

    (A) ambiguous
    (B) influential
    (C) particular
    (D) obscure

5. The word "them" in line 11 refers to

    (A) dealers
    (B) items
    (C) editions
    (D) plates

6. It can be inferred from the passage that The Birds of America project was financed by

    (A) naturalist, William MacGillivray
    (B) the New York Historical Society
    (C) friends of the artist
    (D) Audubon himself

EXERCISE 8:   Popular Culture

Passage One

Independence Day in the United States is observed annually on the Fourth of July. For most communities throughout the nation, the traditional celebration includes parades down the main streets, picnics with hot dogs and lemonade, and, of course, a fireworks display at night. In some towns across the country, however, special events are planned in honor of the occasion. In Bristol, Rhode Island, fire engine teams from
(5)   communities throughout New England compete in a contest to squirt water from their fire hoses. Flagstaff, Arizona hosts a huge three-day powwow, including a rodeo, for twenty Native American tribes. The annual Eskimo games with traditional kayak races are held in Kotzebue, Alaska. Two auto races are always scheduled for the Fourth, including a four-hundred-mile stock car event at the Daytona International Speedway in Daytona, Florida, and an annual auto race up the fourteen-thousand-foot precipice at Pike's
(10) Peak in Colorado.

Several small towns celebrate in other unique ways. Hannibal, Missouri, the hometown of Mark Twain, invites the children to participate in a fence-painting contest, reenacting a scene from Twain's novel *Tom Sawyer.* Lititz, Pennsylvania congregates in the Lititz Springs Park to light thousands of candles and arrange them in various shapes and images.
(15) In Ontario, California, the townspeople combine the traditional with the unusual by setting up tables along Euclid Avenue for what they describe as "the biggest picnic table in the world." In this way, everyone in town has a front-row seat for the two-mile parade.

1. With which of the following topics is the passage primarily concerned?

    (A) Traditional celebrations for the Fourth of July
    (B) Holidays in the United States
    (C) The origin of Independence Day
    (D) Small towns in America

2. How is Independence Day observed in Ontario, California?

    (A) By hosting a powwow and rodeo
    (B) By sponsoring a stock car event
    (C) By squirting water from fire hoses
    (D) By setting up tables along the parade route

3. The author mentions all of the following as ways the Fourth of July is celebrated EXCEPT

    (A) parades
    (B) races
    (C) dances
    (D) fireworks

4. The word "huge" in line 6 could best be replaced by which of the following?

    (A) exciting
    (B) amusing
    (C) complicated
    (D) large

5. The word "them" in line 14 refers to

    (A) shapes
    (B) candles
    (C) children
    (D) images

6. It can be inferred from the passage that

    (A) the Fourth of July is celebrated in Canada as well as in the United States
    (B) towns in the United States celebrate July Fourth in different ways because of their regional customs
    (C) although fireworks are not legal, they are displayed on July Fourth
    (D) The Fourth of July is not celebrated in large cities in the United States

Passage Two

Collectibles have been a part of almost every culture since ancient times. Whereas some objects have been collected for their usefulness, others have been selected for their aesthetic beauty alone. In the United States, the kinds of collectibles currently popular range from traditional objects such as stamps, coins, rare books, and art to more recent items of interest like dolls, bottles, baseball cards, and comic books.

(5)   Interest in collectibles has increased enormously during the past decade, in part because some collectibles have demonstrated their value as investments. Especially during cycles of high inflation, investors try to purchase tangibles that will at least retain their current market values. In general, the most traditional collectibles will be sought because they have preserved their value over the years, there is an organized auction market for them, and they are most easily sold in the event that cash is needed. Some examples of

(10)   the most stable collectibles are old masters, Chinese ceramics, stamps, coins, rare books, antique jewelry, silver, porcelain, art by well-known artists, autographs, and period furniture. Other items of more recent interest include old phonograph records, old magazines, post cards, baseball cards, art glass, dolls, classic cars, old bottles, and comic books. These relatively new kinds of collectibles may actually appreciate faster as short-term investments, but may not hold their value as long-term investments. Once a collectible has had

(15)   its initial play, it appreciates at a fairly steady rate, supported by an increasing number of enthusiastic collectors competing for the limited supply of collectibles that become increasingly more difficult to locate.

1. What is the author's main point?

    (A) Collectibles provide interesting information about culture.
    (B) Collectibles are better than other types of investments.
    (C) New types of collectibles appreciate more rapidly.
    (D) A variety of collectibles have become popular investments in the United States.

2. In comparing new collectibles with more traditional ones, the author observes that

    (A) newer collectibles hold their value
    (B) more traditional collectibles appreciate faster
    (C) after a rapid increase in value, all collectibles have steady rates of appreciation
    (D) newer collectibles make better short-term investments

3. The author mentions all of the following as examples of new types of collectible items EXCEPT

    (A) post cards
    (B) dolls
    (C) bottles
    (D) autographs

4. The word "stable" in line 10 could be replaced by

    (A) prevalent
    (B) reliable
    (C) expensive
    (D) exquisite

5. The word "their" in line 7 refers to

    (A) investors
    (B) tangibles
    (C) values
    (D) cycles

6. The paragraph following the passage most probably discusses

    (A) how collectors locate and purchase collectibles
    (B) why collectibles are risky investments
    (C) where to buy collectible toys
    (D) when to sell a collectible item for profit

Passage Three

Although square dancing is usually considered a typically American form of dance, its origin can be traced to earlier European folk dances. The traditional formation, a square consisting of four couples facing each other, can be found in many old European formation dances, including English Morris dancing, Scottish reels, and Irish jigs, as well as the elegant ballroom dancing of the royal courts.

(5)   Historically, square dancing in America has followed two separate lines of development, referred to as eastern square dance and western or cowboy square dance. The eastern dance was clearly related to New England country dancing, and both closely resembled English country dancing, with the four-couple square. In contrast, western square dance was adapted from Appalachian Mountain dances such as the Kentucky running set. In the running set, couples form a circle of any number of couples, although often traditional

(10)   four-couple circles are preferred. Western dance was also influenced by the dances already found in the region, especially those of Spain and Mexico.

Modern American square dancing includes elements of both the eastern and western varieties. The traditional four-couple square is popular, but all four couples join hands for circle figures around the square as well. Unlike the original dances, which could be memorized, modern dances are more spontaneous.

(15)   Square dancers rely on a caller to cue the steps while they are dancing. They must listen carefully to stay in step with the other dancers in their square.

1. What is the author's main purpose in the passage?

   (A) To trace the history of square dancing in the United States
   (B) To teach the reader some basic square dancing steps
   (C) To compare square dances with European folk dances
   (D) To describe modern square dancing

2. What is the origin of square dancing?

   (A) New England country dances
   (B) Cowboy dances
   (C) European folk dances
   (D) Appalachian Mountain dances

3. Western square dancing is described as all of the following EXCEPT

   (A) It is done in a circle, often with four couples.
   (B) It is adapted from the Kentucky running set.
   (C) It is influenced by both Spanish and Mexican dances.
   (D) It uses a traditional four-couple square formation.

4. The word "spontaneous" in line 14 could best be replaced by which of the following?

   (A) awkward
   (B) intricate
   (C) strenuous
   (D) impulsive

5. The word "those" in line 11 refers to

   (A) couples
   (B) circles
   (C) dances
   (D) elements

6. The paragraph following the passage most probably discusses

   (A) types of cues for square dance steps
   (B) the way that dancers memorize steps
   (C) the popularity of square dancing throughout the world
   (D) the formation of square dance clubs in America

Passage Four

Although he created the game of basketball at the YMCA in Springfield, Massachusetts, Dr. James A. Naismith was a Canadian. Working as a physical education instructor at the International YMCA, now Springfield College, Dr. Naismith noticed a lack of interest in exercise among students during the wintertime. The New England winters were fierce, and the students balked at participating in outdoor
(5)   activities. Naismith determined that a fast-moving game that could be played indoors would fill a void after the baseball and football seasons had ended.

First he attempted to adapt outdoor games such as soccer and rugby to indoor play, but he soon found them unsuitable for confined areas. Finally, he determined that he would have to invent a game.

In December of 1891, Dr. Naismith hung two old peach baskets at either end of the gymnasium at the
(10) school, and, using a soccer ball and nine players on each side, organized the first basketball game. The early rules allowed three points for each basket and made running with the ball a violation. Every time a goal was made, someone had to climb a ladder to retrieve the ball.

Nevertheless, the game became popular. In less than a year, basketball was being played in both the United States and Canada. Five years later, a championship tournament was staged in New York City, which
(15) was won by the Brooklyn Central YMCA.

The teams had already been reduced to seven players, and five became standard in the 1897 season. When basketball was introduced as a demonstration sport in the 1904 Olympic Games in St. Louis, it quickly spread throughout the world. In 1906, a metal hoop was introduced to replace the basket, but the name basketball has remained.

1. What does this passage mainly discuss?

   (A) The Olympic Games in St. Louis in 1904
   (B) The development of basketball
   (C) The YMCA athletic program
   (D) Dr. James Naismith

2. When was the first demonstration game of basketball held during the Olympics?

   (A) 1891
   (B) 1892
   (C) 1897
   (D) 1904

3. The author mentions all of the following as typical of the early game of basketball EXCEPT

   (A) Three points were scored for every basket.
   (B) Running with the ball was not a foul.
   (C) Nine players were on a team.
   (D) The ball had to be retrieved from the basket after each score.

4. The phrase "balked at" in line 4 could best be replaced by

   (A) resisted
   (B) enjoyed
   (C) excelled at
   (D) were exhausted by

5. The word "them" in line 8 refers to

   (A) indoors
   (B) seasons
   (C) games
   (D) areas

6. It can be inferred from the passage that the original baskets

   (A) were not placed very high
   (B) had a metal rim
   (C) did not have a hole in the bottom
   (D) were hung on the same side of the basketball court

Passage Five

Mickey Mouse was not Walt Disney's first successful cartoon creation, but he is certainly his most famous one. It was on a cross-country train trip from New York to California in 1927 that Disney first drew the mouse with the big ears. Supposedly, he took his inspiration from the tame field mice that used to scamper into his old studio in Kansas City. No one is quite sure why he dressed the mouse in the now-

(5) familiar shorts with two buttons and gave him the yellow shoes. But we do know that Disney had intended to call him Mortimer until his wife Lillian intervened and christened him Mickey Mouse.

Capitalizing on the interest in Charles Lindbergh, Disney planned Mickey's debut in the short cartoon *Plane Crazy,* with Minnie as a co-star. In the third short cartoon, *Steamboat Willie,* Mickey was whistling and singing through the miracle of the modern soundtrack. By the 1930s Mickey's image had circled the

(10) globe. He was a superstar at the height of his career.

Although he has received a few minor changes throughout his lifetime, most notably the addition of white gloves and the rounder forms of a more childish body, he has remained true to his nature since those first cartoons. Mickey is appealing because he is nice. He may get into trouble, but he takes it on the chin with a grin. He is both good-natured and resourceful. Perhaps that was Disney's own image of himself. Why

(15) else would he have insisted on doing Mickey's voice in all the cartoons for twenty years? When interviewed, he would say, "There is a lot of the mouse in me." And that mouse has remained one of the most pervasive images in American popular culture.

1. With what topic is the passage primarily concerned?

   (A) The image of Mickey Mouse
   (B) The life of Walt Disney
   (C) The history of cartoons
   (D) The definition of American culture

2. What distinguished *Steamboat Willie* from earlier cartoons?

   (A) Better color
   (B) A sound track
   (C) Minnie Mouse as co-star
   (D) The longer format

3. The first image of Mickey Mouse is described as all of the following EXCEPT

   (A) He was dressed in shorts with two buttons.
   (B) He had big ears.
   (C) He wore yellow shoes.
   (D) He was using white gloves.

4. The word "pervasive" in line 17 could best be replaced by

   (A) well loved
   (B) widespread
   (C) often copied
   (D) expensive to buy

5. The word "those" in line 12 refers to

   (A) cartoons
   (B) forms
   (C) gloves
   (D) changes

6. The paragraph following the passage most probably discusses

   (A) the history of cartoons
   (B) other images in popular culture
   (C) Walt Disney's childhood
   (D) the voices of cartoon characters

EXERCISE 9:   Textbooks/Business

Passage One

Although the composition and role of the board of directors of a company will vary from one organization to the next, a few generalizations may be made. As regards the composition of the board, customarily some directors are prominent men and women selected to give prestige to the group. Others are usually chosen from among retired executives of the organization for their specialized knowledge of the
(5) company.

It is generally true that, as long as the top management maintains the confidence of the board of directors, the directors will not actively intervene to dictate specific policies. This is the same administrative procedure usually followed by the board of trustees of a college or university, and is similar in many respects to the parliamentary system of ministerial responsibility practiced in Great Britain.

1. The title below that best expresses the ideas in this passage is?

   (A) The Board of Directors
   (B) The Board of Trustees
   (C) The Parliamentary System
   (D) Management

2. Who generally formulates policies for a company?

   (A) Top management
   (B) A dictator
   (C) The board of directors
   (D) Retired executives

3. The author mentions all of the following as having similar administrative procedures EXCEPT

   (A) the board of directors of a company
   (B) the board of trustees of a college
   (C) the members of Congress in the United States
   (D) the members of parliament in Great Britain

4. The word "prominent" in line 3 could best be replaced by

   (A) professional
   (B) ethical
   (C) important
   (D) elderly

5. The word "Others" in line 3 refers to

   (A) boards
   (B) directors
   (C) executives
   (D) companies

6. Who would not be a likely candidate to be chosen as a member of the board of directors of City Bank?

   (A) a retired president of City Bank
   (B) a respected lawyer
   (C) a City Bank employee
   (D) a state senator

Passage Two

There are four basic types of competition in business that form a continuum from pure competition through monopolistic competition and oligopoly to monopoly. At one end of the continuum, pure competition results when every company has a similar product. Companies that deal in commodities such as wheat or corn are often involved in pure competition. In pure competition, it is often the ease and efficiency
(5)   of distribution that influences purchase.

In contrast, in monopolistic competition, several companies may compete for the sale of items that may be substituted. The classic example of monopolistic competition is coffee and tea. If the price of one is perceived as too high, consumers may begin to purchase the other. Coupons and other discounts are often used as part of a marketing strategy to influence sales.
(10)   Oligopoly occurs when a few companies control the majority of sales for a product or service. For example, only five airline carriers control more than 70 percent of all ticket sales in the United States. In oligopoly, serious competition is not considered desirable because it would result in reduced revenue for every company in the group. Although price wars do occur, in which all companies offer substantial savings to customers, a somewhat similar tendency to raise prices simultaneously is also usual.
(15)   Finally, monopoly occurs when only one firm sells the product. Traditionally, monopolies have been tolerated for producers of goods and services that have been considered basic or essential, including electricity and water. In these cases, it is government control, rather than competition, that protects and influences sales.

1. Which of the following would be the best title for the passage?

   (A) Monopolies
   (B) The Commodity Market
   (C) The Competition Continuum
   (D) The Best Type of Competition

2. An example of a product in monopolistic competition is

   (A) corn
   (B) electricity
   (C) airline tickets
   (D) coffee

3. The author mentions all of the following as characteristic of monopoly EXCEPT

   (A) the use of coupons or other discounts
   (B) government control
   (C) basic or essential services
   (D) only one firm

4. The word "tolerated" in line 16 could best be replaced by which of the following?

   (A) permitted
   (B) reserved
   (C) criticized
   (D) devised

5. The word "it" in line 12 refers to

   (A) competition
   (B) group
   (C) company
   (D) revenue

6. It can be inferred that this passage was first printed in

   (A) a business textbook
   (B) a government document
   (C) an airline brochure
   (D) a newspaper

Passage Three

Telecommuting is some form of computer communication between employees' homes and offices. For employees whose jobs involve sitting at a terminal or word processor entering data or typing reports, the location of the computer is of no consequence. If the machine can communicate over telephone lines, when the work is completed, employees can dial the office computer and transmit the material to their employers.

(5) A recent survey in *USA Today* estimates that there are approximately 8.7 million telecommuters. But although the numbers are rising annually, the trend does not appear to be as significant as predicted when *Business Week* published "The Portable Executive" as its cover story a few years ago. Why hasn't telecommuting become more popular?

Clearly, change simply takes time. But in addition, there has been active resistance on the part of many

(10) managers. These executives claim that supervising the telecommuters in a large work force scattered across the country would be too difficult, or, at least, systems for managing them are not yet developed, thereby complicating the manager's responsibilities.

It is also true that employees who are given the option of telecommuting are often reluctant to accept the opportunity. Most people feel that they need regular interaction with a group, and many are concerned that

(15) they will not have the same consideration for advancement if they are not more visible in the office setting. Some people feel that even when a space in their homes is set aside as a work area, they never really get away from the office.

1. With which of the following topics is the passage primarily concerned?

   (A) The advantages of telecommuting
   (B) A definition of telecommuting
   (C) An overview of telecommuting
   (D) The failure of telecommuting

2. How many American workers are involved in telecommuting?

   (A) More than predicted in *Business Week*
   (B) More than 8 million
   (C) Fewer than last year
   (D) Fewer than estimated in *USA Today*

3. The author mentions all of the following as concerns of telecommuters EXCEPT

   (A) the opportunities for advancement
   (B) the different system of supervision
   (C) the lack of interaction with a group
   (D) the fact that the work space is in the home

4. The word "resistance" in line 9 could best be replaced by

   (A) alteration
   (B) participation
   (C) opposition
   (D) consideration

5. The word "them" in line 11 refers to

   (A) telecommuters
   (B) systems
   (C) executives
   (D) responsibilities

6. It can be inferred from the passage that the author is

   (A) a telecommuter
   (B) the manager of a group of telecommuters
   (C) a statistician
   (D) a reporter

Passage Four

Although Henry Ford's name is closely associated with the concept of mass production, he should receive equal credit for introducing labor practices as early as 1913 that would be considered advanced even by today's standards. Safety measures were improved, and the work day was reduced to eight hours, compared with the ten- or twelve-hour day common at the time. In order to accommodate the shorter work
(5)   day, the entire factory was converted from two to three shifts.

In addition, sick leaves as well as improved medical care for those injured on the job were instituted. The Ford Motor Company was one of the first factories to develop a technical school to train specialized skilled laborers and an English language school for immigrants. Some efforts were even made to hire the handicapped and provide jobs for former convicts.
(10)   The most widely acclaimed innovation was the five-dollar-a-day minimum wage that was offered in order to recruit and retain the best mechanics and to discourage the growth of labor unions. Ford explained the new wage policy in terms of efficiency and profit sharing. He also mentioned the fact that his employees would be able to purchase the automobiles that they produced—in effect creating a market for the product. In order to qualify for the minimum wage, an employee had to establish a decent home and demonstrate
(15)   good personal habits, including sobriety, thriftiness, industriousness, and dependability. Although some criticism was directed at Ford for involving himself too much in the personal lives of his employees, there can be no doubt that, at a time when immigrants were being taken advantage of in frightful ways, Henry Ford was helping many people to establish themselves in America.

1. What is the author's main purpose in the passage?

   (A) To include mass production and the assembly line among Henry Ford's accomplishments
   (B) To report the origin of the minimum wage
   (C) To credit Henry Ford with industrial reforms
   (D) To defend Henry Ford's practices

2. How many hours did Ford's employees work per shift in his factory?

   (A) Three
   (B) Eight
   (C) Ten
   (D) Twelve

3. The author mentions all of the following as labor practices instituted by Ford EXCEPT

   (A) the five-dollar-a-day minimum wage
   (B) education and training programs
   (C) labor unions
   (D) sick leaves

4. The word "innovation" in line 10 refers to

   (A) an original idea
   (B) an extravagant offer
   (C) a devious plan
   (D) a popular policy

5. The word "that" in line 2 refers to

   (A) the concept
   (B) labor practices
   (C) mass production
   (D) equal credit

6. It can be inferred from the passage that the author

   (A) feels that Ford should be remembered for the concept of mass production
   (B) believes that Ford was too involved in his worker's lives
   (C) favors labor unions
   (D) commends Ford's philanthropy

Passage Five

The increase in international business and in foreign investment has created a need for executives with knowledge of foreign languages and skills in cross-cultural communication. Americans, however, have not been well trained in either area and, consequently, have not enjoyed the same level of success in negotiation in an international arena as have their foreign counterparts.

(5)   Negotiating is the process of communicating back and forth for the purpose of reaching an agreement. It involves persuasion and compromise, but in order to participate in either one, the negotiators must understand the ways in which people are persuaded and how compromise is reached within the culture of the negotiation.

In many international business negotiations abroad, Americans are perceived as wealthy and impersonal.
(10) It often appears to the foreign negotiator that the American represents a large multimillion-dollar corporation that can afford to pay the price without bargaining further. The American negotiator's role becomes that of an impersonal purveyor of information and cash.

In studies of American negotiators abroad, several traits have been identified that may serve to confirm this stereotypical perception, while undermining the negotiator's position. Two traits in particular that cause
(15) cross-cultural misunderstanding are directness and impatience on the part of the American negotiator. Furthermore, American negotiators often insist on realizing short-term goals. Foreign negotiators, on the other hand, may value the relationship established between negotiators and may be willing to invest time in it for long-term benefits. In order to solidify the relationship, they may opt for indirect interactions without regard for the time involved in getting to know the other negotiator.
(20)   Clearly, perceptions and differences in values affect the outcomes of negotiations and the success of negotiators. For Americans to play a more effective role in international business negotiations, they must put forth more effort to improve cross-cultural understanding.

1. What is the author's main point?

   (A) Negotiation is the process of reaching an agreement.
   (B) Foreign languages are important for international business.
   (C) Foreign perceptions of American negotiators are based on stereotypes.
   (D) American negotiators need to learn more about other cultures.

2. According to the author, what is the purpose of negotiation?

   (A) To undermine the other negotiator's position
   (B) To communicate back and forth
   (C) To reach an agreement
   (D) To understand the culture of the negotiators

3. The American negotiator is described as all of the following EXCEPT

   (A) perceived by foreign negotiators as wealthy
   (B) willing to invest time in relationships
   (C) known for direct interactions
   (D) interested in short-term goals

4. The word "undermining" in line 14 is closest in meaning to the phrase

   (A) making known
   (B) making clear
   (C) making brief
   (D) making weak

5. The word "that" in line 12 refers to

   (A) bargaining
   (B) role
   (C) corporation
   (D) price

6. The paragraph following the passage most probably discusses

   (A) ways to increase cross-cultural understanding
   (B) traits that cause cross-cultural misunderstanding
   (C) knowledge of foreign languages
   (D) relationships between negotiators

EXERCISE 10:   Textbooks/Natural Sciences

Passage One

A popular theory explaining the evolution of the universe is known as the Big Bang Model. According to the model, at some time between ten and twenty billion years ago, all present matter and energy were compressed into a small ball only a few kilometers in diameter. It was, in effect, an atom that contained in the form of pure energy all of the components of the entire universe. Then, at a moment in time that
(5)   astronomers refer to as T = 0, the ball exploded, hurling the energy into space. Expansion occurred. As the energy cooled, most of it became matter in the form of protons, neutrons, and electrons. These original particles combined to form hydrogen and helium, and continued to expand. Matter formed into galaxies with stars and planets.

1. Which sentence below best summarizes this passage?

    (A) The Big Bang theory does not account for the evolution of the universe.
    (B) According to the Big Bang Model, an explosion caused the formation of the universe.
    (C) The universe is made of hydrogen and helium.
    (D) The universe is more than ten billion years old.

2. According to this passage, when were the galaxies formed?

    (A) Ten billion years ago
    (B) Fifteen billion years ago
    (C) At T = 0
    (D) Twenty billion years ago

3. The environment before the Big Bang is described as all of the following EXCEPT

    (A) compressed matter
    (B) energy
    (C) all the components of the universe
    (D) protons, neutrons, and electrons

4. The word "compressed" in line 3 could best be replaced by

    (A) excited
    (B) balanced
    (C) reduced
    (D) controlled

5. The word "it" in line 6 refers to

    (A) energy
    (B) space
    (C) expansion
    (D) matter

6. It may be inferred that

    (A) energy and matter are the same
    (B) protons, neutrons, and electrons are not matter
    (C) energy may be converted into matter
    (D) the galaxies stopped expanding as energy cooled

Passage Two

American black bears appear in a variety of colors despite their name. In the eastern part of their range, most of these bears have shiny black fur, but in the west they grow brown, red, or even yellow coats. To the north, the black bear is actually gray or white in color. Even in the same litter, both brown and black furred bears may be born.

(5)   Black bears are the smallest of all American bears, ranging in length from five to six feet, weighing from three hundred to five hundred pounds. Their eyes and ears are small and their eyesight and hearing are not as good as their sense of smell.

Like all bears, the black bear is timid, clumsy, and rarely dangerous, but if attacked, most can climb trees and cover ground at great speeds. When angry or frightened, it is a formidable enemy.

(10)   Black bears feed on leaves, herbs, roots, fruit, and berries, insects, fish, and even larger animals. One of the most interesting characteristics of bears, including the black bear, is their winter sleep. Unlike squirrels, woodchucks, and many other woodland animals, bears do not actually hibernate. Although the bear does not eat during the winter months, sustaining itself from body fat, its temperature remains almost normal, and it breathes regularly four or five times per minute.

(15)   Most black bears live alone, except during mating season. They prefer to live in caves, hollow logs, or dense thickets. A litter of one to four cubs is born in January or February after a gestation period of six to nine months, and they remain with their mother until they are fully grown or about one and a half years old. Black bears can live as long as thirty years in the wild, and even longer in game preserves set aside for them.

1. With what topic is the passage primarily concerned?

    (A) The color of bears
    (B) The characteristics of black bears
    (C) The habitat of black bears
    (D) The similarity of black bears to other bears

2. According to the author, which of the following senses is best in black bears?

    (A) Sight
    (B) Hearing
    (C) Smell
    (D) Taste

3. The black bear is described as all of the following EXCEPT

    (A) It is the smallest American bear.
    (B) It is born with brown, yellow, red, or black fur.
    (C) It is not usually dangerous.
    (D) It is like squirrels and other animals that hibernate.

4. The word "formidable" in line 9 is closest in meaning to

    (A) reluctant
    (B) intimidating
    (C) overestimated
    (D) occasional

5. The word "them" in line 19 refers to

    (A) their mother
    (B) black bears
    (C) thirty years
    (D) game preserves

6. The paragraph following the passage most probably discusses

    (A) black bears from different ranges
    (B) the mating ritual of black bears
    (C) black bears in game preserves
    (D) natural enemies of black bears

Passage Three

Light from a living plant or animal is called bioluminescence, or cold light, to distinguish it from incandescence, or heat-generating light. Life forms could not produce incandescent light without being burned. Their light is produced by chemicals combining in such a way that little or no measurable heat is produced.

(5)   Although bioluminescence is a relatively complex process, it can be reduced to simple terms. Living light occurs when luciferin and oxygen combine in the presence of luciferase. Fireflies require an additional compound called ATP.

Much remains unknown, but many scientists who study bioluminescence believe that the origin of the phenomenon goes back to a time when there was no oxygen in the earth's atmosphere. When oxygen was (10) gradually introduced into the atmosphere, it was poisonous to life forms. Plants and animals produced light to use up the oxygen. Millions of years ago, all life produced light to survive. As the millennia passed, life forms on earth became tolerant of, and finally dependent on oxygen, and the adaptation that produced bioluminescence was no longer necessary, but some primitive plants and animals continued to use the light for new functions such as mating or attracting prey.

1. With what topic is the passage primarily concerned?

    (A) Bioluminescence
    (B) Luciferase
    (C) Primitive plants and animals
    (D) The earth's atmosphere

2. According to the author, why has bioluminescence continued in modern plants and animals?

    (A) For survival
    (B) For mating or attracting prey
    (C) For producing heat
    (D) For burning excess oxygen

3. Bioluminescence is described as all of the following EXCEPT

    (A) a complex chemical process
    (B) an adaptation of early plants and animals to the environment
    (C) a form of cold light
    (D) a poisonous substance

4. The word "primitive" in line 13 is closest in meaning to

    (A) very old
    (B) very large
    (C) very important
    (D) very common

5. The word "it" in line 1 refers to

    (A) a plant
    (B) an animal
    (C) bioluminescence
    (D) incandescence

6. The paragraph following the passage most probably discusses

    (A) incandescence in prehistoric plants and animals
    (B) incandescence in modern plants and animals
    (C) bioluminescence in prehistoric plants and animals
    (D) bioluminescence in modern plants and animals

Passage Four

Hydrogen, the lightest and simplest of the elements, has several properties that make it valuable for many industries. It releases more heat per unit of weight than any other fuel. In rocket engines, tons of hydrogen and oxygen are burned, and hydrogen is used with oxygen for welding torches that produce temperatures as high as 4,000 degrees F and can be used in cutting steel. Fuel cells to generate electricity operate on
(5) hydrogen and oxygen.

Hydrogen also serves to prevent metals from tarnishing during heat treatments by removing the oxygen from them. Although it would be difficult to remove the oxygen by itself, hydrogen readily combines with oxygen to form water, which can be heated to steam and easily removed.

Hydrogen is also useful in the food industry for a process known as hydrogenation. Products such as
(10) margarine and cooking oils are changed from liquids to semisolids by adding hydrogen to their molecules. Soap manufacturers also use hydrogen for this purpose.

Hydrogen is also one of the coolest refrigerants. It does not become a liquid until it reaches temperatures of −425 degrees F. Pure hydrogen gas is used in large electric generators to cool the coils. In addition, in the chemical industry, hydrogen is used to produce ammonia, gasoline, methyl alcohol, and many other
(15) important products.

1. What is the author's main purpose in the passage?

   (A) To explain the industrial uses of hydrogen
   (B) To describe the chemical properties of hydrogen
   (C) To discuss hydrogenation
   (D) To give examples of how hydrogen and oxygen combine

2. How can hydrogen be used to cut steel?

   (A) By cooling the steel to a very low temperature
   (B) By cooling the hydrogen with oxygen to a very low temperature
   (C) By heating the steel to a very high temperature
   (D) By heating the hydrogen with oxygen to a very high temperature

3. The author mentions all of the following as uses for hydrogen EXCEPT

   (A) to remove tarnish from metals
   (B) to produce fuels such as gasoline and methyl alcohol
   (C) to operate fuel cells that generate electricity
   (D) to change solid foods to liquids

4. The word "readily" in line 7 could best be replaced by

   (A) completely
   (B) slowly
   (C) usually
   (D) easily

5. The word "them" in line 7 refers to

   (A) fuel cells
   (B) metals
   (C) treatments
   (D) products

6. It can be inferred from the passage that hydrogen

   (A) is too dangerous to be used for industrial purposes
   (B) has many purposes in a variety of industries
   (C) has limited industrial uses because of its dangerous properties
   (D) is used in many industries for basically the same purpose

Passage Five

The magnetosphere consists of the two strong belts of radiation that lie within an area of weaker radiation surrounding most of the earth. It extends outward for tens of thousands of miles. The magnetosphere is comprised of slow-moving electrons, trapped by the earth's magnetic lines of force. The shape of the magnetosphere is determined by the earth's magnetic field, but it is distorted by electrically charged
(5) particles that emanate from the sun to the earth. These charged particles are often referred to as the solar wind, pushing nearer to the earth on the sunlit side and away from the earth on the dark side. Thus, the higher end of the magnetosphere extends up to forty thousand miles on the sunlit side, and the lower end hovers within a few hundred miles of the earth on the dark side.

There is very little radiation near the earth's north and south poles because the earth's magnetic lines of
(10) force enter the earth near the poles. Conversely, the same lines of forces are far above the earth near the equator.

1. What does this passage mainly discuss?

    (A) The nature of the magnetosphere
    (B) The effects of solar wind
    (C) The amount of radiation near the earth's poles
    (D) The shape of the earth's magnetic fields

2. How far does the magnetosphere extend on the dark side of the earth?

    (A) Several hundred miles
    (B) Ten thousand miles
    (C) Forty thousand miles
    (D) Tens of thousands of miles

3. The magnetosphere is described as all of the following EXCEPT

    (A) a series of slow-moving electrons
    (B) particles referred to as solar wind
    (C) two strong belts of radiation
    (D) a sphere inside an area of weaker radiation that surrounds the earth

4. The word "Conversely" in line 10 could best be replaced by

    (A) Therefore
    (B) On the other hand
    (C) Nevertheless
    (D) In conclusion

5. The word "it" in line 4 refers to

    (A) radiation
    (B) the earth
    (C) the shape
    (D) the earth's magnetic field

6. It can be inferred from the passage that the author's point of view is

    (A) uninterested
    (B) skeptical
    (C) objective
    (D) persuasive

TEST OF WRITTEN
ENGLISH (TWE)

Arguing a Point of View

The most frequent type of question on the TWE is a topic in which you are asked to compare and contrast opposing viewpoints on an issue, and then to take a position and argue in favor of your view.

QUESTION 1

(30 minutes)

Some people say that recycling should be required by law. Others say that it should be a personal choice. Which viewpoint do you agree with? Use specific reasons and examples to support your answer.

NOTES

Use this space for essay notes only. Work done on this work sheet will *not* be scored. Write the complete final version of your essay on the Essay Pages.

Essay Pages

QUESTION 2
(30 minutes)

Some people say that parents should be responsible for the crimes that their underage children commit. Others say that the parent should not be punished for a crime committed by another person. Which viewpoint do you agree with? Use specific reasons and examples to support your answer.

NOTES

Use this space for essay notes only. Work done on this work sheet will *not* be scored. Write the complete final version of your essay on the Essay Pages.

Essay Pages

QUESTION 3
(30 minutes)

Some people say that smoking should be banned in restaurants. Others say that there should be a special smoking section retained for those who wish to smoke. Which viewpoint do you agree with? Use specific reasons and examples to support your answer.

NOTES

Use this space for essay notes only. Work done on this work sheet will *not* be scored. Write the complete final version of your essay on the Essay Pages.

Essay Pages

QUESTION 4

(30 minutes)

Some people say that marriages should be arranged by intermediaries. Others say that young people should be free to choose their marriage partners. Which viewpoint do you agree with? Use specific reasons and examples to support your answer.

NOTES

Use this space for essay notes only. Work done on this work sheet will *not* be scored. Write the complete final version of your essay on the Essay Pages.

Essay Pages

QUESTION 5

(30 minutes)

Some people say that gun sales should be controlled by legislation. Others say that it is the right of all citizens to own a gun if they choose to do so. Which viewpoint do you agree with? Use specific reasons and examples to support your answer.

NOTES

Use this space for essay notes only. Work done on this work sheet will *not* be scored. Write the complete final version of your essay on the Essay Pages.

Essay Pages

QUESTION 6

(30 minutes)

Some people say that children should attend the public schools in their neighborhoods. Others say that parents should be able to use a voucher to send their children to schools of their choice in any neighborhood. Which viewpoint do you agree with? Use specific reasons and examples to support your answer.

NOTES

Use this space for essay notes only. Work done on this work sheet will *not* be scored. Write the complete final version of your essay on the Essay Pages.

Essay Pages

QUESTION 7
(30 minutes)

Some people say that lotteries should be made illegal because many people do not understand that the odds of winning are very small. Others say that lotteries are good because they generate funds for states. Which viewpoint do you agree with? Use specific reasons and examples to support your answer.

NOTES

Use this space for essay notes only. Work done on this work sheet will *not* be scored. Write the complete final version of your essay on the Essay Pages.

Essay Pages

QUESTION 8
(30 minutes)

Some people say that all citizens have a responsibility to vote in every election, and that they should be required by law to do so. Others say that voting is a right, and that citizens should be allowed to vote or not as they choose. Which viewpoint do you agree with? Use specific reasons and examples to support your answer.

NOTES

Use this space for essay notes only. Work done on this work sheet will *not* be scored. Write the complete final version of your essay on the Essay Pages.

Essay Pages

QUESTION 9
(30 minutes)

Some people say that it is right in a democracy to offer college admission to every high school graduate. Others say that admission to college should be offered by examination only. Which viewpoint do you agree with? Use specific reasons and examples to support your answer.

NOTES

Use this space for essay notes only. Work done on this work sheet will *not* be scored. Write the complete final version of your essay on the Essay Pages.

Essay Pages

QUESTION 10
(30 minutes)

Some people say that living in a small town has many advantages. Others say that large cities offer more opportunities for a better lifestyle. Which viewpoint do you agree with? Use specific reasons and examples to support your answer.

NOTES

Use this space for essay notes only. Work done on this work sheet will *not* be scored. Write the complete final version of your essay on the Essay Pages.

Essay Pages

Interpreting a Chart or a Graph

A less-frequently tested question requires you to describe a chart or graph and interpret it.

QUESTION 1

(30 minutes)

This graph shows responses by adults of different age groups to the question "How do you prefer to pay for goods and services?" Using the information in the graph, compare the preferences that different age groups surveyed place on financial alternatives. Explain your conclusions, supporting them with details from the graph.

<u>GRAPH AND NOTES</u>

Use this space for essay notes only. Work done on this work sheet will *not* be scored. Write the complete final version of your essay on the Essay Pages.

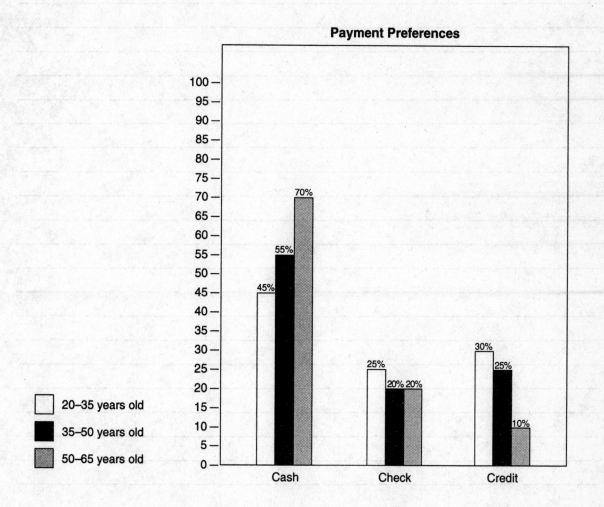

Essay Pages

QUESTION 2

(30 minutes)

This graph shows responses by a group of students to the question "What does success mean to you?" Using the information in the graph, compare the value that students surveyed place on different aspects of their lives.

GRAPH AND NOTES

Use this space for essay notes only. Work done on this work sheet will *not* be scored. Write the complete final version of your essay on the Essay Pages.

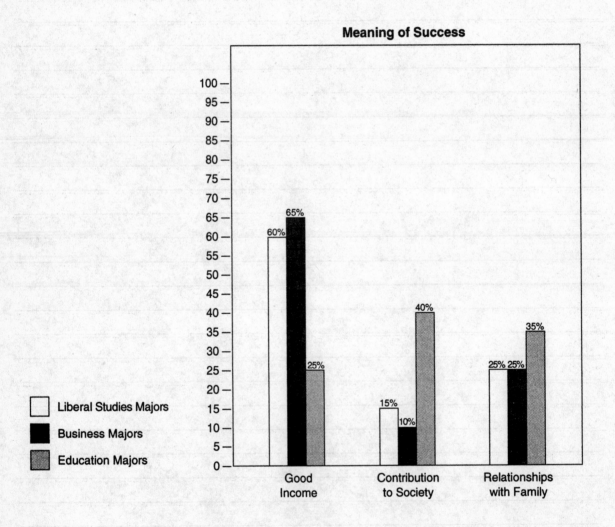

Essay Pages

QUESTION 3

(30 minutes)

This graph shows responses by several families to the question "What would you take with you from your home if you had only one minute to leave?" Using the information in the graph, compare the value that different age groups place on different possessions. Explain your conclusions, supporting them with details from the graph.

<u>GRAPH AND NOTES</u>

Use this space for essay notes only. Work done on this work sheet will *not* be scored. Write the complete final version of your essay on the Essay Pages.

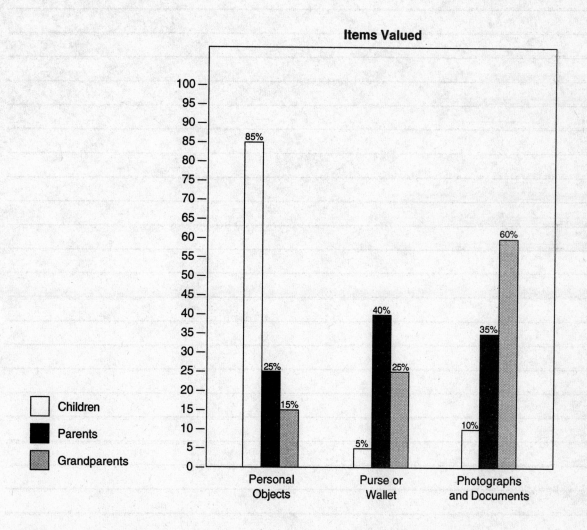

Essay Pages

QUESTION 4

(30 minutes)

This graph shows responses by students, parents, and teachers to the question "What is the most important characteristic of a good teacher?" Using the information in the graph, compare the value that the students, parents, and teachers place on various characteristics. Explain your conclusions, supporting them with details from the graph.

<u>GRAPH AND NOTES</u>

Use this space for essay notes only. Work done on this work sheet will *not* be scored. Write the complete final version of your essay on the Essay Pages.

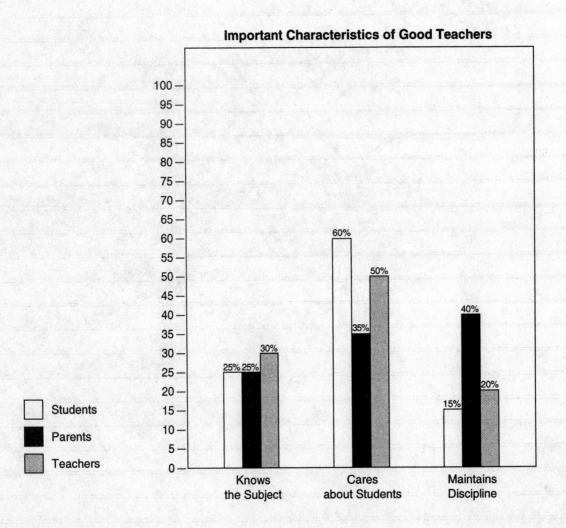

Important Characteristics of Good Teachers

Essay Pages

QUESTION 5

(30 minutes)

This graph shows responses by young long-distance telephone users to the question "Which person do you call the most?" Using the information in the graph, compare the value that different age groups place on relationships. Explain your conclusions, supporting them with details from the graph.

<u>GRAPH AND NOTES</u>

Use this space for essay notes only. Work done on this work sheet will *not* be scored. Write the complete final version of your essay on the Essay Pages.

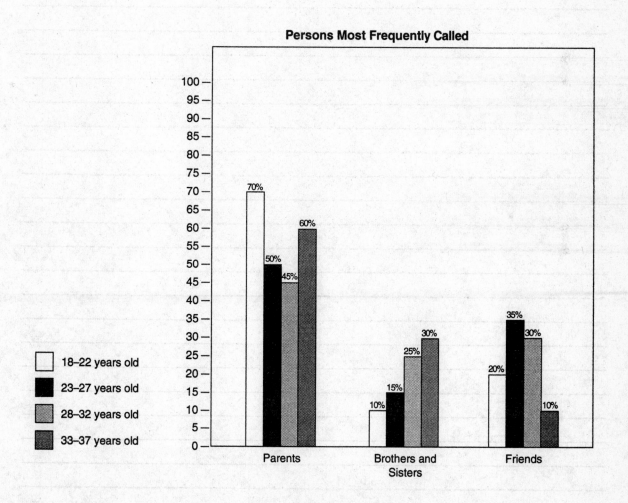

Persons Most Frequently Called

Essay Pages

UNIT THREE

CORRECTING

ANSWER KEY
FOR THE TOEFL

Chapter 3   Listening Comprehension

Part A—Short Conversations

EXERCISE 1: Direct Information

1. (A)	3. (C)	5. (D)	7. (C)	9. (C)
2. (B)	4. (C)	6. (B)	8. (B)	10. (C)

EXERCISE 2: Selections

1. (B)	3. (C)	5. (D)	7. (A)	9. (D)
2. (C)	4. (D)	6. (D)	8. (A)	10. (B)

EXERCISE 3: Reversals

1. (C)	3. (C)	5. (B)	7. (D)	9. (C)
2. (B)	4. (D)	6. (D)	8. (D)	10. (C)

EXERCISE 4: Idiomatic Speech

1. (A)	3. (B)	5. (A)	7. (A)	9. (B)
2. (C)	4. (B)	6. (C)	8. (A)	10. (C)

EXERCISE 5: Computations

1. (D)	3. (C)	5. (C)	7. (D)	9. (C)
2. (C)	4. (B)	6. (D)	8. (B)	10. (D)

EXERCISE 6: Places

1. (B)	3. (A)	5. (C)	7. (B)	9. (B)
2. (B)	4. (B)	6. (A)	8. (A)	10. (C)

EXERCISE 7: Feelings and Emotional Responses

1. (C)	3. (B)	5. (D)	7. (C)	9. (B)
2. (A)	4. (C)	6. (A)	8. (C)	10. (A)

EXERCISE 8: Probabilities

1. (B)	3. (C)	5. (A)	7. (C)	9. (C)
2. (C)	4. (B)	6. (C)	8. (B)	10. (B)

EXERCISE 9: Deductions

1. (C)	3. (D)	5. (C)	7. (B)	9. (C)
2. (C)	4. (B)	6. (D)	8. (A)	10. (D)

EXERCISE 10: Cumulative Review (Part 1)

1. (B)	3. (C)	5. (B)	7. (C)	9. (D)
2. (B)	4. (D)	6. (A)	8. (B)	10. (A)

EXERCISE 11: Cumulative Review (Part 2)

1. (A)	3. (A)	5. (D)	7. (B)	9. (C)
2. (C)	4. (C)	6. (B)	8. (C)	10. (A)

Part B—Extended Conversations

EXERCISE 12: Friends

Conversation One	Conversation Two	Conversation Three	Conversation Four
1. (C)	1. (B)	1. (B)	1. (A)
2. (B)	2. (C)	2. (B)	2. (B)
3. (B)	3. (A)	3. (D)	3. (B)
4. (C)	4. (A)	4. (B)	4. (C)

EXERCISE 13: Service Personnel

Conversation One	Conversation Two	Conversation Three	Conversation Four
1. (C)	1. (A)	1. (A)	1. (C)
2. (C)	2. (A)	2. (D)	2. (A)
3. (C)	3. (C)	3. (C)	3. (B)
4. (B)	4. (C)	4. (A)	4. (A)

EXERCISE 14: University Personnel

Conversation One	Conversation Two	Conversation Three	Conversation Four
1. (C)	1. (B)	1. (A)	1. (B)
2. (A)	2. (B)	2. (A)	2. (D)
3. (C)	3. (C)	3. (A)	3. (C)
4. (A)	4. (B)	4. (A)	4. (B)

EXERCISE 15: University Professors

Conversation One	Conversation Two	Conversation Three	Conversation Four
1. (A)	1. (C)	1. (B)	1. (A)
2. (A)	2. (C)	2. (B)	2. (C)
3. (B)	3. (B)	3. (B)	3. (A)
4. (D)	4. (D)	4. (C)	4. (C)

EXERCISE 16: Class Discussions

Conversation One	Conversation Two	Conversation Three	Conversation Four
1. (A)	1. (B)	1. (A)	1. (D)
2. (C)	2. (D)	2. (A)	2. (B)
3. (C)	3. (A)	3. (B)	3. (A)
4. (B)	4. (A)	4. (C)	4. (B)

EXERCISE 17: Cumulative Review

Conversation One	Conversation Two	Conversation Three	Conversation Four
1. (D)	1. (B)	1. (B)	1. (A)
2. (C)	2. (B)	2. (A)	2. (B)
3. (B)	3. (B)	3. (C)	3. (B)
4. (D)	4. (A)	4. (B)	4. (C)

Part C—Mini Talks

EXERCISE 18: Announcements and Advertisements

Mini Talk One	Mini Talk Two	Mini Talk Three	Mini Talk Four
1. (B)	1. (A)	1. (A)	1. (D)
2. (D)	2. (B)	2. (B)	2. (B)
3. (B)	3. (D)	3. (D)	3. (B)
4. (C)	4. (A)	4. (D)	4. (C)
5. (B)	5. (B)	5. (C)	5. (B)

EXERCISE 19: News and Weather Reports

Mini Talk One	Mini Talk Two	Mini Talk Three	Mini Talk Four
1. (B)	1. (A)	1. (B)	1. (D)
2. (B)	2. (A)	2. (A)	2. (C)
3. (C)	3. (C)	3. (B)	3. (B)
4. (B)	4. (C)	4. (C)	4. (C)
5. (A)	5. (C)	5. (B)	5. (A)

EXERCISE 20: Informative Speeches

Mini Talk One	Mini Talk Two	Mini Talk Three	Mini Talk Four
1. (D)	1. (A)	1. (D)	1. (C)
2. (C)	2. (B)	2. (A)	2. (B)
3. (A)	3. (C)	3. (C)	3. (C)
4. (D)	4. (C)	4. (B)	4. (B)
5. (B)	5. (C)	5. (A)	5. (D)

EXERCISE 21: General Interest Statements

Mini Talk One	Mini Talk Two	Mini Talk Three	Mini Talk Four
1. (B)	1. (A)	1. (B)	1. (B)
2. (C)	2. (D)	2. (A)	2. (A)
3. (D)	3. (C)	3. (C)	3. (B)
4. (A)	4. (D)	4. (C)	4. (A)
5. (C)	5. (C)	5. (D)	5. (C)

EXERCISE 22: Informal Academic Statements

Mini Talk One	Mini Talk Two	Mini Talk Three	Mini Talk Four
1. (C)	1. (B)	1. (A)	1. (C)
2. (D)	2. (D)	2. (D)	2. (C)
3. (A)	3. (B)	3. (C)	3. (C)
4. (B)	4. (B)	4. (D)	4. (A)
5. (A)	5. (C)	5. (D)	5. (C)

EXERCISE 23: Formal Academic Statements

Mini Talk One	Mini Talk Two	Mini Talk Three	Mini Talk Four
1. (C)	1. (C)	1. (D)	1. (A)
2. (B)	2. (A)	2. (B)	2. (B)
3. (B)	3. (B)	3. (A)	3. (B)
4. (B)	4. (B)	4. (A)	4. (B)
5. (C)	5. (B)	5. (B)	5. (C)

EXERCISE 24: Cumulative Review

Mini Talk One	Mini Talk Two	Mini Talk Three	Mini Talk Four
1. (B)	1. (B)	1. (D)	1. (A)
2. (A)	2. (C)	2. (B)	2. (C)
3. (B)	3. (C)	3. (A)	3. (C)
4. (D)	4. (A)	4. (A)	4. (D)
5. (A)	5. (B)	5. (B)	5. (A)

Chapter 4   Structure and Written Expression

Part A—Structure Problems

EXERCISE 1: Verbs (Part 1)

1. (D)	4. (D)	7. (A)	10. (C)	13. (B)
2. (C)	5. (B)	8. (B)	11. (A)	14. (A)
3. (A)	6. (C)	9. (C)	12. (C)	15. (C)

EXERCISE 2: Verbs (Part 2)

1. (B)	4. (B)	7. (C)	10. (D)	13. (A)
2. (A)	5. (C)	8. (A)	11. (D)	14. (D)
3. (B)	6. (A)	9. (C)	12. (B)	15. (A)

EXERCISE 3: Verbs (Part 3)

1. (D)	4. (A)	7. (D)	10. (B)	13. (C)
2. (A)	5. (C)	8. (B)	11. (D)	14. (C)
3. (C)	6. (C)	9. (B)	12. (C)	15. (D)

EXERCISE 4: Pronouns

1. (A)	4. (A)	7. (B)	10. (C)	13. (A)
2. (C)	5. (B)	8. (B)	11. (C)	14. (C)
3. (A)	6. (C)	9. (A)	12. (A)	15. (A)

EXERCISE 5: Nouns

1. (D)	4. (C)	7. (B)	10. (C)	13. (C)
2. (D)	5. (D)	8. (C)	11. (C)	14. (C)
3. (A)	6. (C)	9. (B)	12. (D)	15. (D)

EXERCISE 6: Modifiers (Part 1)

1. (A)	4. (C)	7. (A)	10. (C)	13. (D)
2. (A)	5. (A)	8. (B)	11. (B)	14. (B)
3. (D)	6. (D)	9. (C)	12. (C)	15. (C)

EXERCISE 7: Modifiers (Part 2)

1. (C)	4. (B)	7. (B)	10. (C)	13. (A)
2. (D)	5. (D)	8. (A)	11. (D)	14. (D)
3. (A)	6. (A)	9. (D)	12. (B)	15. (C)

EXERCISE 8: Comparatives

1. (C)	4. (C)	7. (C)	10. (C)	13. (C)
2. (B)	5. (C)	8. (A)	11. (B)	14. (C)
3. (C)	6. (D)	9. (C)	12. (D)	15. (C)

EXERCISE 9: Connectors

1. (A)	4. (C)	7. (C)	10. (B)	13. (D)
2. (C)	5. (C)	8. (D)	11. (C)	14. (C)
3. (C)	6. (A)	9. (B)	12. (B)	15. (B)

EXERCISE 10: Cumulative Review (Part 1)

1. (C)	4. (C)	7. (A)	10. (D)	13. (B)
2. (D)	5. (C)	8. (C)	11. (A)	14. (B)
3. (C)	6. (D)	9. (D)	12. (A)	15. (C)

EXERCISE 11: Cumulative Review (Part 2)

1. (B)	4. (B)	7. (D)	10. (D)	13. (D)
2. (B)	5. (B)	8. (B)	11. (C)	14. (C)
3. (D)	6. (A)	9. (B)	12. (A)	15. (D)

Part B—Written Expression

EXERCISE 12: Point of View

1. (A)	6. (B)	11. (B)	16. (A)	21. (C)
2. (A)	7. (B)	12. (C)	17. (B)	22. (A)
3. (B)	8. (A)	13. (D)	18. (A)	23. (B)
4. (B)	9. (A)	14. (A)	19. (B)	24. (B)
5. (B)	10. (B)	15. (B)	20. (B)	25. (C)

EXERCISE 13: Agreement

1. (B)	6. (B)	11. (C)	16. (B)	21. (C)
2. (C)	7. (A)	12. (D)	17. (B)	22. (C)
3. (B)	8. (C)	13. (D)	18. (C)	23. (B)
4. (C)	9. (A)	14. (A)	19. (C)	24. (B)
5. (B)	10. (B)	15. (B)	20. (C)	25. (A)

EXERCISE 14: Introductory Verbal Modifiers

1. (A)	6. (B)	11. (A)	16. (A)	21. (A)
2. (A)	7. (D)	12. (A)	17. (A)	22. (B)
3. (B)	8. (B)	13. (A)	18. (A)	23. (A)
4. (A)	9. (C)	14. (A)	19. (B)	24. (A)
5. (A)	10. (B)	15. (D)	20. (A)	25. (A)

EXERCISE 15: Parallel Structure

1. (D)	6. (C)	11. (A)	16. (B)	21. (D)
2. (D)	7. (C)	12. (C)	17. (C)	22. (D)
3. (B)	8. (B)	13. (C)	18. (B)	23. (D)
4. (B)	9. (D)	14. (A)	19. (C)	24. (D)
5. (A)	10. (B)	15. (D)	20. (D)	25. (C)

EXERCISE 16: Redundancy

1. (D)	6. (C)	11. (B)	16. (A)	21. (B)
2. (A)	7. (D)	12. (B)	17. (C)	22. (D)
3. (C)	8. (A)	13. (A)	18. (A)	23. (A)
4. (D)	9. (B)	14. (B)	19. (D)	24. (B)
5. (A)	10. (A)	15. (C)	20. (B)	25. (A)

EXERCISE 17: Word Choice

1. (D)	6. (D)	11. (B)	16. (D)	21. (A)
2. (D)	7. (C)	12. (A)	17. (A)	22. (B)
3. (B)	8. (B)	13. (C)	18. (B)	23. (A)
4. (D)	9. (C)	14. (A)	19. (D)	24. (A)
5. (C)	10. (A)	15. (A)	20. (A)	25. (A)

EXERCISE 18: Structure

1. (B)	6. (C)	11. (B)	16. (C)	21. (B)
2. (A)	7. (C)	12. (D)	17. (A)	22. (A)
3. (A)	8. (A)	13. (A)	18. (A)	23. (A)
4. (B)	9. (B)	14. (A)	19. (C)	24. (B)
5. (C)	10. (A)	15. (C)	20. (C)	25. (A)

EXERCISE 19: Cumulative Review (Part 1)

1. (A)	6. (B)	11. (B)	16. (B)	21. (D)
2. (C)	7. (A)	12. (D)	17. (B)	22. (C)
3. (A)	8. (B)	13. (B)	18. (B)	23. (B)
4. (D)	9. (A)	14. (C)	19. (C)	24. (D)
5. (A)	10. (B)	15. (C)	20. (A)	25. (C)

EXERCISE 20: Cumulative Review (Part 2)

1. (D)	6. (D)	11. (C)	16. (D)	21. (B)
2. (A)	7. (D)	12. (C)	17. (B)	22. (A)
3. (C)	8. (A)	13. (B)	18. (A)	23. (C)
4. (C)	9. (B)	14. (D)	19. (B)	24. (B)
5. (B)	10. (C)	15. (A)	20. (C)	25. (A)

Chapter 5   Reading Comprehension

Part A—General Interest

EXERCISE 1: General Interest

Passage One	Passage Two	Passage Three	Passage Four	Passage Five
1. (B)	1. (A)	1. (D)	1. (C)	1. (B)
2. (B)	2. (C)	2. (C)	2. (B)	2. (B)
3. (C)	3. (C)	3. (D)	3. (C)	3. (D)
4. (A)	4. (C)	4. (D)	4. (B)	4. (C)
5. (C)	5. (C)	5. (B)	5. (D)	5. (B)
6. (A)	6. (A)	6. (B)	6. (A)	6. (C)

Part B—Academic Information

EXERCISE 2: Academic Information

Passage One	Passage Two	Passage Three	Passage Four	Passage Five
1. (A)	1. (D)	1. (A)	1. (B)	1. (B)
2. (B)	2. (C)	2. (B)	2. (C)	2. (D)
3. (D)	3. (D)	3. (B)	3. (C)	3. (D)
4. (B)	4. (B)	4. (D)	4. (A)	4. (A)
5. (A)	5. (C)	5. (C)	5. (A)	5. (A)
6. (A)	6. (C)	6. (D)	6. (B)	6. (B)

EXERCISE 3: Textbooks/Biography

Passage One	Passage Two	Passage Three	Passage Four	Passage Five
1. (A)	1. (C)	1. (B)	1. (C)	1. (D)
2. (D)	2. (B)	2. (C)	2. (A)	2. (C)
3. (B)	3. (D)	3. (A)	3. (D)	3. (C)
4. (A)	4. (B)	4. (A)	4. (C)	4. (A)
5. (D)	5. (C)	5. (B)	5. (B)	5. (B)
6. (A)	6. (C)	6. (C)	6. (D)	6. (B)

EXERCISE 4: Textbooks/History and Civics

Passage One	Passage Two	Passage Three	Passage Four	Passage Five
1. (A)	1. (C)	1. (A)	1. (C)	1. (C)
2. (C)	2. (B)	2. (D)	2. (D)	2. (B)
3. (D)	3. (C)	3. (D)	3. (B)	3. (B)
4. (A)	4. (B)	4. (C)	4. (B)	4. (D)
5. (C)	5. (A)	5. (B)	5. (C)	5. (B)
6. (B)	6. (A)	6. (C)	6. (D)	6. (D)

EXERCISE 5: Textbooks/Social Sciences

Passage One	Passage Two	Passage Three	Passage Four	Passage Five
1. (C)	1. (A)	1. (C)	1. (A)	1. (C)
2. (B)	2. (C)	2. (B)	2. (B)	2. (D)
3. (D)	3. (D)	3. (A)	3. (A)	3. (D)
4. (C)	4. (A)	4. (B)	4. (B)	4. (A)
5. (B)	5. (C)	5. (C)	5. (B)	5. (B)
6. (C)	6. (A)	6. (C)	6. (C)	6. (C)

EXERCISE 6: Textbooks/Literature

Passage One	Passage Two	Passage Three	Passage Four	Passage Five
1. (C)	1. (D)	1. (B)	1. (B)	1. (B)
2. (C)	2. (D)	2. (B)	2. (B)	2. (A)
3. (A)	3. (B)	3. (C)	3. (C)	3. (D)
4. (B)	4. (C)	4. (D)	4. (C)	4. (B)
5. (B)	5. (C)	5. (A)	5. (D)	5. (A)
6. (C)	6. (D)	6. (B)	6. (B)	6. (D)

EXERCISE 7: Textbooks/Arts and Entertainment

Passage One	Passage Two	Passage Three	Passage Four	Passage Five
1. (C)	1. (A)	1. (A)	1. (A)	1. (B)
2. (C)	2. (D)	2. (D)	2. (B)	2. (B)
3. (C)	3. (B)	3. (A)	3. (D)	3. (D)
4. (A)	4. (A)	4. (C)	4. (D)	4. (C)
5. (D)	5. (D)	5. (C)	5. (B)	5. (D)
6. (B)	6. (B)	6. (B)	6. (D)	6. (D)

EXERCISE 8: Textbooks/Popular Culture

Passage One	Passage Two	Passage Three	Passage Four	Passage Five
1. (A)	1. (D)	1. (A)	1. (B)	1. (A)
2. (D)	2. (D)	2. (C)	2. (D)	2. (B)
3. (C)	3. (D)	3. (D)	3. (B)	3. (D)
4. (D)	4. (B)	4. (D)	4. (A)	4. (B)
5. (B)	5. (B)	5. (C)	5. (C)	5. (A)
6. (B)	6. (A)	6. (A)	6. (C)	6. (B)

EXERCISE 9: Textbooks/Business

Passage One	Passage Two	Passage Three	Passage Four	Passage Five
1. (A)	1. (C)	1. (C)	1. (C)	1. (D)
2. (A)	2. (D)	2. (B)	2. (B)	2. (C)
3. (C)	3. (A)	3. (B)	3. (C)	3. (B)
4. (C)	4. (A)	4. (C)	4. (A)	4. (D)
5. (B)	5. (A)	5. (A)	5. (B)	5. (B)
6. (C)	6. (A)	6. (D)	6. (D)	6. (A)

EXERCISE 10: Textbooks/Natural Sciences

Passage One	Passage Two	Passage Three	Passage Four	Passage Five
1. (B)	1. (B)	1. (A)	1. (A)	1. (A)
2. (C)	2. (C)	2. (B)	2. (D)	2. (A)
3. (D)	3. (D)	3. (D)	3. (D)	3. (B)
4. (C)	4. (B)	4. (A)	4. (D)	4. (B)
5. (A)	5. (B)	5. (C)	5. (B)	5. (C)
6. (C)	6. (C)	6. (D)	6. (B)	6. (C)

Chapter 6   Test of Written English (TWE)

*Scoring Scale for the TWE

6 shows consistent proficiency

- Is well organized
- Addresses the topic
- Includes examples and details
- Has few errors in grammar and vocabulary

5 shows inconsistent proficiency

- Is well organized
- Addresses the topic
- Includes fewer examples and details
- Has more errors in grammar and vocabulary

4 shows minimal proficiency

- Is adequately organized
- Addresses most of the topic
- Includes some examples and details
- Has errors in grammar and vocabulary that occasionally confuse meaning

3 shows developing proficiency

- Is inadequately organized
- Addresses part of the topic
- Includes few examples and details
- Has many errors in grammar and vocabulary that confuse meaning

2 shows little proficiency

- Is disorganized
- Does not address the topic
- Does not include examples and details
- Has many errors in grammar and vocabulary that consistently confuse meaning

1 shows no proficiency

- Is disorganized
- Does not address the topic
- Does not include examples and details
- Has so many errors in grammar and vocabulary that meaning is not communicated

*Reprinted from *Barron's How to Prepare for the TOEFL*

EXPLANATORY
ANSWERS
FOR THE TOEFL

Chapter 3   Listening Comprehension

Part A—Short Conversations

EXERCISE 1: Direct Information

1. **(A)** "I've been up all night finishing a paper." Choice (B) contradicts the fact that all the man has had to drink is coffee. Choice (D) contradicts the fact that the man has finished the paper. Choice (C) is not mentioned and may not be concluded from information in the conversation.

2. **(B)** "Can I use my credit card . . . ?" Choice (A) refers to the alternative that the woman suggests, not to her preference. Choices (C) and (D) are not mentioned and may not be concluded from information in the conversation.

3. **(C)** "She probably thought that such an expensive gift was inappropriate on such short acquaintance." The word *short* in Choice (A) refers to the acquaintance, not to the man. Choice (B) is true, but it is not the reason Sharon stopped seeing the man. Choice (D) contradicts the fact that the man gave Sharon an expensive gift.

4. **(C)** "This is a standard security procedure." Choice (A) contradicts the fact that the woman denied that he suspected the woman of theft. The word *secure* in Choice (B) and the word *standard* in Choice (D) refer to a standard security procedure, not to securing a purse or to a standard size.

5. **(D)** "Could I borrow yours [your notebook] before the test?" The word *study* in Choice (A) refers to the man's plan to study, not to the woman's request. The word *break* in Choice (C) refers to the man's breaks at work, not to the woman's request. Choice (B) is not mentioned and may not be concluded from information in the conversation.

6. **(B)** "Oh, that's Steve's sister." Choice (C) refers to the owner of the car, not to the driver. Choice (D) refers to the person who had a party, not to the person driving. Choice (A) is not mentioned and may not be concluded from information in the conversation.

7. **(C)** "It [the door] sticks a little." Choice (A) refers to the woman's original conclusion, not to the real reason that the door would not open. The word *key* in Choice (B) refers to the woman's question about a key, not to the reason that the door would not open. Choice (D) is not mentioned and may not be concluded from information in the conversation.

8. **(B)** "Can we use our calculators on the test?" The word *check* in Choice (A) refers to the woman's offer to check the calculators, not to what the man wants to do. Choices (C) and (D) are not mentioned and may not be concluded from information in the conversation.

9. **(C)** "You should call his [your roommate's] family." Choice (A) contradicts the fact that the woman does not think it is fair for the man to be stuck with the bills. The word *family* in Choice (B) refers to the family of the roommate, not of the man. The word *leave* in Choice (D) refers to the roommate's leaving, not the man's leaving.

10. **(C)** "Then I'll review your options with you." Choices (A), (B), and (D) refer to instructions that the woman gives the man for him to do before their interview, not to the way that the woman will help the man at the interview.

EXERCISE 2: Selections

1. **(B)** "... we are just good friends." Choice (A) refers to the way that the man feels about Jack, not to their actual relationship. Choice (C) refers to the woman's assumption, not to the relationship. Choice (D) is not mentioned and may not be concluded from information in the conversation.

2. **(C)** "Well, I know that Steve is looking for a roommate." Because the woman mentions that Steve is looking for a roommate, it may be concluded that she is suggesting that the man and Steve be roommates. Choice (A) contradicts the fact that Frank responded to the man's offer by saying that he was going to live with Geoff. Choices (B) and (D) contradict the fact that Frank and Geoff plan to be roommates.

3. **(C)** "A *C*." Choice (B) refers to Mike's grade, not to the woman's grade. Choice (D) refers to the grades received by almost everyone else. Choice (A) is not mentioned and may not be concluded from information in the conversation.

4. **(D)** "... if I were you, I'd look into some of the special offers through the university." Choices (A) and (C) refer to alternatives that the woman mentions, not to the advice she gives the man. The word *newspaper* in Choice (B) refers to an article about special offers, not to an ad for a computer.

5. **(D)** "You didn't get your grades because your name isn't on the roster." Choice (A) contradicts the fact that the woman paid her fees. Choice (C) contradicts the fact that she attended class. Choice (B) is not mentioned and may not be concluded from information in the conversation.

6. **(D)** "... I think I need a 7½ here." Choices (A) and (B) refer to the size that the woman takes in Europe, not to the size she needs here. Choice (C) refers to the size that the woman takes in Canada.

7. **(A)** "... tell me the last time you had your glasses changed. It really sounds more like eye strain." Choices (B), (C), and (D) refer to the concerns that the woman has about her health, not to the problem that the man suspects.

8. **(A)** "Have you started writing your paper for history?" "Not yet." Choices (B), (C), and (D) refer to assignments that she is doing now, not to an assignment she must begin.

9. **(D)** "Are you glad that you came to Washington?" "Yes, indeed." Choices (A) and (B) refer to places the man considered before coming to Washington. Choice (C) is not mentioned and may not be concluded from information in the conversation.

10. **(B)** "Something is wrong with second gear." Choices (C) and (D) refer to gears that run fine. Choice (A) is not mentioned and may not be concluded from information in the conversation.

EXERCISE 3: Reversals

1. **(C)** "... I have my car back now." Choice (A) refers to the man's offer, and to the woman's first plan, not to the way that the woman will get to the airport. Choices (B) and (D) are not mentioned and may not be concluded from information in the conversation.

2. **(B)** "How about the eggs and pancakes?" Choice (A) refers to the woman's choice before she changes her mind. Choice (D) refers to part of the woman's order, but leaves out the fact that she wants eggs, also. Choice (C) is not mentioned and may not be concluded from information in the passage.

3. **(C)** "Four, no five." Choice (B) refers to the man's first thought, not to his final statement about the number of boxes he ordered. Choices (A) and (D) contradict the fact that the man ordered five boxes of cookies.

4. **(D)** "It's 6-1-9." Choice (A) refers to the man's first response, before he corrects himself. Choices (B) and (C) are not mentioned and may not be concluded from information in the conversation.

5. **(B)** "... it's ten cents a copy when you make fewer than twenty copies, and you have only fifteen." Choice (A) refers to the price per page for twenty copies or more. The number in Choice (C) refers to the number of copies the woman has, not to the price per copy. The number in Choice (D) refers to the number of copies required for the lower price, not to the price per copy.

6. **(D)** "That's $2.50." Choice (B) refers to the price of a one-page domestic fax, not to the overseas transmission that the woman wants to send. The per-minute prices in Choices (A) and (C) are not mentioned and may not be concluded from information in the conversation.

7. **(D)** "... I'd rather go to the movies." Choices (A) and (C) refer to the man's preference, not to the woman's preference. Choice (B) is not mentioned and may not be concluded from information in the passage.

8. **(D)** "... I should take two fifties and the rest twenties." Choice (A) refers to the man's request before he changed his mind. Choices (B) and (C) contradict the fact that he asks for some twenties.

9. **(C)** "... better yet, the Old House." Choice (A) refers to the woman's first suggestion before she changed her mind. Choices (B) and (D) are not mentioned and may not be concluded from information in the conversation.

10. **(C)** "... let's say seven, just to be on the safe side." The time in Choice (A) refers to the man's first estimate, not to the man's final estimate. Choices (B) and (D) contradict the fact that the man acknowledged that he would be home late.

EXERCISE 4: Idiomatic Speech

1. **(A)** "You're putting me on" is an idiomatic expression that means the speaker does not think the other person is serious. Choices (B), (C), and (D) are not paraphrases of the expression.

2. **(C)** "That's just what I need" is an idiomatic expression that means the speaker will be inconvenienced. Choices (A), (B), and (D) are not paraphrases of the expression.

3. **(B)** "... I've run out" is an idiomatic expression that means the speaker has used all of the supply. Choices (A), (C), and (D) are not paraphrases of the expression.

4. **(B)** "No joke" is an idiomatic expression that means the speaker agrees with another person. Choices (A), (C), and (D) are not paraphrases of the expression.

5. **(A)** "You're just not all there ..." is an idiomatic expression that means the speaker does not believe the other person is very attentive. Choices (B), (C), and (D) are not paraphrases of the expression.

6. **(C)** "Mickey Mouse" is an idiomatic expression that describes something easy or without substance. Choices (A), (B), and (D) are not paraphrases of the expression.

7. **(A)** "Don't bother" is an idiomatic expression that means the speaker does not want the other person to take action. Choices (B), (C), and (D) are not paraphrases of the expression.

8. **(A)** "I'll say" is an idiomatic expression that means the speaker agrees with the other person. Choices (B), (C), and (D) are not paraphrases of the expression.

9. **(B)** "I'll believe it when I see it" is an idiomatic expression that means the speaker is doubtful. Choices (A), (C), and (D) are not paraphrases of the expression.

10. **(C)** "Don't ask" is an idiomatic expression that means an emphatic no. Choices (A), (B), and (D) are not paraphrases of the expression.

EXERCISE 5: Computations

1. **(D)** If the man's car gets forty miles per gallon and the woman's car gets twenty, then the man's mileage is two times, or twice, that of the woman. The woman's mileage is half that of the man. Choices (A), (B), and (C) cannot be computed from information in the conversation.

2. **(C)** If the appointment is for 9:00 and the man has to be fifteen minutes, he will probably arrive at fifteen minutes after nine, or 9:15. Choice (A) refers to a time one hour, not fifteen minutes, later. Choice (B) refers to the original time of the appointment, not to the time when the man will actually arrive. Choice (D) refers to a time thirty, not fifteen, minutes later.

3. **(C)** If general-public tickets are ten dollars each and student tickets are half-price, or five dollars, then two general and two student tickets would cost ten dollars times two, or twenty dollars, plus five dollars times two, or ten dollars, for a total of thirty dollars. Choice (A) refers to the price of one general-public or two student tickets. Choice (B) refers to the price of two general-public or four student tickets. Choice (D) refers to the price of four general-public tickets.

4. **(B)** "Twenty-five dollars each . . ." Choice (A) refers to half the sale price of two sweaters. Choice (C) refers to the sale price of two sweaters, not one sweater. Choice (D) refers to the regular, not the sale price, of two sweaters. It was not necessary to make a computation in order to answer this question.

5. **(C)** If it costs $2.55 for the first three minutes, and $1.00 for each additional minute, then a ten-minute call would cost $2.55 plus $1.00 times 7 or $7.00 for a total of $9.55. Choice (B) refers to the price of a ten-minute call if the first three minutes as well as additional minutes cost $1.00 each. Choices (A) and (D) are not mentioned and may not be computed or concluded from information in the conversation.

6. **(D)** If his watch says 1:15, but it is a little fast, it must be before 1:15. Choice (A) contradicts the fact that he told the woman what time it was. Choice (B) contradicts the fact that he told the woman what time it was and the fact that he said that his watch was a little fast. Choice (C) contradicts the fact that his watch was fast.

7. **(D)** If he owes fifteen dollars, and he may write the check for ten dollars over the amount of purchase, he may write the check for fifteen plus ten, or a total of twenty-five dollars. Choice (A) refers to the amount over the purchase, not to the total. Choice (B) contradicts the fact that the woman agrees to his paying by check. Choice (C) contradicts the fact that he may write the check for ten dollars over the amount, not just the amount of purchase.

8. **(B)** If the man has three 15¢ stamps, or 45¢, plus two 25¢ stamps, or 50¢, for a total of 95¢, and he needs one more 5¢ stamp, the total postage is $1.00. Choice (C) refers to the amount of postage he has on the package, not to the amount required. Choices (A) and (D) cannot be computed from information in the conversation.

9. **(C)** If the printer ribbons used to cost $13.00 and the price has gone up $5.00, the ribbons now cost $13.00 plus $5.00, or $18.00. Choice (A) refers to the price of the ribbons before, not now. Choice (B) cannot be computed from information in the conversation. Choice (D) refers to the price of ribbons if the price has gone down, instead of up, $5.00.

10. **(D)** If the woman arrives in Chicago at 11:00 A.M. and she must wait for five hours, she will leave Chicago at five hours after 11:00 A.M. or 4:00 P.M. Choice (A) refers to the time she will leave to go to Chicago, not depart from Chicago. Choice (B) refers to the time she will arrive in, not depart from, Chicago. The number in Choice (C) refers to the flight number, not to the time.

EXERCISE 6: Places

1. **(B)** From the references to the *special, baked chicken, coffee,* and the *check*, it must be concluded that this conversation takes place in a restaurant. Baked pastries, not chicken, may be found in a bakery in Choice (A). Checks, but not chicken and coffee, may be found in a bank in Choice (C). Chickens, but not checks, may be found on a farm in Choice (D).

2. **(B)** From the references to a *prescription* and *refilled,* it must be concluded that this conversation takes place in a drugstore. A prescription may be written, but not refilled, in a dentist's office in Choice (A). It is not customary to get a prescription refilled at the places referred to in Choices (C) and (D).

3. **(A)** From the reference to *bride,* it must be concluded that this conversation takes place at a wedding. The words *honeymoon* and *Florida* in Choices (B) and (C) refer to where the couple is going, not to where they are now. It is not customary for a bride to be recognized at an airport in Choice (D).

4. **(B)** From the references to *press, twelve,* and *where* [he is] *going,* it must be concluded that this conversation takes place in an elevator. It is not customary to press a number in order to go somewhere in the places referred to in Choices (A), (C), and (D).

5. **(C)** From the references to *doctoral candidates* and *black robes,* it must be concluded that this conversation takes place at a graduation. It is customary to wear black colors or black clothing, not black robes, at a funeral in Choice (D). It is not customary to wear black robes at the places referred to in Choices (A) and (B).

6. **(A)** From the references to *glazed doughnuts,* a *loaf,* and French *bread,* it must be concluded that this conversation takes place in a bakery. The word *French* in Choice (C) refers to a kind of bread, not to a place. It is not customary to find baked goods in the places referred to in Choices (B) and (D).

7. **(B)** From the references to *title* and a *book,* it must be concluded that this conversation takes place at a library. The words *God* and *England* in Choices (A) and (C) refer to the title of the book, not to places. It is not customary to be looking for a book in a theater in Choice (D).

8. **(A)** From the reference to *treatments,* it must be concluded that this conversation takes place in a doctor's office. It is not customary to discuss treatments in the places referred to in Choices (B), (C), and (D).

9. **(B)** From the references to *accounts, interest rate,* and *monthly balance,* it must be concluded that this conversation takes place in a bank. The word *club* in Choice (C) refers to a kind of account, not a place. Accounts, but not interest rates, might be found in the places referred to in Choices (A) and (D).

10. **(C)** From the references to *reservation, party of two,* and *table,* it must be concluded that this conversation takes place in a restaurant. The word *reservation* in Choice (A) refers to a place saved, not to an Indian reservation. The word *party* in Choice (B) refers to a group, not to an occasion. In choice (D) the woman says that she will call the man, but a telephone is not mentioned and may not be concluded from information in the conversation.

EXERCISE 7: Feelings and Emotional Responses

1. **(C)** Since the man says that he has had several interviews, and that he can work for his father, and since his tone is confident, it may be concluded that he feels confident. Choice (A) contradicts the fact that the man says he is not worried. Choices (B) and (D) are not mentioned and may not be concluded from information in the conversation.

2. **(A)** Since the man compares the movie to fairy tales, and since his tone is sarcastic, it may be concluded that he thought it was a very unrealistic movie. Choices (B), (C), and (D) are not mentioned and may not be concluded from information in the conversation.

3. **(B)** Since the woman says she knows she did much better, it may be concluded that she thought she improved her score. Choice (A) contradicts the fact that she knows she did much better. The number in Choice (C) refers to the score she received the first time, not this time. Choice (D) contradicts the fact that she knew a lot about several of the reading comprehension passages.

4. **(C)** Since the woman says that the man is not *with it* any day, and since her tone is impatient, it may be concluded that she thinks he never pays attention. Choices (A), (B), and (D) are not mentioned and may not be concluded from information in the conversation.

5. **(D)** Since the man says to forget asking Rick, and since his tone is negative, it may be concluded that he does not want to invite them. Choice (C) contradicts the fact that he does not want to invite Rick. Choices (A) and (B) are not mentioned and may not be concluded from information in the conversation.

6. **(A)** Since the man says *what,* and since his tone is surprised, it may be concluded that the man is surprised by the news. Choices (B), (C), and (D) are not mentioned and may not be concluded from information in the conversation.

7. **(C)** Since the man agrees with the woman, it may be concluded that he does not like the grading system. Choice (A) misinterprets the idiom *to not care for,* which means to not like. Choice (D) contradicts the fact that he agrees with the woman. Choice (B) is not mentioned and may not be concluded from information in the conversation.

8. **(C)** Since the man agrees reluctantly, and since his tone is dubious, it may be concluded that he has his doubts about Terry. Choices (A), (B), and (D) are not mentioned and may not be concluded from information in the conversation.

9. **(B)** Since the man agrees with the woman when she says that she does not want to go to the review session, it may be concluded that he does not want to go. Since he says they should go, it may be concluded that he will go. Choices (A) and (C) contradict the fact that the man does not want to go. Choice (D) contradicts the fact that he will go.

10. **(A)** Since the man says *bummer,* and since his tone is sympathetic, it may be concluded that he thinks Janine would be difficult to live with. Choices (B) and (C) contradict the fact that the man thinks it is a bummer for the woman to have been assigned to live with Janine instead of with Carol. Choice (D) is not mentioned and may not be concluded from information in the conversation.

EXERCISE 8: Probabilities

1. **(B)** Since the man has ordered a large orange juice, he will most probably accept the size orange juice they have. Choice (A) is less probable because they have the drink that he wants. Choice (C) is less probable because there is no reason for him to change his order because of the size glass available. Choice (D) is less probable because the hot tea was ordered in addition to the orange juice, not instead of it.

2. **(C)** Since the woman went to the library last night, and the man suggests that she might have left her book there, the woman will most probably go to the library to look for her book. Choices (A) and (D) are less probable because the kitchen and the table refer to the place where the book was yesterday, not to places where the woman will go to study or eat instead of looking for the lost book. Choice (B) is less probable because in the conversation *chemistry* refers to the book, not a class.

3. **(C)** Since the woman does not know anyone in London, she will most probably refuse the collect call. Choice (A) is less probable because she will probably not accept the charges. Choices (B) and (D) are less probable because she does not know anyone in London.

4. **(B)** Since the man is looking for a copy machine, and the woman directs him to a building across the street, he will most probably go across the street to make a copy. Choice (A) is less probable because she does not have access to a copy machine. Choice (C) is less probable because the building is right across the street. Choice (D) is less probable because the man wants to make copies, but he does not have them now.

5. **(A)** Since the woman says that the offer sounds good to her, she will most probably join the club. Choice (B) is less probable because the $5.00 refers to the cost of joining the club, not the price of a video. Choice (C) is less probable because the offer of one free video after renting ten is available after joining the club. Choice (D) is less probable because she is already in the video store.

6. **(C)** Since the man asks for his call to be directed to reservations, he will most probably make a reservation. Choice (A) is less probable because his call, not he, is being directed. Choice (B) is less probable because he is already on the phone, making a call. Choice (D) is less probable because the woman is directing his call to someone else.

7. **(C)** Since the woman asks where the bus will stop, she will most probably cross the street to wait for the bus. Choices (A) and (D) are less probable because she wants to take a bus. Choice (B) is less probable because the bus stop is on the other side of the street.

8. **(B)** Since the man suggests that the woman call the highway patrol, she will most probably call them. Choice (A) is less probable because the man suggests that she check with the highway patrol before leaving. Choices (C) and (D) are not mentioned and may not be concluded from the information.

9. **(C)** Since the man delivers within three miles of the university, he will most probably make the delivery to the woman if she is close to the university. Choice (A) is less probable because the woman has not indicated that she is at the university. Choice (B) is less probable because the woman may be within the delivery area. Choice (D) is not mentioned and may not be concluded from information in the conversation.

10. **(B)** Since the man does not have twenty minutes to wait, he will most probably wait five minutes to be seated in the smoking section. Choice (A) is less probable because the man says he does not have twenty minutes to wait. Choice (C) is less probable because both sections have a waiting list. Choice (D) is not mentioned and may not be concluded from the information in the conversation.

EXERCISE 9: Deductions

1. **(C)** Since the man says that he will come back tonight, he implies that he will check the book out before closing. Choice (A) is less likely because he plans to return to the library. Choice (B) is less likely because he leaves the library. Choice (D) is less likely because the book is already on reserve.

2. **(C)** Since the man says that there is a machine downstairs, he implies that the woman should go downstairs to get a soda. Choice (A) is less likely because there is a soda machine downstairs. Choice (B) is less likely because he gives directions to the woman. Choice (D) contradicts the fact that he gives directions to a soda machine.

3. **(D)** Since the man expresses surprise that the woman will have to take the TOEFL, and mentions that he thought those who graduated from an American high school were exempted from taking it, we know that the woman graduated from an American high school. Choice (B) is less likely because she is making application to American universities now. Choice (C) contradicts the fact that she thought she would not be required to take the TOEFL but has been required to do so by the universities to which she applied. Choice (A) is not mentioned and may not be concluded from information in the conversation.

4. **(B)** Since the man says the woman was lucky to be in line for two hours, the man most probably means that he was in line longer than the woman. Choice (A) is true, but it is not what the man means by his comment. Choice (C) contradicts the fact that the man thought the woman's two-hour wait was lucky compared to his. Choice (D) contradicts the fact that it took the woman two hours to register.

5. **(C)** Because the man offers an argument against taking a plane, it must be concluded that he prefers to take a bus. Choice (B) refers to the way that the woman, not the man prefers to travel. Choices (A) and (D) are not mentioned and may not be concluded from information in the conversation.

6. **(D)** Because she can't pay twenty-six dollars for the leather gloves, it must be concluded that she will buy the vinyl ones. Choices (A), (B), and (C) contradict the fact that she can't pay twenty-six dollars for the leather gloves.

7. **(B)** Because the man has never seen Bob go out so often with the same person, it must be concluded that Bob is serious about Sally. Choice (D) contradicts the fact that Bob has never gone out so often with the same person. Choices (A) and (C) are not mentioned and may not be concluded from information in the conversation.

8. **(A)** From the references to *metric units, meters, grams, feet,* and *pounds,* it must be concluded that the people are discussing weights and measures. The phrase *European nations* refers to the countries using the metric system, not to politics, in Choice (B). The word *employ* refers to use, not employment, in Choice (C). The word *pounds* refers to weight, not money, in Choice (D).

9. **(C)** Because the man says that Jane always says she is going to quit her job, it must be concluded that he does not take her seriously. Choice (A) contradicts the fact that the man does not believe Jane will quit. Choice (B) refers to the way that the woman, not Jane, feels. The word *present* in Choice (D) refers to a going-away present for Jane, not for the man.

10. **(D)** Because they do not see her there, it must be concluded that Betty was not at the play. Choices (A) and (C) contradict the fact that she told the man she would be at the play. Choice (B) contradicts the fact that the man and woman don't see her at the play.

EXERCISE 10: Short Conversations/Cumulative Review (Part 1)

1. **(B)** "But then I took a few courses in the engineering department, and I was hooked." Choice (A) refers to the major that the woman started to pursue before engineering. Choice (C) refers to a career that the woman considered before she chose engineering. Choice (D) is not mentioned and may not be concluded from information in the conversation.

2. **(B)** If the in-store special is twelve hundred dollars, and the manufacturer's coupon is worth an extra one-hundred-dollar rebate, then the computer will cost twelve hundred minus one hundred, or eleven hundred dollars. Choice (A) refers to the in-store price without the rebate. Choice (C) refers to the list price, not the in-store price, minus the rebate. Choice (D) refers to the list price.

3. **(C)** "I thought we were going to meet at seven-thirty . . ." Choice (A) refers to the time the woman arrived, not to the time that they agreed to meet. Choice (B) refers to the time now. Choice (D) confuses the word *fifty* with *fifteen,* and refers to the time now.

4. **(D)** ". . . their number [the chemistry department's] is almost like ours [the psychology department's]." Choice (A) refers to the reason that the man tried to call the chemistry department, not the psychology department. Choice (B) contradicts the fact that the numbers are similar, but not the same. Choice (C) contradicts the fact that he was trying to call the chemistry department, not the psychology department.

5. **(B)** ". . . this afternoon after one-thirty it'll be ready." The number in Choice (A) refers to the number of copies of each original that the woman wants. The number in Choice (C) refers to the one hundred and twenty pages that the woman wants to have copied, not to the number of minutes that it will take to copy the originals. The number in Choice (D) refers to the time, one-thirty, that the copies will be ready, not to the number of minutes that it will take.

6. **(A)** If the library stays open until two o'clock in the morning, and will be closing in a few minutes, then the time is a few minutes before two o'clock. Choice (B) contradicts the fact that they will be closing in a few minutes. Choices (C) and (D) contradict the fact that they close at two o'clock, and they are still open now.

7. **(C)** From the reference to the *second window* and the request to *please drive forward,* it must be concluded that the conversation takes place at a fast-food drive-through. A sandwich and a soda may be found in a grocery store, a restaurant, or a cafeteria, as in Choices (A), (B), and (D), but it is not customary to drive to a window to pick up the food at any of the places except the fast-food drive-through.

8. **(B)** Since the woman suggest that they meet later tonight, it must be concluded that she wants to meet the man. Choice (A) contradicts the fact that the man knows the woman's class schedule. Choice (D) contradicts the fact that the man wants to meet after the woman's class. Choice (C) is not mentioned and may not be concluded from information in the conversation.

9. **(D)** "Call me at 674-9521 if you get back before nine o'clock." Choice (A) contradicts the fact that the woman wants the man to call her at home after nine o'clock. Choice (B) contradicts the fact that the woman wants the man to call her at home after, not before, nine o'clock. Choice (C) contradicts the fact that Jack is the man who should return the call.

10. **(A)** "Why not eat with me in the cafeteria?" Choice (B) refers to the place where the man left his lunch, not to the woman's suggestion. Choice (C) contradicts the fact that the woman suggests the cafeteria, not her house, for lunch. Choice (D) contradicts the fact that the woman invites the man to go with her to the cafeteria to eat.

EXERCISE 11: Cumulative Review (Part 2)

1. **(A)** "I am [working at the bookstore]." Choice (B) refers to the purpose for the woman's part-time job, which she took in order to buy Christmas presents, not to her place of employment. Choice (C) refers to the place where the woman is working part time, not full time. Choice (D) refers to the location of the bookstore, near the dormitory.

2. **(C)** If they can't move until the twentieth, and that is five more days, then today is twenty minus five, or August 15. Choice (A) would be twenty plus, not minus, five. Choice (B) refers to the date that they can move, not to today's date. The number in Choice (D) refers to the number of days that they must stay in the hotel, not to today's date.

3. **(A)** ". . . and change again in Los Angeles for Hawaii." Choice (B) refers to the city where the woman must make her final change of planes, not to her final destination. Choices (C) and (D) refer to cities where the woman must change planes en route.

4. **(C)** Since the woman has made the dean's list, an honor roll for academic excellence, we must conclude that she is a good student. The term *dean* in Choice (A) refers to the list, not to the woman. Choice (D) contradicts the fact that she was on the dean's list last semester. Choice (B) is not mentioned and may not be concluded from information in the conversation.

5. **(D)** From the references to the *license, test results,* an *eye exam,* and the *officer,* it must be concluded that the conversation takes place in the Bureau of Motor Vehicles. Although a photograph might be taken in a photographer's studio as in Choice (A), a test might be given in a classroom in Choice (B), and an eye exam might be verified in an optometrist's office as in Choice (C), it is not probable that the combination of activities would occur in any of these choices.

6. **(B)** ". . . turn in the main entrance [of the university] and it's the first building you see. . . ." Choice (A) refers to the street that takes you to the entrance of the university. Choice (C) refers to the place where you should make your left turn. Choice (D) contradicts the fact that you go to the first light, turn, and travel on Circle Drive.

7. **(B)** "The one [bank] closest to the college." Choice (A) refers to the fact that the woman wants to find the bank closest to the college, not the college itself. Choice (C) refers to the name of a street, not to a grant that provides financial assistance. Choice (D) contradicts the fact that she chooses the bank on Grant Avenue, not the one on First Street.

8. **(C)** "Please don't bother" is an idiomatic expression that means the speaker does not want to cause work. Choices (A), (B), and (D) are not paraphrases of the expression.

9. **(C)** "No way" is an idiomatic expression that means the speaker will not agree under any circumstances. Choices (A), (B), and (D) may not be concluded as the speaker's attitude, expressed by this idiom.

10. **(A)** Since the woman says *after all,* it must be concluded that she was under the opposite impression. Choice (B) refers to the man's state of mind, not to that of the woman. Choice (C) contradicts the fact that the woman and man are making plans for the trip. Choice (D) is not mentioned and may not be concluded from information in the conversation.

Part B—Extended Conversations

EXERCISE 12: Friends

Conversation One

1. **(C)** "Look, I know how you feel about my smoking. You don't have to tell me every day." Choices (A), (B), and (D) are mentioned in reference to the main topic of the conversation, "the man's smoking."

2. **(B)** "Why don't you go to a doctor? . . . I mean a general practitioner." Choice (A) contradicts the fact that the woman, not the man, will rethink their plans. Choice (C) refers to the man's interpretation of the suggestion, not to what the woman suggests. Choice (D) refers to a source of stress, not to the woman's suggestion.

3. **(B)** "I can't believe it!" Choice (C) refers to the woman's feelings, not to those of the man. Choices (A) and (D) are not mentioned and may not be concluded from information in the conversation.

4. **(C)** Since the man says that the woman does not have to tell him how she feels about his smoking every day, it may be concluded that she has asked the man to quit smoking many times. Choice (B) contradicts the fact that she is engaged. Choice (D) contradicts the fact that she loves the man. Choice (A) is not mentioned and may not be concluded from information in the conversation.

Conversation Two

1. **(B)** "Did you see that TV special on Norman Rockwell last night?" Choices (A), (C), and (D) are mentioned in reference to the main topic of the conversation, "the TV program about Norman Rockwell."

2. **(C)** "It never occurred to me that he would have actually employed models. . . . But it does make sense to use photographs of real people . . ." Choice (A) refers to the woman's assumption, not to Rockwell's method. Choice (B) refers to Rockwell's finished work, not to the source of the interesting faces. Choice (D) contradicts the fact that the picture tells a story.

3. **(A)** "And to think that he [Rockwell] created several hundred of those [paintings]." Choices (B), (C), and (D) are not mentioned and may not be concluded from information in the conversation.

4. **(A)** "I'd like to see it [the exhibit], too. Let's go." Choice (B) contradicts the fact that they already saw the special. Choice (C) contradicts the fact that the television special aired last night, not now. Choice (D) contradicts the fact that they are in Miami now.

Conversation Three

1. **(B)** "I can't figure out how to put the page numbers on." Choice (A) contradicts the fact that the man is using the computer, and only needs help with a specific operation. Choice (D) contradicts the fact that the man is using the computer to put page numbers on a document. Choice (C) is mentioned in reference to the main topic, "the woman showing the man how to put page numbers on a document."

2. **(B)** "Well, that's the problem then. The numbers don't show up on the screen. But they will on the printed copy." Choice (A) contradicts the fact that the man has already done that. Choice (D) contradicts the fact that the numbers don't show up on the screen. Choice (C) is not mentioned and may not be concluded from information in the conversation.

3. **(D)** " . . . it would be better if you let me talk you through it." Choice (B) refers to the man's suggestion, not to what the woman wants the man to do. Choices (A) and (C) are not mentioned and may not be concluded from information in the conversation.

4. **(B)** "This is my job [teaching people about computers]." Choice (C) contradicts the fact that she tells the man not to worry and offers to coach him. Choice (D) contradicts the fact that she answers all the man's questions. Choice (A) is not mentioned and may not be concluded from information in the conversation.

Conversation Four

1. **(A)** " . . . I'm hungry." Choice (B) contradicts the fact that Bill, not John, noticed the time. Choices (C) and (D) are true but not the reasons for the conversation.

2. **(B)** "It's [the test is] not until Monday but I want to go home this weekend." Choice (A) contradicts the fact that the test is on Monday, not that night. Choices (C) and (D) are not mentioned and may not be concluded from information in the conversation.

3. **(B)** Because the cafeteria is going to close in half an hour and it is six o'clock now, it must be concluded that the cafeteria closes thirty minutes later, or at six-thirty. Choice (A) refers to the time it is now, not to the time the cafeteria closes. Choice (C) refers to when John is going to go home. Choice (D) refers to when John has a test.

4. **(C)** "Well, knock on my door if you decide to get that pizza later." Choice (D) contradicts the fact that Bill tells John what is being served in the cafeteria. Choices (A) and (B) are not mentioned and may not be concluded from information in the conversation.

EXERCISE 13: Service Personnel

Conversation One

1. **(C)** "Well, I'm not sure [whether I need to get a driver's license]. You see, I have an international driver's license." Choice (A) contradicts the fact that the man has an international driver's license. Choices (B) and (D) refer to what the man is directed to do, not to what he wants to do.

2. **(C)** "Then you can apply for a limited license. . . . Oh yes you do [have to take a driver's test]." Choice (A) refers to the procedure for an application, but not to what the man has to do in order to drive legally. Choice (B) contradicts the fact that the man, as a student, will be temporarily residing in the state, and therefore, cannot use his international driver's license. Choice (D) is not mentioned and may not be concluded from information in the conversation.

3. **(C)** ". . . a limited license [is] . . . a five-year license." Choice (A) refers to the time limit for legal use of an international license. Choice (B) refers to the number of years that the man will stay in the United States. Choice (D) refers to the number of dollars that a limited license costs, not to the number of years that the license is valid.

4. **(B)** "I don't have ID with me, but I can go get it." Choices (A) and (D) refer to requirements that the man will have to fulfill after he shows his ID. Choice (C) is not mentioned and may not be concluded from information in the conversation.

Conversation Two

1. **(A)** "I'd like to put an ad in the newspaper, please." Choices (B), (C), and (D) are not mentioned and may not be concluded from information in the conversation.

2. **(A)** "I want to sell my furniture." Choice (B) refers to the name of the boulevard where the man lives, not to what he is trying to sell. Choice (C) refers to the name of the apartment building where the man lives. Choice (D) is not mentioned and may not be concluded from information in the conversation.

3. **(C)** "I'm just going to pay cash." Choice (A) refers to checking the wording of an ad, not to a method of payment. Choices (B) and (D) contradict the fact that the man does not wish to be billed.

4. **(C)** "So, if you want to use abbreviations, that might save you some money." Choice (B) contradicts the fact that abbreviations make the ad shorter, not longer. Choices (A) and (D) are not mentioned and may not be concluded from information in the conversation.

Conversation Three

1. **(A)** "And thank you for shopping at the Family Store." Choice (B) is a secondary theme used to develop the main theme of the conversation. Choice (C) refers to the fact that the clerk asks the woman to put her telephone number on the front of the check, not to his showing her how to write a check. Choice (D) refers to the woman's college ID, not to her registration at the college.

2. **(D)** "Both money and checks are considered cash." Choice (A) is considered correct, but incomplete. Choices (B) and (C) contradict the fact that money and checks, not charge cards, are considered cash.

3. **(C)** "Well, here's my driver's license. I don't have any charge cards, but I do have my student ID card from City College." Choice (A) contradicts the fact that the woman doesn't have any charge cards. Choice (B) refers to identification that can be used, not to the identification that the woman actually uses. Choice (D) refers to the fact that she must put her telephone number on the front of the check, but it is not a piece of identification.

4. **(A)** Since the man thanks the woman for shopping at the Family Store, it may be concluded that he is a clerk. It is not as probable that the persons in Choices (B), (C), and (D) would help a woman with a purchase.

Conversation Four

1. **(C)** From the references to *this bus, gate eleven,* and *these baggage checks,* it must be concluded that this conversation takes place at a bus station. Choice (A) refers to the place where the woman is going, not to where she is now. Choice (B) refers to the time that the passengers should be at the door. Choice (D) refers to the purpose of the conversation, not the place.

2. **(A)** "Two-fifteen at gate eleven." The number in Choice (B) refers to the gate, not the time. Choice (C) refers to the time that the passengers should be at the door. Choice (D) refers to a time fifteen minutes before the passengers should be at the door and half an hour before the bus leaves.

3. **(B)** "Just two. I'll carry the other one with me." Choice (A) refers to the number of suitcases she will carry, not to the number she will check. Choice (C) refers to the total number of suitcases she has to check and to carry. Choice (D) refers to twice the number of suitcases she will check.

4. **(A)** Because the woman says that the fare was only twenty dollars the last time she took the bus, it must be concluded that she has taken this trip before. Choices (B), (C), and (D) are not mentioned and may not be concluded from the conversation.

EXERCISE 14: University Personnel

Conversation One

1. **(C)** "I can't let you take someone else's test. . . . the privacy act won't permit it." Choices (A), (B), and (D) are mentioned in reference to the main topic of the conversation, "school policy."

2. **(A)** "I can only give a test to the student whose name appears on it. . . . that's the law." Choice (B) contradicts the fact that she can't even give it [the test] to a family member. Choice (D) contradicts the fact that Jim wants to pick up the test that Terry took. Choice (C) is not mentioned and may not be concluded from information in the conversation.

3. **(C)** "My last name is Raleigh." Choice (A) is the name of the man's friend. Choice (B) is the name of the professor. Choice (D) is the name of the secretary.

4. **(A)** "Okay. I'll tell Terry." Choice (B) contradicts the fact that the man is in the office and has picked up his test. Choice (D) contradicts the fact that the man has already taken the test. Choice (C) is not mentioned and may not be concluded from information in the conversation.

Conversation Two

1. **(B)** ". . . the books for Chem 100 aren't in yet." Choices (A), (C), and (D) are mentioned in reference to the main topic of the conversation, "a book for a class the man is taking."

2. **(B)** "I didn't do that well in chemistry in high school." Choices (A), (C), and (D) are not mentioned and may not be concluded from information in the conversation.

3. **(C)** "Where's the bulletin board?" Choice (A) contradicts the fact that the book would be on reserve, and not available to be checked out. Choice (B) contradicts the fact that the man considered making copies of a few pages, not the whole book. Choice (D) refers to the man's original plan, not to what he will do before he leaves.

4. **(B)** Since the man wants to buy a book, it may be concluded that the conversation most probably took place in a bookstore. Choice (A) refers to the place where the man might locate a copy of the book on reserve. Choice (C) refers to the fact that there are T-shirts and clothing near the front door in the bookstore. Choice (D) refers to the place where the man lives, not to where the conversation takes place.

Conversation Three

1. **(A)** "I'm here because I want to change roommates." Choice (D) refers to the plan that the head resident suggests, not to the purpose of the conversation. Choices (B) and (C) are not mentioned and may not be concluded from information in the conversation.

2. **(A)** "Well, David is really into having fun . . ." Choice (B) contradicts the fact that David isn't on scholarship. Choice (C) contradicts the fact that Bill has talked with David about the problem. Choice (D) is not mentioned and may not be concluded from information in the conversation.

3. **(A)** ". . . he [the roommate] has so many people in our room all the time that I can't study. And the stereo is on constantly." Choice (B) contradicts the fact that the man's roommate doesn't take him seriously when they talk. Choice (C) contradicts the fact that the man and his roommate were good friends. Choice (D) contradicts the fact that the man and his roommate are from the same home town.

4. **(A)** "Come back to see me next Monday." Choice (C) contradicts the fact that the head resident, not the man, will talk to David. Choice (D) contradicts the fact that he is speaking with the head resident now. Choice (B) is not mentioned and may not be concluded from information in the conversation.

Conversation Four

1. **(B)** "I have been looking for information about scholarships . . . but . . . I haven't found anything for foreign students. . . ." Choices (A), (C), and (D) are mentioned in reference to the main topic of the conversation, "financial aid for international students."

2. **(D)** "It's for my friend." Choices (A), (B), and (C) contradict the fact that the information is for the woman's friend.

3. **(C)** "It's highly competitive, but there are no restrictions on nationality." Choice (A) contradicts the fact that the scholarship is highly competitive. Choice (B) is the reason that the woman's friend would qualify for the scholarship, not the reason the advisor chose the scholarship for him. Choice (D) refers to Mr. Williams, not to the woman's friend.

4. **(B)** Since the man is giving advice about scholarships, it may be concluded that he is a financial aid officer. Choice (A) refers to the person who helped the woman before she came to the man's office. Choice (C) refers to Mr. Williams. Choice (D) is not mentioned and may not be concluded from information in the conversation.

EXERCISE 15: University Professors

Conversation One

1. **(A)** ". . . I'm not upset that you couldn't keep the appointment, but it is common courtesy to call." Choices (B), (C), and (D) are mentioned in reference to the main topic of the conversation, "the man's last appointment."

2. **(A)** "That's two o'clock . . . Tuesday." Choices (B) and (C) refer to alternative times that the professor suggests, not to the time that the student chooses for the appointment. Choice (D) refers to the time that the student suggests.

3. **(B)** ". . . it is common courtesy to call." Choice (A) contradicts the fact that he had an appointment that he did not keep. Choice (C) contradicts the fact that the professor is not upset because he couldn't keep the appointment. Choice (D) is not mentioned and may not be concluded from information in the conversation.

4. **(D)** From the tone of the conversation, it may be concluded that the professor is annoyed because the student did not call to cancel his appointment. Choice (B) refers to the student's attitude, not to that of the professor. Choices (A) and (C) are not mentioned and may not be concluded from information in the conversation.

Conversation Two

1. **(C)** "I need to ask you to let me take the final early." Choices (A) and (B) are mentioned in reference to the main topic of the conversation, "a change in the date of the woman's exam." Choice (D) contradicts the fact that the woman has already scheduled her flight.

2. **(C)** "Truthfully, I just made a mistake [scheduling the trip]." Choice (B) is true, but it is not the problem that is the concern of the conversation. Choice (D) contradicts the fact that the woman has not yet taken the final exam. Choice (A) is not mentioned and may not be concluded from information in the conversation.

3. **(B)** "You can take the exam on Monday." Choice (A) contradicts the fact that the woman has not taken the exam yet. Choice (D) refers to the woman's suggestion, not to the professor's decision. Choice (C) is not mentioned and may not be concluded from information in the conversation.

4. **(D)** Since the woman bought a ticket to go home for Christmas, and her flight leaves on Tuesday, it may be concluded that the conversation took place in December. Choices (A), (B), and (C) are not close enough to Christmas.

Conversation Three

1. **(B)** ". . . I wanted to tell you that I have nominated you for the outstanding student award." Choices (A), (C), and (D) are mentioned in reference to the main topic of the conversation, "the woman's nomination for an award."

2. **(B)** "Oh, I should have told you more when I saw you after class, but there were so many students waiting to ask questions." Choice (A) contradicts the fact that he saw her after class. Choice (C) refers to the award that the woman, not the man, will receive. Choice (D) is not mentioned and may not be concluded from information in the conversation.

3. **(B)** ". . . you'll receive five hundred dollars along with the certificate of honor." Choice (A) refers to the nomination, not to the award. Choice (D) refers to the interview for the award, not for a position. Choice (C) is not mentioned and may not be concluded from information in the conversation.

4. **(C)** "I'm really honored." Choice (B) refers to the way the woman feels when she first hears the news, not to how she feels at the end of the conversation. Choices (A) and (D) are not mentioned and may not be concluded from information in the conversation.

Conversation Four

1. **(A)** ". . . I should have your scores on the test by then and we can get you registered." Choices (B) and (D) are secondary themes used to develop the main theme of the conversation. Choice (C) is not mentioned and may not be concluded from information in the conversation.

2. **(C)** "That's only three classes." Choice (A) refers to the number of hours that the two-hour laboratory meets per week. Choice (B) refers to the number of hours that each five-hour class meets per week. Choice (D) refers to the total number of hours that the classes meet per week.

3. **(A)** "A driver's license will be fine." Choice (B) refers to the man's suggestion, not to what he needs. Choice (D) contradicts the fact that the man needs identification to be admitted to the examination. Choice (C) is not mentioned and may not be concluded from information in the conversation.

4. **(C)** Because the woman says that she advises first-year students, it must be concluded that the student is a first-year student, or a freshman. Choice (A) contradicts the fact that he is an engineering student. Choice (B) contradicts the fact that he has had two courses in chemistry. Choice (D) is not mentioned and may not be concluded from information in the conversation.

EXERCISE 16: Class Discussions

Conversation One

1. **(A)** "Let's talk about the results of your laboratory experiment." Choices (B) and (C) are secondary themes used to develop the main theme of the discussion. Choice (D) contradicts the fact that the students had already done the lab experiment.

2. **(C)** "And carbon deposits began to form on the bottom of the bottle." Choice (A) refers to the ribbon that was lit, not to the deposits. Choice (B) refers to the material that was put in the bottle at the beginning of the experiment, not to what was deposited at the end. Choice (D) refers to the method of collection, water displacement.

3. **(C)** "The burning magnesium broke the carbon-oxygen bonds in the carbon dioxide, and then the oxygen combined with the magnesium to produce magnesium oxide." Choices (A), (B), and (D) contradict the fact that burning magnesium broke the carbon-oxygen bonds.

4. **(B)** Since the students are able to explain the procedures for the experiment, it may be concluded that they performed the experiment correctly. Choice (C) contradicts the fact that in spite of a little problem, the students completed the experiment. Choice (D) refers to the fact that there is burning magnesium, not a fire in the lab. Choice (A) is not mentioned and may not be concluded from information in the discussion.

Conversation Two

1. **(B)** "The TOEFL and Michigan are good English proficiency tests [for college admissions]." Choice (A) refers to the name of a test, the Michigan Test, not to admissions standards at the University of Michigan. Choice (C) is a secondary theme used to develop the main theme of the talk. Choice (D) refers to the topic assigned for Wednesday, not to the main theme of the talk.

2. **(D)** "I don't agree with having the tests, Professor Ayers, and that's my position." Choice (A) refers to Sally's, not Paul's opinion. Choices (B) and (C) are not mentioned and may not be concluded from information in the discussion.

3. **(A)** ". . . Sally believes that the tests are good, but that many people don't use them for their intended purpose." Choice (C) refers to what the admissions officers do, not to what Sally believes they should do. Choices (B) and (D) refer to what Paul believes admissions officers should do, not to what they actually do.

4. **(A)** "Okay, class." From the reference to *class,* it must be concluded that this conversation took place in a classroom. Choices (B), (C), and (D) are not mentioned and may not be concluded from information in the discussion.

Conversation Three

1. **(A)** "Dr. Anderson, could you please clarify the requirements for this course?" Choice (B) refers to one student, Tom, not to all the students. Choice (C) contradicts the fact that the professor is clarifying the requirements he has previously explained. Choice (D) is not mentioned and may not be concluded from information in the talk.

2. **(A)** "What kind of research paper did you have in mind? An original study? A report? A book review, perhaps?" "A report." Choices (B) and (C) refer to options that the student, not the professor, mentions. Choice (D) is not mentioned and may not be concluded from information in the discussion.

3. **(B)** "One hundred multiple-choice questions covering both the lectures and the outside readings. From the reference to *multiple-choice* questions, it must be concluded that it is an objective test. Choices (A), (C), and (D) are not mentioned and may not be concluded from information in the discussion.

4. **(C)** From the reference to current trends in *U.S. foreign policy,* it must be concluded that Dr. Anderson teaches political science. Choices (A), (B), and (D) are not mentioned and may not be concluded from information in the discussion.

Conversation Four

1. **(D)** "Since so many of you have asked me how to learn a language, I thought that it might be useful to take some class time to discuss it." Choices (A), (B), and (C) are secondary themes used to develop the main theme of the talk.

2. **(B)** "... I think that travel has probably been the most helpful to me." Choice (C) refers to what Betty did before traveling. Choice (D) refers to what helped Bill, not Betty. Choice (A) is not mentioned and may not be concluded from information in the discussion.

3. **(A)** "Probably the best way to learn is to combine all of these ideas: traveling, talking with people, going to movies, watching TV, listening to the radio, and reading books, newspapers and magazines." Choice (B) is true, but incomplete. Choice (D) refers to Betty's opinion, not to Professor Baker's opinion. Choice (C) is not mentioned and may not be concluded from information in the discussion.

4. **(B)** Since Professor Baker encourages the students to express their opinions, it may be concluded that he is respectful of them. Choice (A) contradicts the fact that Professor Baker rephrases the students' comments and combines them into a better answer. Choice (C) contradicts the fact that the students interact informally without waiting to be called on. Choice (D) refers to Betty, not to Professor Baker.

EXERCISE 17: Cumulative Review

Conversation One

1. **(D)** "Let's go swimming. . . . How about dinner . . . ? I just want to spend time with you." Choices (A), (B), and (C) are mentioned in reference to the main topic of the conversation, "plans for the evening."

2. **(C)** "I'd like to, but I have a paper due on Friday. . . ." Choice (A) refers to the test that the man, not the woman, has to take. Choice (B) contradicts the fact that the woman refuses the invitation to go swimming. Choice (D) contradicts the fact that the woman agrees with the man that she wants to spend time with him.

3. **(B)** "I'll go over there [to the library] with you after dinner, and you can do your research. . . ." Choice (A) refers to the place where they will have dinner, not to the place where they will go after dinner. Choice (C) refers to the place where the man originally suggested that they spend the evening, not to the place where they agreed to go after dinner. Choice (D) refers to the place where they will go after they finish their work at the library.

4. **(D)** Because the man wanted to go swimming, but he agreed to go to the Grill for dinner, and then to the library, it must be concluded that he is willing to compromise. Choice (A) contradicts the fact that the man has a test to study for. Choice (B) contradicts the fact that the man plans to study. Choice (C) contradicts the fact that the man is concerned about the woman walking home alone after dark.

Conversation Two

1. **(B)** "Dr. Williams, I need to talk with you about changing my major." Choices (A), (C), and (D) are mentioned in reference to the main purpose of the conversation, "to discuss a change of major."

2. **(B)** "I'm majoring in chemical engineering." Choice (A) refers to the type of engineering, not to the major field. Choice (C) refers to the major that the woman wants to declare, not to her major now. Choice (D) refers to one of the classes that the woman must take if she changes her major.

3. **(B)** "One semester, [extra] full time." Choice (A) contradicts the fact that the woman doesn't need any more electives. Choice (C) refers to the official form that she has filed to major in chemical engineering, not to an official form for her change of major. Choice (D) contradicts the fact that the woman has already finished all the math courses.

4. **(A)** "That's okay [that one semester, full time, will be added to the program of studies]. I really want to do this." Choice (B) contradicts the fact that she agrees to comply with the extra requirements in order to change her major. Choice (C) contradicts the fact that engineering courses will be used under additional electives. Choice (D) refers to the number of hours in engineering that the woman has completed, not to the number of hours that she will take this semester.

Conversation Three

1. **(B)** "I don't understand . . . [the parking] ticket on my car." Choices (A), and (C) are mentioned in reference to the event that prompted this conversation, "the man received a parking ticket." Choice (D) contradicts the fact that the man had already purchased a parking permit.

2. **(A)** "Well, are you a student at the university?" "Yes." The *cousin* in Choice (B) refers to the person who lent the man a car, not to a relative of the woman. Choice (C) refers to the woman, not to the man. Choice (D) refers to a type of parking space, not to the man in the conversation.

3. **(C)** "That's the problem, then. Your parking permit is good for your car only." Choice (A) contradicts the fact that the man bought a parking permit. Choice (B) contradicts the fact that he parked in a student parking area. Choice (D) contradicts the fact that he is a student at the university.

4. **(B)** "I'm afraid I'll have to charge you the ten-dollar fine." Choice (A) refers to the car that the man used when he received the ticket, not to the car that he will use now. Choice (C) contradicts the fact that the man has a parking permit. Choice (D) refers to the kind of permit that the man will need if he uses someone else's car, not to what he will do now.

Conversation Four

1. **(A)** "I'd like a ticket to the Spring Symphony Concert at the Opera House, please." Choices (B), (C), and (D) are mentioned in reference to the main topic of the conversation, "the purchase of a ticket."

2. **(B)** "And the ten-dollar seats . . . [are] . . . On the extreme sides of the first balcony. . . ." Choices (A) and (C) refer to the twenty-dollar seats, not to the ten-dollar seats. Choice (D) refers to the fifty-dollar seats.

3. **(B)** "Do you have any twenty-dollar seats left?" "We do." Choices (A), (C), and (D) contradict the fact that the man asks for a twenty-dollar ticket.

4. **(C)** "Just one [ticket]?" "Yes." Choice (A) contradicts the fact that the man buys a ticket. Choice (B) is less probable because he does not buy a season ticket. Choice (D) is not mentioned and may not be concluded from information in the conversation.

EXERCISE 18: Announcements and Advertisements

Mini Talk One

1. **(B)** ". . . remember, a phone call means so much more than a letter." Choice (A) contradicts the fact that a phone call means more. Choices (C) and (D) are secondary themes used to develop the main theme of the talk.

2. **(D)** "Rates on direct calls are . . . lowest after eleven o'clock at night." Choice (C) refers to a time when rates are cheaper, but not the cheapest. Choices (A) and (B) are not mentioned and may not be concluded from information in the advertisement.

3. **(B)** "In fact, you can make a ten-minute call anywhere in the Continental United States for just $2.70." Choices (A), (C), and (D) are not mentioned and may not be concluded from information in the advertisement.

4. **(C)** "Now calls to many overseas locations may be dialed direct. Check your telephone directory for overseas area codes." Choice (A) refers to what you should do in order to make a collect, credit card, person-to-person, or pay phone call. Choice (B) contradicts the fact that you should check the phone book for overseas area codes, not for the overseas operator's number. Choice (D) refers to the sponsor of the message, not to what you should do to call overseas.

5. **(B)** Since a call is less expensive during evening, night, or weekend hours, it may be concluded that daytime calls have the most expensive rates. Choice (A) contradicts the fact that collect, credit card, person-to-person, and pay phone calls require the services of an operator. Choices (C) and (D) are not mentioned and may not be concluded from information in the talk.

Mini Talk Two

1. **(A)** "Appalachian Airlines will begin passenger service . . ." Choice (B) refers to the use of Charlotte's finest restaurants for catering on the airline, not to advertising for the restaurants. Choice (C) contradicts the fact that the speaker encourages passengers who are tired of large airplanes to use the new service. Choice (D) contradicts the fact that the speaker advises travelers to call a toll-free number for reservations.

2. **(B)** "Appalachian Airlines will use comfortable Boeing 737 twin jets. . . . Fly comfortably." Choice (A) contradicts the fact that unlike large airplanes, Appalachian seats only 106 passengers. Choice (D) contradicts the fact that Appalachian Airlines will begin passenger service at Charlotte Airport Thursday. Choice (C) is not mentioned and may not be concluded from information in the advertisement.

3. **(D)** ". . . morning and afternoon departures daily to Atlanta." Choices (A) and (B) are correct but incomplete. Choice (C) contradicts the fact that departures leave daily. Service begins on Thursday.

4. **(A)** ". . . the Appalachian Airlines toll-free number: 800-565-7000." Choices (B), (C), and (D) are not mentioned and may not be concluded from information in the advertisement.

5. **(B)** Since the service will begin at Charlotte Airport, it may be concluded that the audience for the announcement is directed toward residents of the Charlotte area. Choice (A) would be less interested because the Atlanta area is only one of many destinations from Charlotte. Choice (D) would not be interested because Florida is not one of the designated destinations. Choice (C) is not mentioned and may not be concluded from information in the talk.

Mini Talk Three

1. **(A)** "If you drink, don't drive." Choices (B), (C), and (D) are not mentioned and may not be concluded from information in the announcement.

2. **(B)** Because one-half of all fatal traffic accidents involve alcohol, it must be concluded that fifty percent of all fatal accidents resulting in death are caused by drunk driving. The number in Choice (C) refers to the amount of the fine, not to the number of accidents resulting in death. Thousands of people are killed, but the numbers in Choices (A) and (D) are not mentioned and may not be concluded from information in the announcements.

3. **(D)** "If you are convicted of drunk driving you will be sentenced to at least three days in jail, and your license will be suspended for thirty days." The jail sentence in Choice (A) is correct, but the thirty-dollar fine is not mentioned and may not be concluded from information in the announcement. The jail sentence in Choice (B) refers to the amount of time that the court can sentence, not to the minimum required sentence, and the thirty-dollar fine is not mentioned and may not be concluded from information in the announcement. Choice (C) contradicts the fact that the minimum required sentence is three, not thirty days.

4. **(D)** ". . . the court can sentence you to as much as six months in jail." Choice (A) refers to the minimum sentence, not to the length of time that the court can sentence. Choice (B) refers to the length of time that a license can be suspended. Choice (C) is not mentioned and may not be concluded from information in the announcement.

5. **(C)** Since the talk is a public service announcement, it most probably takes place on a television station. It is less probable that a public service announcement would take place at any of the locations in Choices (A), (B), and (D).

Mini Talk Four

1. **(D)** "Here is your weekend guide to what is going on at the University of Colorado. . . ." Choices (A), (B), and (C) are secondary themes used to develop the main theme of the talk.

2. **(B)** "To reserve seats, call the Student Union . . . or drop by the box office." Choice (A) refers to the name of the performer, not the way to get a ticket to the concert. Choices (C) and (D) are not mentioned and may not be concluded from information in the announcement.

3. **(B)** "In addition to the famous rock and mineral collection and the exhibits of early people, there will be a special exhibit of American Indian pottery and sand paintings." Choices (A), (C), and (D) are mentioned but not referred to as famous.

4. **(C)** "Snow Valley is reporting good conditions. . . . Pine Mountain is reporting very good conditions. . . . Oak Creek Canyon Resort is reporting very good conditions . . ." Choices (A), (B), and (D) contradict the fact that good and very good conditions only were mentioned.

5. **(B)** "You are listening to WKID in Boulder, Colorado." It is less probable that the persons mentioned in Choices (A), (C), and (D) would be giving a weekend guide on the local radio station.

EXERCISE 19: News and Weather Reports

Mini Talk One

1. **(B)** "Nancy Anne Brown was crowned Miss State University in the Centennial Hall auditorium . . ." Choice (A) refers to the pageant in which Miss State University will participate next May, not to the subject of the speaker's story. Choice (C) refers to the candidate's home town, not to a pageant. Choice (D) refers to the candidate's home state, not to a pageant.

2. **(B)** "A blue-eyed blond from Los Angeles, Miss Brown is 5 feet 10 inches tall and weighs 120 pounds." The word *brown* in Choices (A), (C), and (D) refers to the last name of the new Miss State University, not the color of her hair or eyes.

3. **(C)** "She placed . . . third in the talent competition." Choice (A) refers to her place in the swimming suit and evening gown competitions, her place in the beauty category, and her overall place. Choice (B) refers to her place in the intelligence competition. Choice (D) is not mentioned and may not be concluded from information in the report.

4. **(B)** "Miss Brown received a check for $1,000 and a scholarship award for $2,000." Choice (A) refers to the amount of the check, not the scholarship. Choice (C) refers to the total amount of the check and the scholarship. Choice (D) is not mentioned and may not be concluded from information in the report.

5. **(A)** "After graduating, she hopes to pursue a career in the theater." Since Miss Brown is a junior at State University, it may be concluded that she will return to the University in order to finish her senior year and graduate. Choices (B) and (C) refer to the responsibilities that Miss Brown will have during her reign, not after. Choice (D) refers to Miss Brown's plans for after graduation.

Mini Talk Two

1. **(A)** "The cost is going up for just about everything, and college tuition is no exception." Choices (B), (C), and (D) are secondary themes used to develop the main theme of the talk.

2. **(A)** ". . . tuition at most American universities will be on an average of 9 percent higher this year than last." The number 90 in Choice (C) sounds like 9, but it is not mentioned and may not be concluded from information in the report. Choice (D) refers to the percentage increase in the last decade, not in the last year. The number in Choice (B) sounds like 200, but it is not mentioned and may not be concluded from information in the report.

3. **(C)** ". . . $11,200 for tuition. . . . Ten years ago the tuition was $5,300." If the tuition is $11,200 today and was $5,300 ten years ago, then the cost has increased by $11,200 minus $5,300 or $5,900. The number in Choice (A) refers to the percentage increase, not to the dollar increase. Choice (B) refers to the cost of tuition ten years ago, not to the increase in cost. Choice (D) refers to the cost of tuition today.

4. **(C)** ". . . foreign students who are not eligible for scholarships." Choice (D) contradicts the fact that they are not eligible for scholarships. Choices (A) and (B) are not mentioned and may not be concluded from information in the report.

5. **(C)** Since the speaker provides statistics and facts, it may be concluded that the tone of the talk is informative. Choices (A), (B), and (D) are less probable because the speaker does not personalize the talk by using critical, persuasive, or defensive words.

Mini Talk Three

1. **(B)** "... a tornado watch ... [which] means that weather conditions are favorable for the formation of a funnel cloud ..." Choices (A) and (D) contradict the fact that no tornado warnings have been issued. Choice (C) is not mentioned and may not be concluded from information in the talk.

2. **(A)** "The watch will be in effect until ten o'clock tonight or until cancellation by the Weather Service." The number in Choice (D) refers to the number of counties affected, not to the time. Choices (B) and (C) are not mentioned and may not be concluded from information in the report.

3. **(B)** "A tornado *warning* means that a funnel cloud has been sighted." Choice (D) refers to the definition of a tornado watch, not warning. Choices (A) and (C) are not mentioned and may not be defined from information in the report.

4. **(C)** "... a tornado watch for the following five counties ..." The number in Choice (D) refers to the time that the watch will be canceled, not to the number of counties affected. Choice (A) contradicts the fact that five counties are included in the watch. Choice (B) is not mentioned and may not be concluded from information in the report.

5. **(B)** Since the watch will be in effect until ten o'clock, it may be concluded that the listeners will stay tuned until that time. Choice (A) contradicts the fact that the watch will be in effect until, not after, ten o'clock. Choice (C) is less probable because the bulletin was issued by the National Weather Service. Choice (D) contradicts the fact that no tornado warnings have been issued.

Mini Talk Four

1. **(D)** "The showers and thunderstorms moved north of us leaving all stations in the Tri-State Area with reports of sunny skies and warm temperatures." Choice (B) refers to the weather that moved north, not to the weather in the Tri-State Area. Choices (A) and (C) are not mentioned and may not be concluded from information in the report.

2. **(C)** "The current temperature reading here at Philadelphia is eighty-five degrees ..." Choice (D) refers to the temperature expected tomorrow, not now. Choices (A) and (B) are not mentioned and may not be concluded from information in the report.

3. **(B)** "The showers and thunderstorms moved north of us ..." Choice (D) contradicts the fact that the rain moved north, not south of us. Choices (A) and (C) are not mentioned and may not be concluded from information in the report.

4. **(C)** "... no rain in sight until Thursday or Friday." Choice (A) contradicts the fact that today there are reports of sunny skies and warm temperatures. Choice (B) contradicts the fact that fair weather is predicted for tomorrow. Choice (D) is not mentioned and may not be concluded from information in the report.

5. **(A)** "For tomorrow, more fair weather ... and no rain in sight until Thursday or Friday." Since the prediction includes a day before Thursday and Friday, it may be concluded that the broadcast probably occurred on Tuesday. Choices (B), (C), and (D) contradict the fact that the prediction includes a day before Thursday.

EXERCISE 20: Informative Speeches

Mini Talk One

1. **(D)** "... it is one of my more pleasant duties to welcome you on behalf of State University. ... In the meantime, I would like to take a few moments to thank some of the people who have worked so hard to make this evening possible." Choices (A), (B), and (C) are not mentioned and may not be concluded from information in the speech.

2. **(C)** "As director of the Office of International Student Affairs ..." Choice (A) refers to one of the people the speaker thanks, not to the speaker. Choice (B) refers to the person who is providing music, not to the speaker. Choice (D) refers to Mr. Sim Lee, not to the speaker.

3. **(A)** "Right now coffee from Brazil and Colombia is being served at the tables, and for those of you who prefer tea, there is a selection . . ." Choice (B) contradicts the fact that people were served earlier. Choice (C) refers to what people will do later, not now. Choice (D) is not mentioned and may not be concluded from information in the speech.

4. **(D)** "After the program, may I invite you to stay to dance to music . . ." Choices (A) and (B) contradict the fact that they are invited to stay, not to go somewhere else. Choice (C) contradicts the fact that the students will dance to music, not listen to it.

5. **(B)** Since the food was prepared by students from thirty-five countries, it may be concluded that there are foreign students from many countries attending State University. Choice (D) contradicts the fact that the dinner is a large, annual event. Choices (A) and (C) are not mentioned and may not be concluded from information in the talk.

Mini Talk Two

1. **(A)** "Today Dr. Taylor will speak to us about federal regulations for urban development . . ." Choices (B), (C), and (D) refer to areas of Dr. Taylor's expertise, but not to the topic of the lecture.

2. **(B)** "Dr. Taylor received his B.A. degree . . . at Yale. . . . a masters degree . . . and a Ph.D. . . . from Cornell University." Choice (A) refers to the university where Dr. Taylor received his B.A., not his Ph.D. Choice (C) refers to the university where he taught. The place in Choice (D) refers to the city where Dr. Taylor worked, not to the university where he received his Ph.D.

3. **(C)** "Last year Dr. Taylor resigned from the university in order to accept a research position with the Department of Housing and Urban Development . . ." Choice (A) refers to the place where Dr. Taylor was employed after he received his Ph.D., not to where he is employed now. Choice (B) refers to a building that Dr. Taylor designed, not to the place where he works. Choice (D) refers to the place where Dr. Taylor's articles are published.

4. **(C)** Because the speaker says that he can think of no one more qualified to speak than Dr. Taylor, it must be concluded that he respects him. Choice (A) contradicts the fact that the speaker says it is a great honor to introduce Dr. Taylor. Choice (B) contradicts the fact that Dr. Taylor is well known to all of us. Choice (D) contradicts the fact that the speaker can think of no one more qualified.

5. **(C)** Since the purpose of the talk is to introduce Dr. Taylor, it may be concluded that the speaker and audience will listen to Dr. Taylor's speech next. Choices (A), (B), and (D) are not mentioned and may not be concluded from information in the talk.

Mini Talk Three

1. **(D)** "I thought I would break from tradition today in order to share some anecdotes from the life of a man [Edison], who like you, enjoyed reading." Choices (A), (B), and (C) are secondary themes used to develop the main theme of the talk.

2. **(A)** ". . . when I was asked to speak at the Community Book Club luncheon, I thought about several topics that might be of interest to a group of avid readers . . ." The word *inventor* in Choice (D) refers to the topic, not to the audience. Choices (B) and (C) are not mentioned and may not be concluded from information in the speech.

3. **(C)** ". . . life of a man, who, like you, enjoyed reading." Choice (A) is true, but it is not the reason that the speaker chose to talk about Edison. Choices (B) and (D) are not mentioned and may not be concluded from information in the speech.

4. **(B)** "Whenever he was paid for an invention, he used the money for his two loves—more experiments and more books." Choices (A), (C), and (D) are not mentioned and may not be concluded from information in the speech.

5. **(A)** Since Edison spent only three months in school and spent most of his time reading, it may be concluded that he received most of his education from reading. Choice (B) contradicts the fact that Edison attended school for three months. Choice (C) contradicts the fact that Edison's mother taught him to read at an early age. Choice (D) contradicts the fact that Edison tried to read all the books in the Detroit Public Library regardless of subject.

Mini Talk Four

1. **(C)** "And so, State is a different place, but like University Tower, it is built of the same brick." Choice (A) contradicts the fact that it is built of the same brick, or that we are still committed to the same age-old ideals. Choice (B) contradicts the fact that University Tower has been torn down, a belltower has been built, and parking lots have been replaced by grass, trees, and pedestrian walkways. Choice (D) contradicts the fact that State is a different place.

2. **(B)** "It is a great privilege for me to be invited to speak at the tenth-year reunion of State University's graduating class." Choice (A) contradicts the fact that the occasion is the reunion of a graduating class, not a graduation. Choices (C) and (D) are not mentioned and may not be concluded from information in the speech.

3. **(C)** "We are still committed to the same age-old ideals of quality education . . ." Choice (A) contradicts the facts that University Tower was torn down, a bell tower was built, and parking lots were replaced by grass, trees, and pedestrian walkways. Choice (B) contradicts the fact that many young people from abroad have been added to the student population. Choice (D) contradicts the fact that the Division of Continuing Education has been expanded, including a Saturday and summer enrichment program for children, and an afternoon and evening special interest program for adults.

4. **(B)** "Two years ago University Tower was inspected and found to be unsafe." Choice (A) contradicts the fact that the belltower was constructed after the tower was found to be unsafe and had to be torn down. Choice (C) contradicts the fact that the parking lots were replaced by grass, trees, and pedestrian walkways, and the fact that a belltower, not a parking lot, was constructed over the site. Choice (D) contradicts the fact that there were efforts to restore it.

5. **(D)** Since the new belltower was constructed on the same site using the good brick from the original building, and the original bells were preserved, it may be concluded that the campus planners made efforts to preserve a sense of history in planning the new construction. Choice (A) refers to the location of the new parking garages, not to land that had been purchased. Choice (B) contradicts the fact that parking lots were replaced by green areas. Choice (C) refers to the creation and expansion of the Division of Continuing Education, not to actual consultation with the community.

EXERCISE 21: General Interest Statements

Mini Talk One

1. **(B)** "Fast-food restaurants are responding to the consumer demand for healthier meals." Choices (A), (C), and (D) are secondary themes that are used to develop the main theme of the talk.

2. **(C)** "Hamburgers traditionally have been fried with ten or even fifteen teaspoons of fat!" Choices (A), (B), and (D) are not mentioned and may not be concluded from information in the talk.

3. **(D)** "Americans spend more than fifty *billion* dollars on fast food every year." Choices (A), (B), and (C) are not mentioned and may not be concluded from information in the talk.

4. **(A)** ". . . there is a chart posted to inform consumers about the fat content, sodium content, cholesterol count, and calorie count of each item on the menu." Choices (B), (C), and (D) are not mentioned and may not be concluded from information in the talk.

5. **(C)** Since consumers are demanding healthier meals with less fat, it may be concluded that they are careful about the fat content of their food. Choice (B) contradicts the fact that sixty-six million Americans eat at least one meal a day away from home. Choice (D) contradicts the fact that there are several options that will keep them on their diets. Choice (A) is not mentioned and may not be concluded from information in the talk.

Mini Talk Two

1. **(A)** "Winning the lottery should be a dream come true, but ... people underestimate the effect that their winnings will have on their taxes." Choices (B), (C) and (D) are secondary themes that are used to develop the main theme of the talk.

2. **(D)** "... taxes on early installments are lower than taxes on later ones ..." Choices (A), (B), and (C) contradict the fact that taxes on early installments are lower.

3. **(C)** "Most countries don't tax winnings from lotteries, including Canada, where winners are given their million dollar prize in a lump sum tax free." Choices (A), (B), and (D) contradict the fact that no taxes are charged against winnings.

4. **(D)** "But in the United States, the public is being subjected to six kinds of taxation.... taxes on the money they earn to buy tickets.... state operating expenses.... taxes by local, state, and federal governments.... inheritance taxes ..." Choice (A) contradicts the fact that lottery winners are taxed. Choices (B) and (C) are correct but incomplete.

5. **(C)** Since the government taxes lottery winners, it may be concluded that the speaker means the government is the big winner because of the tax revenue. Choice (B) is true but the revenue from sales represents only a small amount of money compared with the amount collected in taxes. Choice (D) contradicts the fact that estates are subject to inheritance taxes, not to the remainder of installments. Choice (A) is not mentioned and may not be concluded from information in the talk.

Mini Talk Three

1. **(B)** "By 1792, Congress passed an act authorizing the coinage of gold eagles.... by the turn of the century ... gold disappeared from circulation until 1834.... The financial uncertainty during the Great Depression ... encouraged hoarding of gold.... Now, there are no restrictions." Choices (A), (C), and (D) are secondary themes that are used to develop the main theme of the talk.

2. **(A)** "By 1792.... gold coins were standardized to silver on a fifteen to one ratio." Choice (C) refers to the value by the turn of the century or 1800. Choices (B) and (D) are not mentioned and may not be concluded from information in the talk.

3. **(C)** "The new interest and demand for gold encouraged the Mint to strike twenty-dollar double eagles ..." Choice (A) refers to the gold half eagles coined in 1792, not to the double eagle. Choice (B) refers to the eagle. Choice (D) refers to the limited number of gold coins struck at the same time as the double eagles.

4. **(C)** "Now, there are no restrictions regarding the export, import, purchase, sale, or collecting of gold coins in the United States." Choice (A) refers to restrictions imposed during the Great Depression, not now. Choice (D) refers to restrictions in the years after the Great Depression. Choice (B) is not mentioned and may not be concluded from information in the talk.

5. **(D)** Since coins were hoarded during the Great Depression, it may be concluded that during times of financial insecurity the interest in coin collecting increases. Choice (A) contradicts the fact that restrictions occurred during the financial uncertainty during the Great Depression. Choices (B) and (C) are not mentioned and may not be concluded from information in the talk.

Mini Talk Four

1. **(B)** "... there is no such thing as a safe tan." Choice (A) is mentioned objectively as it refers to protecting oneself from overexposure to the sun, not as an ad. Choice (C) contradicts the fact that outdoor sports are a cause of sun damage. Choice (D) is a secondary theme that is used to develop the main theme of the talk.

2. **(A)** "... in order to get tanned, you have to get injured first." Choice (B) contradicts the fact that the melanin does not totally protect the skin. Choice (D) refers to a potential danger, not to a definite result. Choice (C) is not mentioned and may not be concluded from information in the talk.

3. **(B)** "People with fair complexions should use an SPF 30 formula, which provides thirty times the protection to skin that an untreated area receives." Choice (A) refers to the fact that people who enjoy outdoor activities should use a sunscreen. Choice (C) refers to people who insist on a dark tan, not to people with fair complexions. Choice (D) contradicts the fact that the author advises against getting a tan.

4. **(A)** ". . . other people . . . insist that a dark tan makes them look and feel healthier . . ." Choices (C) and (D) refer to reasons that people spend time in the sun, not to why people try to get a tan. Choice (B) is not mentioned and may not be concluded from information in the talk.

5. **(C)** Since SPF 30 screens thirty times the amount of sun that unprotected skin does, it may be concluded that SPF 15 screens fifteen times the amount of sun. Choice (A) contradicts the fact that the speaker recommends SPF 30 to people with fair complexions. Choice (B) contradicts the fact that the speaker suggests that people with fair complexions use a sun screen with a higher SPF number. Choice (D) contradicts the fact that the speaker suggests that people with dark skin use a sun screen with an SPF 15.

EXERCISE 22: Informal Academic Statements

Mini Talk One

1. **(C)** ". . . SQ3R. The letters stand for five steps in the reading process . . ." Choices (A), (B), and (D) are not mentioned and may not be concluded from information in the statement.

2. **(D)** "*Survey* means to look quickly." The first step in Choice (A) refers to the order in the five steps that surveying occupies, not to the meaning of survey. Choice (B) refers to the last step *recite,* not survey. Choice (C) refers to the second step, *question*.

3. **(A)** "Think about what you are reading as a series of ideas, not just a sequence of words." Choice (B) contradicts the fact that some students prefer to underline important points, and that seems to be just as useful as note taking. Choice (C) refers to step one, *survey,* not to step three, *read.* Choice (D) contradicts the fact that readers should think about what they are reading as a series of ideas, not just a sequence of words.

4. **(B)** "The last step is recite." Choice (A) refers to the third, not the last step. Choice (C) refers to the fourth step. Choice (D) is not included in the five steps and may not be concluded from information in the statement.

5. **(A)** Since the purpose of the talk is to help students with a study skills reading method, it can be concluded that the talk most probably took place in a freshman orientation course. It is less probable that a lesson would take place at any of the locations in Choices (B), (C), and (D).

Mini Talk Two

1. **(B)** "Your test on Friday will cover material from both of your textbooks, my lecture notes and your lab assignments." Choice (A) refers to the first lecture, not to this lecture. Choice (C) refers to the test on Friday. Choice (D) refers to the material to be tested, not to the purpose of the lecture.

2. **(D)** "The multiple-choice will count half of your grade [on the test]." Choice (A) refers to the credit toward the final grade for attendance, not to the credit on the test for multiple-choice questions. Choice (B) refers to the credit toward the final grade for the test and for the lab report, not to the credit for the multiple-choice questions. Choice (C) refers to the credit toward the final grade for the final exam.

3. **(B)** "Oh yes, this test represents twenty-five percent of your total grade for the semester." Choice (A) refers to the credit toward the final grade for attendance, not for the test. Choice (C) refers to the credit toward the final grade for the final exam. Choice (D) refers to the credit on the test for the multiple-choice questions and for the essay questions.

4. **(B)** "I will tell you right now that there won't be any math problems . . ." Choice (A) refers to the notes from the first lecture, not to all of the notes. Choice (C) contradicts the fact that the speaker reveals that there will be no math problems on the test. Choice (D) contradicts the fact that the speaker encourages students to review the formulas.

5. **(C)** "Your test on Friday will cover material from both of your textbooks, my lecture notes, and your lab assignments. . . . there won't be any math problems, but that doesn't mean that you shouldn't review the formulas . . ." Choices (A), (B), and (D) would be less likely to have *lab assignments* and *formulas*.

Mini Talk Three

1. **(A)** "I would like to clarify the differences among paraphrasing, quoting [which are legitimate strategies], and plagiarizing." Choices (B) and (C) are secondary themes used to develop the main theme of the talk. Choice (D) is not mentioned and may not be concluded from information in the talk.

2. **(D)** "If you do not cite the source, then you are plagiarizing." Choices (B) and (C) refer to quoting, not to plagiarizing. Choice (A) is not mentioned and may not be concluded from information in the lecture.

3. **(C)** ". . . whereas paraphrasing and quoting are legitimate writing strategies . . ." Choices (A) and (B) contradict the fact that plagiarizing is not a legitimate writing strategy. Choice (D) contradicts the fact that copying [without citing the source] is not a legitimate writing strategy.

4. **(D)** "If I discover that you have plagiarized on your term paper, you will receive a zero for the paper and an F for the course." Choices (A), (B), and (C) are not mentioned as alternatives, and may not be concluded from information in the lecture.

5. **(D)** Since the speaker is teaching the audience how to write a term paper, it may be concluded that the speaker is a teacher. Choices (A) and (B) refer to the audience, not to the speaker. Choice (C) is less probable because a librarian does not usually assign term papers.

Mini Talk Four

1. **(C)** "Let's take a few minutes to look at the policies and procedures listed on page three . . ." Choices (A) and (B) are secondary themes that are used to develop the main theme of the talk. Choice (D) is not mentioned and may not be concluded from information in the talk.

2. **(C)** "The grade for a late assignment will be lowered by one letter for each day past the due date." Choice (A) contradicts the fact that assignments must be submitted on the due date for students to receive full credit. Choice (B) contradicts the fact that grades for late assignments will be lowered. Choice (D) is not mentioned and may not be concluded from information in the talk.

3. **(C)** ". . . the make-ups are quite a bit more difficult than the regularly scheduled exams." Choice (A) contradicts the fact that a make-up exam must be arranged within one week of the scheduled date of the exam. Choice (B) contradicts the fact that he gives essay instead of multiple-choice tests for make-ups. Choice (D) refers to the regularly scheduled exam, not to the make-up exam.

4. **(A)** ". . . you must submit a request form with a signed statement of explanation. . . ." Choice (B) refers to the procedure for being absent from an exam, not to the procedure for an incomplete. Choice (C) refers to the procedure for a make-up exam. Choice (D) refers to the consequences of failing to comply with the procedure, not to the procedure itself.

5. **(C)** Since the professor tells students that his home phone is listed in the telephone directory, it must be concluded that he does not mind if students call him at home. Choice (A) contradicts the fact that he has explicit policies and procedures on his syllabus. Choice (B) contradicts the fact that the policies and procedures are fair. Choice (D) is not mentioned and may not be concluded from information in the talk.

EXERCISE 23: Formal Academic Statements

Mini Talk One

1. **(C)** ". . . research at the University of Texas at Arlington has shown that the order of one's birth in relationship to brothers and sisters may be a significant factor." Choices (A), (B), and (D) are secondary themes that are used to develop the main theme of the lecture.

2. **(B)** "As you know from your text, both heredity and environment play a role in the development of the personality." Choice (A) refers to the topic of the lecture, not to what students should know before the lecture. Choices (C) and (D) refer to the information in the lecture.

3. **(B)** "Those born first tend to develop personality traits that make them domineering, ambitious, and highly motivated to achieve." Choices (A) and (D) refer to traits exhibited by children born later, not by firstborn children. Choice (C) is not mentioned and may not be concluded from information in the lecture.

4. **(B)** "... a woman with older brothers and a man with older sisters seem to be able to interact more easily with the opposite sex." Choice (A) contradicts the fact that a man with older sisters is able to interact more easily. Choices (C) and (D) contradict the fact that a woman with older brothers is able to interact more easily.

5. **(C)** "... children born later in the family tend to be more socially adept, likable, talkative individuals." Choices (A) and (B) refer to children who develop traits that make them domineering, ambitious, and highly motivated to achieve, not sociable. Choice (D) is not mentioned and may not be concluded from information in the talk.

Mini Talk Two

1. **(C)** "Yesterday we discussed ... inflation. ... We concluded. ... We also talked about ..." Choice (A) contradicts the fact that yesterday we discussed inflation. Choices (B) and (D) are not mentioned and may not be concluded from information in the statement.

2. **(A)** "... rising prices, or in the economist's terms, inflation." Choice (B) refers to pensions, not to inflation. Choice (C) refers to the ability to purchase goods and services. Choice (D) refers to how much it costs to maintain a standard of living.

3. **(B)** "... stockholders and persons with business interests and investments would probably benefit most from inflation ..." Choice (A) contradicts the fact that an employee with a salary agreed to in a long-term contract will be most seriously affected by inflation. Choice (C) contradicts the fact that persons with fixed incomes, for example, the elderly who depend on pensions, will be most seriously affected by inflation. Choice (D) contradicts the fact that persons with slow-rising incomes will be most seriously affected by inflation.

4. **(B)** "... while their dollar incomes stay the same, the cost of goods and services rises, and in effect, real income decreases; that is, they are able to purchase less with the same amount of money." Choice (A) contradicts the fact that inflation is rising prices. Choice (C) contradicts the fact that they are able to purchase less with the same amount of money. Choice (D) contradicts the fact that dollar incomes stay the same.

5. **(B)** "And now, before we begin today's lecture, are there any questions about the term inflation or any of the examples ... ?" Choice (A) contradicts the fact that the questions have not yet been asked. Choices (C) and (D) have already taken place.

Mini Talk Three

1. **(D)** "Today we will discuss what occurs when the balance of nature is disturbed, either by a geological change such as a change of climate, or a local agitation such as a fire." Choices (A), (B), and (C) are secondary ideas that are used to develop the main idea.

2. **(B)** "... a local agitation such as a fire. ... After the balance of nature has been disturbed, a period of rehabilitation must occur. ... The final stage ... is called a climax association." Choice (C) contradicts the fact that the balance of nature is disturbed, either by a geologic change such as a change of climate, or a local agitation such as a fire. Choice (D) refers to the total complex of relationships in ecology, not to the forest fire example. Choice (A) is not mentioned and may not be concluded from information in the statement.

3. **(A)** "The pioneer life is temporary and soon replaced by other forms of life . . . preparing the environment for the forms that will replace them." Choice (B) contradicts the fact that it is temporary and soon replaced by other forms of life. Choices (C) and (D) contradict the fact that pioneer plants are replaced by shrubs and shrubs are replaced by trees.

4. **(A)** "What is essential is that the balance of nature permits the association to continue in spite of other organic competition . . ." Choice (B) contradicts the fact that the climax association may not have the same kinds of plants and animals as the association that was prevalent before the fire. Choice (C) contradicts the fact that a climax association is the final stage, not the stage before the final stage. Choice (D) contradicts the fact that a climax association is stable, not a state of disturbance.

5. **(B)** Since the lecture includes plants, and animals as well as minerals, it may be concluded that the talk most probably took place in a biology class. Choice (A) is not as probable because the reference to minerals is secondary to the theme of plants and animals. Choices (C) and (D) are not mentioned and may not be concluded from information in the talk.

Mini Talk Four

1. **(A)** "I propose that the popular detachment of science from engineering has not provided us with a useful model for comparison, and perhaps not even an historically correct one." Choice (B) is a secondary theme used to develop the main theme of the talk. Choices (C) and (D) contradict the fact that the speaker asserts that the distinction between science and engineering has not been valid.

2. **(B)** "Whereas the scientist was thought of as an intellectual . . . the engineer was thought of as a busy, practical person. . . . The scientist might discover the laws of nature, but the engineer would be the one to exploit them . . ." Choice (A) contradicts the fact that the engineer, not the scientist, would be the one to exploit the laws of nature. Choice (C) contradicts the fact that the scientist, not the engineer, was thought of as an intellectual. Choice (D) contradicts the fact that the engineer, not the scientist, would be the one to exploit nature for use, that is, to apply science.

3. **(B)** "Christian Huygens, a Dutch astronomer, mathematician, and physicist who developed theorems on centrifugal force and wave motion, also developed the first accurate timepiece." Choice (A) refers to Louis Pasteur, not to Christian Huygens. Choice (C) refers to Sir Isaac Newton. Choice (D) is not mentioned and may not be concluded from information in the statement.

4. **(B)** "I propose that the popular detachment of science from engineering has not provided us with a useful model for comparison, and perhaps not even an historically correct one." Choices (A), (C), and (D) contradict the fact that the detachment has not provided us with a useful model.

5. **(C)** "In every century, noted theoretical scholars were deeply involved in the practical application of their own work." Choice (A) contradicts the fact that they made practical application of their own work. Choice (B) contradicts the fact that the scientists were identified as noted theoretical scholars, not the best of each century. Choice (D) contradicts the fact that they were theoretical scholars, not engineers.

EXERCISE 24: Mini Talks/Cumulative Review

Mini Talk One

1. **(B)** "Welcome to Carlsbad Caverns. . . ." Choices (A), (C), and (D) are secondary themes used to develop the main theme of the talk, "Carlsbad Caverns."

2. **(A)** "Welcome to Carlsbad Caverns. . . . the rooms that you will see when we descend into the caverns themselves." Because the group is present at the location and will go into the caverns, it must be concluded that they are tourists. It is not as probable that the *scholars* in Choice (B) would be present on site for the talk. Choice (D) refers to the *football field* that is used to explain the size of the rooms in the caverns, not to the group of people listening to the talk. Choice (C) is not mentioned and may not be concluded from information in the talk.

3. **(B)** "The largest [room in the caverns] could hold ten football fields." Choices (A), (C), and (D) are mentioned in reference to the caverns, but do not refer to the size of the caves.

4. **(D)** ". . . about one million years ago . . . the dripping formed a stalactite." Choice (A) refers to what occurred sixty million years ago, not one million years ago. Choice (B) refers to what occurred over a long period of time, not a specified time. Choice (C) refers to what occurred before one million years ago.

5. **(A)** ". . . the rooms that you will see when we descend into the caverns themselves." Because the speaker refers to aspects of the caverns that the group will see, it must be concluded that he will take them into the caves. Choices (B), (C), and (D) are not mentioned and may not be concluded from information in the talk.

Mini Talk Two

1. **(B)** "I realize that some of you are concerned about my holistic scoring system for your essays, so I thought we should take a little time to look at it together." Choice (A) contradicts the fact that the talk was an informal explanation, not a formal lecture. Choice (D) contradicts the fact that the system will be used on the listeners' [students'] essays. Choice (C) is not mentioned and may not be concluded from information in the talk.

2. **(C)** "Although holistic scoring is based on a general impression of the writing, it is not merely a subjective score." Choice (A) contradicts the fact that holistic scoring is not a subjective score. Choice (B) contradicts the fact that the teacher has example essays with letter grades for the students to review. Choice (D) refers to one of five criteria for the teacher's total holistic score.

3. **(C)** "I also read for grammar and punctuation, but only as one of the five criteria." Choice (A) contradicts the fact that grammar is one of the five criteria. Choice (B) refers to handwriting, not grammar. Choice (D), the relative importance, is not mentioned and may not be concluded from information in the talk.

4. **(A)** Because the speaker will be scoring their essays, it must be concluded that the relationship is that of teacher-students. It is not as probable that the speaker would score the essays of colleagues, readers, or supervisors in Choices (B), (C), and (D).

5. **(B)** The tone of the talk is informative. Because the speaker agrees to explain the system, it must be concluded that he is neither defensive nor uncooperative as in Choices (A) and (C). Choice (D) may not be concluded from information in the talk.

Mini Talk Three

1. **(D)** "Almost all of the fourteen varieties of geese are found in the Northern Hemisphere." Choices (A), (B), and (C) are secondary themes used to develop the main theme of the lecture, "geese in the Northern Hemisphere."

2. **(B)** ". . . and the male [goose], called a gander . . ." Choices (A), (C), and (D) are not included in the definition of a *gander*.

3. **(A)** "The males and females [geese] do not mate until they are three years old, but when they do, they mate for life." The number in Choice (B) refers to the age at which geese begin to mate, not to the frequency of mating. Choice (C) contradicts the fact that the offspring remain with their parents for one year. Choice (D) contradicts the fact that the coloring of the female and the male is similar.

4. **(A)** ". . . the movement of air by the wings of each bird in the formation makes the task of flying easier for the bird behind it." Choice (C) contradicts the fact that several geese take turns leading the group on long migrations. Choices (B) and (D) are not mentioned and may not be concluded from information in the talk.

5. **(B)** Because the talk was about varieties of geese, it must be concluded that it took place as part of a zoology lecture. Choice (A) refers to the explanation of the vee formation that might have taken place in a physics class, but it is not as probable that the physics lecturer would also refer to the mating habits. Choices (C) and (D) are not mentioned and may not be concluded from information in the lecture.

Mini Talk Four

1. **(A)** ". . . public lands for the purpose of establishing colleges. . . . Seventy-five percent of all . . . degrees . . . are awarded by land grant colleges. . . . the children of many middle class families . . . have found their opportunity . . . at the land grant schools. . . ." Choices (B), (C), and (D) are secondary themes used to develop the main theme of the talk, "land grant colleges."

2. **(C)** "Proceeds from the sale of the [public] land were to be used in the state as a perpetual fund, the interest of which was to be used to support the state college." Choices (A), (B), and (C) refer to funding sources for colleges today, not to the way that state colleges were funded originally.

3. **(C)** Since Justin Smith Morrill introduced a bill in Congress establishing land grant colleges, it must be concluded that the Morrill Act was named for him. Choices (A), (B), and (D) are not mentioned and may not be concluded from information in the talk.

4. **(D)** "Seventy-five percent of all bachelor's degrees conferred in the United States . . . are awarded by land grant colleges." The number in Choice (A) refers to the percentage of funding from federal sources, not to the percentage of degrees conferred. Choice (B) refers to the percentage of engineering degrees, not bachelor's degrees conferred. Choice (C) refers to the percentage of funding from state governments.

5. **(A)** ". . . the tuition and other fees paid by students has traditionally been kept low, with . . . funding . . . by the state government, and . . . the federal government." Choice (B) is a result of the low tuition, not a cause. Choice (C) refers to the fact that the sale of public land supported the establishment of land grant colleges, not to the location of the colleges themselves. Choice (D) is not mentioned and may not be concluded from information in the talk.

Chapter 4   Structure and Written Expression

Part A—Structure Problems

EXERCISE 1: Verbs (Part 1)

1. **(D)** *That* is used before the subject *he* and the verb word *rest* in the clause after the verb *insists*.

2. **(C)** *Neither* is used before the auxiliary *does* followed by the subject *she*. *She doesn't either* would also be correct.

3. **(A)** *Hadn't* and the participle *had* are used after the verb *wish* in the main clause.

4. **(D)** *Wouldn't* is used before the subject *you* and the verb *like* in an invitation.

5. **(B)** *Do not* is used before the verb word *submit* to express a negative command.

6. **(C)** *Am* is used before the verb phrase *used to* followed by the *-ing* form *eating* to express habit.

7. **(A)** *Had* is used before the person *them* followed by the verb word *practice* to express an activity caused by *the coach*.

8. **(B)** The *-ing* form *answering* is used after the verb phrase *not mind*.

9. **(C)** *Had better* is used before the verb word *reserve* to express advice.

10. **(C)** *Weren't* is used after *if* to express a condition contrary to fact.

11. **(A)** *Didn't she* is used to agree with *your sister* and *used to visit* in the main clause.

12. **(C)** *Had* is used before the participle *come* in the conditional clause.

13. **(B)** *Would rather* is used before the subject *you* and the past verb *didn't* followed by the verb word *do* to express preference.

14. **(A)** *Must have* is used before the participle *left* to express a logical conclusion.

15. **(C)** *Had* is used before the participle *rung* to refer to an activity *already* in the past.

EXERCISE 2: Verbs (Part 2)

1. **(B)** *That* is used before the subject *he* followed by *would* and the verb word *call* after the verb phrase *had hoped*.

2. **(A)** *Did* is used before the subject *I* to agree with *lived* in the main clause. *And I did too* would also be correct.

3. **(B)** *Know how* is used before the infinitive *to take* to express ability or skill. *Does your new secretary know shorthand* would also be correct.

4. **(B)** *Had* is used before the person *his big brother* followed by the verb word *tie* to express an activity caused by *Tommy*.

5. **(C)** *Were* is used after the verb *wish* in the main clause.

6. **(A)** The verb word *begin* is used in the clause after the verb *recommends*.

7. **(C)** *Shall we* is used to agree with *let's* in the main clause.

8. **(A)** *Would ['d] rather* is used before *not* and the verb word *have* to express preference.

9. **(C)** *Would you please* is used before *not* followed by the verb word *write* to express a negative command.

10. **(D)** *Was* is used before the verb phrase *used to* followed by the *-ing* form *sitting* to express a habit.

11. **(D)** *Were* is used after *if* to express a condition contrary to fact.

12. **(B)** *Hadn't* is used before the participle *had* in the conditional clause.

13. **(A)** *Hasn't he* is used to agree with *he's [he has]* in the main clause.

14. **(D)** The *-ing* form *seeing* is used after the verb phrase *looking forward to.*

15. **(A)** The verb word *be* is used in the clause after the impersonal expression *it is imperative.*

EXERCISE 3: Verbs (Part 3)

1. **(D)** *Need* is used before the *-ing* form *adjusting* to express necessity for repair. *The brakes need to be adjusted* would also be correct.

2. **(A)** *Could* is used before the verb *go* after the verb *wish* in the main clause.

3. **(C)** *Knows how* is used before the infinitive *to use* to express ability or skill. *Miss Smith knows the equipment* would also be correct.

4. **(A)** *Used to* is used before the verb word *go* to express a habit in the past.

5. **(C)** *Must have* is used before the participle *misunderstood* to express a logical conclusion.

6. **(C)** *Wouldn't* is used before the subject *you* followed by *rather* and the verb word *sit* to express preference.

7. **(D)** *That* is used before the subject *he* and the verb word *stay* in the clause after the verb *insisted.*

8. **(B)** The participle *written* is used after *had* to refer to an activity in the past.

9. **(B)** *Neither* is used before the auxiliary *would* followed by the subject *the other driver. The other driver wouldn't either* would also be correct.

10. **(B)** *Doesn't* is used in the clause of condition to agree with *we'll [we will]* in the clause of result.

11. **(D)** *Have* is used before the thing *your temperature* followed by the participle *taken* to express an activity caused by someone else.

12. **(C)** The infinitive *to pass* is used after the verb *fails.*

13. **(C)** *That* is used before the subject *she* followed by *would* and the verb word *answer* after the verb phrase *had hoped.*

14. **(C)** The verb word *start* is used after the verb phrase *had better* and the *-ing* form *getting up* is used after the verb *start.*

15. **(D)** *Is it* is used to agree with the subject *today's weather* and the verb *is* in the main clause.

EXERCISE 4: Pronouns

1. **(A)** *Whom* is used to refer to the person *foreigner* as the complement of the verb *saw.*

2. **(C)** The *-ing* form *asking* is used after the verb phrase *forgot about,* and the possessive pronoun *our* is used to modify the *-ing* form *asking.*

3. **(A)** The object pronoun *me* is used as the complement of the verb *invites.*

4. **(A)** *Who* is used to refer to the person *student* as the subject of the verb *is.*

5. **(B)** The *-ing* form *offering* is used after the verb *appreciate,* and the possessive pronoun *your* is used to modify the *-ing* form *offering.*

6. **(C)** *Who* is used to refer to the person *woman* as the subject of the verb *was hurt.*

7. **(B)** The object pronoun *them* is used after the preposition *for.*

8. **(B)** The object pronoun *us* is used after the preposition *of.*

9. **(A)** *Who* is used to refer to the person *woman* as the subject of the verb *posed.*

10. **(C)** The object pronoun *him* is used after the preposition *with.*

11. **(C)** The object pronoun *me* is used as the complement of the verb *let.*

12. **(A)** The subject pronoun *who* is used to refer to the person *he,* the subject of the verb *was.*

13. **(A)** The object pronoun *her* is used as the complement of the verb *ask.*

14. **(C)** *Which* is used to refer to the thing *notebooks.*

15. **(A)** The *-ing* form *watching* is used after the verb phrase *not mind,* and the possessive pronoun *their* is used to modify the *-ing* form *watching.*

EXERCISE 5: Nouns

1. **(D)** *The* is used with the ordinal number *third* before the noun *window. Window three,* without the article *the,* would also be correct.

2. **(D)** *Ears* to express a plural number with the noun *corn* is idiomatic.

3. **(A)** The cardinal number *two* is used after the noun *volume. The second volume* would also be correct.

4. **(C)** *A few* is used before the plural count noun *dollars. A little money* would also be correct.

5. **(D)** *The* is used with the ordinal number *tenth* before the noun *chapter. Chapter ten* would also be correct.

6. **(C)** *Pieces of* is used before the noncount noun *jewelry* to express a plural number.

7. **(B)** *So little* is used before the noncount noun *time. So little* has a negative meaning. *It is good that you have a little time* would also be correct. *A little* has a positive meaning.

8. **(C)** *Much* is used before the noncount noun *news. We have had some news* would also be correct.

9. **(B)** *The* is used with the ordinal number *thirty-fifth* before the noun *president.*

10. **(C)** *Two pieces of* is used before the noncount noun *toast* to express a plural number.

11. **(C)** The cardinal number *six* is used after the noun *gate.*

12. **(D)** *A little* is used before the noncount noun *information.*

13. **(C)** *A piece of* is used before the noncount noun *mail* to express a singular number.

14. **(C)** The cardinal number *two* is used after the noun *lane. The second lane* would also be correct.

15. **(D)** *Much* is used before the noncount noun *homework.*

EXERCISE 6: Modifiers (Part 1)

1. **(A)** *Since* is used before the duration of time *three years* followed by *ago. She hasn't seen her family for three years* would also be correct.

2. **(A)** *The* is used before the noun *hall,* which is used as an adjective to describe the second count noun *closet.* Adjectives do not have plural endings in English.

3. **(D)** *Ago* is used after the duration of time *thirty years. Bill has worked at the University for thirty years* would also be correct.

4. **(C)** The adjective *strong* is used after the verb of the senses *tastes.*

5. **(A)** *The* is used before the noun *tea,* which is used as an adjective to describe the second count noun *cup.* Adjectives do not have plural endings in English.

6. **(D)** The hyphenated adjective *two-month-old* is used before the noun *baby.* Adjectives do not have plural endings in English.

7. **(A)** *So* is used before the adjective *expensive* followed by *that* and the clause of result *I couldn't afford it.*

8. **(B)** *I haven't gone* is used before *for* and the duration of time *the past five seasons.*

9. **(C)** *Such a* is used before the adjective *snowy* and the noun *day* followed by *that* and the clause of result *travel advisories have been issued.*

10. **(C)** *The* is used before the ordinal number *sixth* followed by *of* and the month *June* to identify a date.

11. **(B)** The adverb of manner *attentively* is used to describe how *they listened.*

12. **(C)** *So* is used before the adjective *good* followed by *that* and the clause of result *I ate them all.*

13. **(D)** The noun *department* is used as an adjective to describe the second noun *stores.* Adjectives do not have plural endings in English.

14. **(B)** *Such a* is used before the adjective *big* and the noun *mistake.*

15. **(C)** The adjective *good* is followed by *enough* to express sufficiency.

EXERCISE 7: Modifiers (Part 2)

1. **(C)** The adverb of manner *carefully* is used to describe how *Sam does his work.*

2. **(D)** The adjective *bad* is used after the verb of the senses *tastes.*

3. **(A)** *She's [has] lived here* is used before *since* and the specific point in time *1976.*

4. **(B)** *There* is used before the adjective *fast* followed by *enough* to express sufficiency.

5. **(D)** The adverb *late* does not have an *-ly* form.

6. **(A)** *Such* is used before the adjective *nice* and the noncount noun *weather* followed by *that* and the clause of result *we went camping.*

7. **(B)** *The* is used with the ordinal number *second* followed by *of* and the month *September* to identify a date.

8. **(A)** *So* is used before the adjective *late* followed by *that* and the clause of result *she missed her bus.*

9. **(D)** The noun *room* is used as an adjective to describe the second noun *numbers.* Adjectives do not have plural endings in English.

10. **(C)** The adjective *light* is followed by *enough* to express sufficiency.

11. **(D)** *So* is used before the adjective *beautiful* followed by the determiner *a* and the noun *day. Such a beautiful day* would also be correct.

12. **(B)** The noun *mathematics,* which always has an *-s* ending, is used as an adjective to describe the second noun *teachers.* Adjectives do not have plural endings in English.

13. **(A)** The hyphenated adjective *two-bedroom* is used before the noun *apartment.* Adjectives do not have plural endings in English.

14. **(D)** *For* is used before the duration of time *several months.*

15. **(C)** The adverb of manner *clearly* is used to describe how *we can see.*

EXERCISE 8: Comparatives

1. **(C)** *As soon as* is used before the subject *I* and the present tense verb *finish* to express a future activity.

2. **(B)** *The* is used before the comparative *more* in the clause of condition followed by *the* before the comparative *worse* in the clause of result.

3. **(C)** *The same* is used before *as* followed by the pronoun *mine* in a comparison. *Yours and mine are almost the same* would also be correct.

4. **(C)** The cardinal number *three* is used before *times* followed by *as much as* in a multiple number.

5. **(C)** The adjective *pretty* is used with *-er* followed by *than* in a comparison. *As pretty as her sister* would also be correct.

6. **(D)** *As soon as* is used before the subject *we* and the present verb *finish* to express a future activity.

7. **(C)** *Different* is used before *from* followed by the noun *the others* in a comparison. *This new soap and the others are not much different* would also be correct.

8. **(A)** *As* is used before the adjective *nice* followed by *as* in a comparison.

9. **(C)** The comparative adjective *larger* is used before *than* followed by *those* to refer to the *rooms*.

10. **(C)** *As soon as* is used before the subject *we* and the present verb *find* to express a future activity.

11. **(B)** *Like* is used before the noun *the midterm* in a comparison. *The final and the midterm will be alike* would also be correct.

12. **(D)** The comparative adjective *friendlier* is followed by *than* in a comparison.

13. **(C)** *As high as* is used before the amount of money *six thousand dollars* to establish a limit.

14. **(C)** *The* is used before the comparative *more* in the clause of condition followed by *the* before the comparative *more* in the clause of result.

15. **(C)** *Twice* is used before *as much* in a multiple number.

EXERCISE 9: Connectors

1. **(A)** *What* is used before the subject *the taxes* and the verb *are* to maintain subject-verb word order after a question word connector.

2. **(C)** *Because of* is used before the noun *the noise* to express cause. *Because it was noisy* would also be correct.

3. **(C)** *What* is used before the subject *the professor* and the verb *said* to maintain subject-verb word order after a question word connector.

4. **(C)** *So that* is used before the clause of purpose *he could finish*.

5. **(C)** The subject *he* and the verb *went* are used after the connector *where* to maintain subject-verb word order after a question word connector.

6. **(A)** *As well as* is used before the third name *Jane*.

7. **(C)** *Because* is used before the subject *the bus* and the verb *was* to express cause. *Because of the bus* would also be correct.

8. **(D)** *Despite* is used before the noun *the light rain* in the clause of concession. *In spite of the light rain* would also be correct.

9. **(B)** The subject *she* and the verb *wants* are used after the connector *what* to maintain subject-verb word order after a question word connector.

10. **(B)** *And* is used before the adjective *honored* in coordination with *both* and the adjective *pleased*.

11. **(C)** *How much* is used before the subject *these shoes* and the verb *cost* to maintain subject-verb word order after a question word connector.

12. **(B)** *So that* is used before the clause of purpose *we could hear.*

13. **(D)** *But also* is used before the phrase *on the baseball team* in coordination with *not only* and the phrase *on the basketball squad.*

14. **(C)** *In spite of* is used before the noun *his wealth* in the clause of concession. *Despite his wealth* would also be correct.

15. **(B)** The subject *the nearest bus stop* and the verb *is located* are used after the connector *where* to maintain subject-verb word order after a question word connector.

EXERCISE 10: Cumulative Review (Part 1)

1. **(C)** The *-ing* form adjective *interesting* is used to describe the noun *data.*

2. **(D)** *Much too much* is a phrase that is used to express excess. *The cost is too much for most businesses* would also be correct.

3. **(C)** *There* is used before *is* to refer to the noun *salt* at the specific place *in the ocean.*

4. **(C)** The *-ing* form *cracking* is used after the preposition *without.*

5. **(C)** *Will have* is used before the participle *decreased* to express the future viewpoint *by the second year of production.*

6. **(D)** *For* is used before the phrase *four terms* to express a duration of time.

7. **(A)** *A* refers to the count noun *state.* All other choices are redundant.

8. **(C)** *Virtually* qualifies the phrase *all types of,* which expresses classification.

9. **(D)** *Are* is used before *there* to refer to the noun *notes* at the specific place in the musical scale, and to maintain word order for questions.

10. **(D)** *By* is used before the *-ing* form *increasing* to express method.

11. **(A)** *If* is used before the noun *endangered species* and the verb *are* followed by the infinitive *to be* to express the result of a condition with *must.*

12. **(A)** The *-ing* form *engaging* is used after the noun *ants* to describe them.

13. **(B)** *From* is used before the *-ing* form *watching* to express cause.

14. **(B)** The preposition *to* is used after the verb *prefer.*

15. **(C)** The infinitive *to complete* is used to express purpose.

EXERCISE 11: Cumulative Review (Part 2)

1. **(B)** *Ought* is used before *to* to express obligation. *A healthy heart should pump* would also be correct.

2. **(B)** *Not* is used before the infinitive *to be* in the clause after the verb *agreed. Doctors agreed that they shouldn't be truthful* would also be correct.

3. **(D)** *No* is used before the noun *earthquakes. The New England states have not had any serious earthquakes* would also be correct.

4. **(B)** *Almost* is used before *all* to express approximation. *Nearly all* would also be correct.

5. **(B)** *In* is used before the month *December.*

6. **(A)** *In* is used after *interested.* The *-ing* form *establishing* is used after the preposition *in.*

7. **(D)** The past verb *borrowed* is used. *An English company lent the Pilgrims seven thousand dollars* would also be correct.

8. **(B)** *When* is used before the subject *it* and the present verb *ages* to express a general truth.

9. **(B)** *But* is used before the noun *smell* to express exception.

10. **(D)** *Others* is used consecutively with *some*.

11. **(C)** The infinitive *to communicate* is used to express purpose.

12. **(A)** *Let* is used before the complement *their offspring* followed by the verb word *build* to express permission.

13. **(D)** The noun phrase *medical diagnosis* is used with *cooking* and *telecommunications* to maintain parallel structure.

14. **(C)** The subject *art* is used before the verb phrase *tends to be* followed by *worth* and the indefinite amount *more* to express value.

15. **(D)** *Won't* is used before *be* followed by the participle *developed* in a passive to express the importance of the cure. *Scientists won't develop a cure until more funds are allocated* would also be correct to express the importance of the *scientists*.

Part B—Written Expressions

EXERCISE 12: Point of View

1. **(A)** The adverbial phrase *in 1970* establishes a point of view in the past. *Are* should be *were* to maintain the point of view.

2. **(A)** The verb *did not make* establishes a point of view in the past. *Changes* should be *changed* to maintain the point of view.

3. **(B)** The adverbial phrase *this year* establishes a point of view in the present. *Were* should be *are* to maintain the point of view.

4. **(B)** The verb *said* establishes a point of view in the past. *Is* should be *was* to maintain the point of view.

5. **(B)** The verb *were* establishes a point of view in the past. *Will* should be *would* to maintain the point of view.

6. **(B)** The adverbial phrase *last April* establishes a point of view in the past. *Is working* should be *worked* to maintain the point of view.

7. **(B)** The verb *found* establishes a point of view in the past. *Wants* should be *wanted* to maintain the point of view.

8. **(A)** The verb *thought* establishes a point of view in the past. *Will* should be *would* to maintain the point of view.

9. **(A)** The reference to an activity before the subject's death establishes a point of view in the past. *Publishes* should be *published* to maintain the point of view.

10. **(B)** The adverbial phrase *last Friday* establishes a point of view in the past. *Does* should be *did* to maintain the point of view.

11. **(B)** The adverbial phrase *seven o'clock in the morning when the sun comes up* establishes a point of view in the present. *Disappeared* should be *disappears* to maintain the point of view.

12. **(C)** The verb *was* establishes a point of view in the past. *Want* should be *wanted* to maintain the point of view.

13. **(D)** The verb *is* establishes a point of view in the present. *Invited* should be *invites* to maintain the point of view.

14. **(A)** The verb *thought* establishes a point of view in the past. *Are* should be *were* to maintain the point of view.

15. **(B)** The adverbial phrase *October 19, 1781* establishes a point of view in the past. *Surrenders* should be *surrendered* to maintain the point of view.

16. **(A)** The adverbial phrase *last month* establishes a point of view in the past. *Is* should be *was* to maintain the point of view.

17. **(B)** The reference to an activity before the subject's death establishes a point of view in the past. *Lives* should be *lived* to maintain the point of view.

18. **(A)** The verb *said* establishes a point of view in the past. *Is* should be *was* to maintain the point of view.

19. **(B)** Both the phrase *In 1990* and the verb *reported* establish a point of view in the past. *Believe* should be *believed* to maintain the point of view.

20. **(B)** Both the phrase *last year* and the verb *told* establish a point of view in the past. *Is* should be *was* to maintain the point of view.

21. **(C)** The verb *are* establishes a point of view in the present. *Were* should be *are* to maintain the point of view.

22. **(A)** The adverb *yesterday* establishes a point of view in the past. *Does* should be *did* to maintain the point of view.

23. **(B)** The verb *give* establishes a point of view in the present. *Deposited* should be *deposit* to maintain the point of view.

24. **(B)** The verb *accelerated* establishes a point of view in the past. *Qualifies* should be *qualified* to maintain the point of view.

25. **(C)** The verb *is* establishes a point of view in the present. *Included* should be *includes* to maintain the point of view.

EXERCISE 13: Agreement

1. **(B)** There must be agreement between pronoun and antecedent. *You* should be *one* or *his* to agree with the impersonal antecedent *one*.

2. **(C)** There must be agreement between subject and verb. *Were* should be *was* to agree with the singular subject *what happened*.

3. **(B)** There must be agreement between subject and verb. *Are* should be *is* to agree with the third person singular subject *the governor*.

4. **(C)** There must be agreement between pronoun and antecedent. *Their* should be *our* to agree with the second person antecedent *those of us*.

5. **(B)** There must be agreement between subject and verb. *Is* should be *are* to agree with the plural subject *both*.

6. **(B)** There must be agreement between subject and verb. *Are* should be *is* to agree with the singular subject *money*.

7. **(A)** There must be agreement between subject and verb. *Have* should be *has* to agree with the inverted singular subject *little rain*.

8. **(C)** There must be agreement between pronoun and antecedent. *Their* should be *his* to agree with the singular subject *everyone*.

9. **(A)** There must be agreement between subject and verb. *Were* should be *was* to agree with the singular subject *the popularity*.

10. **(B)** There must be agreement between subject and verb. *Develop* should be *develops* to agree with the singular subject *not one*.

11. **(C)** There must be agreement between subject and verb. *Have* should be *has* to agree with the inverted singular subject *little change*.

12. **(D)** There must be agreement between pronoun and antecedent. *Their* should be *its* to agree with the third person singular neuter noun *the eagle.*

13. **(D)** There must be agreement between subject and verb. *Require* should be *requires* to agree with the singular subject *the Blue Spruce.*

14. **(A)** There must be agreement between subject and verb. *Is* should be *are* to agree with the plural subject *few airports.*

15. **(B)** There must be agreement between subject and verb. *Were* should be *was* to agree with the singular subject *work.*

16. **(B)** There must be agreement between subject and verb. *Are* should be *is* to agree with the singular subject *the president.*

17. **(B)** There must be agreement between pronoun and antecedent. *Their* should be *his* to agree with the singular subject *each voter.*

18. **(C)** There must be agreement between pronoun and antecedent. *Their* should be *our* to agree with the second person antecedent *those of us.*

19. **(C)** There must be agreement between subject and verb. *Were* should be *was* to agree with the singular subject *neither.*

20. **(C)** There must be agreement between pronoun and antecedent. *You* should be *one* or *he* to agree with the impersonal antecedent *one.*

21. **(C)** There must be agreement between subject and verb. *Are* should be *is* to agree with the singular subject *one.*

22. **(C)** There must be agreement between subject and verb. *Know* should be *knows* to agree with the singular subject *one.*

23. **(B)** There must be agreement between pronoun and antecedent. *They* should be *one* or *he* to agree with the impersonal antecedent *one.*

24. **(B)** There must be agreement between subject and verb. *Were* should be *was* to agree with the inverted singular subject *a serious objection.*

25. **(A)** There must be agreement between subject and verb. *Are* should be *is* to agree with the singular subject *a large percentage.*

EXERCISE 14: Introductory Verbal Modifiers

1. **(A)** An introductory verbal phrase followed by a comma should immediately precede the noun that it modifies. *After finishing Roots* is misplaced because it does not precede the noun it modifies, *author Alex Haley.*

2. **(A)** An introductory verbal phrase followed by a comma should immediately precede the noun that it modifies. *A competitive sport* is misplaced because it does not modify the noun it precedes, *gymnasts.*

3. **(B)** An introductory verbal phrase followed by a comma should immediately precede the noun that it modifies. *Carefully soaking* should be *(you) carefully soak them* to provide a noun and a verb for the introductory verbal phrase *to remove stains from permanent press clothing.*

4. **(A)** An introductory verbal phrase followed by a comma should immediately precede the noun that it modifies. *Found in Tanzania by Mary Leakey* is misplaced because it does not precede the noun it modifies, *the three-million-year-old fossils.*

5. **(A)** An introductory verbal phrase followed by a comma should immediately precede the noun that it modifies. *After fighting the blaze for three days* is misplaced because it does not precede the noun it modifies, *the firefighters.*

6. **(B)** An introductory verbal phrase followed by a comma should immediately precede the noun that it modifies. *After finishing their degrees* is misplaced because it does not precede the noun it modifies, *the students.*

7. **(D)** An introductory verbal phrase followed by a comma should immediately precede the noun that it modifies. *Columbus's final resting place* should be *Columbus is now buried* because the man, not the place, is modified by the verbal phrase *Originally having been buried in Spain.*

8. **(B)** An introductory verbal phrase followed by a comma should immediately precede the noun that it modifies. *New York audiences received the new play* should be *the new play was received by New York audiences* because the play, not the audiences, is modified by the verbal phrase *written by Neil Simon.*

9. **(C)** An introductory verbal phrase followed by a comma should immediately precede the noun that it modifies. *Survival is assured* should be *animals ensure survival* because the animals, not the survival, is modified by the verbal phrase *by migrating to a warmer climate every fall.*

10. **(B)** An introductory verbal phrase followed by a comma should immediately precede the noun that it modifies. *A memorial fund will be established* should be *family and friends will establish a memorial fund* because the family and friends, not the memorial fund, are modified by the verbal phrase *saddened by the actor's sudden death.*

11. **(A)** An introductory verbal phrase followed by a comma should immediately precede the noun that it modifies. *Dental floss should be used* should be *(you) use dental floss* to provide a noun for the introductory verbal phrase *to prevent cavities.*

12. **(A)** An introductory verbal phrase followed by a comma should immediately precede the noun that it modifies. *The Senate committee's discovery* should be *The Senate committee discovered* because the committee, not the discovery, is modified by the verbal phrase *while researching the problem of violent crime.*

13. **(A)** An introductory verbal phrase followed by a comma should immediately precede the noun that it modifies. *Trying to pay for a purchase with cash* is misplaced because it does not precede the noun it modifies, *customers.*

14. **(A)** An introductory verbal phrase followed by a comma should immediately precede the noun that it modifies. *After reviewing the curriculum* is misplaced because it does not precede the noun it modifies, *faculty.*

15. **(D)** An introductory verbal phrase followed by a comma should immediately precede the noun that it modifies. *Hank Aaron's record* should be *Hank Aaron* because the man, not the record, is modified by the verbal phrase *having hit more home runs than any other player in the history of baseball.*

16. **(A)** An introductory verbal phrase followed by a comma should immediately precede the noun that it modifies. *Banned in the U.S.* is misplaced because it does not precede the noun it modifies, *fluorocarbons.*

17. **(A)** An introductory verbal phrase followed by a comma should immediately precede the noun that it modifies. *To avoid jet lag* is misplaced because it does not precede the noun it modifies, *patients.*

18. **(A)** An introductory verbal phrase followed by a comma should immediately precede the noun that it modifies. *After cooking in the microwave oven for five minutes* is misplaced because it does not precede the noun it modifies, *most meat dishes.*

19. **(B)** An introductory verbal phrase followed by a comma should immediately precede the noun that it modifies. *Traditionally named for women* is misplaced because it does not precede the noun it modifies, *a hurricane.*

20. **(A)** An introductory verbal phrase followed by a comma should immediately precede the noun that it modifies. *Their answers* should be *the witnesses* because it is the people, not their answers, who are modified by the verbal phrase *before testifying.*

21. **(A)** An introductory verbal phrase followed by a comma should immediately precede the noun that it modifies. *By reading the instructions carefully* is misplaced because it does not modify the noun it precedes, *mistakes.*

22. **(B)** An introductory verbal phrase followed by a comma should immediately precede the noun that it modifies. *Having been divorced* is misplaced because it does not modify the noun that it precedes, *her credit.*

23. **(A)** An introductory verbal phrase followed by a comma should immediately precede the noun that it modifies. *Attempting to smuggle drugs into the country* is misplaced because it does not precede the noun it modifies, *the criminals.*

24. **(A)** An introductory verbal phrase followed by a comma should immediately precede the noun that it modifies. *While trying to build a tunnel through the Blue Ridge Mountains* is misplaced because it does not precede the noun it modifies, *workmen.*

25. **(A)** An introductory verbal phrase followed by a comma should immediately precede the noun that it modifies. *Founded in 1919* is misplaced because it does not precede the noun it modifies, *the Institute for International Education.*

EXERCISE 15: Parallel Structure

1. **(D)** Ideas in a series should be expressed by parallel structures. *That it would adjourn* should be *to adjourn* to provide parallelism with the infinitives *to cancel* and *to approve.*

2. **(D)** Ideas in a series should be expressed by parallel structures. *It is* should be deleted to provide parallelism among the adjectives *fast, safe,* and *convenient.*

3. **(B)** Ideas after inclusives should be expressed by parallel structures. *Not only popular* should be *popular not only* to provide parallelism between the adverbial phrases *in the United States* and *abroad.*

4. **(B)** Ideas in a series should be expressed by parallel structures. *Turning* should be *turn* to provide parallelism with the verb words *lock* and *walk.*

5. **(A)** Ideas in a series should be expressed by parallel structures. *Making* should be *to make* to provide parallelism with the infinitive *to control.*

6. **(C)** Ideas in a series should be expressed by parallel structures. *To modify* should be *by modifying* to provide parallelism with the phrase *by changing.*

7. **(C)** Ideas in a series should be expressed by parallel structures. *Awareness* should be *aware* to provide parallelism with the adjectives *intelligent* and *capable.*

8. **(B)** Ideas after inclusives should be expressed by parallel structures, and inclusives should be used in coordinating pairs. *But* should be *but also* to coordinate with *not only.*

9. **(D)** Ideas in a series should be expressed by parallel structures. *Signing your name* should be *the signature* to provide parallelism with the nouns *the address, the inside address, the salutation, the body,* and *the closing.*

10. **(B)** Ideas in a series should be expressed by parallel structures. *To do* should be *doing* to provide parallelism with *using.*

11. **(A)** Ideas in a series should be expressed by parallel structures. *Being introduced* should be *to be introduced* to provide parallelism with the infinitive *to read.*

12. **(C)** Ideas after exclusives should be expressed by parallel structures, and exclusives should be used in coordinating pairs. *And not* should be *nor* to coordinate with *neither.*

13. **(C)** Ideas in a series should be expressed by parallel structures. *Who* should be deleted to provide parallelism among the verbs *understands, knows,* and *works.*

14. **(A)** Ideas in a series should be expressed by parallel structures. *Ice skating* should be *to go ice skating* to provide parallelism with the infinitive *to go skiing.*

15. **(D)** Ideas in a series should be expressed by parallel structures. *The operation was begun* should be *began the operation* to provide parallelism with the past, active verb *examined.*

16. **(B)** Ideas in a series should be expressed by parallel structures. *Because of the time* should be *because there was little time* to provide parallelism with the clause *because we were not sure.*

17. **(C)** Ideas in a series should be expressed by parallel structures. *Avoiding* should be *avoid* to provide parallelism with the verb words *drink* and *eat.*

18. **(B)** Ideas after inclusives should be expressed by parallel structures. *A key* should be *with a key* to provide parallelism with the phrase *with an element.*

19. **(C)** Ideas in a series should be expressed by parallel structures. *Warning* should be *to warn* to provide parallelism with the infinitive *to report.*

20. **(D)** Ideas in a series should be expressed by parallel structures. *Had finished* should be *finishing* to provide parallelism with the *-ing* forms *traveling* and *visiting.*

21. **(D)** Ideas in a series should be expressed by parallel structures. *There are* should be deleted to provide parallelism among the nouns *the flag, the airplane,* and *the gowns.*

22. **(D)** Ideas in a series should be expressed by parallel structures. *Less* should be *least* to provide parallelism with the superlative adjectives *the smallest* and *most recently published.*

23. **(D)** Ideas after inclusives should be expressed by parallel structures. *The House of Representatives* should be *by the House of Representatives* to provide parallelism with the phrase *by the Senate.*

24. **(D)** Ideas in a series should be expressed by parallel structures. *With ease* should be *easily* to provide parallelism with the adverbs *safely* and *efficiently.*

25. **(C)** Ideas after exclusives should be expressed by parallel structures and exclusives should be used in coordinating pairs. *But also* should be *but* to coordinate with *not.*

EXERCISE 16: Redundancy

1. **(D)** Repetition of a word by another word with the same meaning is redundant. *Again* should be deleted because it means *repeat.*

2. **(A)** Repetition of the subject by a subject pronoun is redundant. *It* should be deleted.

3. **(C)** Repetition of a word by another word with the same meaning is redundant. *Or purchasing* should be deleted because it means *buying.*

4. **(D)** Indirect phrases instead of adverbs are redundant. *In an impartial manner* should be *impartially.*

5. **(A)** Indirect phrases are redundant. *There was not any clarity* should be *it was not clear.*

6. **(C)** Repetition of the subject by the subject pronoun is redundant. *They* should be deleted.

7. **(D)** Repetition of a word by another word with the same meaning is redundant. *Back* should be deleted because it means *return.*

8. **(A)** Repetition of a word by another word with the same meaning is redundant. *Who knows a great deal* should be deleted because it means *an authority.*

9. **(B)** Words or phrases that do not add information are redundant. *In terms of* should be *to.*

10. **(A)** Repetition of the subject by a subject pronoun is redundant. *He* should be deleted.

11. **(B)** Repetition of a word by another word with the same meaning is redundant. *Enough* should be deleted because it means *sufficiently.*

12. **(B)** Words or phrases that do not add information are redundant. *In nature* should be deleted.

13. **(A)** Repetition of the subject by a subject pronoun is redundant. *He* should be deleted.

14. **(B)** Indirect phrases instead of adverbs are redundant. *In a careful manner* should be *carefully.*

15. **(C)** Repetition of the subject by a subject pronoun is redundant. *They* should be deleted.

16. **(A)** Repetition of the subject by a subject pronoun is redundant. *She* should be deleted.

17. **(C)** Repetition of a word by another word with the same meaning is redundant. *New* should be deleted because it means *innovations*.

18. **(A)** Words or phrases that do not add information are redundant. *More* should be deleted because *perfect* cannot be improved.

19. **(D)** Repetition of a word by another word with the same meaning is redundant. *By name* should be deleted

20. **(B)** Repetition of a word by another word with the same meaning is redundant. *Forward* should be deleted because it means *advances*.

21. **(B)** Repetition of the subject by a subject pronoun is redundant. *It* should be deleted.

22. **(D)** Indirect phrases instead of adverbs are redundant. *With rapidity* should be *rapidly*.

23. **(A)** Repetition of the subject by a subject pronoun is redundant. *She* should be deleted.

24. **(B)** Words or phrases that do not add information are redundant. *In politics* should be deleted.

25. **(A)** Repetition of the subject by a subject pronoun is redundant. *It* should be deleted.

EXERCISE 17: Word Choice

1. **(D)** *Equal to* is a prepositional idiom. *As* should be *to*.

2. **(D)** *Lie* means *to occupy a place*. *Laying* should be *lying*.

3. **(B)** *Raise* means *to move to a higher place*. *Is risen* should be *is raised*.

4. **(D)** *Broke* is a colloquial expression. *Broke* should be *bankrupt*.

5. **(C)** *Compare with* is a prepositional idiom. *Comparing* should be *compared with*.

6. **(D)** *To give someone their walking papers* is a colloquial expression. *Gave them their walking papers* should be *dismissed them*.

7. **(C)** *Similar to* is a prepositional idiom. *As* should be *to*.

8. **(B)** *Near to* is not idiomatic. *To* should be *deleted*.

9. **(C)** *Effects on* is a prepositional idiom. *In* should be *on*.

10. **(A)** *Carefulness* is not the correct part of speech. *Carefulness* should be *care*.

11. **(B)** *Real* is an adjective used in colloquial speech as an adverb. *Real great* should be *very great*.

12. **(A)** *Formerly* means *in the past*. *Formally* should be *formerly*.

13. **(C)** *Let* means *allow*. *Leave* should be *let*.

14. **(A)** *Bored with* is a prepositional idiom. *Of* should be *with*.

15. **(A)** *Effective* is not the correct part of speech. *Effective* should be *effect*.

16. **(D)** *Considerate* means *polite*. *Considerable* should be *considerate*.

17. **(A)** *Can't hardly* is not idiomatic. *Can't hardly* should be *can hardly*.

18. **(B)** *Rise* means *to go up*. *Raised* should be *risen*.

19. **(D)** *In conflict* is a prepositional idiom. *On* should be *in*.

20. **(A)** *The cops* is a colloquial expression. *The cops* should be *the police*.

21. **(A)** *With regard to* is a prepositional idiom. *Of* should be *to*.

22. **(B)** *Lie* means *to occupy a place*. *To lay* should be *to lie*.

23. **(A)** *Except for* is a prepositional idiom. *Excepting for* should be *except for*.

24. **(A)** *To suspicion* is not idiomatic. *Suspicioned* should be *suspected*.

25. **(A)** *Menkind* is not idiomatic. *Menkind* should be *mankind*.

EXERCISE 18: Structure

1. **(B)** *The best* should be *the better* because two, not three or more lectures, are being compared.

2. **(A)** *Knows to assist* should be *knows how to assist* because *knows how* is used before the infinitive *to assist*.

3. **(A)** *Wrote* should be *written* because a participle, not a past form, is used with *had*.

4. **(B)** *Differently* should be *different* because an adjective, not an adverb, is used after the verb of the senses *seem*.

5. **(C)** *So* should be *so that* because it introduces a clause of purpose.

6. **(C)** *Do* should be *doing* or *to do* because an *-ing* form or an infinitive, not a verb word, is used after the verb *continue*.

7. **(C)** *Which* should be *who* because it refers to people, not things.

8. **(A)** *Understands* should be *understood* because a past form, not a present form, is used after the verb *wishes*.

9. **(B)** *From* should be deleted because a preposition is not used after the verb *forbid*.

10. **(A)** *Ran* should be *run* because a participle, not a past form, is used with *had*.

11. **(B)** *Ninety-days* should be *ninety-day* because an adjective does not use a plural form.

12. **(D)** *Badly* should be *bad* because an adjective, not an adverb, is used after the verb of the senses *taste*.

13. **(A)** *I* should be *me* because an objective pronoun is used after *let*.

14. **(A)** *Investigates* should be *investigate* because the word *recommendation* requires a verb word.

15. **(C)** *As* should be *than* because *than* is used after the comparative *younger*.

16. **(C)** *In spite* should be *in spite of* because *in spite of* introduces a condition with an unexpected result. *Despite* would also be correct.

17. **(A)** *Lately* should be *late* because the adverb form of *late* does not have an *-ly* ending.

18. **(A)** *Would have been* should be *had been* because *had* and a participle are used in the condition and *would have* and a participle are used in the result.

19. **(C)** *The worst* should be *the worse* because comparative forms are used with *the* in double comparisons that express cause and result.

20. **(C)** *Much* should be *many* because *many* is used with the count noun *movies*.

21. **(B)** *Whom* should be *who* because it is the subject of the verb *will win*.

22. **(A)** *Would have checked* should be *had checked* because *had* and a participle are used in the condition and *would have* and a participle are used in the result.

23. **(A)** *Her* should be *she* because a subject pronoun is used after *it was*.

24. **(B)** *Taking* should be *to take* because an infinitive, not an *-ing* form, is used after the verb *fail*.

25. **(A)** *Will sign* should be *sign* because a verb word is used after the impersonal expression *is it necessary*.

EXERCISE 19: Cumulative Review (Part 1)

1. **(A)** Repetition of the subject clause by a subject pronoun is redundant. *It* should be deleted.

2. **(C)** *Lay* should be *laid*. *Lay* is the past form of *to lie*, which means to recline. *Laid* is the past form of *to lay*, which means to put in a place.

3. **(A)** Repetition of the subject by a subject pronoun is redundant. *It* should be deleted.

4. **(D)** *The same* is used with a quality noun such as *age* followed by *as* in comparisons. *Old* is an adjective. *Old* should be *age*.

5. **(A)** *An understand* is not the correct part of speech. *Understand* should be *understanding*.

6. **(B)** A passive sentence is used to focus on the structures rather than on the builders. In a passive sentence, a form of *be* is followed by a participle. *Build* should be *built*.

7. **(A)** *The classify* is not the correct part of speech. *Classify* should be *classification*.

8. **(B)** *The same* is used with a quality noun such as *color* followed by *as* in comparisons. *Than* should be *as*.

9. **(A)** Every sentence must have a main verb. *Having* should be *has*.

10. **(B)** An introductory verbal phrase followed by a comma should immediately precede the noun that it modifies. *The Library of Congress is where Archibald MacLeish worked* should be *Archibald MacLeish worked at the Library of Congress* to provide an appropriate noun for the introductory verbal phrase *born in 1892*.

11. **(B)** The comparative adjective *better* is used for separate comparisons of two, including *images . . . and . . . signals*, and *images . . . and tapes*. *Best* should be *better*.

12. **(D)** Ideas after exclusives should be expressed by parallel structures. *Writing* should be *write* to provide parallelism with the verb word *read*.

13. **(B)** There must be agreement between subject and verb. *Have* should be *has* to agree with the singular subject *a mature grove*.

14. **(C)** The adverbial phrase *seven months before the stock market crashed in 1929,* and the verb *said* establish a point of view in the past. *Are* should be *were* to maintain the point of view.

15. **(C)** Ideas in a series should be expressed by parallel structures. *Also they* should be deleted to provide parallelism among the verb words *stick out, move*, and *retract*.

16. **(B)** *Such as* introduces an example. *Such* should be *such as* before the examples of metals.

17. **(B)** An introductory verbal phrase followed by a comma should immediately precede the noun that it modifies. *Tours by* should be deleted because the *S.S. Constitution*, not the tours, is modified by the verbal phrase, *refurbished as a cruise vessel*.

18. **(B)** Every sentence must have a main verb. *Composed* should be *are composed*.

19. **(C)** Ideas after inclusives should be expressed by parallel structures, and inclusives should be used in coordinating pairs. *Also* should be *but also* to coordinate with *not only*.

20. **(A)** The adverbial clause *although we once thought* establishes a point of view in the past. *Has* should be *had* to maintain the point of view.

21. **(D)** There must be agreement between subject and verb. *Is* should be *are* to agree with the plural subject *coins*.

22. **(C)** There must be agreement between subject and verb. *Are* should be *is* to agree with the inverted singular subject *evidence*.

23. **(B)** The adverbial phrase *for about twelve thousand years* establishes a point of view that begins in the past. *Are living* should be *have been living* to maintain the point of view.

24. **(D)** There must be agreement between subject and verb. *Are contained* should be *is contained* to agree with the singular subject *the urinary system*.

25. **(C)** Ideas in a series should be expressed by parallel structures. *How much energy* should be *the energy* to provide parallelism with the noun *the heat*.

EXERCISE 20: Cumulative Review (Part 2)

1. **(D)** Ideas in a series should be expressed by parallel structures. *Move* should be *the movement of* to provide parallelism with the noun phrase *the maintenance of.*

2. **(A)** *Because* introduces a clause with a subject and verb. *Because of* introduces a phrase. *Because* should be *because of* before the nouns *expense . . . and concern. Because traditional fuels were expensive, there was concern . . .* would also be correct.

3. **(C)** There must be agreement between subject and verb. *Was* should be *were* to agree with the plural subject *dinosaurs.*

4. **(C)** The adverbial phrase *in the Middle Ages* establishes a point of view in the past. *Is completed* should be *was completed* to maintain the point of view.

5. **(B)** *So* is used before the adjective *great* to express cause. *As* should be *that* to introduce the clause of result.

6. **(D)** *When* is used before the subject and a present verb to express a future activity. *Will sleep* should be *sleep.*

7. **(D)** There must be agreement between subject and verb. *Were* should be *was* to agree with the singular subject *art deco.*

8. **(A)** Repetition of the subject by a subject pronoun is redundant. *They* should be deleted.

9. **(B)** The adverbial phrase *before the 1800s* establishes a point of view in the past. *Can* should be *could* to maintain the point of view.

10. **(C)** There must be agreement between subject and verb. *Are* should be *is* to agree with the singular subject *temperature.*

11. **(C)** The adverbial phrase *in 1991* establishes a point of view in the past. *Are passed* should be *were passed* to maintain the point of view.

12. **(C)** There must be agreement between subject and verb. *Thinks* should be *think* to agree with the plural subject *scientists.*

13. **(B)** Indirect phrases instead of adverbs are redundant. *In a uniform manner* should be *uniformly.*

14. **(D)** An introductory verbal phrase followed by a comma should immediately precede the noun that it modifies. *Ernest Hemingway wrote* A Farewell to Arms should be A Farewell to Arms, *written by Ernest Hemingway,* because the book, not the author, is modified by the verbal phrase, *published by Penguin Press.*

15. **(A)** *In* is used between numbers to express a fraction. *On* should be *in.*

16. **(D)** Ideas in a series should be expressed by parallel structures. *To improve* should be *by improving* to provide parallelism with the phrase *by increasing.*

17. **(B)** *The most longest* should be *the longest.* Because *long* is a one-syllable adjective, the superlative is formed by adding *-est. Most* is used with two-syllable adjectives that do not end in *-y.*

18. **(A)** *The develop* is not the correct part of speech. *Develop* should be *development.*

19. **(B)** There must be agreement between subject and verb. *Lives* should be *live* to agree with the plural subject *nine* [people].

20. **(C)** *Any other* excludes all others. *The other* should be *other.*

21. **(B)** There must be agreement between subject and verb. *Has* should be *have* to agree with the plural subject *remains.*

22. **(A)** Repetition of a word by another word with the same meaning is redundant. *Approximately* should be deleted because it means *about*.

23. **(C)** Repetition of the subject by a subject pronoun, and addition of a second main verb is redundant. *It is* should be deleted.

24. **(B)** The past form of the verb *to spend* is *spent*. *Spended* should be *spent*.

25. **(A)** *As a whole* is a phrase that means generally. *As whole* should be *as a whole*.

Chapter 5   Reading Comprehension

Part A—General Interest

EXERCISE 1: General Interest
Passage One

1. **(B)** "To save the most money, use the following strategies when you negotiate [to buy a car]." Choice (D) is a secondary idea used to support the main idea, "to offer advice to prospective car buyers." Choices (A) and (C) are not mentioned and may not be concluded from information in the passage.

2. **(B)** "... try to buy your new car at the end of the year, just before the next year's models arrive in the fall." Choice (A) refers to the end of the calendar year, not to the time just before the new models arrive. Choice (C) contradicts the fact that the author recommends buying at the end, not the beginning of the month. Choice (D) is not mentioned and may not be concluded from information in the passage.

3. **(C)** Choice (A) is mentioned in lines 2–4. Choice (B) is mentioned in lines 6–7. Choice (D) is mentioned in line 9. The author implies that by paying cash or using a bank, one can avoid paying a dealer's commission.

4. **(A)** In the context of this passage, an *inventory* means the goods that a business has available for purchase. Choices (B), (C), and (D) are not accepted meanings of the word *inventory*.

5. **(C)** "The dealer has to pay insurance and finance charges for every car in the inventory, and is usually willing to sell one [a car] for less money in order to reduce the overhead expenses." Choices (A), (B), and (D) would change the meaning of the sentence.

6. **(A)** Since the author states that buying a car is one of the few purchases that allows for negotiation, it may be concluded that negotiating a price for most purchases is not common in the United States. Choices (B), (C), and (D) are not mentioned and may not be concluded from information in the passage.

Passage Two

1. **(A)** A rental agreement, also called a lease, is a legal document. "Your signature on this legal document indicates that you have read and understood its contents ..." Choices (B), (C), and (D) are included in sections of the rental agreement.

2. **(C)** "The security deposit shall be refunded ... if notice in writing of termination has been given thirty (30) days in advance ..." The number in Choice (A) refers to the number of days in advance that written termination, not the keys, must be given. Choice (B) contradicts the fact that the deposit shall be refunded if the premises are undamaged. Choice (D) is not mentioned and may not be concluded from information in the passage.

3. **(C)** Choice (A) is mentioned in line 4. Choice (B) is mentioned in lines 5–7. Choice (D) is mentioned in lines 10–11.

4. **(C)** In the context of this passage, *premises* are property. Choices (A), (B), and (D) are not accepted meanings of the word *premises*.

5. **(C)** "Your signature on this legal document indicates that you have read and understood its [the document's] contents and agree to abide by its conditions." Choices (A), (B), and (D) would change the meaning of the sentence.

6. **(A)** "... notice in writing of termination ... [must be] given thirty (30) days in advance ..." Choice (B) refers to a date two weeks, not thirty days in advance of the move. Choice (C) refers to a date thirty days after, not in advance, of the move. Choice (D) refers to the date of the move.

Passage Three

1. **(D)** "General Appliance Company guarantees the product to be free of manufacturing defects for one year after the original date of purchase." Choice (A) would seem to be true but does not summarize the information in the passage. Choice (B) contradicts the fact that General Appliance will repair or replace the product free of charge, provided that damage has not resulted from accident. Choice (C) is not mentioned and may not be concluded from information in the passage.

2. **(C)** "Deliver the product to any one of the authorized service facilities . . ." Choice (B) refers to the place where questions should be addressed, not to the place where products are repaired or replaced. Choice (D) refers to the company that guarantees the product. Choice (A) is not mentioned and may not be concluded from information in the passage.

3. **(D)** Choice (A) is mentioned in lines 4–5. Choice (B) is mentioned in lines 5–6. Choice (C) is mentioned in lines 4–5.

4. **(D)** In the context of this passage, a *warranty* is a guarantee. Choices (A), (B), and (C) are not accepted meanings of the word *warranty.*

5. **(B)** "If the product should become defective within the warranty period, General Appliance will repair or replace it [the product] free of charge, provided that damage to the product has not resulted from accident or misuse." Choices (A), (C), and (D) would change the meaning of the sentence.

6. **(B)** "General Appliance Company guarantees the product to be free from manufacturing defects for one year . . . provided that damage . . . has not resulted from accident or misuse." Choice (A) contradicts the fact that the guarantee is for one year (twelve months), not fourteen months. Choice (C) contradicts the fact that the guarantee does not apply to damage from accident. Choice (D) refers to a situation in which no replacement would be necessary.

Passage Four

1. **(C)** The passage provides information without subjective commentary. Choices (A), (B), and (D) would provide more subjective commentary and opinion.

2. **(B)** "On the date that your telephone is to be installed, a responsible person, such as an apartment manager, must be at home to unlock the door for the serviceman." Choice (A) refers to the person in the telephone store who helps customers select a telephone, not to the person who installs it. Choice (C) refers to the person who may unlock an apartment for the serviceman. Choice (D) refers to the person whose name must be given to the sales representative as a reference.

3. **(C)** Choice (A) is mentioned in line 1. Choice (B) is mentioned in lines 3–4. Choice (D) is mentioned in line 5. Choice (C) contradicts the fact that a responsible person must be at home to unlock the door for the serviceman.

4. **(B)** In the context of this passage, *samples* are examples. Choices (A), (C), and (D) are not accepted meanings of the word *samples.*

5. **(D)** "Students on scholarships should provide their [the students'] sponsor's name instead of an employer's name." Choices (A), (B), and (C) would change the meaning of the sentence.

6. **(A)** "A sales representative will be glad to show you samples of the designs and colors [of telephones] available." Choice (B) contradicts the fact that a responsible person, such as an apartment manager, can unlock the door. Choice (C) contradicts the fact that students on scholarship should provide their sponsor's name as a reference. Choice (D) contradicts the fact that the deposit may be paid by Mastercard or Visa.

Passage Five

1. **(B)** "Please use these procedures in order to make a machine withdrawal . . ." Choice (A) contradicts the fact that the withdrawal must be made from an existing account. Choice (C) contradicts the fact that it is necessary to have a card in order to follow the procedure. Choice (D) contradicts the fact that the procedure is for withdrawals only, not for deposits and withdrawals.

2. **(B)** "Remove your card from the slot. The drawer will open with receipt and your cash withdrawal in fifty-dollar packets." Choice (A) refers to what happens after you enter the number. Choice (D) refers to what happens after you enter the amount of withdrawal. Choice (C) is not mentioned and may not be concluded from information in the passage.

3. **(D)** Choice (A) is mentioned in line 4. Choice (B) is mentioned in line 3. Choice (C) is mentioned in line 6. Choice (D) contradicts the fact that you should remove your card from the slot. You must claim your card in person only when the machine retains it.

4. **(C)** In the context of this passage, *a slot* is an opening. Choices (A), (B), and (D) are not accepted meanings of the word *slot*.

5. **(B)** "If you attempt to withdraw more than the limited number of times, your card will be retained in the machine, and you will have to reclaim it [the card] in person at your main branch bank." Choices (A), (C), and (D) would change the meaning of the sentence.

6. **(C)** "Enter the amount of withdrawal, either fifty or one hundred dollars. . . . All customers are limited to two withdrawals in one twenty-four hour period." Choice (A) contradicts the fact that the withdrawals are in fifty-dollar packets. Choice (B) contradicts the fact that the identification numbers are four-, not five-digit numbers. Choice (D) contradicts the fact that withdrawals can be made from your City Bank checking or savings accounts.

Part B—Academic Information

EXERCISE 2: Academic Information

Passage One

1. **(A)** "The legal residence status of all students is determined at the time of their enrollment in State University . . ." Choices (B), (C), and (D) are secondary ideas used to support the main idea, "residency requirements for students."

2. **(B)** "This is true [that in-state residents pay less] because State University is supported by state funds contributed in part by the taxpayers who reside in the state." Choice (A) contradicts the fact that resident aliens may apply for in-state status after twelve months. Choice (C) contradicts the fact that ownership of property in the state will not be acceptable proof for in-state resident status. Choice (D) contradicts the fact that a resident of another state would be correctly classified as out-of-state.

3. **(D)** ". . . tax records . . . will not be acceptable proof [of in-state residence]." Choice (A) is mentioned in line 12. Choice (B) is mentioned in line 13. Choice (C) is mentioned in line 11.

4. **(B)** In the context of this passage, *consecutive* means continuous. Choices (A), (C), and (D) are not accepted meanings of the word *consecutive*.

5. **(A)** ". . . a nonresident minor . . . or adult who establishes legal residence in the state and maintains it [residence] for twelve months may petition for a change of status." Choices (B), (C), and (D) would change the meaning of the sentence.

6. **(A)** Since in-state residents pay one-fifth the tuition of out-of-state residents, it may be concluded that out-of-state residents pay five times the amount that in-state residents pay. None of the other choices—(B), (C), or (D)—compute correctly.

Passage Two

1. **(D)** "To drop a course on the day of open registration. . . . To add a course. . . . To drop or add a course after the second day of classes . . ." Choice (A) refers to the procedure before dropping and adding courses. Choice (B) refers to one kind of change on a class schedule, not to both dropping and adding courses. Choice (C) is not mentioned and may not be concluded from information in the passage.

2. **(C)** "To drop or add a course after the second day of classes . . . take it [a petition] to the instructor of the course . . ." Choice (A) refers to the person who must give permission to add a course after the first fifteen days of each quarter. Choice (B) refers to the person who must give permission to add a course on the day of open registration. Choice (D) refers to the person who must be paid, not to the person who must give permission to add a course.

3. **(D)** Choice (A) is mentioned in line 1. Choice (B) is mentioned in line 2. Choice (C) is mentioned in line 2.

4. **(B)** In the context of this passage, to *drop* means to withdraw from. Choices (A), (C), and (D) are not accepted meanings of the word *drop*.

5. **(C)** ". . . obtain a drop-add petition from your college office, complete it [the petition] and take it to the instructor of the course in question for his or her signature." Choices (A), (B), and (D) would change the meaning of the sentence.

6. **(C)** ". . . take it [the drop-add petition] . . . to your academic advisor . . ." Since students must take petitions to their academic advisors, it must be concluded that they are all assigned one. Choice (A) contradicts the fact that the dean of the college may give permission after the first fifteen days. Choice (B) contradicts the fact that no drops or adds will be permitted after the first fifteen days of each quarter, not semester. Choice (D) contradicts the fact that students must take their petitions from the college office to the registration area in the Student Union.

Passage Three

1. **(A)** Choices (B) and (C) are true but are not a complete summary. Choice (D) refers to the fact that business majors must earn a grade of C or better in business courses in their specialization, not in all courses. The average must be C in all courses.

2. **(B)** "Candidates . . . must earn a minimum grade of C or better in each course in the area of specialization." Choices (A), (C), and (D) are grades below a C.

3. **(B)** Choice (A) is mentioned in line 2. Choice (C) is mentioned in lines 4–5. Choice (D) is mentioned in lines 3–4. The number in Choice (B) refers to the quality points, not to the quarter hours.

4. **(D)** In the context of this passage, a *specialization* is a major field of study. Choices (A), (B), and (C) are not accepted meanings of the word *specialization*.

5. **(C)** "They [students] must earn a C or better in each accounting course." Choices (A), (B), and (D) would change the meaning of the sentence.

6. **(D)** "Candidates for the bachelor of business administration degree must complete 186 quarter hours of course work . . ." Since 186 hours is required to graduate, it must be concluded that a student who had completed 170 hours would be in his or her last year, that is, the senior year. Choices (A), (B), and (C) are the first, second, and third years, respectively.

Passage Four

1. **(B)** A notice provides information without subjective commentary. Choice (A) refers to the notice of an occasion with a time, date, and place mentioned. Choice (C) refers to a series of questions. Choice (D) refers to a form with personal and professional information on it.

2. **(C)** "A change in the federal regulations now requires that every international student admitted to the United States on an F-1 visa be assigned a social security number." Choice (A) contradicts the fact that the number may not be used for off-campus employment purposes. Choice (B) contradicts the fact that if they do not have them [social security numbers], they are asked to depart the country. Choice (D) contradicts the fact that they are granted F-1 visas before they are assigned the social security numbers.

3. **(C)** Choice (A) is mentioned in line 3. Choice (B) is mentioned in line 3. Choice (D) is mentioned in lines 1–2.

4. **(A)** In the context of this passage, *regulations* are rules. Choices (B), (C), and (D) are not accepted meanings of the word *regulations*.

5. **(A)** "The record will be marked to indicate that it [the number] is a nonwork number and may not be used for off-campus employment purposes." Choices (B), (C), and (D) would change the meaning of the sentence.

6. **(B)** "Students who wish to work on campus may do so without notifying INS." Choices (A) and (C) contradict the fact that students may not work off campus. Choice (C) contradicts the fact that students may work on campus.

Passage Five

1. **(B)** "Accreditation is a system for setting national standards of quality in education." Choices (A), (C), and (D) are secondary ideas that are used to develop the main idea, "accreditation."

2. **(D)** "If you are not sure about [the accreditation of] a certain school, don't hesitate to check its reputation with an education officer at the nearest U.S. Embassy." Choice (B) contradicts the fact that the accreditation system is not administered by the government. Choice (C) contradicts the fact that students should make certain that the institution is accredited before registering. Choice (A) is not mentioned and may not be concluded from information in the passage.

3. **(D)** Choice (A) is mentioned in line 10. Choice (B) is mentioned in lines 8–9. Choice (C) is mentioned in lines 6–7. Choice (D) contradicts the fact that the United States is unique in the world because its accreditation system is not administered by the government.

4. **(A)** In the context of this passage, *unique* means unusual. Choices (B), (C), and (D) are not accepted meanings of the word *unique*.

5. **(A)** "If you are not sure about a certain school, don't hesitate to check its [the school's] reputation with an education officer at the nearest U.S. embassy." Choices (B), (C), and (D) would change the meaning of the sentence.

6. **(B)** ". . . a student should make certain that the institution is accredited in order to assure that the school has a recognized standard of . . . financial support." Choice (A) contradicts the fact that other governments or future employers may not recognize a degree earned from a school that has not received accreditation. Choice (C) contradicts the fact that the government does not administer the accreditation system. Choice (D) contradicts the fact that students should make certain that a school is accredited before registering.

EXERCISE 3: Textbooks/Biography

Passage One

1. **(A)** ". . . but he [King] was able to maintain unity and extend Canadian autonomy while acting within a difficult federal system." Choices (B), (C), and (D) are secondary ideas used to support the main idea, "that King made a valuable contribution to Canada."

2. **(D)** ". . . he earned the respect of most Canadians for his political astuteness and . . . his essential Canadianness." Choice (A) contradicts the fact that King was criticized for procrastination. Choice (B) refers to a characteristic of King, but not to a reason that he was admired. The word *frustration* in Choice (C) refers to the result of King's methods, not to his ability to deal with it.

3. **(B)** Choice (A) is mentioned in line 6. Choice (C) is mentioned in line 6. Choice (D) is mentioned in line 5.

4. **(A)** In the context of this passage, *autonomy* is independence. Choices (B), (C), and (D) are not accepted meanings of the word *autonomy*.

5. **(D)** "He served his fellow Canadians in many appointed and elected offices, including among them [the offices] a seat in the parliament, before being elected prime minister in 1921." Choices (A), (B), and (C) would change the meaning of the sentence.

6. **(A)** Since William Lyon Mackenzie King was named for his grandfather and was greatly influenced by him, it may be concluded that he was proud of his family. Choice (B) contradicts the fact that he held the office of prime minister for twenty-one years. Choice (C) contradicts the fact that he graduated from the University of Toronto and studied at both Harvard and Chicago Universities. Choice (D) contradicts the fact that he was often criticized for procrastination.

Passage Two

1. **(C)** "Edwin Hubble was an American astronomer whose research led to discoveries about galaxies and the nature of the universe." Choices (A), (B), and (D) are secondary ideas used to support the main idea, "Edwin Hubble's research."

2. **(B)** "Hubble's Constant, a standard relationship between a galaxy's distance from the earth and its speed of recession . . ." Choices (A) and (D) refer to the islands universe theory, not to Hubble's Constant. Choice (C) refers to a phenomenon for which Hubble provided observational evidence.

3. **(D)** Choice (A) is mentioned in line 7. Choice (B) is mentioned in line 6. Choice (C) is mentioned in line 3.

4. **(B)** In the context of this passage, *capability* is capacity. Choices (A), (C), and (D) are not accepted meanings of the word *capability*.

5. **(C)** "His work pushed the one-hundred-inch Mount Wilson telescope beyond its [the telescope's] capability, and provided strong impetus for the construction of an instrument twice its size at Mount Palomar, which Hubble used during his last years of research." Choices (A), (B), and (D) would change the meaning of the sentence.

6. **(C)** Since the last sentence of this passage mentions the size and age of the universe, it may be concluded that the following passage discusses the size and age of the universe. Choice (A) refers to the topic of this passage, not to that of the next passage. Choices (B) and (D) are mentioned briefly, but not at the end of the passage as a topic for the following passage.

Passage Three

1. **(B)** ". . . the first woman to join the Marine Corps was Lucy Brewer. . . . The first woman officially documented in Marine records . . . was Orpha Johnson. . . . By 1985, Gail Reals . . . achieved the grade of Brigadier General. . . ." Choices (A), (C), and (D) are secondary ideas used to support the main idea, "women in the Marine Corps."

2. **(C)** "Gail Reals competed for and achieved the grade of Brigadier General, becoming the first woman to be so promoted." Choice (A) refers to Orpha Johnson. Choice (B) refers to Lucy Brewer. Choice (D) is not mentioned by name and may not be concluded from information in the passage.

3. **(A)** Choice (B) is mentioned in line 10. Choice (C) is mentioned in line 9. Choice (D) is mentioned in line 10. Choice (A) refers to duties performed by men, not by women.

4. **(A)** In the context of this passage, to *enlist* means to join. Choices (B), (C), and (D) are not accepted meanings of the word *enlist*.

5. **(B)** "After working as a civilian clerk at Marine Corps headquarters, she [Orpha Johnson] entered the Marine Corps reserve in 1918." Choices (A), (C), and (D) would change the meaning of the sentence.

6. **(C)** Since the last sentence of this passage mentions the fact that women can be found in every branch and occupation of the United States Marine Corps, it may be concluded that the paragraph following the passage most probably discusses the role of women in today's Marine Corps. Choices (A) and (B) are mentioned earlier, not at the end of the passage as a topic for the following passage. Choice (D) is not mentioned and may not be concluded from information in the passage.

Passage Four

1. **(C)** "Ogden Nash was a poet, storyteller, humorist, and philosopher." Choices (A), (B), and (D) are secondary ideas used to support the main idea, "the life and work of Ogden Nash."

2. **(A)** "After a brief attendance at Harvard University, he became a mail clerk on Wall Street . . ." Choice (B) refers to his promotion after his first job. Choices (C) and (D) refer to later jobs.

3. **(D)** Choice (A) is mentioned in line 1. Choice (B) is mentioned in line 1. Choice (C) is mentioned in lines 11–12.

4. **(C)** In the context of this passage, *leading* means prominent. Choices (A), (B), and (D) are not accepted meanings of the word *leading*.

5. **(B)** "His verses are filled with humor and wry wit as well as the unexpected or improbable rhymes that have come to characterize them [the verses]." Choices (A), (C), and (D) would change the meaning of the sentence.

6. **(D)** Since candy is a traditional gift during courtship, it may be concluded that Nash means liquor promotes romantic feelings faster than candy does. Choices (A), (B), and (C) are not mentioned and may not be concluded from information in the passage.

Passage Five

1. **(D)** "Among his more noteworthy contributions to society are those that bear his name. . . . Few Americans have been left untouched by Andrew Carnegie's generosity." Choices (A), (B), and (C) are secondary ideas used to support the main idea, "the philanthropy of Andrew Carnegie."

2. **(C)** "His contributions of more than five million dollars established 2,500 libraries . . ." Choice (D) refers to the amount of money that Carnegie contributed to the library system, not to the number of libraries that were established. Choices (A) and (B) are not mentioned and may not be concluded from information in the passage.

3. **(C)** Choice (A) is mentioned in line 10. Choice (B) is mentioned in line 11. Choice (D) is mentioned in line 13.

4. **(A)** In the context of this passage, *fortunes* are assets. Choices (B), (C), and (D) are not accepted meanings of the word *fortunes*.

5. **(B)** "Among his more noteworthy contributions to society are those [contributions] that bear his name, including the Carnegie Institute of Pittsburgh which has a library, a museum of fine arts, and a museum of natural history." Choices (A), (C), and (D) would change the meaning of the sentence.

6. **(B)** Since Carnegie used his money for the benefit of society, it may be concluded that he meant that rich people should use their money for the benefit of society. Choices (A), (C), and (D) are not mentioned and may not be concluded from information in the passage.

EXERCISE 4: Textbooks/History and Civics

Passage One

1. **(A)** Choice (B) contradicts the fact that immigration in the twentieth century is also mentioned. Choice (C) contradicts the fact that Asian, African, and Latin American immigration is also mentioned. Choice (D) refers to the many contributions by immigrants to urban and agricultural development cited to support the main idea, "immigration."

2. **(C)** "By 1880, large numbers of central and southern Europeans began to find their way to America." Choice (A) refers to the year when most Americans came from England. Choice (B) refers to the year when many Irish, Dutch, German, Swedish, Scottish, and French settlers came to America. Choice (D) refers to the recent years when many Hungarians, Cubans, Lebanese, Syrians, and West Indians have come.

3. **(D)** Choice (A) is mentioned in line 3. Choice (B) is mentioned in line 2. Choice (C) is mentioned in line 3. The Italian immigration occurred in 1880, not 1800.

4. **(A)** In the context of this passage, a *majority* is the largest number. Choices (B), (C), and (D) are not accepted meanings of the word *majority*.

5. **(C)** "The United States is unique in the world, because, with the notable exception of the Native Americans, all Americans are immigrants or the descendants of them [immigrants]." Choices (A), (B), and (D) would change the meaning of the sentence.

6. **(B)** The account is historical. There is no evidence of the attitudes referred to in Choices (A), (C), and (D).

Passage Two

1. **(C)** "Federal policy toward the Native Americans has a long history of inconsistency, reversal, and failure." Choice (A) contradicts the fact that the policies have been inconsistent. Choice (B) contradicts the fact that today, government policies are unclear. Choice (D) is a secondary idea used to support the main idea, "inconsistent and unclear policies."

2. **(B)** ". . . expulsion of the major Southeastern tribes to . . . what is now Oklahoma . . . which the Cherokee Nation refers to as the 'Trail of Tears' . . ." Choice (A) refers to the Dawes Severalty Act, not to the "Trail of Tears." Choice (C) refers to policies before the "Trail of Tears." Choice (D) refers to policies in the 1950s.

3. **(C)** Choice (A) is mentioned in line 1. Choice (B) is mentioned in line 13. Choice (D) is mentioned in line 19.

4. **(B)** In the context of this passage, *ambivalent* means experiencing contradictory feelings. Choices (A), (C), and (D) are not accepted meanings of the word *ambivalent*.

5. **(A)** "At the same time, the government supported missionary groups in their efforts to build churches, schools, and model farms for those tribes that permitted them [missionary groups] to live in their midst." Choices (B), (C), and (D) would change the meaning of the sentence.

6. **(A)** Since the last sentence of this passage mentions the ambivalence of the Native Americans about the role of the federal government in their affairs, it may be concluded that the paragraph following the passage most probably discusses the Native Americans' point of view regarding government policies today. Choices (B), (C), and (D) are not mentioned and may not be concluded from information in the passage.

Passage Three

1. **(A)** "This was the Dust Bowl." Choices (B), (C), and (D) are secondary ideas used to support the main idea, "the Dust Bowl."

2. **(D)** ". . . settlers fled . . . along Route 66 to California." Choices (A), (B), and (C) refer to the Great Plains, where the homesteaders had their farms, not to where they went when they abandoned them.

3. **(D)** Choice (A) is mentioned in line 2. Choice (B) is mentioned in line 2. Choice (C) is mentioned in lines 8–9.

4. **(C)** In the context of this passage, to *flee* means to run away. *Fled* is the past form of *flee*. Choices (A), (B), and (D) are not accepted meanings of the word *flee*.

5. **(B)** "It [the Dust Bowl] choked cattle and sickened the people who stayed." Choices (A), (C), and (D) would change the meaning of the sentence.

6. **(C)** Since the increased demand for wheat during World War I encouraged farmers to plow and plant even wider areas in the Great Plains, it may be concluded that the Great Plains is a wheat-producing region in the United States. In the context of this passage, the word *buffalo* that appears in Choice (A) refers to a variety of grass, not to the animal. Choices (B) and (D) are not mentioned and may not be concluded from information in the passage.

Passage Four

1. **(C)** ". . . Kennedy spoke directly to the television viewers. . . . Later, Kennedy claimed that the debates were the single most important factor. . . . the debates had to have made the difference." Choice (A) contradicts the fact that television debates are a very powerful tool. Choices (B) and (D) are secondary ideas used to support the main idea, "the effect of Kennedy's style in the debates."

2. **(D)** ". . . Kennedy had gained at least 2 million votes as a result of the televised programs." Choice (A) refers to the percentage of American families who owned a television in 1960. Choice (B) refers to the margin of votes by which Kennedy won. Choice (C) is not mentioned and may not be concluded from information in the passage, although some of the numbers correspond to the date of the debate, 1960.

3. **(B)** Choice (A) is mentioned in line 5. Choice (C) is mentioned in lines 6–7. Choice (D) is mentioned in lines 7–8. Choice (B) contradicts the fact that no provision was made for dialogue between the candidates.

4. **(B)** In the context of this passage, *dynamic* means energetic. Choices (A), (C), and (D) are not accepted meanings of the word *dynamic*.

5. **(C)** "In contrast, Kennedy spoke directly to the television viewers, concentrating on creating a dynamic and appealing image in order to influence them [the viewers]." Choices (A), (B), and (D) would change the meaning of the passage.

6. **(D)** Since the last sentence of this passage mentions later candidates, it may be concluded that the paragraph following the passage most probably discusses television debates by candidates after 1960. Choice (A) refers to a book that analyzed the Kennedy-Nixon debates, not to a topic for the following paragraph. Choices (B) and (C) are not mentioned and may not be concluded from information in the passage.

Passage Five

1. **(C)** "Canada is a constitutional monarchy with a parliamentary system of government modeled after that of Great Britain." Choices (A), (B), and (D) are secondary ideas used to support the main idea, "the Canadian system of government."

2. **(B)** "When a government loses its majority support in a general election, a change of government occurs." Choices (A), (C), and (D) contradict the fact that the government is elected by the voters. In Choice (A), the governor general represents the queen but he does not appoint the government. In Choice (C) the prime minister chooses a cabinet, not a government. In Choice (D), the House of Commons holds a great deal of power in the government, but does not choose the government.

3. **(B)** Choice (A) is mentioned in lines 3–4. Choice (C) is mentioned in line 3. Choice (D) is mentioned in line 10. Choice (B) contradicts the fact that the actual head of government is the prime minister.

4. **(D)** In the context of this passage, *dissolved* means dismissed. Choices (A), (B), and (C) are not accepted meanings of the word *dissolved*.

5. **(B)** "The system is referred to as responsible government, which means that the cabinet members sit in parliament and are directly responsible to it [parliament], holding power only as long as a majority of the House of Commons shows confidence by voting with them." Choices (A), (C), and (D) would change the meaning of the sentence.

6. **(D)** Since a change of government occurs when a government loses its majority support in a general election, it may be concluded that the voters in Canada determine when a change of government should occur. Choice (A) contradicts the fact that the prime minister chooses the cabinet. Choice (C) contradicts the fact that the members of the House of Commons are elected directly by voters in general elections. Choice (B) is not mentioned and may not be concluded from information in the passage.

Exercise 5: Textbooks/Social Sciences

Passage One

1. **(C)** "Although behavioral psychologists use many different kinds of equipment in operant conditioning experiments, one device that is frequently employed is the Skinner Box." Choices (A), (B), and (D) are secondary ideas used to support the main idea, "the Skinner Box."

2. **(B)** ". . . the animal [rat] learned that it could get food by pressing the bar." Choice (A) refers to the rat's activity before obtaining food. Choice (D) refers to the rat's activity after obtaining food. Choice (C) is not mentioned and may not be concluded from information in the passage.

3. **(D)** Choice (A) is mentioned in line 4. Choice (B) is mentioned in line 4. Choice (C) is mentioned in lines 6–7.

4. **(C)** In the context of this passage, to *deprive* means to deny. Choices (A), (B), and (D) are not accepted meanings of the word *deprive*.

5. **(B)** "The Skinner Box is a small, empty box except for a bar with a cup underneath it [the bar]." Choices (A), (C), and (D) would change the meaning of the sentence.

6. **(C)** "The food stimulus reinforced the bar pressing response." Choice (A) contradicts the fact that behavioral psychologists use many different kinds of equipment. Choice (B) contradicts the fact that behavioral psychologists use (present tense) many different kinds of equipment in operant conditioning experiments. Choice (D) refers to one specific experiment with a hungry rat, not to operant conditioning in general.

Passage Two

1. **(A)** "This population trend has been referred to as the graying of America." Choices (B), (C), and (D) are secondary ideas used to support the main idea, "the graying of America."

2. **(C)** "Among females, the life span is projected to increase from the current 78.3 years . . ." Choice (A) refers to the average male life span now. Choice (B) refers to the average male life span in 2005. Choice (D) refers to the average female life span in 2005, not now.

3. **(D)** Choice (A) is mentioned in lines 6–7. Choice (B) is mentioned in lines 13–14. Choice (C) is mentioned in line 9.

4. **(A)** In the context of this passage, a *pool* is a group of people. Choices (B), (C), and (D) are not accepted meanings of the word *pool*.

5. **(C)** "Because the birth rates among this specialized population were very high, their [young adults'] children, now among the elderly, are a significant segment of the older population." Choices (A), (B), and (D) would change the meaning of the sentence.

6. **(A)** Since older people tend to get gray hair, it may be concluded that the word *gray* is a reference to the hair color of older people. Choices (B), (C), and (D) are not mentioned and may not be concluded from information in the passage.

Passage Three

1. **(C)** "Whether one is awake or asleep, the brain emits electrical waves. During wakefulness . . . small waves. With . . . sleep, the waves become larger. . . ." Choices (A), (B), and (D) are secondary ideas used to support the main idea, "two types of sleep."

2. **(B)** "In a period of eight hours, most sleepers experience from three to five instances of REM sleep." Choice (A) refers to the number of hours, not the times per night. Choice (C) refers to the number of minutes that each instance of REM sleep lasts. Choice (D) refers to the number of minutes interval between instances of REM sleep.

3. **(A)** Choice (B) is mentioned in line 6. Choice (C) is mentioned in line 7. Choice (D) is mentioned in line 8. Choice (A) refers to slow-wave sleep, not to REM sleep.

4. **(B)** In the context of this passage, *vague* means indefinite. Choices (A), (C), and (D) are not accepted meanings of the word *vague*.

5. **(C)** "Sleep is essential because it [sleep] regenerates the brain and the nervous system." Choices (A), (B), and (D) would change the meaning of the sentence.

6. **(C)** Since REM sleep is important for mental activity, it may be concluded that students who are writing term papers need REM sleep to restore mental functioning. Choice (A) contradicts the fact that slow-wave sleep is helpful in restoring muscle control, not mental activity. Choice (B) contradicts the fact that one kind of sleep will not compensate for the lack of another kind of sleep. Choice (D) is not mentioned and may not be concluded from information in the passage.

Passage Four

1. **(A)** "Although the stated goal of most prison systems . . . is to rehabilitate the inmates . . . the systems themselves do not support such a result. . . . If prisons are . . . to achieve the goal . . . then the prisons themselves will have to change." Choice (D) contradicts the fact that the goal is rehabilitation and reintegration. Choices (B) and (C) are secondary ideas used to support the main idea, "that prisons must be restructured."

2. **(B)** ". . . only one-third of the inmates have vocational training opportunities or work release options." Choice (D) refers to the percentage rate for rearrest. Choices (A) and (C) are not mentioned and may not be concluded from information in the passage.

3. **(A)** Choice (B) is mentioned in line 10. Choice (C) is mentioned in lines 12–13. Choice (D) is mentioned in line 11.

4. **(B)** In the context of this passage, *recidivism* refers to people who return to a former activity, in this case to criminal activity that leads to prison after release. Choices (A), (C), and (D) are not accepted meanings of the word *recidivism*.

5. **(B)** "Although the stated goal of most prison systems, on both federal and state levels, is to rehabilitate the inmates and reintegrate them [the inmates] into society, the systems themselves do not support such a result." Choices (A), (C), and (D) would change the meaning of the sentence.

6. **(C)** Since the last sentence of this passage mentions models for collaborative efforts between the criminal justice system and the community, it may be concluded that the paragraph following the passage most probably discusses examples of models for community collaboration. Choices (A) and (D) have already been discussed earlier in the passage. Choice (B) is not mentioned and may not be concluded from information in the passage.

Passage Five

1. **(C)** "Standard usage. . . . Colloquialisms. . . . Slang. . . ." Choices (A), (B), and (D) are secondary ideas used to support the main idea, "different types of usage."

2. **(D)** "Slang . . . refers to words and expressions understood by a large number of speakers but not accepted as good formal usage by the majority." Choice (A) refers to standard usage. Choice (B) contradicts the fact that colloquial expressions and even slang may be found in standard dictionaries. Choice (C) is not mentioned and may not be concluded from information in the passage.

3. **(D)** Choice (A) is mentioned in lines 15–16. Choice (B) is mentioned in lines 12–13. Choice (C) is mentioned in lines 16–17.

4. **(A)** In the context of this passage, *appropriate* means suitable. Choices (B), (C), and (D) are not accepted meanings of the word *appropriate*.

5. **(B)** "In some cases, the majority never accepts certain slang phrases, but nevertheless retains them [slang phrases] in their collective memories." Choices (A), (C), and (D) would change the meaning of the sentence.

6. **(C)** Since the author states without judgment that most speakers of English will select and use standard, colloquial, and slang expressions in appropriate situations, it may be concluded that the author approves of slang and colloquial speech in appropriate situations. Choices (A), (B), and (D) contradict the fact that the author points out there are appropriate situations for slang and colloquial speech.

EXERCISE 6: Textbooks/Literature

Passage One

1. **(C)** ". . . his work chronicled his life." Choice (A) contradicts the fact that the first six lines of the passage describe his life before he began writing. Choice (B) contradicts the fact that the last twelve lines of the passage describe his work. Choice (D) refers to the fact that his characters were portraits of himself and his family, not to the theme of the passage.

2. **(C)** "The play [*Beyond the Horizon*] won the Pulitzer prize for the best play of the year. O'Neill was to be awarded the prize again in 1922, 1928, and 1957." Choice (A) refers to the number of times that O'Neill won the Nobel, not the Pulitzer prize. Choice (B) refers to the number of times that O'Neill won the Pulitzer prize in addition to the first time. Choice (D) refers to the total number of times that O'Neill was awarded the Pulitzer and Nobel prizes.

3. **(A)** Choice (B) is mentioned in line 6. Choice (C) is mentioned in line 15. Choice (D) is mentioned in line 15.

4. **(B)** In the context of this passage, *briefly* means for a short time. Choices (A), (C), and (D) are not accepted meanings of the word *briefly*.

5. **(B)** "It [the one-act *Bound East for Cardiff*] was produced on Cape Cod by the Provincetown Players, an experimental theater group that was later to settle the famous Greenwich Village theater district in New York." Choices (A), (C), and (D) would change the meaning of the sentence.

6. **(C)** ". . . several themes emerge, including the ambivalence of family relationships, the struggle between the sexes, the conflict between spiritual and material desires, and the vision of modern man as a victim." Choice (A) contradicts the fact that the themes mentioned were controversial. Choice (B) contradicts the fact that most of the characters were portraits of himself and his family. Choice (D) contradicts the fact that O'Neill's plays won so many awards.

Passage Two

1. **(D)** "At the age of sixty-five, Laura Ingalls Wilder began writing a series of novels . . ." Choices (A), (B), and (C) are secondary ideas used to support the main idea, "Wilder's career."

2. **(D)** "At the age of sixty-five, Laura Ingalls Wilder began writing a series of novels . . ." Choices (A), (B), and (C) contradict the fact that Wilder began writing at age sixty-five.

3. **(B)** Choice (A) is mentioned in line 3. Choice (C) is mentioned in line 8. Choice (D) is mentioned in line 9. Choice (B) contradicts the fact that she never graduated.

4. **(C)** In the context of this passage, *sporadically* means at irregular intervals. Choices (A), (B), and (D) are not accepted meanings of the word *sporadically*.

5. **(C)** Written from the perspective of a child, they [more books] have remained popular with young readers from many nations." Choices (A), (B), and (D) would change the meaning of the sentence.

6. **(D)** Since the Wilder books have been translated into fourteen languages, it may be concluded that the books have universal appeal. Choice (A) contradicts the fact that the television series was produced after Wilder's death. Choice (C) contradicts the fact that Wilder's daughter was a nationally known journalist. Choice (B) is not mentioned and may not be concluded from information in the passage.

Passage Three

1. **(B)** "Edgar Allan Poe is today regarded as one of the premier authors of horror stories . . ." Choices (A), (C), and (D) are secondary ideas used to support the main idea, "the work of Edgar Allan Poe."

2. **(B)** "'The Gold Bug' was published, selling 300,000 copies . . ." Choices (A) and (D) refer to two of Poe's best-known stories, but not to tales that sold 300,000 copies. Choice (C) refers to a popular poem.

3. **(C)** Choice (A) is mentioned in line 9. Choice (B) is mentioned in line 9. Choice (D) is mentioned in line 10. Choice (C) contradicts the fact that the narrator is despondent.

4. **(D)** In the context of this passage, *recognition* means appreciation. Choices (A), (B), and (C) are not accepted meanings of the word *recognition*.

5. **(A)** "Twenty-five of his greatest stories were published in a collection called *Tales of the Grotesque and Arabesque* which appeared in 1840, but at the time little notice was taken of it [the collection]." Choices (B), (C), and (D) would change the meaning of the sentence.

6. **(B)** Since Poe received almost no money for his stories while he lived, it may be concluded that he lived in poverty. Choice (A) refers to the theme of a poem, not to Poe's life. Choices (C) and (D) are not mentioned and may not be concluded from information in the passage.

Passage Four

1. **(B)** ". . . the Western genre was established." Choices (A), (C), and (D) are secondary ideas used to support the main idea, "the Western genre."

2. **(B)** "With the appearance in 1902 of *The Virginian* by Owen Wister, the western genre was established." Choice (A) refers to the novels that came earlier. Choices (C) and (D) refer to a novel that influenced the development of the genre, but appeared after the genre had been established.

3. **(C)** Choice (A) is mentioned in line 16. Choice (B) is mentioned in line 15. Choice (D) is mentioned in lines 15–16.

4. **(C)** In the context of this passage, *stock* describes things that recur so often that they are recognizable. Choices (A), (B), and (D) are not accepted meanings of the word *stock*.

5. **(D)** "Told simply, and less dramatically, it [*The Log*] was nonetheless popular and influential in the development of the new genre." Choices (A), (B), and (C) would change the meaning of the sentence.

6. **(B)** Since the last paragraph of this passage mentions easterners who wrote novels about the west, it may be concluded that the theme will continue. Choice (C) refers to a theme of the novels, not to a topic for the next passage. Choices (A) and (D) are not mentioned and may not be concluded from information in the passage.

Passage Five

1. **(B)** "In spite of its apparent simplicity, however, there are several levels to appreciate in reading *The Pearl*." Choices (A), (C), and (D) are secondary ideas used to support the main idea, that "there are many levels to appreciate in *The Pearl*."

2. **(A)** ". . . this latitude for personal interpretation within the universal themes gives *The Pearl* such enduring appeal." Choices (B), (C), and (D) are all true, but they do not explain why *The Pearl* has remained so popular.

3. **(D)** Choice (A) is mentioned in lines 10–11. Choice (B) is mentioned in lines 5–6. Choice (C) is mentioned in line 16. Choice (D) contradicts the fact that the legend had already been created when Steinbeck retold it.

4. **(B)** In the context of this passage, *authentic* means realistic. Choices (A), (C), and (D) are not accepted meanings of the word *authentic*.

5. **(A)** "'If this story is a parable, perhaps everyone takes his own meaning from it [the parable] and reads his own life into it.'" Choices (B), (C), and (D) would change the meaning of the sentence.

6. **(D)** Since the author states that latitude for personal interpretation gives *The Pearl* enduring appeal, it may be concluded that the author feels that reading *The Pearl* is a personal experience. Choice (B) contradicts the fact that the author encourages personal interpretation. Choice (C) contradicts the fact that the author judges the work to have universal appeal. Choice (A) is not mentioned and may not be concluded from information in the passage.

EXERCISE 7: Textbooks/Arts and Entertainment

Passage One

1. **(C)** "The practice of signing and numbering individual prints was introduced by James Abbott McNeill Whistler . . ." Choices (A) and (B) are secondary ideas used to support the main idea, "the practice of signing prints." Choice (D) is not mentioned and may not be concluded from information in the passage.

2. **(C)** "As soon as Whistler and Haden began signing and numbering their prints, their work began to increase in value." Choice (A) is not mentioned as a reason why Whistler's work was more valuable. Choice (B) refers to Whistler's best-known work, but not to the reason that his work increased in value. Choice (D) refers to the prints that were signed along with those of Whistler.

3. **(C)** Choice (A) is mentioned in line 6. Choice (B) is mentioned in line 6. Choice (D) is mentioned in lines 4–5. Choice (C) is true, but it is not a reason why a collector prefers a signed print.

4. **(A)** In the context of this passage, to *speculate* means to guess. Choices (B), (C), and (D) are not accepted meanings of the word *speculate*.

5. **(D)** "Wherever the artist elects to sign it [a print], a signed print is still valued above an unsigned one, even in the same edition." Choices (A), (B), and (C) would change the meaning of the sentence.

6. **(B)** Since Whistler's brother-in-law speculated that collectors would find prints more attractive if there were only a limited number of copies produced and an artist could guarantee and personalize each print, it may be concluded that artists number their prints to guarantee a limited edition. Choice (C) contradicts the fact that there are a limited number. Choice (D) contradicts the fact that the placement of the signature and the number is a matter of personal choice. Choice (A) is not mentioned and may not be concluded from information in the passage.

Passage Two

1. **(A)** "Jazz originated in the southern United States after the Civil War." Choices (B), (C), and (D) are secondary ideas used to support the main idea, "the history of jazz."

2. **(D)** "Jazz originated in the southern United States . . ." Choice (B) refers to one of the origins of jazz, not to where jazz was first heard. Choices (A) and (C) are not mentioned and may not be concluded from information in the passage.

3. **(B)** Choice (A) is mentioned in lines 10–11. Choice (C) is mentioned in lines 7–8. Choice (D) is mentioned in line 4. Choice (B) contradicts the fact that jazz does not exist in the form of printed scores.

4. **(A)** In the context of this passage, a *blend* is a mixture. Choices (B), (C), and (D) are not accepted meanings of the word *blend*.

5. **(D)** "The term jazz itself is of obscure, and possibly nonmusical origin, but it [the term] was first used to describe this particular kind of musical expression in about 1915." Choices (A), (B), and (C) would change the meaning of the sentence.

6. **(B)** Since the last sentence of this passage mentions contemporary artists, it may be concluded that the paragraph following the passage most probably discusses modern jazz musicians. Choices (A), (C), and (D) have already been discussed earlier in the passage.

Passage Three

1. **(A)** "Alfred Hitchcock's precut scripts are legendary. More than any other director, Hitchcock insisted on working from precise and detailed plans." Choice (C) contradicts the fact that the author is involved in praising, not criticizing Hitchcock. Choices (B) and (D) are secondary ideas used to support the main idea, "Hitchcock's directing style."

2. **(D)** ". . . storyboarding, a series of framed drawings of his shots . . ." Choices (A), (B), and (C) are mentioned but are not referred to by name in the passage.

3. **(A)** Choice (B) is mentioned in lines 3–4. Choice (C) is mentioned in lines 6–7. Choice (D) is mentioned in line 8. Choice (A) contradicts the fact that Hitchcock was less interested in the story than in the telling of it.

4. **(C)** In the context of this passage, *juxtaposition* is the close placement of objects or activities that contrast. Choices (A), (B), and (D) are not accepted meanings of the word *juxtaposition*.

5. **(C)** "By the time he had finished such a detailed plan, Hitchcock knew the script so well that he rarely had to refer to it [the script]." Choices (A), (B), and (D) would change the meaning of the sentence.

6. **(B)** Since the last sentence of this passage mentions sequences that provide the viewer with a juxtaposition of contradictory sensations, it may be concluded that the paragraph following the passage most probably discusses examples of scenes in Hitchcock films that elicited contradictory emotions. Choice (C) has already been discussed earlier in the passage. Choices (A) and (D) are not mentioned and may not be concluded from information in the passage.

Passage Four

1. **(A)** "Chiefly through the efforts of Steiglitz, modern photography [the Photo-Secession Movement] had seceded from painting, and had emerged as a legitimate art form." Choices (B), (C), and (D) are secondary ideas used to support the main idea, "The Photo-Secession Movement."

2. **(B)** ". . . they [earlier photographs] were cloudy. . . . In contrast, the straightforward photographers produced images that were sharp and clear." Choices (C) and (D) refer to modern, not earlier photographs. Choice (A) is not mentioned and may not be concluded from information in the passage.

3. **(D)** Choice (A) is mentioned in line 12. Choice (B) is mentioned in lines 14–15. Choice (C) is mentioned in lines 6–7. Choice (D) refers to the Aesthetic Movement, not to the Photo-Secession Movement.

4. **(D)** In the context of this passage, a *defect* is an imperfection. Choices (A), (B), and (C) are not accepted meanings of the word *defect*.

5. **(B)** "Since they [aesthetic prints] were cloudy because of the gum bichromate plate that allowed for manual intervention, the aesthetic prints were easily distinguished from the more modern prints, which came to be called straightforward photographs." Choices (A), (C), and (D) would change the meaning of the sentence.

6. **(D)** Since the author credits Steiglitz with the establishment of modern photography and the publication of one of the most beautiful journals ever produced, it may be concluded that the author admired Alfred Steiglitz. Choices (B) and (C) contradict the fact that the author praises Steiglitz for his work. Choice (A) is not mentioned and may not be concluded from information in the passage.

Passage Five

1. **(B)** "Audubon enjoys a unique place in American art." Choices (A), (C), and (D) are secondary ideas used to support the main idea, "the art of John James Audubon."

2. **(B)** "His reputation, however, rests on the original watercolors of the birds series . . ." Choices (A), (C), and (D) refer to work by Audubon, but not to his best-known work.

3. **(D)** Choice (A) is mentioned in line 16. Choice (B) is mentioned in lines 11. Choice (C) is mentioned in line 16. Choice (D) contradicts the fact that the work was sold by subscription and plates may be purchased today through galleries and art dealers.

4. **(C)** In the context of this passage, *specialized* means for a particular purpose. Choices (A), (B), and (D) are not accepted meanings of the word *specialized*.

5. **(D)** "All of them [the plates] were well-received upon publication and remain popular today, but the 'Wild Turkey Cock' is perhaps his most requested plate." Choices (A), (B), and (C) would change the meaning of the sentence.

6. **(D)** Since Audubon made oil paintings to raise funds for his publications of *Birds of America,* it may be concluded that the project was financed by Audubon himself. Choices (A), (B), and (C) contradict the fact that Audubon sold the series by subscription and raised funds for the publications.

EXERCISE 8: Textbooks/Popular Culture

Passage One

1. **(A)** "Independence Day in the United States is observed annually on the Fourth of July. For most communities throughout the nation, the traditional celebration includes . . ." Choice (D) is a secondary idea used to support the main idea, "traditional celebrations for the Fourth of July." Choices (B) and (C) are not mentioned and may not be concluded from information in the passage.

2. **(D)** "In Ontario, California, the townspeople combine the traditional with the unusual by setting up . . . 'the biggest picnic table in the world' for the two-mile parade." Choice (A) refers to the celebration in Flagstaff, Arizona, not to that in Ontario, Canada. Choice (B) refers to the event in Daytona, Florida. Choice (C) refers to the event in Bristol, Rhode Island.

3. **(C)** Choice (A) is mentioned in line 2. Choice (B) is mentioned in line 7. Choice (D) is mentioned in line 3 Choice (C) is true, but is not mentioned and may not be concluded from information in the passage.

4. **(D)** In the context of this passage, *huge* means large. Choices (A), (B), and (C) are not accepted meanings of the word *huge*.

5. **(B)** "Lititz, Pennsylvania congregates in the Lititz Springs Park to light thousands of candles and arrange them [the candles] in various shapes and images." Choices (A), (C), and (D) would change the meaning of the sentence.

6. **(B)** Since examples of various kinds of celebrations are mentioned in the passage, it may be concluded that towns in the United States celebrate July Fourth in different ways because of their regional customs. Choice (D) contradicts the fact that Daytona, Florida, is a large city. Choices (A) and (C) are not mentioned and may not be concluded from information in the passage.

Passage Two

1. **(D)** "In the United States, the kinds of collectibles currently popular range from traditional objects . . . to more recent items of interest . . ." Choices (A) and (C) are secondary ideas used to support the main idea, "a variety of collectibles." Choice (B) is not mentioned and may not be concluded from information in the passage.

2. **(D)** ". . . relatively new kinds of collectibles may actually appreciate faster as short-term investments, but may not hold their value as long-term investments." Choice (A) contradicts the fact that traditional collectibles, not newer ones, hold their value. Choice (B) contradicts the fact that newer collectibles, not traditional ones, appreciate faster initially. Choice (C) refers to newer collectibles, not all collectibles.

3. **(D)** Choice (A) is mentioned in line 12. Choice (B) is mentioned in line 12. Choice (C) is mentioned in line 13. Choice (D) refers to traditional collectibles, not new types of collectibles.

4. **(B)** In the context of this passage, *stable* means reliable. Choices (A), (C), and (D) are not accepted meanings of the word *stable*.

5. **(B)** "Especially during cycles of high inflation, investors try to purchase tangibles that will at least retain their [the tangibles'] current market values." Choices (A), (C), and (D) would change the meaning of the sentence.

6. **(A)** Since the last sentence of this passage mentions collectors' competing for collectibles that may be difficult to locate, it may be concluded that the following passage most probably discusses how collectors locate and purchase collectibles. Choice (B) contradicts the fact that some collectibles have demonstrated their value as investments. Choices (C) and (D) are not mentioned and may not be concluded from information in the passage.

Passage Three

1. **(A)** "Although square dancing is usually considered a typically American form of dance, its origin can be traced . . ." Choices (B), (C), and (D) are secondary ideas used to support the main idea, "the history of square dancing in the United States."

2. **(C)** ". . . its origin can be traced to earlier European folk dances." Choices (A), (B), and (D) refer to elements in the development of square dancing, but not to the origin of modern square dancing.

3. **(D)** Choice (A) is mentioned in line 10. Choice (B) is mentioned in lines 8–9. Choice (C) is mentioned in lines 10–11. Choice (D) refers to eastern, not western, square dancing.

4. **(D)** In the context of this passage, *spontaneous* means impulsive. Choices (A), (B), and (C) are not accepted meanings of the word *spontaneous*.

5. **(C)** "Western dance was also influenced by the dances already found in the region, especially those [dances] of Spain and Mexico." Choices (A), (B), and (D) would change the meaning of the sentence.

6. **(A)** Since the last paragraph of this passage mentions listening to a caller who cues the steps, it may be concluded that the paragraph following the passage most probably discusses types of cues for square dance steps. Choices (B), (C), and (D) are not mentioned and may not be concluded from information in the passage.

Passage Four

1. **(B)** "Although he created the game of basketball . . ." Choices (A), (C), and (D) are secondary ideas used to support the main idea, "the development of basketball."

2. **(D)** ". . . basketball was introduced as a demonstration sport in the 1904 Olympic Games . . ." Choice (A) refers to the date that Naismith organized the first basketball game, not to its introduction in the Olympics. Choice (C) refers to the date that five players became standard. Choice (B) is not mentioned and may not be concluded from information in the passage.

3. **(B)** Choice (A) is mentioned in line 11. Choice (C) is mentioned in line 10. Choice (D) is mentioned in line 12. Choice (B) contradicts the fact that running with the ball was a violation.

4. **(A)** In the context of this passage, to *balk* means to resist. Choices (B), (C), and (D) are not accepted meanings of the word *balk*.

5. **(C)** "First he attempted to adapt outdoor games such as soccer and rugby to indoor play, but he soon found them [games] unsuitable for confined areas." Choices (A), (B), and (D) would change the meaning of the sentence.

6. **(C)** Since someone had to climb a ladder to retrieve the ball every time a goal was made, it may be concluded that the original baskets did not have a hole in the bottom. Choice (A) contradicts the fact that someone had to climb a ladder to retrieve the ball. Choice (B) contradicts the fact that a metal hoop was introduced in 1906. Choice (D) contradicts the fact that the baskets were hung at either side of the gymnasium.

Passage Five

1. **(A)** "Mickey Mouse was not Walt Disney's first successful cartoon creation, but he is certainly his most famous one." Choices (B), (C), and (D) are secondary ideas used to support the main idea, "the image of Mickey Mouse."

2. **(B)** "In the third short cartoon, *Steamboat Willie,* Mickey was whistling and singing through the miracle of the modern sound track." Choice (C) contradicts the fact that Minnie was a co-star in the first cartoon, *Plane Crazy.* Choices (A) and (D) are not mentioned and may not be concluded from information in the passage.

3. **(D)** "Choice (A) is mentioned in line 5. Choice (B) is mentioned in line 3. Choice (C) is mentioned in line 5. Choice (D) contradicts the fact that the gloves were added later.

4. **(B)** In the context of this passage, *pervasive* means widespread. Choices (A), (C), and (D) are not accepted meanings of the word *pervasive.*

5. **(A)** "Although he has received a few minor changes throughout his lifetime, most notably the addition of white gloves and the rounder forms of a more childish body, he has remained true to his nature since those [cartoons] first cartoons." Choices (B), (C), and (D) would change the meaning of the sentence.

6. **(B)** Since the last sentence of this passage mentions one image in popular culture, it may be concluded that the paragraph following the passage most probably discusses other images in popular culture. Choices (A) and (D) are referred to only as they relate to the Mickey Mouse image. Choice (C) is not mentioned and may not be concluded from information in the passage.

EXERCISE 9: Textbooks/Business

Passage One

1. **(A)** "Although the composition and role of the board of directors of a company will vary . . . a few generalizations may be made." Choice (B) refers to the fact that the board of directors and the board of trustees of a college follow the same administrative procedure, not to the main idea in the passage. Choice (C) refers to the fact that the procedure used by the board of directors is similar to the parliamentary system, not to the main idea. Choice (D) refers to the group who must maintain the confidence of the board of directors.

2. **(A)** "... as long as the top management maintains the confidence of the board of directors, the directors will not actively intervene to dictate specific policies." Choice (C) contradicts the fact that the directors will not actively intervene. Choice (D) refers to the membership of the board of directors, not to those who formulate policy. Choice (B) is not mentioned and may not be concluded from information in the passage.

3. **(C)** Choice (A) is mentioned in lines 7–9. Choice (B) is mentioned in line 8. Choice (D) is mentioned in line 9.

4. **(C)** In the context of this passage, *prominent* means important. Choices (A), (B), and (D) are not accepted meanings of the word *prominent*.

5. **(B)** "Others [other directors] are usually chosen from among retired executives of the organization for their specialized knowledge of the companies." Choices (A), (C), and (D) would change the meaning of the sentence.

6. **(C)** "... customarily some directors are prominent men and women.... Others are usually chosen from among retired executives of the organization...." Choice (A) contradicts the fact that some directors are chosen from retired executives of the organization [City Bank]. Choices (B) and (D) contradict the fact that some directors are prominent men and women.

Passage Two

1. **(C)** "There are four basic types of competition in business that form a continuum ..." Choices (A) and (B) are secondary ideas used to support the main idea, "the competition continuum." Choice (D) is not mentioned and may not be concluded from information in the passage.

2. **(D)** "The classic example of monopolistic competition is coffee and tea." Choice (A) is an example of pure competition, not monopolistic competition. Choice (B) is an example of a monopoly, not monopolistic competition. Choice (C) is an example of an oligopoly.

3. **(A)** Choice (B) is mentioned in line 17. Choice (C) is mentioned in line 16. Choice (D) is mentioned in line 15. Choice (A) refers to monopolistic competition, not to monopoly.

4. **(A)** In the context of this passage, to *tolerate* means to permit. Choices (B), (C), and (D) are not accepted meanings of the word *tolerate*.

5. **(A)** "In oligopoly, serious competition is not considered desirable because it [competition] would result in reduced revenue for every company in the group." Choices (B), (C), and (D) would change the meaning of the sentence.

6. **(A)** Since the purpose of the passage is to teach the differences among the basic types of competition in business, it may be concluded that the passage was first printed in a business textbook. It is not as probable that an expository passage of this kind would be printed in any of the other choices—(B), (C), or (D).

Passage Three

1. **(C)** "Telecommuting is ... computer communication.... there are ... 8.7 million telecommuters.... active resistance on the part of many managers.... employees ... are reluctant...." Choices (A) and (B) are secondary ideas used to support the main idea, "an overview of telecommuting." Choice (D) contradicts the fact that there are 8.7 million telecommuters.

2. **(B)** "A recent survey in *USA Today* estimates that there are approximately 8.7 million telecommuters." Choice (A) contradicts the fact that the trend is not as significant as was predicted in *Business Week*. Choice (C) contradicts the fact that numbers are rising annually. Choice (D) contradicts the fact that the number was reported in *USA Today*.

3. **(B)** Choice (A) is mentioned in line 15. Choice (C) is mentioned in line 14. Choice (D) is mentioned in lines 16–17. Choice (B) refers to a concern of managers, not telecommuters.

4. **(C)** In the context of this passage, *resistance* is opposition. Choices (A), (B), and (D) are not accepted meanings of the word *resistance*.

5. **(A)** "These executives claim that supervising the telecommuters in a large work force scattered across the country would be too difficult, or, at least, systems for managing them [the telecommuters] are not yet developed, thereby complicating the manager's responsibilities." Choices (B), (C), and (D) would change the meaning of the sentence.

6. **(D)** Since the passage is written from an objective point of view, it may be concluded that the author is a reporter. Choices (A), (B), and (C) would probably have more subjective points of view.

Passage Four

1. **(C)** "Although Henry Ford's name is closely associated with the concept of mass production, he should receive equal credit for introducing labor practices . . ." Choice (A) contradicts the fact that Ford's name is closely associated with mass production. Choices (B) and (D) are secondary ideas used to support the main idea, "to credit Henry Ford with industrial reforms."

2. **(B)** ". . . the work day was reduced to eight hours . . ." Choice (A) refers to the number of shifts, not to the hours per shift. Choices (C) and (D) refer to the number of hours in the average work day at the time, not to the number that Ford's employees worked.

3. **(C)** Choice (A) is mentioned in line 10. Choice (B) is mentioned in lines 7–8. Choice (D) is mentioned in line 6. Choice (C) contradicts the fact that Ford tried to discourage the growth of labor unions.

4. **(A)** In the context of this passage, an *innovation* is an original idea or change. Choices (B), (C), and (D) are not accepted meanings of the word *innovation*.

5. **(B)** "Although Henry Ford's name is closely associated with the concept of mass production, he should receive equal credit for introducing labor practices as early as 1913 that [labor practices] would be considered advanced even by today's standards." Choices (A), (C), and (D) would change the meaning of the sentence.

6. **(D)** Since the author states that Ford should receive credit for introducing advanced labor practices, it may be concluded that the author commends Ford's philanthropy. Choice (A) contradicts the fact that the author notes that Ford is already associated with mass production. Choice (B) refers to criticism by others, not by the author. Choice (C) is not probable because the author mentions, without criticism, Ford's efforts to discourage labor unions.

Passage Five

1. **(D)** "For Americans to play a more effective role in international business negotiations, they must put forth more effort to improve cross-cultural understanding." Choices (A), (B), and (C) are secondary ideas that are used to support the main idea, "that American negotiators need to learn more about other cultures."

2. **(C)** "Negotiating is the process of communicating back and forth for the purpose of reaching an agreement." Choice (B) refers to the process, not to the purpose of negotiation. Choice (D) refers to an important aspect of international negotiations. Choice (A) is not mentioned and may not be concluded from information in the passage.

3. **(B)** Choice (A) is mentioned in line 9. Choice (C) is mentioned in line 15. Choice (D) is mentioned in line 16. Choice (B) refers to foreign negotiators, not to the American negotiator.

4. **(D)** In the context of this passage, to *undermine* is to make weak, often in secret. Choices (A), (B), and (C) are not accepted meanings of the word *undermine*.

5. **(B)** "The American negotiator's role becomes that [the role] of an impersonal purveyor of information and cash." Choices (A), (C), and (D) would change the meaning of the sentence.

6. **(A)** Since the last sentence of this passage mentions efforts to improve cross-cultural understanding, it may be concluded that the paragraph following the passage most probably discusses ways to increase cross-cultural understanding. Choices (B), (C), and (D) have already been discussed earlier in the passage.

EXERCISE 10: Textbooks/Natural Sciences

Passage One

1. **(B)** Choice (A) contradicts the fact that the Big Bang Model is a popular theory explaining the evolution of the universe. Choices (C) and (D) are secondary ideas used to support the main idea, "the Big Bang theory."

2. **(C)** "Then, at a moment in time that astronomers refer to as T = 0, . . . Matter formed into galaxies with stars and planets." Choices (A), (B), and (D) refer to an estimate of the time when matter and energy compressed into a ball prior to the explosion that formed the galaxies.

3. **(D)** Choice (A) is mentioned in lines 2–3. Choice (B) is mentioned in lines 2–3. Choice (C) is mentioned in line 4. Protons, neutrons, and electrons appeared after, not before, the Big Bang.

4. **(C)** In the context of this passage, *compressed* means reduced. Choices (A), (B), and (D) are not accepted meanings of the word *compressed*.

5. **(A)** "As the energy cooled, most of it [the energy] become matter in the form of protons, neutrons, and electrons." Choices (B), (C), and (D) would change the meaning of the sentence.

6. **(C)** "As the energy cooled, most of it became matter in the form of protons, neutrons, and electrons." Choice (A) contradicts the fact that energy changed into matter. Choice (B) contradicts the fact that matter is in the form of protons, neutrons, and electrons. Choice (D) contradicts the fact that as energy cooled and became matter, the particles continued to expand.

Passage Two

1. **(B)** "American black bears appear in a variety of colors. . . . are the smallest of all American bears. . . . [are] timid, clumsy, and rarely dangerous. . . . feed on leaves, herbs, etc. . . . live alone. . . ." Choices (A), (C), and (D) are secondary ideas that are used to support the main idea, "the characteristics of black bears."

2. **(C)** ". . . their eyesight and hearing are not as good as their sense of smell." Choices (A) and (B) contradict the fact that their eyesight and hearing are not as good. Choice (D) is not mentioned and may not be concluded from information in the passage.

3. **(D)** Choice (A) is mentioned in line 5. Choice (B) is mentioned in line 2. Choice (C) is mentioned in line 8. Choice (D) contradicts the fact that bears do not actually hibernate.

4. **(B)** In the context of this passage, *formidable* means intimidating. Choices (A), (C), and (D) are not accepted meanings of the word *formidable*.

5. **(B)** "Black bears can live as long as thirty years in the wild, and even longer in game preserves set aside for them [black bears]." Choices (A), (C), and (D) would change the meaning of the sentence.

6. **(C)** Since the last sentence of this passage mentions game preserves, it may be concluded that the paragraph following the passage most probably discusses black bears in game preserves. Choice (A) has already been discussed earlier in the passage. Choices (B) and (D) are not mentioned and may not be concluded from information in the passage.

Passage Three

1. **(A)** "Light from a living plant or animal is called bioluminescence. . . ." Choices (B), (C), and (D) are secondary ideas that are used to support the main idea, "bioluminescence."

2. **(B)** ". . . some primitive plants and animals continue to use the light for new functions such as mating or attracting prey." Choices (A) and (D) refer to the original purposes of bioluminescence, not to the reason it has continued in modern plants and animals. Choice (C) refers to incandescence, not to bioluminescence.

3. **(D)** Choice (A) is mentioned in line 5. Choice (B) is mentioned in line 11. Choice (C) is mentioned in line 1. Choice (D) refers to oxygen in the earth's early atmosphere, not to bioluminescence.

4. **(A)** In the context of this passage, *primitive* means very old; at an early stage of development. Choices (B), (C), and (D) are not accepted meanings of the word *primitive*.

5. **(C)** "Light from a living plant or animal is called bioluminescence, or cold light, to distinguish it [bioluminescence] from incandescence, or heat-generating light." Choices (A), (B), and (D) would change the meaning of the sentence.

6. **(D)** Since the last sentence of this passage mentions that some primitive plants and animals continue to use bioluminescence for new functions, it may be concluded that the paragraph following the passage most probably discusses bioluminescence in modern plants and animals. Choices (A), (B) and (C) have already been discussed earlier in the passage.

Passage Four

1. **(A)** "Hydrogen . . . has several properties that make it valuable for many industries." Choices (B), (C), and (D) are secondary ideas that are used to support the main idea, "the industrial uses of hydrogen."

2. **(D)** ". . . hydrogen is used with oxygen for welding torches that produce temperatures as high as 4,000 degrees F and can be used in cutting steel." Choice (A) contradicts the fact that the hydrogen is heated, and the steel is not cooled. Choice (B) contradicts the fact that the hydrogen is heated, not cooled. Choice (C) contradicts the fact that the hydrogen, not the temperature of the steel, is heated.

3. **(D)** Choice (A) is mentioned in line 6. Choice (B) is mentioned in line 14. Choice (C) is mentioned in lines 4–5. Choice (D) contradicts the fact that liquids are changed to semi-solids, not the reverse.

4. **(D)** In the context of this passage, *readily* means easily. Choices (A), (B), and (C) are not accepted meanings of the word *readily*.

5. **(B)** "Hydrogen also serves to prevent metals from tarnishing during heat treatments by removing the oxygen from them [metals]." Choices (A), (C), and (D) would change the meaning of the sentence.

6. **(B)** Since several uses for hydrogen in a number of industries are mentioned in the passage, it may be concluded that hydrogen has many purposes in a variety of industries. Choices (A) and (D) contradict the fact that several industrial purposes are mentioned in the passage. Choice (C) contradicts the fact that hydrogen has several properties that make it valuable for many industries.

Passage Five

1. **(A)** "The magnetosphere consists of the two strong belts of radiation that lie within an area of weaker radiation surrounding most of the earth." Choices (B), (C), and (D) are secondary ideas that are used to support the main idea, "the nature of the magnetosphere."

2. **(A)** ". . . the lower end hovers within a few hundred miles of the earth on the dark side." Choices (B) and (D) refer to the two strong belts of radiation, not to the magnetosphere on the dark side of the earth. Choice (C) refers to the distance on the sunlit side, not on the dark side.

3. **(B)** Choice (A) is mentioned in line 3. Choice (C) is mentioned in line 1. Choice (D) is mentioned in lines 1–2. Choice (B) refers to electrically charged particles that distort the magnetosphere, not to the magnetosphere itself.

4. **(B)** In the context of this passage, *conversely* means on the other hand. Choices (A), (C), and (D) are not accepted meanings of the word *conversely*.

5. **(C)** "The shape of the magnetosphere is determined by the earth's magnetic fields, but it [the shape] is distorted by electrically charged particles that emanate from the sun to the earth." Choices (A), (B), and (D) would change the meaning of the sentence.

6. **(C)** Since the author presents facts without commentary, it may be concluded that the author's point of view is objective. Choices (A), (B), and (D) contradict the fact that the author does not include any subjective comments.

Chapter 6   Test of Written English (TWE)

The following example test would receive a score of 6 on the TWE. It is well organized, it addresses the topic, it includes examples and details, and it has some but not many errors in grammar and vocabulary.

Read and study this example test before you grade the exercises. Use the scoring scale on page 224.

Example Test

TOPIC: Some students in the United States work while they are earning their degrees in college; others receive support from their families. How should a student's education be supported? Argue both sides of the issue and defend your position.

Notes

friends praise initiative
(WORK) — *future employers be impressed*
student satisfaction

friends praise efforts for family
(FAMILY) — *future employers not expect*
every family member benefit
Society

300

Some students in the United States work while they are earning their degrees; others receive support from their families. Both approaches have advantages and disadvantages. In this essay, I will name some of the advantages of each approach, and I will argue in favor family support.

In a society where independence and individual accomplishment are value, a student who earned his degree by working would be greatly admired. Friends would praise him for his initiative and perseverence. Future employers might be impressed by his work record. He might derive greater satisfaction from his personal investment in it.

On the other hand, in a society where cooperation and family dependence are value, a student who received support would be better understood. Friends would praise him for his efforts on behalf of his family. Future employers would not expect a work record from a student. He might feel greater responsibility toward others in his family because the accomplishment was shared. Thus, not one but every family member would assured some opportunity or benefit.

For my part, I must argue in favor of family support. While I study at an American University, my older brother will send me money every month. When I finish my degree and find a good job, I will send my younger sister to a school or university. It may not be a better way, but it is the way that my society rewards.

Reader's Comments

This writing sample is well organized with a good topic sentence and good support statements. It addresses the question, and does not digress from the topic. There is a logical progression of ideas. Excellent language proficiency, as evidenced by a variety of grammatical structures and appropriate vocabulary. There are only a few grammatical errors that have been corrected below:

Line 7   ⟶   in favor of
Line 9   ⟶   are valued
Lines 18–19 ⟶ are valued
Line 28   ⟶   would be assured

Score: 6

Reprinted from *Barron's How to Prepare for the TOEFL*

APPENDIX

TRANSCRIPT FOR LISTENING COMPREHENSION

Script for the tapes: This transcript is for all the Listening Comprehension Practice Exercises in Chapter 3. It includes Exercises 1 to 24, which are available on cassette tapes. (See page 353 for information on ordering cassette tapes.)

Important: Do not read this transcript until after you have finished the Practice Exercises.

Listening Comprehension

Part A—Short Conversations

Directions: In Part A you will hear short conversations between two speakers. At the end of each conversation, a third voice will ask a question about what was said. The question will be spoken just one time. After you hear a conversation and the question about it, read the four possible answers in your test book and decide which one is the best answer to the question you heard. Then, on your answer sheet, find the number of the question and fill in the space that corresponds to the letter of the answer you have chosen.

EXERCISE 1: Direct Information

1. Woman: You look awful. Do you have a hangover?
   Man: No. I've been up all night finishing a paper. All I've had to drink is coffee.
   Third Voice: What is the man's problem?

2. Woman: Can I use my credit card to pay my fees, or do I have to give you a check?
   Man: Your card is fine as long as your credit approval goes through.
   Third Voice: How does the woman want to pay?

3. Woman: No wonder Sharon won't see you. She probably thought that such an expensive gift was inappropriate on such short acquaintance.
   Man: It certainly is different here. In my country, men are supposed to show women that they care for them by giving them jewelry.
   Third Voice: Why did Sharon stop seeing the man?

4. Woman: Why do you need to check my purse? Do you think I stole something?
   Man: Not at all. This is a standard security procedure.
   Third Voice: Why did the man look through the woman's purse?

5. Woman: I lost my notebook. Could I borrow yours before the test?
   Man: I'm sorry. I'd like to help you, but I just can't. I have to take it with me to work so I can study on my breaks.
   Third Voice: What does the woman want the man to do?

6. Woman: That looks like Steve's car, but who is that girl driving it?
   Man: Oh, that's Steve's sister. I met her last night at Mary Anne's party.
   Third Voice: Who is driving Steve's car?

7. Woman: The door seems to be locked. Do I need a key for the bathroom?
   Man: No. Just push hard. It sticks a little.
   Third Voice: Why won't the door open?

8. Man: Can we use our calculators on the test?
   Woman: Yes, if you bring them to me at the beginning of the test, I'll check them out and return them right away so you can use them.
   Third Voice: What does the man want to do?

9. Man: My roommate left, and he didn't pay his share, so I'm stuck with all the rent and utilities for last month.
   Woman: That's not fair. You should call his family.
   Third Voice: What is the woman's advice?

10. Man: I want to apply for a student loan, please.
    Woman: All right. Fill out these forms and bring in your income tax records from last year. Then I'll review your options with you.
    Third Voice: How will the woman help the man?

EXERCISE 2: Selections

1. Woman: Is Jack your cousin?
   Man: No. He seems more like a brother, really, but we are just good friends.
   Third Voice: What is the relationship between Jack and the man?

2. Man: So I asked Frank if we could live together next semester, and he said that he was going to room with Geoff.
   Woman: Oh, that's too bad. Well, I know that Steve is looking for a roommate.
   Third Voice: What does the woman suggest?

3. Man: What did you get on the calculus exam?
   Woman: A C. And I feel lucky to have it. Mike got a B, but almost everyone else got Ds and Fs.
   Third Voice: What grade did the woman receive?

4. Man: Where can I buy a computer? It doesn't have to be the best on the market. I'm just going to use it to do word processing.
   Woman: Umhum. You could go to a computer store, or a discount store, but if I were you, I'd look into some of the special offers through the university. I saw something in the paper just last night.
   Third Voice: What advice does the woman give the man?

5. Man: You didn't get your grades because your name isn't on the roster. Did you attend the class and take the exams?
   Woman: I certainly did. And I paid my fees, too.
   Third Voice: Why didn't the woman receive a grade for the course?

6. Man: What size do you need?
   Woman: I'm not too sure. I wear a five and a half or a six in Europe, and a seven in Canada, but I think I need a seven and a half here.
   Third Voice: What size will the man probably bring?

7. Woman: I have been having the worst headaches. I know some of it is stress, but I'm worried that I might have something more serious, such as high blood pressure.
   Man: Well, we'll check that out, of course, but first, tell me the last time you had your glasses changed. It really sounds more like eye strain.
   Third Voice: What does the man suspect?

8. Man: Have you started writing your paper for history?
   Woman: Not yet. I'm still writing up my laboratory assignments for chemistry and studying for my midterms in English and French.
   Third Voice: For which class must the woman begin to prepare?

9. Woman: Are you glad that you came to Washington?
    Man: Yes, indeed. I'd considered going to New York or Boston, but I've never regretted my
                  decision.
    Third Voice: Where does the man live?

10. Man: Something is wrong with second gear. It seems to run fine in reverse, and drive, but when I
                  shift it into second, the motor stalls out.
    Woman: I hope that it won't be too difficult to fix.
    Third Voice: Which gear needs to be fixed?

EXERCISE 3: Reversals

1. Man: Do you need a ride to the airport?
    Woman: Thanks, anyway. I thought I would, but I have my car back now.
    Third Voice: How will the woman get to the airport?

2. Man: Okay. What'll you have?
    Woman: Give me the eggs and potatoes. Oh, wait a minute. How about the eggs and pancakes?
    Third Voice: What does the woman want to eat?

3. Woman: How many boxes of Girl Scout cookies did you order?
    Man: Four, no, five.
    Third Voice: How many boxes of cookies did the man order?

4. Man: What is the area code from which you are calling?
    Woman: 6-9-1. Oops, that's not right. It's 6-1-9.
    Third Voice: What is the correct area code for the woman?

5. Woman: I thought you said it was five cents a copy.
    Man: I did, but it's ten cents a copy when you make fewer than twenty copies, and you have only
                  fifteen.
    Third Voice: How much per copy will the woman pay?

6. Woman: How much to send a one-page fax?
    Man: One dollar. Oh, wait a minute. This is an overseas transmission. That's two-fifty.
    Third Voice: How much will the woman pay?

7. Man: Let me see. There's a documentary about wolves on Channel Three.
    Woman: That sounds pretty interesting, but I'd rather go to the movies.
    Third Voice: What does the woman want to do?

8. Woman: Do you want large bills or twenties?
    Man: Give me twenties, please. Oh, wait, maybe I should take two fifties and the rest in twenties.
    Third Voice: What does the man want the woman to do?

9. Man: Where shall we go for lunch? It's your turn to choose.
    Woman: How about The Country Kitchen, or better yet, The Old House. They have great salads.
    Third Voice: Where will the man and woman eat lunch?

10. Woman: Will you be home late again tonight?
    Man: I'm afraid so. But I should be able to get away by six, or let's say seven, just to be on the safe
                  side.
    Third Voice: When will the man be home?

EXERCISE 4: Idiomatic Speech

1. Man: Let's go to Florida on spring break.
   Woman: You're putting me on!
   Third Voice: What does the woman mean?

2. Man: Can you believe it? It says in the paper that tuition is going up another hundred dollars a semester.
   Woman: That's just what I need.
   Third Voice: What does the woman mean?

3. Man: Can you let me borrow some paper? This lecture is so long that I've run out.
   Woman: Sure. Here you go.
   Third Voice: What did the man do?

4. Woman: That test was not what I studied for.
   Man: No joke. I hope I passed it.
   Third Voice: How does the man feel about the test?

5. Man: What did you say?
   Woman: Honestly, Will. You're just not all there sometimes.
   Third Voice: What does the woman mean?

6. Woman: I can't believe that I signed up for this class.
   Man: Neither can I. It is such a Mickey Mouse course.
   Third Voice: On what do the speakers agree?

7. Man: I'll pick you up after class.
   Woman: Don't bother.
   Third Voice: What does the woman mean?

8. Woman: Do you like ice cream?
   Man: I'll say!
   Third Voice: What does the man mean?

9. Man: Did you know that Joan is going to move back to Maine?
   Woman: I'll believe it when I see it.
   Third Voice: What does the woman mean?

10. Woman: How was your day?
    Man: Don't ask.
    Third Voice: What does the man mean?

EXERCISE 5: Computations

1. Man: My car gets forty miles per gallon.
   Woman: Really? Mine only gets twenty.
   Third Voice: How does the man's mileage compare with that of the woman?

2. Man: Hello. This is Tom Davis. I have an appointment with Mrs. Jones for nine o'clock this morning, but I'm afraid I'll have to be about fifteen minutes late.
   Woman: That's all right, Mr. Davis. She doesn't have another appointment scheduled until ten o'clock.
   Third Voice: When will Mr. Davis most probably meet with Mrs. Jones?

3. Man: How much are the tickets?
   Woman: They're ten dollars each for the general public, but student tickets are half price.
   Third Voice: How much will the man pay for two general tickets and two student tickets?

4. Man: How much are these sweaters?
   Woman: They're on sale today, sir. Twenty-five dollars each, or two for forty dollars.
   Third Voice: How much does one sweater cost?

5. Man: I'd like to place a station-to-station call to Ann Arbor, please. How much will that be?
   Woman: That's two dollars and fifty-five cents for the first three minutes, and one dollar for each additional minute.
   Third Voice: How much will the man pay for a ten-minute call?

6. Woman: Excuse me. Do you have the time?
   Man: Yes ma'am. I have 1:15, but my watch is a little bit fast.
   Third Voice: What time is it?

7. Woman: That's fifteen dollars, sir.
   Man: I'd like to pay by check. May I make it out for more than that?
   Woman: Certainly. There's a ten-dollar limit over the amount of purchase, though.
   Third Voice: What is the maximum amount for which the man may write his check?

8. Man: Do I have enough postage on this package?
   Woman: Let's see. You already have three fifteen-cent stamps and two twenty-five cent stamps on it. You only need one five-cent stamp.
   Third Voice: What is the total amount of postage required to mail the package?

9. Woman: I thought that these printer ribbons cost thirteen dollars.
   Man: They used to, but the price has gone up five dollars.
   Third Voice: How much do the printer ribbons cost now?

10. Woman: Aren't there any direct flights?
    Man: I'm sorry. Your best bet would be a nine A.M. departure on flight twelve arriving at Chicago at eleven A.M., with a five-hour wait for your connecting flight to Los Angeles.
    Third Voice: What time will the woman leave Chicago?

EXERCISE 6: Places

1. Woman: The special today is baked chicken and dressing.
   Man: No thank you. Just bring me a cup of coffee and the check, please.
   Third Voice: Where did this conversation most probably take place?

2. Man: I need to get this prescription filled, please.
   Woman: Certainly, sir. It will be about fifteen minutes.
   Third Voice: Where did this conversation most probably take place?

3. Woman: Isn't Mary Ellen a beautiful bride?
   Man: She is indeed. John looks very happy too, doesn't he? He told me that they'll be going to Florida on their honeymoon.
   Third Voice: Where did this conversation most probably take place?

4. Woman: Press twelve, please. (Pause.) Thank you.
   Man: You're welcome. That's where I'm going too.
   Third Voice: Where did this conversation most probably take place?

5. Woman: They'll call the doctoral candidates' names next. Have you found Larry yet?
   Man: No. They all look alike with those black robes on.
   Third Voice: Where did this conversation most probably take place?

6. Woman: I'd like a dozen glazed doughnuts and a loaf of French bread, please.
    Man: Yes, ma'am. That's a dollar ninety-five plus ten cents tax.
    Third Voice: Where did this conversation most probably take place?

7. Woman: What was that title again?
    Man: *God Is an Englishman.* It's a very famous book. I'm sure you must have it.
    Third Voice: Where did this conversation most probably take place?

8. Woman: Are these treatments really necessary? They don't seem to help very much.
    Man: I'm afraid so, Mrs. Jones. Just be patient and I'm sure you'll see some results soon.
    Third Voice: Where did this conversation most probably take place?

9. Woman: We have several kinds of accounts, Mr. Brown. The best interest rate is for the customer club account, but you must maintain a monthly balance of three hundred dollars.
    Man: That will be fine.
    Third Voice: Where did this conversation most probably take place?

10. Man: The name is Wilson. We don't have a reservation, but we have time to wait.
    Woman: Party of two? It shouldn't be more than ten minutes, Mr. Wilson. We'll call you when we have a table set up.
    Third Voice: Where did this conversation most probably take place?

EXERCISE 7: Feelings and Emotional Responses

1. Woman: Are you worried about getting a job after graduation?
    Man: No. I've had several good interviews, and I can always work for my dad for a while.
    Third Voice: How does the man feel?

2. Woman: That was a great movie!
    Man: Sure, if you like fairy tales.
    Third Voice: How did the man feel about the movie?

3. Man: Did you get your TOEFL scores yet?
    Woman: Not yet, but I think I got more than 500. I had 490 the first time I took it, and I know I did much better this time because I knew a lot about several of the reading comprehension passages.
    Third Voice: How does the woman feel about the TOEFL?

4. Man: What page are we on? I'm just not with it today.
    Woman: Or any other day.
    Third Voice: How does the woman feel about the man?

5. Woman: If you invite Lucy, you'll have to ask Rick, too.
    Man: Forget it!
    Third Voice: How does the man feel about Rick?

6. Woman: I heard that Professor Saunders has retired.
    Man: What?
    Third Voice: What is the man's reaction to the news?

7. Woman: I don't care much for the way that our lab assistant grades our assignments.
    Man: Neither do I.
    Third Voice: How does the man feel about the assignments?

8. Woman: You are wrong about Terry.
   Man: If you say so.
   Third Voice: Which word best describes the man's opinion of Terry?

9. Woman: I don't want to go to that review session.
   Man: Neither do I, but I think we should.
   Third Voice: How does the man feel about the review session?

10. Woman: I was going to room with Carol, but when I got here, I had been assigned to live with Janine.
    Man: Bummer.
    Third Voice: How does the man feel about Janine?

EXERCISE 8: Probabilities

1. Man: I'll have hot tea and a large glass of orange juice.
   Woman: We only have one size orange juice. It's pretty big, though. About like that.
   Third Voice: What will the man probably do?

2. Woman: Have you seen my chemistry book?
   Man: It was on the kitchen table yesterday. Did you have it with you when you went to the library last night? Maybe you left it there.
   Third Voice: What will the woman probably do?

3. Man: You have a long-distance call from London. Will you accept the charges?
   Woman: I don't know anyone in London.
   Third Voice: What will the woman probably do?

4. Man: Is there a copy machine in this building?
   Woman: No. But there is one in the building across the street.
   Third Voice: What will the man probably do?

5. Man: Tuesdays you can rent two videos for the price of one. Wednesdays you can rent any video you want for ninety-nine cents. And every time you have rented a total of ten, you get one free. But you have to join the club, and that costs five dollars.
   Woman: Okay. That sounds good to me.
   Third Voice: What will the woman probably do?

6. Woman: How may I direct your call?
   Man: Reservations, please.
   Third Voice: What does the man probably want to do?

7. Woman: Is this where the bus to the mall stops?
   Man: No. It's on the other side of the street.
   Third Voice: What will the woman probably do?

8. Woman: Did you drive in on I-17?
   Man: Yes, and it was already starting to get slick. By now it should be really bad. You'd better call the highway patrol before you leave to make sure it's still open.
   Third Voice: What will the woman probably do?

9. Woman: Do you deliver?
   Man: That depends. We do if you are within three miles of the university.
   Third Voice: What will the man do?

10. Woman: It will be about a twenty-minute wait if you want to sit in the non-smoking section. We can
                   seat you in smoking in five minutes.
     Man: Okay. I don't have twenty minutes to wait.
     Third Voice: What will the man probably do?

EXERCISE 9: Deductions

1. Woman: That book is on reserve, so you can't take it out of the library. You can use it here for two
                  hours, though. Or, you can wait until an hour before closing and check it out until the library
                  opens at eight in the morning.
    Man: Okay. I'll come back tonight.
    Third Voice: What does the man imply?

2. Woman: Do you know where I can get a soda?
    Man: Isn't there a machine downstairs?
    Third Voice: What does the man imply?

3. Man: Why do *you* have to take the TOEFL? I thought if you graduated from an American high
                  school you didn't have to take it.
    Woman: I thought so, too. But the universities where I applied required a score even with an American
                  diploma.
    Third Voice: What do we know about the woman?

4. Woman: How long did it take you to register? I was in line for two hours.
    Man: You were lucky.
    Third Voice: What did the man mean?

5. Woman: If I were you, I would take a plane instead of a bus. It will take you forever to get there.
    Man: But flying makes me so nervous.
    Third Voice: What does the man prefer to do?

6. Man: These gloves are quite a bit cheaper than the leather ones. They are vinyl, but frankly I can't
                  tell much difference.
    Woman: I really like the leather, but I can't pay twenty-six dollars.
    Third Voice: What will the woman probably do?

7. Woman: Do you think that Bob is serious about Sally?
    Man: Well, I know this. I've never seen him go out so often with the same person.
    Third Voice: What conclusion does the man want us to draw from his statement?

8. Woman: Whereas European nations have traditionally employed metric units such as meters and
                  grams, the United States has employed English units such as feet and pounds.
    Man: Both systems are now in use in the U.S., though.
    Third Voice: What are these people most probably discussing?

9. Woman: Jane told me that she was going to quit her job. I'll certainly be sorry to see her go.
    Man: Oh, she always says that! I wouldn't buy her a going-away present if I were you.
    Third Voice: What does the man think about Jane?

10. Man: I wonder what happened to Betty Thompson? I don't see her anywhere.
    Woman: I don't know. She told me that she would be here at the play tonight.
    Third Voice: What do we learn about Betty from this conversation?

EXERCISE 10: Cumulative Review (Part 1)

1. Man: Did you always want to be an engineer?
   Woman: No. I started out majoring in math. I thought I might like to teach on the college level. But then I took a few courses in the engineering department, and I was hooked.
   Third Voice: What career is the woman pursuing?

2. Man: How much would a new computer cost?
   Woman: Well, the list price is sixteen hundred dollars, but our in-store special is twelve hundred. Then, you can use your sales receipt and this coupon to send in to the manufacturer for an extra one-hundred-dollar rebate.
   Third Voice: How much will the computer cost the man?

3. Man: Am I late? I thought we were going to meet at seven-thirty, and it's only seven-fifteen now.
   Woman: No, I'm early. I got here about seven o'clock.
   Third Voice: What time had the man and woman agreed to meet?

4. Man: Psychology? Oops! I'm calling the chemistry department to make an appointment.
   Woman: Yes, well, their number is almost like ours. Try 344-6782.
   Third Voice: Why did the man call the psychology department?

5. Woman: How soon can I have these copied? I only need one copy of each original.
   Man: One hundred and twenty pages. If you come back this afternoon after one-thirty it'll be ready.
   Third Voice: When can the woman pick up her copies?

6. Woman: I thought the library was open all night during finals week.
   Man: No. Just until two in the morning. We'll be closing in a few minutes.
   Third Voice: What time is it now?

7. Man: I'd like a regular roast beef sandwich and a large diet soda, please.
   Woman: Your total is $3.01 at the second window. Please drive forward.
   Third Voice: Where does this conversation probably take place?

8. Man: Meet me at the Union after your class.
   Woman: I can't. How about later tonight?
   Third Voice: What do we know from this conversation?

9. Man: Leave your name and phone number at the tone. I'll get back to you.
   Woman: Jack, this is Beverly. Call me at 674-9521 if you get back before nine o'clock. After that, call me at home. Thanks!
   Third Voice: What does the woman want the man to do?

10. Man: Oh, no. I forgot my lunch at home.
    Woman: Why not eat with me in the cafeteria?
    Third Voice: What does the woman suggest?

EXERCISE 11: Cumulative Review (Part 2)

1. Man: I thought you were working at the bookstore over by the dorm.
   Woman: I am. I just work here at the pizza parlor part time on weekends to pay for Christmas presents.
   Third Voice: Where does the woman work full time?

2. Man: We can't move in until the twentieth.
   Woman: Oh no. That's five more days in this hotel!
   Third Voice: What is today's date?

3. Man: Are you getting off in Atlanta, too?
   Woman: No. I go on to Saint Louis, then I change planes for Los Angeles, and change again in Los Angeles for Hawaii.
   Third Voice: What is the man's final destination?

4. Man: So did you make the dean's list? You worked hard enough last semester.
   Woman: Yeah, I made it.
   Third Voice: What do we know about the woman?

5. Woman: You need to get your picture taken for the license. Let me have your test results and verification of your eye exam.
   Man: I left them with the officer at the counter.
   Third Voice: Where does this conversation most probably take place?

6. Man: Can you tell me how to get to Rosenthal Auditorium?
   Woman: Sure. Go to the first light and turn left. That's Circle Drive. Stay on Circle until you get to the university, then turn in the main entrance, and it's the first building you see on the right.
   Third Voice: Where is Rosenthal Auditorium?

7. Man: Which branch do you want? First National has a bank on First Street and one on Grant Avenue.
   Woman: The one closest to the college. I guess that would be Grant.
   Third Voice: What does the woman want to do?

8. Woman: Shall I get you something to drink?
   Man: Please don't bother.
   Third Voice: What does the man mean?

9. Man: Why don't you go with Bob if Randy can't take you?
   Woman: No way!
   Third Voice: How does the woman feel about Bob?

10. Woman: Great! So you are coming with us after all.
    Man: Yes. I changed my mind.
    Third Voice: What had the woman assumed?

Part B—Extended Conversations

<u>Directions:</u> In this part of the test, you will hear several extended conversations between two speakers. After each conversation, you will be asked some questions. The conversations and questions will be spoken just one time. They will not be written out for you, so you will have to listen carefully to understand what the speaker says.

After you hear a question, read the four possible answers in your test book and decide which one is the best answer to the question you heard. Then, on your answer sheet, find the number of the question and fill in the space that corresponds to the answer you have chosen.

EXERCISE 12: Friends

Conversation One

Man: We seem to be having this conversation over and over again.
Woman: You're right.
Man: Look, I know how you feel about my smoking. You don't have to tell me every day.
Woman: I'm sorry. I worry about you.
Man: I know. But work and school have me so stressed out. Maybe I'll be able to quit after I graduate.
Woman: Let's be honest. There's always going to be a reason not to. After you graduate, it's going to be hard to find a job, then there will be the stress from just starting a job, then . . .
Man: Okay, I get your point. It's just so hard. You don't really understand because you never smoked.
Woman: You need some help. Why don't you go to a doctor?
Man: You mean a psychiatrist.
Woman: No, I don't. I mean a general practitioner. Maybe you can get a patch, or some pills, well, I don't know, something to help you with the withdrawal. Because that's what it is.
Man: Really, I believe I can just quit on my own. But I'll think about it. I will.
Woman: All right. I won't mention it for a week. Then I want to know your decision. Because if you don't get some help, I need to rethink our plans.
Man: You mean you'd break our engagement over this? I can't believe it!
Woman: I don't know. I love you, but I'm not sure I could accept everything that goes along with the smoking.

1. What is the main topic of this conversation?
2. What does the woman suggest?
3. How does the man feel about the woman's decision?
4. What can we infer about the woman?

Conversation Two

Man: Did you see that TV special on Norman Rockwell last night?

Woman: Yes, I did. It was really good, wasn't it?

Man: It sure was. I thought it was really interesting how he developed the paintings in stages starting with photographs.

Woman: Yes, I did, too. It never occurred to me that he would have actually employed models. I just assumed that he invented all those wonderful characters.

Man: I know. But it does make sense to use photographs of real people to solve as many of the composition problems as possible before starting to paint.

Woman: True. Anyway, you know what I like most about his work?

Man: What?

Woman: Well, when you look at one of the magazine covers . . . which magazine was it?

Man: *The Saturday Evening Post.*

Woman: Yes, you can just tell what the people are thinking and feeling. The picture really tells a story.

Man: You're right. I like that, too. And to think that he created several hundred of those.

Woman: Amazing. Of course, that was over a period of almost sixty years, but still . . .

Man: I'd like to see them when that exhibit comes to Miami.

Woman: What exhibit?

Man: The one they mentioned after the special.

Woman: Oh, I must have turned it off before the announcement. I'd like to see it, too. Let's go.

1. What do the speakers mainly discuss?
2. How did Rockwell paint such interesting faces?
3. What do we know abut Rockwell?
4. What will the couple probably do?

Conversation Three

Woman: What's the problem?

Man: I can't figure out how to put the page numbers on. I've done everything and they aren't showing up.

Woman: Let's see. Did you press Shift, F-8?

Man: Yes, I did that. Then I hit P for page and N for number.

Woman: That's good. Did you type in the page number where you want the numbering to start?

Man: Yes. I typed the number 1.

Woman: Right. Did you press Enter?

Man: Yes.

Woman: How about F-7 to return to the document?

Man: I did that. But no numbers showed up on the screen.

Woman: Unhuh. Did you print it?

Man: No, I don't want to print it until I see the numbers.

Woman: Well, that's the problem then. The numbers don't show up on the screen. But they will on the printed copy. Let's try that.

Man: Okay. You do it this time, and I'll watch.

Woman: Well, I'll do it if you want, but it would be better if you let me talk you through it.

Man: I don't know.

Woman: Really. Once you've done it with someone coaching you, it's easier to do it on your own. Don't worry. This is my job.

Man: Oh, all right. Shift, F-8.

Woman: Now hit P for page and N for number.

Man: And the page number I want to start with which is number 1.

Woman: Great. Just press Enter, then F-7 to return to the document, and you're all set to print. Then you'll see those numbers.

1. What is the main purpose of this conversation?
2. According to the woman, what is the problem that the man is having?
3. What does the woman want the man to do?
4. What do we infer about the woman?

Conversation Four

Bill: Want to go down to dinner, John? The line is going to close in about half an hour, and I'm hungry.
John: What time is it?
Bill: Six o'clock. You had better go now if you want to eat. They're serving fish cakes and baked potatoes.
John: I don't think I'll go.
Bill: Oh, come on. Get yourself a big salad if you don't want fish. The dessert will probably be good.
John: No, thanks Bill. I think that I'll keep studying for a while, and then maybe I'll order a pizza later.
Bill: Suit yourself. Do you have a test or something?
John: Yeah. It's not until Monday but I want to go home this weekend.
Bill: Lucky you. Two days of home cooking.
John: It sure beats the cafeteria at this place.
Bill: True. Well, knock on my door if you decide to get that pizza later.
John: Why? Aren't you going to eat either?
Bill: Sure. But I'll be hungry again by ten.

1. What prompted this conversation?
2. Why is John studying?
3. When will the cafeteria close?
4. What does Bill want John to do?

EXERCISE 13: Service Personnel

Conversation One

Man: Hello. I need to talk with someone about my driver's license.
Woman: Yes. How may I help you? Do you have a driver's license, or do you need to get one?
Man: Well, I'm not sure. You see, I have an international driver's license.
Woman: Uhuh. And how long will you be staying in the United States?
Man: Probably four years, until I finish my degree.
Woman: Oh. Then you will need to get an Arizona driver's license.
Man: Do I have to take a driver's test to do that?
Woman: Yes, you do. You need to come in and take a written exam and an eye exam, and then you need to take a road test with a parallel parking test. Did you say that you are a student?
Man: Yes, I'm a student at the university. I don't have ID with me, but I can go get it.
Woman: Okay. Then you can apply for a limited license. Just come back and show your student ID, and you can make application for a five-year license.
Man: Great. That's what I want. So I don't have to take the driver's test then.
Woman: Oh, yes you do. But the license only costs you ten dollars. A regular license would cost you a lot more than that, but it is valid for more than five years.
Man: Why can't I just use my international driver's license?
Woman: You could if you were just visiting for less than a year. But as a student, you will be temporarily residing in our state.
Man: Okay. So that's why my friend can use his international license. He is a tourist.
Woman: Right.

1. What is the main purpose of the conversation?
2. What does the man have to do in order to drive legally?
3. For how long is a limited license valid?
4. What will the man most probably do next?

Conversation Two

Man: I'd like to put an ad in the newspaper, please.
Woman: A classified ad?
Man: Yes. I want to sell my furniture. I'm moving.
Woman: I see. May I have your name, please?
Man: Bill Martyn.
Woman: M-A-R-T-I-N?
Man: Y-N.
Woman: Okay. M-A-R-T-Y-N. And your address, Mr. Martyn?
Man: For the next few weeks I'll be at the Garden Apartments on Book Boulevard.
Woman: Is that where you want to be billed?
Man: No. I'll probably be gone before a bill could be sent. I'm just going to pay cash.
Woman: Okay. The rates are by the inch, not by the word. So, if you want to use abbreviations, that might save you some money.
Man: Oh, that's a good idea. I have everything written out here, but I'll just check it over before I give it to you. Maybe I can use some shorter words, too.
Woman: Okay. You can use that table over there to make your revisions. Just bring it back to me when you are ready.

1. What prompted the conversation?
2. What does the man want to sell?
3. How will the man pay?
4. Why does the man decide to revise what he has written?

Conversation Three

Man: Will that be cash or charge?
Woman: I want to pay by check if I may.
Man: Certainly. That's cash, then.
Woman: Cash?
Man: Yes. Both money and checks are considered cash. Only credit cards are charge.
Woman: Oh.
Man: Just make the check out to the Family Store.
Woman: Okay.
Man: And I'll need two pieces of identification. A driver's license and a major credit card.
Woman: Well, here's my driver's license. I don't have any charge cards, but I do have my student ID card from City College. Will that be all right?
Man: I think so. I need two numbers. Your student number is on the ID, isn't it?
Woman: Yes, it is. Do you need anything else?
Man: Just put your telephone number on the front of the check.
Woman: Okay.
Man: Good. Now let me give you your license, your ID, and your package. And thank you for shopping at the Family Store.
Woman: Thank *you*.

1. What is the purpose of the conversation?
2. What is meant by the term cash?
3. What did the woman use as identification?
4. Who is the man in this conversation?

Conversation Four

Woman: Good morning.
Man: Good morning. What can I do for you?
Woman: I'd like a ticket to Pittsburgh, please.

Man: Round trip?

Woman: No. One way.

Man: Okay. That'll be twenty-two dollars.

Woman: Twenty-two? Last time I took this bus it was only twenty.

Man: I know. The rates went up this month.

Woman: Just like everything else.

Man: Yeah.

Woman: Does the bus still leave at two-fifteen?

Man: Two-fifteen at gate eleven. You ought to be at the door by two o'clock, though. The driver usually begins loading fifteen minutes before he pulls out.

Woman: Fine.

Man: Do you want to check your suitcases?

Woman: Just two. I'll carry the other one with me.

Man: That's good. We can only check two of them anyway. Give these baggage checks to the driver when you get to Pittsburgh.

Woman: Okay. Thanks a lot.

Man: You're welcome. Have a good trip.

1. Where does this conversation take place?
2. What time does the driver leave?
3. How many suitcases does the woman want to check?
4. What do we know about the woman from the conversation?

EXERCISE 14: University Personnel

Conversation One

Man: Hello, Mrs. Kelly. I'd like to pick up my test, please.

Woman: Sure. Whose class are you in?

Man: Dr. Purcell's math class.

Woman: And your name?

Man: My last name is Raleigh. R-A-L-E-I-G-H.

Woman: That's right. Jim Raleigh. Here it is.

Man: Thank you. And Terry Young's test, too, please.

Woman: Oh, I'm sorry. I can't let you take someone else's test.

Man: He's sick, and he can't come in to get it. He's my roommate.

Woman: I understand. But the privacy act won't permit it.

Man: Really? Maybe you could call him.

Woman: Not even then. I can only give a test to the student whose name appears on it. I can't even give it to a family member.

Man: That's weird.

Woman: I think so, too, frankly, but that's the law.

Man: Okay. I'll tell Terry. Thanks anyway.

Woman: You're welcome. Tell him I'll just keep his test here until he feels better and can come in for it himself.

Man: Okay. I'll do that.

Woman: Have a nice day, Jim.

Man: You, too, Mrs. Kelly.

1. What do the speakers mainly discuss?
2. Why can't the woman give Terry Young's test to the man?
3. What is the man's last name?
4. What will the man most probably do?

Conversation Two

Woman: Look, I'm sorry, but the books for Chem 100 aren't in yet.

Man: Why not? School started last week.

Woman: I really don't know. Maybe the professor ordered them late, or the publisher ran out of them and they are on back order.

Man: This is awful. I'm worried about this course anyway. I didn't do that well in chemistry in high school.

Woman: I know what you mean. Did you check the used book section?

Man: Yes. No luck there.

Woman: Okay. Look, why don't you go over to the library? I'll bet that the professor put at least one copy on reserve.

Man: Do you think so? That would be great. At least I could make copies of the pages that I need until the books come in. Oh, wait. If there's only one copy, everyone will be trying to do that.

Woman: True. Well, we do have a bulletin board. You could put a notice up that you are looking for a book for Chemistry 100, and maybe someone who has it will want to sell it directly to you. Do you have a phone in the dorm?

Man: Yeah. I'll just put my name and phone number on the notice. That's a great idea! Where's the bulletin board?

Woman: By the T-shirts and clothing near the front door. Oh, and be sure to put down the exact title of the book, too, because they don't always use the same one.

Man: Thanks. You've been a big help.

1. What do the speakers mainly discuss?
2. Why is the man worried about the course?
3. What will the man do before he leaves?
4. Where does this conversation most probably take place?

Conversation Three

Man: Are you the head resident?

Woman: Yes.

Man: I'm Bill Miller. I'm here because I want to change roommates.

Woman: Really? That surprises me. I thought that you and David were good friends.

Man: We were. You see, we knew each other before. We are from the same home town, but it looks like we had different reasons for coming to college.

Woman: How so?

Man: Well, David is really into having fun, which is great. But he has so many people in our room all the time that I can't study. And the stereo is on constantly.

Woman: Have you talked to him about it?

Man: Yes, but he just doesn't take me seriously.

Woman: I see.

Man: Miss Todd, I have to study. I'm on scholarship. David isn't.

Woman: Okay. Here's what we can do. Let me talk to David, and then you see how it goes. Just one week.

Man: But . . .

Woman: If you still have a problem at the end of the week, I'll authorize a room change. Come back to see me next Monday.

1. What is the purpose of this conversation?
2. What does the man say about David?
3. What is the man's problem?
4. What will the man most probably do?

Conversation Four

Woman: I have been looking for information about scholarships in the library, but so far I haven't found anything for foreign students, so I thought I'd try your office.

Man: I'm not surprised. Unfortunately, the University offers very little in the way of financial support for nonresident students. I would say about eighty percent of the scholarships go to Illinois residents.

Woman: What about the other twenty percent?

Man: Grants and scholarships for specific fields of study. But most of them are restricted to citizens of the U.S. What's your major?

Woman: Oh, it isn't for me. I'm a citizen. It's for a friend. His major is engineering.

Man: Engineering. Well, he might qualify for the Williams Memorial Scholarship. Mr. Williams was a very successful engineer in Chicago, and his family arranged for a scholarship in his name. It's highly competitive, but there are no restrictions on nationality. How are your friend's grades?

Woman: He has a 3.9.

Man: Well, that's good enough to try for it.

Woman: Is there anything else, in case that doesn't work out?

Man: Has your friend considered work-study? He would have to work twenty hours a week. It's usually office work, although occasionally there are jobs in the library or one of the labs.

Woman: Can he do that on a student visa? He doesn't have a work permit.

Man: That's okay. He is allowed to work part time as long as it's on campus.

1. What is the main topic of the conversation?
2. Who needs the information?
3. Why does the man suggest the Williams Memorial Scholarship?
4. Which of the positions listed does the man most probably hold?

EXERCISE 15: University Professors

Conversation One

Man: I'm really sorry, Professor Irwin. I was sick yesterday.

Woman: Look, I'm not upset that you couldn't keep the appointment, but it is common courtesy to call. You know that.

Man: Yes, I do.

Woman: During registration I have to see all my students, and sometimes they have to wait several days to get in. When someone doesn't show and doesn't call, that deprives someone else of an appointment time.

Man: You're right. I apologize. I didn't feel well, and I guess I just wasn't thinking straight at the time.

Woman: Okay. Apology accepted. Now, I suppose you need to set up another appointment.

Man: Yes, I do. Can you see me now if I wait?

Woman: No. I can see you at three o'clock this afternoon, or during my office hour on Tuesday or Thursday.

Man: Great. Your office hour is best. That's two o'clock, right?

Woman: That's right. Which day do you prefer?

Man: Tuesday.

Woman: Okay. Be there this time.

Man: I will be. Thanks a lot.

1. What is the main subject of the conversation?
2. When is the man's new appointment scheduled?
3. What should the man have done about his first appointment?
4. What word best describes Professor Irwin's attitude toward the student?

Conversation Two

Woman: Dr. Newbury, could I speak with you?

Man: Sure. Come on in.

Woman: I need to ask you to let me take the final early.

Man: May I ask why?

Woman: Yes. It's because I bought a ticket to go home for Christmas, and my flight leaves on Tuesday. That's the day before the exam.

Man: Yes, well, Penny, the exam schedule is printed in the registration materials. You had to know the dates. Why didn't you buy your ticket for the day after the exam?

Woman: Truthfully, I just made a mistake. And now, I've got a real problem because the ticket is nonrefundable, and I can't afford to buy another one.

Man: Hmmn.

Woman: Dr. Newbury, I live too far away to get home for Thanksgiving and Spring Break like the other students do. This is my only chance to see my family during the school year. I'm sorry that it happened, but couldn't you make an exception this time? Or could you give me an incomplete and let me make it up next semester?

Man: Okay. Anyone can make a mistake. You can take the exam on Monday.

Woman: Thank you. I really appreciate this.

1. What is the woman's main purpose in this conversation?
2. Why does the woman have a problem?
3. What does the professor decide to do?
4. When does this conversation most probably take place?

Conversation Three

Man: You're probably wondering why I asked you to come see me.

Woman: Yes, I am. I have been a little worried about it all morning.

Man: Oh, I should have told you more when I saw you after class, but there were so many students waiting to ask questions. Jean, I wanted to tell you that I have nominated you for the outstanding student award.

Woman: Really?

Man: You are clearly the best student in my class, and, as I understand, in the rest of your classes as well. I have talked with your other professors. You see, in order to be chosen for the award, you need to have three professors sign the nomination. Dr. Jones, Dr. Harvey, and Dr. Small were more than glad to do so.

Woman: This is such a surprise. I can hardly take it in.

Man: Well, I think you have a very good chance to win it.

Woman: Dr. Foley, the fact that you think highly enough of me to make the nomination is more than enough for me. I'm really happy just to be nominated.

Man: You deserve it. The selection committee will be calling you to set up an interview. Call me when they do, and I'll meet with you to give you some suggestions on how to prepare. If you get the award, you'll receive five hundred dollars along with the certificate of honor.

Woman: Thank you so much, Dr. Foley. I'm really honored.

1. What is the main topic of the conversation?
2. Why didn't Professor Foley talk with Jean after class?
3. What will the woman receive if she is chosen?
4. Which word best describes the woman's feelings at the end of the conversation?

Conversation Four

Woman: I usually advise first-year engineering students to take mathematics, chemistry, and an introductory engineering course the first quarter.

Man: Oh. That's only three classes.

Woman: Yes. But I'm sure that you'll be busy. They're all five-hour courses, and you'll have to meet each class every day. The chemistry course has an additional two-hour laboratory.

Man: So that would be seventeen hours of class a week.

Woman: That's right.

Man: Okay. Which mathematics course do you think I should take?

Woman: Have you taken very much math in high school?

Man: Four years. I had algebra, geometry, trigonometry . . .

Woman: Good. Then I suggest that you take the math placement test. It's offered this Friday at nine o'clock in the morning in Tower Auditorium.

Man: Do I need anything to be admitted? I mean a permission slip?

Woman: No. Just identification. A driver's license will be fine.

Man: Do I take a chemistry test too?

Woman: No. Chemistry 100 is designed for students who have never taken a chemistry course, and Chemistry 200 is for students who have had chemistry in high school.

Man: I've had two courses.

Woman: Then you should take Chemistry 200, Orientation to Engineering, and either Mathematics 130 or 135, depending on the results of your placement test. Come back Friday afternoon. I should have your score on the test by then and we can finish getting you registered.

1. What is the purpose of this conversation?
2. How many classes does the woman advise the man to take?
3. What does the man need to be admitted to the examination?
4. What do we know about the student?

EXERCISE 16: Class Discussions

Conversation One

Smith: Let's talk about the results of your laboratory experiment. Did you have any problems with it?

Bob: Yes, Professor Smith. We did.

Smith: Who's your lab partner, Bob?

Bob: Anne Wilson.

Smith: Well, Anne, can you and Bob go over the procedure for the class?

Anne: Sure. First we put ten grams of crushed limestone in a bottle.

Smith: Anything special about the bottle?

Bob: It was a gas-collecting bottle with a one-hole stopper and bent glass tubing.

Smith: Very good. So you put the limestone in a gas-collecting bottle. Then what?

Anne: Then we poured in ten milligrams of hydrochloric acid, put on the stopper, and collected a bottle of carbon dioxide.

Smith: Right. What was the method of collection?

Anne: Water displacement.

Smith: Good.

Anne: Then, we lit a magnesium ribbon and put it in the bottle of carbon dioxide.

Bob: And carbon deposits began to form on the bottom of the bottle. You see, we didn't have any problem with procedure. . . .

Anne: Well, we had a little problem getting the magnesium ribbon to stay lit until we could get it into the bottle.

Bob: Okay. But we did it. The big problem was that we really didn't understand what happened. Did the magnesium combine with the oxygen in the carbon dioxide?

Smith: You have just answered your own question, Bob. The burning magnesium broke the carbon-oxygen bonds in the carbon dioxide, and then the oxygen combined with the magnesium to produce magnesium oxide.

Anne: And the carbon was freed to deposit itself on the bottle.

Smith: Exactly.

1. What is the purpose of this class discussion?
2. What was deposited on the bottom of the gas bottle?
3. What caused the deposits?
4. What can we infer from this discussion?

Conversation Two

Sally: I'm sorry. I just don't agree with you at all.

Paul: Look. Take the example of an international student applying for university admission. If the student has a 500 on the TOEFL or an 80 on the Michigan Test, most admissions officers will accept the applicant. The student with a 499 or 79 won't be considered. The officer won't even look at transcripts.

Sally: Right. But I think that proves my point, not yours.

Paul: How?

Sally: Well, it's the admissions officer who decides *how* to use the test. The TOEFL and the Michigan are good English proficiency tests, but that's all they are. And English proficiency is necessary for success in an American university, but so are several other factors, including good academic preparation.

Paul: Good academic preparation is more important.

Sally: Maybe. I don't really know. But what I'm trying to explain to you is that admissions officers should use the proficiency test as one of many considerations, and as such, they really shouldn't insist on a rigid cut-off score like 500 or 80.

Ayers: Isn't this the basic disagreement: that Paul thinks the tests are bad in themselves, and Sally believes that the tests are good, but that many people don't use them for their intended purpose.

Paul: I don't agree with having the tests, Professor Ayers, and that's my position.

Sally: But Paul, what would you do to evaluate the English proficiency of a student ten thousand miles away without a standardized test?

Paul: I admit that's a big problem.

Sally: It sure is.

Ayers: Okay, class. For Wednesday, let's consider the problem of evaluation without standardized tests like the TOEFL, the SAT, GMAT, and GRE. Paul says that there ought to be an alternative. Sally doesn't seem to believe that there is an appropriate alternative. Please bring in your ideas and suggestions, and we'll discuss them.

1. What do the speakers mainly discuss?
2. What is Paul's opinion about the TOEFL and the Michigan Test?
3. What does Sally say about the admissions officers?
4. Where did this discussion most probably take place?

Conversation Three

Tom: Dr. Anderson, could you please clarify the requirements for this course? Some of us are a little bit confused about the final examination.

Anderson: Oh? Well, you have two options in this course. You can either take a final examination or you can write a research paper instead.

Tom: Excuse me, Dr. Anderson. That's the point I need you to clarify. What kind of research paper did you have in mind? An original study? A report? A book review, perhaps?

Anderson: A report. A summary really, based upon current research in the field.

Jane: How long should the reports be?

Anderson: Length is really not important. I should think that it would take at least ten pages in order to develop the topic, however.

Jane: And should we check the topic with you before we begin writing?

Anderson: You may, if you wish. But the only requirement is that it relate to current trends in United States foreign policy. Are you considering writing a paper, Jane?

Jane: I'm not sure. I think that I'd like to know a little bit more about the examination.

Anderson: All right. One hundred multiple-choice questions covering both the lectures and the outside readings.

Tom: Didn't you say that you would give us one hour for the examination?

Anderson: Yes, I did.

Tom: I'm going to do the paper, then.

Jane: Me too.

1. What prompted the discussion?
2. What kind of research paper has Dr. Anderson assigned?
3. What kind of examination has Dr. Anderson prepared?
4. Based upon the class discussion, which course does Dr. Anderson most probably teach?

Conversation Four

Baker: Since so many of you have asked me about how to learn a language, I thought that it might be useful to take some class time today to discuss it. Betty, you speak several languages, don't you?

Betty: Yes, I speak Spanish and French.

Baker: And what helped you most in learning those languages?

Betty: What helped me most. . . . Well, I studied both languages in high school, and I'm still studying Spanish here at the University, but I think that travel has probably been the most help to me. You see, I've been lucky in that I've lived in Europe. Believe me, I didn't speak very well before I moved there.

Bill: You're right, Betty. After studying a language, practice is very useful. When you live in a country where the language is spoken, it's ideal. But, you know, sometimes it's difficult to make friends in a new place, even when the people are very friendly.

Betty: Yes, I know what you mean. Especially if you don't speak the language too well. I had some problems when I first moved to Europe.

Baker: And, of course, some people are shy.

Betty: That's true.

Bill: Professor Baker, whether or not I'm living in a country where the language is spoken, I always go to movies, and whenever I can, I watch TV or listen to the radio in the language I'm trying to learn.

Betty: Me too. And reading is another good way to learn. Books are good, but I think that newspapers and magazines are even better.

Baker: Probably the best way to learn is to combine all of these ideas: traveling, talking with people, going to movies, watching TV, listening to the radio, and reading books, newspapers and magazines. What do you think?

Betty: I agree with that, Professor Baker.

Bill: So do I. But I don't believe that it's possible to take advantage of practice opportunities without some knowledge of the language first.

Betty: Sure. First it's a good idea to study grammar, vocabulary. . . .

Bill: . . . and listening, perhaps even reading.

Betty: Then practice is very, very helpful.

1. What do the speakers mainly discuss?
2. What helped Betty most in learning Spanish?
3. What is Professor Baker's opinion?
4. How can we best describe Professor Baker?

EXERCISE 17: Cumulative Review

Conversation One

Man: Let's go swimming over at the student center.

Woman: I'd like to, but I have a paper due on Friday, and I haven't even started it yet.

Man: Just an hour. I've got a test tomorrow, so I won't be able to stay very long.

Woman: I need the exercise, but I just can't spare the time.

Man: Okay. How about dinner at the Grill? You have to eat sometime, and it's right by the library. I'll go over there with you after dinner, and you can do your research while I study for my test.

Woman: Well . . .

Man: Come on. You'll probably want to stay late, and you shouldn't walk home after dark. I'll stay until you're ready to go.

Woman: That would be nice, but . . .

Man: Look, we really wouldn't be wasting any time. We'd just be doing everything we need to do, but we'd be doing it together. I just want to spend time with you.

Woman: Me, too. Okay. I need to go home first, then I'll meet you at the Grill about six. Is that all right?

Man: That's great! We'll get everything done. You'll see.

1. What do the speakers mainly discuss?
2. Why does the woman refuse the man's invitation?
3. What does the man suggest that they do after dinner?
4. What do we learn about the man?

Conversation Two

Woman: Dr. Williams, I need to talk with you about changing my major.

Man: Oh, hello, Sarah. Come on in.

Woman: Thanks.

Man: Let me look at your file. Have you declared your major yet? Officially, I mean?

Woman: Yes, I'm majoring in chemical engineering.

Man: Oh yes, here's the form. And what do you want to change to?

Woman: Business. It's not because engineering is hard, though, Dr. Williams. I've finished all the math courses already. I just like the business courses I'm taking.

Man: Well, you have eighteen hours in engineering, Sarah, and only six hours in business. And the problem is you don't need any more electives, so the eighteen hours in engineering will be extra work for you on your program. I just don't have any place to put them except under additional electives.

Woman: I see. So how much longer will it take me to graduate if I change to business?

Man: One semester, full time. You'll have to take twelve hours of business courses that term including accounting.

Woman: That's okay. I really want to do this.

1. What is the purpose of this conversation?
2. What is the woman's major now?
3. What advice does the man provide?
4. What does the woman decide?

Conversation Three

Man: I don't understand. I got a ticket on my car.

Woman: Unhuh. Well, are you a student of the university?

Man: Yes.

Woman: And did you buy a parking permit?

Man: I certainly did! And I was parked in a student parking area. The one behind the Student Union.

Woman: I see. Let me look it up, then. What's your student ID number?

Man: 972-38-4401.

Woman: Mr. Warren?

Man: That's right.

Woman: Yes, your parking permit is current. Let me see your ticket.

Man: Here it is.

Woman: Oh. But this ticket is for a 1994 blue Ford and we show your permit for a 1990 red Chevrolet.

Man: My car was in the shop so I drove my cousin's car.

Woman: That's the problem, then. Your parking permit is good for your car only. When you have to use a different car, you should get a temporary permit here at Campus Police before you use one of the student lots. Otherwise, just park in a visitor's space.

Man: And how much do they cost?

Woman: They are free to students who have regular permits. In the meantime, I'm afraid I'll have to charge you the ten-dollar fine.

1. What prompted this conversation?
2. Who is the man?
3. Why did the man have a problem?
4. What will the man most probably do now?

Conversation Four

Man: I'd like a ticket to the Spring Symphony Concert at the Opera House, please.
Woman: Which day? Saturday the seventeenth is sold out, but we have a few tickets for Friday the sixteenth and both Friday and Saturday the twenty-third and twenty-fourth.
Man: The Saturday ticket, please.
Woman: The twenty-fourth?
Man: Yes.
Woman: Just one?
Man: Yes.
Woman: Okay. We have ten-dollar seats, twenty-dollar seats, and fifty-dollar seats, depending on where you want to sit. And, of course, we have season tickets for the entire concert series.
Man: Where are the twenty-dollar seats?
Woman: At the front in the middle of the first balcony or the back of the ground floor.
Man: And the ten-dollar seats?
Woman: On the extreme sides of the first balcony and the back of the first balcony as well as the entire second balcony.
Man: Do you have any twenty-dollar seats left at the front of the first balcony?
Woman: We do. Seat AA-twelve. It's here on the chart.
Man: Oh, okay. That's good. I'll take that one.
Woman: For Saturday?
Man: Yes.

1. What is the main topic of the conversation?
2. Which of the seats would cost ten dollars?
3. Which seat did the man purchase?
4. What can we infer about the man?

Listening Comprehension

Part C—Mini Talks

Directions: In this part of the test, you will hear several short mini talks. After each talk or conversation, you will be asked some questions. The talks and questions will be spoken just one time. They will not be written out for you, so you will have to listen carefully to understand what the speaker says.

After you hear a question, read the four possible answers in your test book and decide which one is the best answer to the question you heard. Then, on your answer sheet, find the number of the question and fill in the space that corresponds to the answer you have chosen.

EXERCISE 18: Announcements and Advertisements

Mini Talk One

Are you thinking of writing someone a letter? Call instead. It isn't that expensive, especially when you call during evening, night, or weekend hours. In fact, you can make a ten-minute call anywhere in the continental United States for just two dollars and seventy cents.

For even greater savings, always dial direct, that is, without an operator's assistance. Rates on direct calls are lower after five o'clock in the evening and lowest after eleven o'clock at night. Collect, credit card, person-to-person, and pay phone calls require the services of an operator, and they cost more than direct calls.

Need to call out of the country? Now calls to many overseas locations may be dialed direct. Check your telephone directory for overseas area codes.

Next time you have good news, or you just want to stay in touch, remember, a phone call means so much more than a letter. This has been a message from Southern Telephone Company.

1. What is the purpose of the announcement?
2. According to this talk, when is a direct dial telephone call cheapest?
3. How much does it cost to make a ten-minute call within the continental United States?
4. What should one do in order to make an overseas call?
5. What can be inferred about daytime calls?

Mini Talk Two

Appalachian Airlines will begin passenger service at Charlotte Airport Thursday with morning and afternoon departures daily to Atlanta, and nonstop service to Washington, D.C., with connections in Washington for Cleveland, New York, and Boston.

Tired of being crowded aboard large airplanes? Appalachian Airlines will use comfortable Boeing 737 twin jets with a capacity to seat one hundred and six passengers. There is more room for your underseat luggage, and more room for you.

Most flights will include breakfast and lunch catered by Charlotte's finest restaurants and served by one of Appalachian's courteous flight attendants.

Next time you need to travel, be good to yourself. Fly comfortably. Fly Appalachian Airlines. For reservations or more information, call your travel agent, or call the Appalachian Airlines toll-free number: 800-565-7000. That is 800-565-7000 for reservations to Atlanta, Washington, D.C., Cleveland, New York, or Boston.

1. What is the purpose of the announcement?
2. What is an advantage of taking Appalachian Airlines?
3. When do flights leave Charlotte for Atlanta?
4. What is the telephone number for Appalachian Airlines?
5. Who is the audience for this announcement?

Mini Talk Three

The National Highway Traffic Safety Administration estimates that one-half of all fatal traffic accidents involve alcohol. Every year, thousands of passengers and pedestrians are killed because of reckless, irresponsible behavior by a drunk driver.

Ohio law prohibits persons who are under the influence of alcohol to drive. If you do drive while under the influence of alcohol, you can be arrested. If you are convicted of drunk driving, you will be sentenced to at least three days in jail, and your license will be suspended for thirty days. But did you know that the court can sentence you to as much as six months in jail and fine you in the amount of five-hundred dollars in addition to the mandatory three-day sentence? Think about it the next time you leave a party.

If you drink, don't drive.

This has been a public service announcement by the Ohio Safety Commission.

1. What is the main idea of this announcement?
2. How many accidents resulting in death are caused by drunk driving?
3. What is the minimum required sentence for driving under the influence of alcohol in Ohio?
4. How much time may the court require an offender to spend in jail for driving under the influence of alcohol?
5. Where does this announcement most probably take place?

Mini Talk Four

Here is your weekend guide to what is going on at the University of Colorado. . . .

And it is a good weekend for football. The Colorado Buffaloes will play the Oklahoma Sooners Friday night at Oklahoma, and they will return home to face the Nebraska Cornhuskers Saturday night on the University of Colorado field. The Buffaloes are expected to win both games, fans. Tickets are available from the ticket office at the sports arena.

There are also a few tickets available for the Saturday night concert by Walter Murphy and the Big Apple Band. Most of the tickets are ten dollars, although a very few five-dollar seats are still on sale. To reserve seats, call the Student Union at 666-5771, or stop by the box office.

The University Museum will be open from ten o'clock A.M. until five o'clock P.M. Saturday and Sunday. In addition to the famous rock and mineral collection and the exhibits of early people, there will be a special exhibit of American Indian pottery and sand painting. Admission is free.

And now a report on snow conditions at area ski resorts. Snow Valley is reporting good conditions with six inches of new snow in the last twenty-four hours; Pine Mountain is reporting very good conditions with eight inches of new snow; and the Oak Creek Canyon Resort is reporting very good conditions with nine inches of new snow.

This has been the weekend guide. You are listening to WKID in Boulder, Colorado.

1. What is the main purpose of this announcement?
2. How can one get a ticket to the Walter Murphy concert?
3. Why is the University Museum famous?
4. What are the general snow conditions at ski resorts?
5. Who is the speaker?

EXERCISE 19: News and Weather Reports

Mini Talk One

Nancy Anne Brown was crowned Miss State University in the Centennial Hall auditorium last night after a week-long pageant that included preliminary competitions in the categories of beauty, intelligence, and talent.

A blue-eyed blonde from Los Angeles, California, Miss Brown is five feet, ten inches tall and weighs one hundred-twenty pounds. She won both the swimming suit and the evening gown competitions to place first in the beauty category. She placed second in the intelligence competition for her extemporaneous response to questioning by a panel of judges, and third in the talent competition, to give her an overall first-place ranking. In the talent competition, Miss Brown sang "I Feel Pretty" from the Broadway musical *West Side Story*.

As Miss State University, Miss Brown received a check for one thousand dollars and a scholarship award for two thousand dollars. She will represent State University at the Miss University U.S.A. Pageant in Washington, D.C., next May.

If she wins the title in Washington, she will take a one-year leave of absence from her studies at State University in order to devote her time to travel and other responsibilities associated with the title. Miss Brown is a junior majoring in speech and drama. After graduating, she hopes to pursue a career in the theater.

1. What is the main subject of the speaker's story?
2. How does the new Miss State University look?
3. What place did Nancy Anne Brown receive in the talent competition?
4. How much was the scholarship offered as one of the prizes?
5. What will Miss Brown probably do after her reign has ended?

Mini Talk Two

The cost is going up for just about everything, and college tuition is no exception. According to a nationwide survey published by the College Board's Scholarship Service, tuition at most American universities will be on an average of 9 percent higher this year than last.

The biggest increase will occur at private colleges. Public colleges, heavily subsidized by tax funds, will also increase their tuition, but the increase will be a few percentage points lower than their privately sponsored neighbors.

As a follow up, the United Press International did their own study at several private colleges. At Ivy League schools, most advisors recommended that students have $16,800 available for one year's expenses, including $11,200 for tuition, $4,800 for room and board, and $800 for books and supplies. Ten years ago the tuition was $5,300. To put that another way, the cost has climbed more than 200 percent in the last decade.

An additional burden is placed on out-of-state students who must pay extra charges and foreign students who are not eligible for scholarships at state-funded universities.

On the brighter side, the survey revealed that college graduates are entering the best job market since the middle 1960s. Job offers are up 16 percent from last year, and salaries are good, at least for graduates in technical fields. For example, a recent graduate in petroleum engineering can expect to make as much as $40,000 per year. A student with a liberal arts degree might expect to make about half that salary.

1. What is the main subject of the speaker's story?
2. What is the average increase in tuition expenses at American universities this year over last?
3. How much did tuition increase at Ivy League schools over a ten-year period?
4. According to the reporter, what is a problem for foreign students at state universities?
5. Which word best describes the tone of this talk?

Mini Talk Three

We interrupt this program to bring you a special weather bulletin. The National Weather Service has issued a tornado watch for the following five counties: Douglas, Johnson, Jefferson, Leavenworth, and Franklin. The watch will be in effect until ten o'clock tonight or until cancellation by the Weather Service.

Remember, a tornado *watch* means that weather conditions are favorable for the formation of a funnel cloud. A tornado *warning* means that a funnel cloud has been sighted and you should find shelter. As yet, no tornado warnings have been issued for any of the counties in the area.

1. What is the purpose of this weather bulletin?
2. Until what time will the tornado watch be in effect?
3. What is the definition of a tornado warning?
4. How many counties have been included in the tornado watch?
5. What will the listeners most probably do next?

Mini Talk Four

On the satellite map we can see how the rain and showers in Kansas and Nebraska moved into Illinois and Indiana overnight, crossed Lake Michigan, and dissipated in upstate New York and Canada.

The showers and thunderstorms moved north of us leaving all stations in the Tri-State Area with reports of sunny skies and warm temperatures. Trenton is reporting eighty-five degrees with fair skies. Eighty-seven degrees in Wilmington, and the sun is still shining in New Brunswick with eighty degrees. The current temperature reading here in Philadelphia is eighty-five degrees under sunny skies. The barometric pressure is 30.05 and holding steady. Southwesterly winds at five to ten miles per hour.

For tomorrow, more fair weather with a high expected near ninety degrees, a low of about seventy, and no rain in sight until Thursday or Friday.

1. In general terms, what is the weather like in the Tri-State Area?
2. What is the average temperature for Philadelphia and surrounding cities now?
3. According to the weatherman, what happened to the thundershowers yesterday?
4. When is it likely to rain in Philadelphia?
5. What can we infer about the date of this talk?

EXERCISE 20: Informative Speeches

Mini Talk One

As director of the Office of International Student Affairs, it is one of my more pleasant duties to welcome you on behalf of State University to the annual International Dinner. This year the food that you are enjoying was prepared by students from thirty-five countries. Right now coffee from Brazil and Colombia is being served at the tables, and for those of you who prefer tea, there is a selection of teas from Japan, India, and Ireland at the beverages booth. Please serve yourselves.

In the meantime, I would like to take a few moments to thank some of the people who have worked so hard to make this evening possible, especially Mr. Abdul Al-Husseini, president of the International Student Association; Miss Isabel Ruiz and Mrs. Benne Singh, chairpersons of the food committee; Mr. Sim Lee, chairperson of the program committee; and Mr. and Mrs. George Pappas, chairpersons of the publicity and ticket committee. I am sure that the dinner could not have been such a success without their time and efforts.

And now, as I see, almost everyone has been served, and we will be able to begin our program. First, a fashion show, featuring the typical dress of fifteen countries, followed by a number of traditional songs and dances from around the world.

After the program, may I invite you to stay to dance to music compliments of Jim Johnson, here with us from WQAD radio.

1. What is the main purpose of the talk?
2. Who is the speaker?
3. What are the people doing while they are listening to the speaker?
4. After the program, what will the students do?
5. What can we infer about State University?

Mini Talk Two

It is a great honor for me to introduce today's guest lecturer; Dr. C. Henry Taylor, a colleague who is so well known to all of us for his many accomplishments and contributions to the field of architecture and planning that it hardly seems necessary to recount them here. Nevertheless, as customary, I will summarize his long experience as a prelude to his address.

Dr. Taylor received his B.A. degree in urban history at Yale University in 1955. Five years later, he was awarded a masters degree in architecture and a Ph.D. in urban design from Cornell University. Upon graduating, he accepted a teaching position in the Department of Architecture and Fine Arts at Illinois University, where he was promoted to chairman of the department in 1969. Last year Dr. Taylor resigned from the University in order to accept a research position with the Department of Housing and Urban Development in Washington as director of planning.

In addition to teaching and research, Dr. Taylor has devoted much time to designing, writing, and lecturing. Some of his most famous buildings are right here in the Chicago area, and include the Twin Towers office building and the Saint Lawrence Seaway Recreation Center. His many articles on functional architecture and urban planning have appeared in scores of journals over the past twenty years, and a half dozen textbooks are to his credit, including one of the books that we use for this seminar, *Trends in Urban Design.*

Today Dr. Taylor will speak to us about federal regulations for urban development, and frankly, I know of no one more qualified to address the subject.

Ladies and gentlemen, please welcome Dr. C. Henry Taylor, scholar, designer, and author.

1. What is the topic of Dr. Taylor's lecture?
2. From which university did Dr. Taylor receive his Ph.D.?
3. Where is Dr. Taylor employed now?
4. How does the speaker feel about Dr. Taylor?
5. What will the speaker and audience most probably do next?

Mini Talk Three

When I was asked to speak at the Community Book Club luncheon, I thought about several topics that might be of interest to a group of avid readers, and I considered doing a book review or discussing the life of a well known literary figure, but I thought that I would break with tradition today in order to share some anecdotes from the life of a man, who, like you, enjoyed reading.

In spite of the fact that Thomas Alva Edison had almost no formal education, spending only three months in school, his mother taught him to read at quite an early age. Between the ages of nine and twelve, he read such difficult volumes as Humes' *History of England,* Gibbon's *Decline and Fall of the Roman Empire,* and Newton's *Principia.*

As a young man, Mr. Edison decided to read all of the books in the Detroit public library, systematically, shelf by shelf. After finishing the first fifteen feet, he decided to reconsider the task.

A few years later, in Cincinnati, his love for reading almost cost him his life. Having stayed at the library until very late, Mr. Edison started home with a pile of old magazines for which he had paid the large sum of two dollars. Suspecting that he might be a thief, a policeman ordered him to stop. But Mr. Edison was too deaf to hear the order. The policeman shot, and missed.

In addition to the electric light, Thomas Edison is known for inventing the phonograph, microphone, mimeograph, electric storage battery, and photographic film. Whenever he was paid for an invention, he used the money for his two loves—more experiments and more books.

A friend described Edison's life in those busy days. "I went to visit Tom," he said, "and I found him sitting behind a pile of books five feet high which he had ordered from New York, London, and Paris. He studied them night and day, eating at his desk and sleeping in his chair. In six weeks he had read all of the books and had performed more than two thousand experiments using the formulas that he had studied."

1. What is the main topic of this talk?
2. Who is the audience for this talk?
3. Why did the speaker choose to talk about Thomas Edison?
4. What did Mr. Edison do with the money that he earned from his inventions?
5. What can we infer about Edison?

Mini Talk Four

It is a great privilege for me to be invited to speak at the tenth-year reunion of State University's graduating class. When you arrived on campus today, after a decade, you were probably impressed by two changes at State: one, the absence of University Tower, the first building constructed on the campus, and an historic landmark for many years; and two, the disappearance of parking lots on main campus.

Two years ago University Tower was inspected and found to be unsafe. In spite of efforts to restore it, it was necessary to level the building. A belltower was constructed on the same site, built for the most part using the good brick that was saved from the original building. The original bells were also preserved.

As for the parking lots, they have been replaced by grass, trees, and pedestrian walkways. Parking is now located in parking garages on the North and West sides of the campus.

Two more subtle changes have occurred within the past decade. One is the creation and expansion of the Division of Continuing Education for the Community, including a Saturday and summer enrichment program for children, and an afternoon and evening special interest program for adults. The other is the addition to the student population of many young people from abroad, especially students from Japan, Latin America, and the Middle East. Most international students are enrolled in the College of Engineering and the College of Business.

And so, State is a different place, but like University Tower, it is built of the same brick. We are still committed to the same age-old ideals of quality education for our citizens, but we have extended our commitment beyond the borders of our state and nation to encompass the citizens and nations of the world.

1. What is the main idea of the man's talk?
2. What is the occasion for the man's speech?
3. How is State University the same?
4. Why was University Tower torn down?
5. What can we infer about the campus planners?

EXERCISE 21: General Interest Statements

Mini Talk One

Fast-food restaurants are responding to the consumers' demand for healthier meals. Now, salad bars are in place in many chains along with healthier options on the menu, including grilled chicken breasts, vegetables, and oat bran buns.

Hamburgers traditionally have been fried with ten or even fifteen teaspoons of fat! Now, there are a growing number of consumers who don't want fried food, or who insist that their burgers and french fries be prepared in vegetable oil. Low-fat yogurt is offered as an alternative to ice cream.

Americans spend more than fifty *billion* dollars on fast food every year. And sixty-six million of us eat at least one meal a day away from home. But now, with these changes in menus, eating out doesn't have to ruin your diet. At McDonald's you can order a salad with reduced-calorie dressing and low-fat yogurt; at Arby's, eat french fries fried in corn oil; at Burger King, have a skinless chicken breast on an oat bran roll; and at Domino's Pizza, order a pizza with a vegetable topping.

In many of the large franchise restaurants, there is a chart posted to inform consumers about the fat content, sodium content, cholesterol count, and calorie count of each item on the menu. If you don't see a poster, just ask for the information at the counter when you order your meal. You will find several options that will keep you on your diet.

1. What is the main topic of this talk?
2. How much fat was used to prepare a hamburger in the traditional way?
3. How much money do Americans spend on fast food every year?
4. What is listed on the chart at many franchises?
5. From this talk, what can we infer about Americans?

Mini Talk Two

Winning the lottery should be a dream come true, but for some winners, it is a nightmare. Many people underestimate the effect that their winnings will have on their taxes. Among the millionaires who receive their winnings in twenty annual installments of fifty thousand dollars each, first-year federal income taxes range from nine thousand dollars to twenty-four thousand dollars, with an average tax bite of seventeen thousand dollars. Even worse, taxes on early installments have traditionally been lower than taxes on later ones because most winners have used their previous lower incomes in a method called income averaging to pay at a lower rate. But after the first five years, their new, higher incomes have made income averaging ineffective. By then, winners have had to return half of their yearly installments in taxes.

Many lottery experts, including the national Commission on Gambling, believe that taxes on winnings adversely affect ticket sales. Most countries don't tax winnings from lotteries, including Canada, where winners are given their million-dollar prize in a lump sum tax free. But in the United States, the public is being enticed by the promise of instant wealth while they are being subjected to six kinds of taxation. First, they pay taxes on the money they earn to buy tickets. Then, the state withholds a percentage of the money from ticket sales for operating expenses. When they win, they are taxed by local, state, and federal governments. And, finally, after their death, their estates are subject to inheritance taxes. In the lottery, it is clear that the biggest winners are the state and federal governments.

1. What does the speaker mainly discuss?
2. When have lottery winnings been taxed at the highest rates?
3. How do most countries treat winners of a lottery?
4. How many kinds of taxation are lottery winners subject to in the United States?
5. What does the speaker mean when he says that the government is the big winner in the lottery?

Mini Talk Three

By 1792, Congress had passed an act authorizing the coinage of gold eagles valued at ten dollars, half eagles valued at five dollars, and quarter eagles valued at two dollars and fifty cents. These gold coins were standardized to silver on a fifteen to one ratio, that is, fifteen ounces of silver to one ounce of gold. Although the ratio was reasonable at the time that the bill was passed, by the turn of the century, the ratio in Europe had reached fifteen and three quarters to one, and the overvalued gold coins in the United States were either smuggled out of the country or melted down. Gold therefore disappeared from circulation until 1834 when a new law reduced the weight of gold pieces. Soon afterward, gold coins appeared in a smaller size and returned to circulation. The new interest and demand for gold encouraged the Mint to strike twenty-dollar double eagles and a smaller number of fifty-dollar gold coins.

The financial uncertainty during the Great Depression of 1929 encouraged hoarding of gold coins by individuals, a situation that became so serious that the government finally ordered all gold coins to be turned in. During the next several years, a number of amendments exempted certain kinds of gold coins and allowed limited collecting. Since then, the interest in collecting gold coins has increased, and the restrictions have decreased. Now, there are no restrictions regarding the export, import, purchase, sale, or collecting of gold coins in the United States.

1. What is the main topic of this talk?
2. What was the value of silver to gold in 1792?
3. How much was the double eagle worth in the mid-1800s?
4. What are the restrictions on collecting gold coins today?
5. What most probably happens during times of financial insecurity?

Mini Talk Four

My colleague, Dr. Rigel at New York University, explains it this way: There is no such thing as a safe tan. Why do you think the body tans? Any ideas? Well, the body tans because it is being injured by ultraviolet radiation. The radiation causes the body to produce melanin, which is the dark pigment that skin cells need to screen out damaging rays from the sun. To put that another way, in order to get tanned, you have to get injured first.

Ultraviolet radiation accelerates the aging process in skin by promoting changes in collagen, the protein in the skin's connective tissues. Even worse, it can lead to cell and tissue damage resulting in skin cancer and impairment of the immune system.

So why do so many people insist on damaging their skin by overexposure to the sun's rays? For some people, being in the sun is simply a byproduct of enjoying an outdoor activity such as playing tennis, swimming, or participating in water sports. A simple solution for them is to use a sun screen. People with fair complexions should use an SPF thirty formula, which provides thirty times the protection to skin that an untreated area receives. People with darker skin can use SPF fifteen. For people who insist that a dark tan makes them look and feel healthier, the solution isn't so simple. These people require education about the serious effects of sun damage. They may feel healthier, but they are putting themselves at risk.

1. What is the purpose of this talk?
2. According to this passage, what happens when you get a tan?
3. According to the speaker, how should people with fair complexions protect themselves from the sun?
4. Why do many people try to get a dark tan?
5. What can we infer about SPF from this talk?

EXERCISE 22: Informal Academic Statements

Mini Talk One

Today I want to help you with a study reading method known as SQ3R. The letters stand for five steps in the reading process: Survey, Question, Read, Review, Recite. Each of the steps should be done carefully and in the order mentioned.

In all study reading, a *survey* should be the first step. Survey means to look quickly. In study reading you need to look quickly at titles, words in darker or larger print, words with capital letters, illustrations, and charts. Don't stop to read complete sentences. Just look at the important divisions of the material.

The second step is *question*. Try to form questions based on your survey. Use the question words *who, what, when, where, why,* and *how*.

Now you are ready for the third step. *Read*. You will be rereading the titles and important words that you looked at in the survey. But this time you will read the examples and details as well. Sometimes it is useful to take notes while you read. I have had students who preferred to underline important points, and it seemed to be just as useful as note-taking. What you should do, whether you take notes or underline, is to read actively. Think about what you are reading as a series of ideas, not just a sequence of words.

The fourth step is *review*. Remember the questions that you wrote down before you read the material? You should be able to answer them now. You will notice that some of the questions were treated in more detail in the reading. Concentrate on those. Also review material that you did not consider in your questions.

The last step is *recite*. Try to put the reading into your own words. Summarize it either in writing or orally.

SQ3R—survey, question, read, review, and recite.

1. What do the letters in the SQ3R method represent?
2. What does the word *survey* mean?
3. What does the lecturer say about *reading,* step three in the SQ3R method?
4. What is the last step in the SQ3R method?
5. Where does this talk most probably take place?

Mini Talk Two

Your test on Friday will cover material from both of your textbooks, my lecture notes, and your lab assignments. There will be fifty multiple-choice questions and five short answer essay questions. The multiple-choice will count half of your grade and the essay questions will count half of your grade.

I will tell you right now that there won't be any math problems, but that doesn't mean that you shouldn't review the formulas and know what they are used for.

I wouldn't bother much with the notes from my first lecture since that was an overview of the course, but you'll probably want to look at them when you study for the final.

Oh yes, this test represents twenty-five percent of your total grade for the semester. The lab reports are twenty-five percent, attendance ten, and your final forty.

Any questions?

1. What is the purpose of the announcement?
2. On this test, how much will the multiple-choice questions count?
3. What percentage of the total grade will this test count?
4. What does the speaker say about math problems?
5. In which class would this announcement occur?

Mini Talk Three

Before you start writing your term papers, I would like to clarify the differences among paraphrasing, quoting, and plagiarizing. All of these activities involve the use of someone else's ideas, but whereas paraphrasing and quoting are legitimate writing strategies, plagiarizing is a serious offense.

In your term papers, I expect you to paraphrase, that is, to summarize someone else's ideas in your own words. I also expect you to quote, that is to copy information from another source and enclose it in quotation marks in your paper.

When you paraphrase and quote, be sure to cite the source of your information. If you do not cite the source, then you are plagiarizing. You are stealing the ideas and using them as your own. If I discover that you have plagiarized on your term paper, you will receive a zero for the paper and an F for the course.

1. What is the main topic of this talk?
2. What is plagiarizing?
3. What are two legitimate writing strategies?
4. What will happen to a student who plagiarizes on the term paper?
5. Who is the speaker?

Mini Talk Four

Let's take a few minutes to look at the policies and procedures listed on page three of the course syllabus. Refer to the section under assignments first, please. You will notice that all assignments must be typewritten and submitted on the due date in order for you to receive full credit. The grade for a late assignment will be lowered by one letter for each day past the due date.

Now, look at the section under examinations. As you see, all exams must be completed on the dates and times scheduled in the syllabus. If you must be absent for an exam, try to call me to let me know what your problem is. My office phone is on the syllabus, and my home phone is listed in the telephone directory. A make-up exam must be arranged within one week of the scheduled date of the exam. And, I must warn you, the questions on the make-up will not be the same as the questions on the regular exam. In fact, I usually give multiple choice tests, but I always give essay tests for make-ups. And, so my students tell me, the make-ups are quite a bit more difficult than the regularly scheduled exams.

One more thing, if you need to request an incomplete, please remember that I only approve them for illness or for a serious personal problem, not just because you ran out of time. And you must submit a request form with a signed statement of explanation to my office in order for your incomplete to be considered. Otherwise, you will have to register and take the entire course over again to get credit.

1. What is the main purpose of this talk?
2. What is the speaker's policy for late assignments?
3. What is the professor's policy for make-up exams?
4. What is the procedure for a student to receive a grade of incomplete?
5. What can we infer about the speaker?

EXERCISE 23: Formal Academic Statements

Mini Talk One

Good morning. I trust that you have all read the assignment and that we can proceed with today's lecture. As you know from your text, both heredity and environment play a role in the development of the personality.

In addition, research at the University of Texas at Arlington has shown that the order of one's birth in relationship to brothers and sisters may be a significant factor. Those born first tend to develop personality traits that make them domineering, ambitious, and highly motivated to achieve. And the same is true for only children. In contrast, children born later in the family tend to be more socially adept, likable, talkative individuals.

Also interesting in the research is the fact that a woman with older brothers and a man with older sisters seem to be able to interact more easily with the opposite sex. Having older opposite-sex siblings seems to be important in being able to establish social relationships with members of the opposite sex.

1. What is the main subject of this lecture?
2. What should the students know before they hear this lecture?
3. What personality traits do firstborn children exhibit?
4. Which one of the people listed in question four would probably be the most comfortable interacting with a member of the opposite sex?
5. Which of the children listed in question five would probably be the most social?

Mini Talk Two

Yesterday we discussed the problem of rising prices, or, in the economist's terms, inflation. We noted that, during periods of inflation, all prices and incomes do not rise at the same rate. Some incomes rise more slowly than the cost of living, and a few do not rise at all. Other incomes rise more rapidly than the cost of living.

We concluded that persons with fixed incomes, as, for example, the elderly who depend upon pensions, and persons with slow-rising incomes as, for example, an employee with a salary agreed to in a long-term contract, will be most seriously affected by inflation. Please recall that while their dollar incomes stay the same, the cost of goods and services rises, and in effect, real income decreases; that is, they are able to purchase less with the same amount of money.

We also talked about the fact that stockholders and persons with business interests and investments would probably benefit most from inflation, since high prices would increase sales receipts, and profits would likely rise faster than the cost of living.

And now, before we begin today's lecture, are there any questions about the term inflation or any of the examples given in our discussion so far?

1. What is the main purpose of the talk?
2. According to the lecture, what is inflation?
3. Who benefits most from inflation?
4. What happens when income rises more slowly than the cost of living?
5. What is the audience probably going to do next?

Mini Talk Three

To review from yesterday's lecture, ecology is the study of organisms in relation to their environment. The total complex of relationships is referred to as the "web of life."

You will remember that when their relationships do not change much from year to year, we observe a balance of nature.

Today we will discuss what occurs when the balance of nature is disturbed, either by a geological change such as a change of climate, or a local agitation such as a fire.

After the balance of nature has been disturbed, a period of rehabilitation must occur. The first life to appear is called pioneer flora and fauna. The pioneer life is temporary and soon replaced by other forms of life. In turn, these forms are replaced by others. That is, a series of transitional life forms successively appears, preparing the environment for the forms that will replace them.

Eventually, a new balance is established. The final stage in the relationships of plants and animals in transition tends to be stable for a long time. It is called a *climax association*.

For example, after a forest fire, pioneer plants will appear, usually herbs or ground cover. Soon they will be replaced by shrubs. Shrubs will be replaced by trees. And so it goes, until ultimately, a permanent climax flora will establish itself in balance with the fauna, minerals, and water supply.

Interestingly enough, the climax association may not have the same kinds of plants and animals as the association that was prevalent before the fire. What is essential is that the balance of nature permits the association to continue in spite of other organic competition for the area.

1. What is the main topic of today's lecture?
2. Why is the example of a forest fire used?
3. According to the lecturer, why is pioneer life important?
4. What is essential in the identification of a climax association?
5. Where does this lecture most probably take place?

Mini Talk Four

In an earlier age, there was a great distinction in the public mind between science and engineering. Whereas the scientist was thought of as an intellectual, motivated by a desire for knowledge and order, the engineer was thought of as a busy, practical person, involved in producing something for which the public was willing to pay. The scientist might discover the laws of nature, but the engineer would be the one to exploit them for use and profit.

Historically, however, the distinction has not been valid. In every century, noted theoretical scholars were deeply involved in the practical application of their own work. For example, in the seventeenth century, Christian Huygens, a Dutch astronomer, mathematician, and physicist who developed theorems on centrifugal force and wave motion, also developed the first accurate timepiece. In the eighteenth century, the British mathematician and philosopher Sir Isaac Newton was credited not only with advancing theories of mechanics and optics, but also with inventing the reflecting telescope, a direct application of his theory. In the nineteenth century, the French chemist and bacteriologist Louis Pasteur first proposed theories of disease, and then set about the discovery of vaccines for anthrax and rabies, as well as the process for purification that bears his name to this day.

I propose that the popular detachment of science from engineering has not provided us with a useful model for comparison, and perhaps not even an historically correct one.

1. What is the main purpose of the lecture?
2. According to public opinion in the past, how was a scientist different from an engineer?
3. Who was Christian Huygens?
4. What was the lecturer's opinion about science?
5. Why did the lecturer discuss the work of Huygens, Newton, and Pasteur?

EXERCISE 24: Cumulative Review

Mini Talk One

Welcome to Carlsbad Caverns, considered the most spectacular system of caverns in North America. Carlsbad began a long history of development some sixty million years ago, which was long before our human ancestors. Gradually, over a long period of time, rain and rivers ate away at the rock here in Carlsbad. This rock is limestone and is fairly soft, the kind of rock that can be dissolved by a weak acid. As rain fell, the drops picked up carbon dioxide from the air and the soil, and the carbon dioxide changed the rainwater into carbonic acid, the same kind of fizz water that you drink in sodas. As the rainwater fell on the limestone, thin cracks began to appear. Then more rain fell, and widened the cracks into paths, tunnels, and finally the rooms that you will see when we descend into the caverns themselves. Some of these rooms are about a thousand feet long. The largest would hold ten football fields.

The process stopped when the earth folded and the beds of limestone became part of a mountain range, draining the rock-walled rooms of the water. Then, about one million years ago, a single drop of rain dripped from the ceiling of the cave, and as time passed, the dripping formed a stalactite. Some drops of water dripped to the floor and formed a stalagmite. The lime in the stalactites and stalagmites crystallized and created the stone formations that you will see hanging from the ceiling and growing from the floor of the caverns.

1. What is the main topic of the talk?
2. What group is the speaker addressing?
3. What does the speaker say about the size of the caves?
4. What happened about one million years ago?
5. What will probably happen next?

Mini Talk Two

I realize that some of you are concerned about my holistic scoring system for your essays, so I thought we should take a little time to look at it together.

Although holistic scoring is based on a general impression of the writing, it is not merely a subjective score. I do have criteria that identify general characteristics of quality, including focus, organization, development, style, and mechanics. I read for clarity of thought and analysis. Clear thinking results in clear writing. I also read for grammar and punctuation, but only as one of the five criteria. And I ignore handwriting as long as I can read it, as well as moral and factual judgments that may not correspond to my own.

I maintain a file of sample essays with *A, B, C, D,* and *F* grades for you to review. I also distribute a rubric that describes each of these letter grade performance levels. If you would like a copy of the rubric, let me know. You can see the sample essays in my office any time during my office hours.

1. What prompted this talk?
2. What kind of grading system is holistic scoring?
3. What does the speaker say about grammar and punctuation?
4. What is the relationship of the speaker to the listeners?
5. Which word best describes the speaker's attitude?

Mini Talk Three

Almost all of the fourteen varieties of geese are found in the Northern Hemisphere. Like ducks, they make long migrations in the winter, although they do not travel as far as most ducks do. Geese are usually larger than ducks and smaller than swans, but there is a great variation within the family of geese. Some varieties weigh as little as two pounds, while others weigh as much as twenty pounds.

Unlike the case of ducks, it is difficult to distinguish between the female, called a goose, and the male, called a gander, because their coloring is so similar. The males and females do not mate until they are three years old, but when they do, they mate for life. The offspring, called goslings, remain with their parents for one year. Then the young ganders establish their own nesting territory and begin to defend it from intruders. These territories are often located in the grassy shorelines that provide the materials for their nests, including grass, twigs, and reeds. The gander stays with the female to protect and raise the young goslings, especially urgent during the first forty to eighty-five days that it takes for the young to master flight.

Many species of geese fly in a vee formation. The group has a leader, and the movement of air by the wings of each bird in the formation makes the task of flying easier for the bird behind it. On long migrations, several geese will take turns leading the group.

1. What is the main topic of the lecture?
2. What is a *gander*?
3. What do we know about the mating habits of geese?
4. What is the purpose of the vee formation?
5. What can we infer about this lecture?

Mini Talk Four

In 1857, Justin Smith Morrill introduced a bill in Congress to provide the states with public lands for the purpose of establishing colleges to train students in agriculture and mechanical arts. Twenty thousand acres were to be proportioned for each Senator and Representative that the state had in Congress. Proceeds from the sale of the land were to be used in the state as a perpetual fund, the interest on which was to be used to support the state college. Within a period of five years, a college had to be established. Although the bill passed both houses by narrow margins, President Buchanan vetoed it, and the vote in the House was insufficient to override the veto. Four years later, Morrill introduced a similar bill, increasing the acreage to thirty thousand for each Representative and Senator, and President Abraham Lincoln signed it into law.

From their inception, land grant institutions have played an important role in the development of agriculture, veterinary medicine, home economics, and engineering. Seventy-five percent of all bachelor's degrees conferred in the United States and two fifths of all engineering degrees are awarded by land grant colleges. Earle Ross has called these institutions *democracy's colleges* because the tuition and other fees paid by students has traditionally been kept low, with forty-one percent of the funding appropriated by the state government, and another thirty percent by the federal government. For this reason, the children of many middle class families in the United States have found their opportunity for higher education at the land grant schools in their states.

1. What does the speaker mainly discuss?
2. How were state colleges funded originally?
3. Why is legislation that established land grant colleges called the Morrill Act?
4. How many bachelor's degrees are awarded by land grant colleges in the United States?
5. Why is the tuition at a land grant college lower than that of other colleges?

ANSWER SHEETS
FOR THE TOEFL

There are now two versions of the TOEFL answer sheet. One is horizontal and the other is vertical. When you take the TOEFL examination, you will receive only one version of the answer sheet.

Answer Sheet for Chapter 3

Part A—Short Conversations

EXERCISE 1: Direct Information

1 Ⓐ Ⓑ Ⓒ Ⓓ   3 Ⓐ Ⓑ Ⓒ Ⓓ   5 Ⓐ Ⓑ Ⓒ Ⓓ   7 Ⓐ Ⓑ Ⓒ Ⓓ   9 Ⓐ Ⓑ Ⓒ Ⓓ
2 Ⓐ Ⓑ Ⓒ Ⓓ   4 Ⓐ Ⓑ Ⓒ Ⓓ   6 Ⓐ Ⓑ Ⓒ Ⓓ   8 Ⓐ Ⓑ Ⓒ Ⓓ   10 Ⓐ Ⓑ Ⓒ Ⓓ

EXERCISE 2: Selections

1 Ⓐ Ⓑ Ⓒ Ⓓ   3 Ⓐ Ⓑ Ⓒ Ⓓ   5 Ⓐ Ⓑ Ⓒ Ⓓ   7 Ⓐ Ⓑ Ⓒ Ⓓ   9 Ⓐ Ⓑ Ⓒ Ⓓ
2 Ⓐ Ⓑ Ⓒ Ⓓ   4 Ⓐ Ⓑ Ⓒ Ⓓ   6 Ⓐ Ⓑ Ⓒ Ⓓ   8 Ⓐ Ⓑ Ⓒ Ⓓ   10 Ⓐ Ⓑ Ⓒ Ⓓ

EXERCISE 3: Reversals

1 Ⓐ Ⓑ Ⓒ Ⓓ   3 Ⓐ Ⓑ Ⓒ Ⓓ   5 Ⓐ Ⓑ Ⓒ Ⓓ   7 Ⓐ Ⓑ Ⓒ Ⓓ   9 Ⓐ Ⓑ Ⓒ Ⓓ
2 Ⓐ Ⓑ Ⓒ Ⓓ   4 Ⓐ Ⓑ Ⓒ Ⓓ   6 Ⓐ Ⓑ Ⓒ Ⓓ   8 Ⓐ Ⓑ Ⓒ Ⓓ   10 Ⓐ Ⓑ Ⓒ Ⓓ

EXERCISE 4: Idiomatic Speech

1 Ⓐ Ⓑ Ⓒ Ⓓ   3 Ⓐ Ⓑ Ⓒ Ⓓ   5 Ⓐ Ⓑ Ⓒ Ⓓ   7 Ⓐ Ⓑ Ⓒ Ⓓ   9 Ⓐ Ⓑ Ⓒ Ⓓ
2 Ⓐ Ⓑ Ⓒ Ⓓ   4 Ⓐ Ⓑ Ⓒ Ⓓ   6 Ⓐ Ⓑ Ⓒ Ⓓ   8 Ⓐ Ⓑ Ⓒ Ⓓ   10 Ⓐ Ⓑ Ⓒ Ⓓ

EXERCISE 5: Computations

1 Ⓐ Ⓑ Ⓒ Ⓓ   3 Ⓐ Ⓑ Ⓒ Ⓓ   5 Ⓐ Ⓑ Ⓒ Ⓓ   7 Ⓐ Ⓑ Ⓒ Ⓓ   9 Ⓐ Ⓑ Ⓒ Ⓓ
2 Ⓐ Ⓑ Ⓒ Ⓓ   4 Ⓐ Ⓑ Ⓒ Ⓓ   6 Ⓐ Ⓑ Ⓒ Ⓓ   8 Ⓐ Ⓑ Ⓒ Ⓓ   10 Ⓐ Ⓑ Ⓒ Ⓓ

EXERCISE 6: Places

1 Ⓐ Ⓑ Ⓒ Ⓓ   3 Ⓐ Ⓑ Ⓒ Ⓓ   5 Ⓐ Ⓑ Ⓒ Ⓓ   7 Ⓐ Ⓑ Ⓒ Ⓓ   9 Ⓐ Ⓑ Ⓒ Ⓓ
2 Ⓐ Ⓑ Ⓒ Ⓓ   4 Ⓐ Ⓑ Ⓒ Ⓓ   6 Ⓐ Ⓑ Ⓒ Ⓓ   8 Ⓐ Ⓑ Ⓒ Ⓓ   10 Ⓐ Ⓑ Ⓒ Ⓓ

EXERCISE 7: Feelings and Emotional Responses

1 Ⓐ Ⓑ Ⓒ Ⓓ   3 Ⓐ Ⓑ Ⓒ Ⓓ   5 Ⓐ Ⓑ Ⓒ Ⓓ   7 Ⓐ Ⓑ Ⓒ Ⓓ   9 Ⓐ Ⓑ Ⓒ Ⓓ
2 Ⓐ Ⓑ Ⓒ Ⓓ   4 Ⓐ Ⓑ Ⓒ Ⓓ   6 Ⓐ Ⓑ Ⓒ Ⓓ   8 Ⓐ Ⓑ Ⓒ Ⓓ   10 Ⓐ Ⓑ Ⓒ Ⓓ

EXERCISE 8: Probabilities

1 Ⓐ Ⓑ Ⓒ Ⓓ   3 Ⓐ Ⓑ Ⓒ Ⓓ   5 Ⓐ Ⓑ Ⓒ Ⓓ   7 Ⓐ Ⓑ Ⓒ Ⓓ   9 Ⓐ Ⓑ Ⓒ Ⓓ
2 Ⓐ Ⓑ Ⓒ Ⓓ   4 Ⓐ Ⓑ Ⓒ Ⓓ   6 Ⓐ Ⓑ Ⓒ Ⓓ   8 Ⓐ Ⓑ Ⓒ Ⓓ   10 Ⓐ Ⓑ Ⓒ Ⓓ

EXERCISE 9: Deductions

1 Ⓐ Ⓑ Ⓒ Ⓓ   3 Ⓐ Ⓑ Ⓒ Ⓓ   5 Ⓐ Ⓑ Ⓒ Ⓓ   7 Ⓐ Ⓑ Ⓒ Ⓓ   9 Ⓐ Ⓑ Ⓒ Ⓓ
2 Ⓐ Ⓑ Ⓒ Ⓓ   4 Ⓐ Ⓑ Ⓒ Ⓓ   6 Ⓐ Ⓑ Ⓒ Ⓓ   8 Ⓐ Ⓑ Ⓒ Ⓓ   10 Ⓐ Ⓑ Ⓒ Ⓓ

EXERCISE 10: Cumulative Review (Part 1)

1 Ⓐ Ⓑ Ⓒ Ⓓ   3 Ⓐ Ⓑ Ⓒ Ⓓ   5 Ⓐ Ⓑ Ⓒ Ⓓ   7 Ⓐ Ⓑ Ⓒ Ⓓ   9 Ⓐ Ⓑ Ⓒ Ⓓ
2 Ⓐ Ⓑ Ⓒ Ⓓ   4 Ⓐ Ⓑ Ⓒ Ⓓ   6 Ⓐ Ⓑ Ⓒ Ⓓ   8 Ⓐ Ⓑ Ⓒ Ⓓ   10 Ⓐ Ⓑ Ⓒ Ⓓ

EXERCISE 11: Cumulative Review (Part 2)

1 Ⓐ Ⓑ Ⓒ Ⓓ   3 Ⓐ Ⓑ Ⓒ Ⓓ   5 Ⓐ Ⓑ Ⓒ Ⓓ   7 Ⓐ Ⓑ Ⓒ Ⓓ   9 Ⓐ Ⓑ Ⓒ Ⓓ
2 Ⓐ Ⓑ Ⓒ Ⓓ   4 Ⓐ Ⓑ Ⓒ Ⓓ   6 Ⓐ Ⓑ Ⓒ Ⓓ   8 Ⓐ Ⓑ Ⓒ Ⓓ   10 Ⓐ Ⓑ Ⓒ Ⓓ

Part B—Extended Conversations

EXERCISE 12: Friends

Conversation One	Conversation Two	Conversation Three	Conversation Four
1 Ⓐ Ⓑ Ⓒ Ⓓ	1 Ⓐ Ⓑ Ⓒ Ⓓ	1 Ⓐ Ⓑ Ⓒ Ⓓ	1 Ⓐ Ⓑ Ⓒ Ⓓ
2 Ⓐ Ⓑ Ⓒ Ⓓ	2 Ⓐ Ⓑ Ⓒ Ⓓ	2 Ⓐ Ⓑ Ⓒ Ⓓ	2 Ⓐ Ⓑ Ⓒ Ⓓ
3 Ⓐ Ⓑ Ⓒ Ⓓ	3 Ⓐ Ⓑ Ⓒ Ⓓ	3 Ⓐ Ⓑ Ⓒ Ⓓ	3 Ⓐ Ⓑ Ⓒ Ⓓ
4 Ⓐ Ⓑ Ⓒ Ⓓ	4 Ⓐ Ⓑ Ⓒ Ⓓ	4 Ⓐ Ⓑ Ⓒ Ⓓ	4 Ⓐ Ⓑ Ⓒ Ⓓ

EXERCISE 13: Service Personnel

Conversation One	Conversation Two	Conversation Three	Conversation Four
1 Ⓐ Ⓑ Ⓒ Ⓓ	1 Ⓐ Ⓑ Ⓒ Ⓓ	1 Ⓐ Ⓑ Ⓒ Ⓓ	1 Ⓐ Ⓑ Ⓒ Ⓓ
2 Ⓐ Ⓑ Ⓒ Ⓓ	2 Ⓐ Ⓑ Ⓒ Ⓓ	2 Ⓐ Ⓑ Ⓒ Ⓓ	2 Ⓐ Ⓑ Ⓒ Ⓓ
3 Ⓐ Ⓑ Ⓒ Ⓓ	3 Ⓐ Ⓑ Ⓒ Ⓓ	3 Ⓐ Ⓑ Ⓒ Ⓓ	3 Ⓐ Ⓑ Ⓒ Ⓓ
4 Ⓐ Ⓑ Ⓒ Ⓓ	4 Ⓐ Ⓑ Ⓒ Ⓓ	4 Ⓐ Ⓑ Ⓒ Ⓓ	4 Ⓐ Ⓑ Ⓒ Ⓓ

EXERCISE 14: University Personnel

Conversation One	Conversation Two	Conversation Three	Conversation Four
1 Ⓐ Ⓑ Ⓒ Ⓓ	1 Ⓐ Ⓑ Ⓒ Ⓓ	1 Ⓐ Ⓑ Ⓒ Ⓓ	1 Ⓐ Ⓑ Ⓒ Ⓓ
2 Ⓐ Ⓑ Ⓒ Ⓓ	2 Ⓐ Ⓑ Ⓒ Ⓓ	2 Ⓐ Ⓑ Ⓒ Ⓓ	2 Ⓐ Ⓑ Ⓒ Ⓓ
3 Ⓐ Ⓑ Ⓒ Ⓓ	3 Ⓐ Ⓑ Ⓒ Ⓓ	3 Ⓐ Ⓑ Ⓒ Ⓓ	3 Ⓐ Ⓑ Ⓒ Ⓓ
4 Ⓐ Ⓑ Ⓒ Ⓓ	4 Ⓐ Ⓑ Ⓒ Ⓓ	4 Ⓐ Ⓑ Ⓒ Ⓓ	4 Ⓐ Ⓑ Ⓒ Ⓓ

EXERCISE 15: University Professors

Conversation One	Conversation Two	Conversation Three	Conversation Four
1 Ⓐ Ⓑ Ⓒ Ⓓ	1 Ⓐ Ⓑ Ⓒ Ⓓ	1 Ⓐ Ⓑ Ⓒ Ⓓ	1 Ⓐ Ⓑ Ⓒ Ⓓ
2 Ⓐ Ⓑ Ⓒ Ⓓ	2 Ⓐ Ⓑ Ⓒ Ⓓ	2 Ⓐ Ⓑ Ⓒ Ⓓ	2 Ⓐ Ⓑ Ⓒ Ⓓ
3 Ⓐ Ⓑ Ⓒ Ⓓ	3 Ⓐ Ⓑ Ⓒ Ⓓ	3 Ⓐ Ⓑ Ⓒ Ⓓ	3 Ⓐ Ⓑ Ⓒ Ⓓ
4 Ⓐ Ⓑ Ⓒ Ⓓ	4 Ⓐ Ⓑ Ⓒ Ⓓ	4 Ⓐ Ⓑ Ⓒ Ⓓ	4 Ⓐ Ⓑ Ⓒ Ⓓ

EXERCISE 16: Class Discussions

Conversation One	Conversation Two	Conversation Three	Conversation Four
1 Ⓐ Ⓑ Ⓒ Ⓓ	1 Ⓐ Ⓑ Ⓒ Ⓓ	1 Ⓐ Ⓑ Ⓒ Ⓓ	1 Ⓐ Ⓑ Ⓒ Ⓓ
2 Ⓐ Ⓑ Ⓒ Ⓓ	2 Ⓐ Ⓑ Ⓒ Ⓓ	2 Ⓐ Ⓑ Ⓒ Ⓓ	2 Ⓐ Ⓑ Ⓒ Ⓓ
3 Ⓐ Ⓑ Ⓒ Ⓓ	3 Ⓐ Ⓑ Ⓒ Ⓓ	3 Ⓐ Ⓑ Ⓒ Ⓓ	3 Ⓐ Ⓑ Ⓒ Ⓓ
4 Ⓐ Ⓑ Ⓒ Ⓓ	4 Ⓐ Ⓑ Ⓒ Ⓓ	4 Ⓐ Ⓑ Ⓒ Ⓓ	4 Ⓐ Ⓑ Ⓒ Ⓓ

EXERCISE 17: Cumulative Review

Conversation One	Conversation Two	Conversation Three	Conversation Four
1 Ⓐ Ⓑ Ⓒ Ⓓ	1 Ⓐ Ⓑ Ⓒ Ⓓ	1 Ⓐ Ⓑ Ⓒ Ⓓ	1 Ⓐ Ⓑ Ⓒ Ⓓ
2 Ⓐ Ⓑ Ⓒ Ⓓ	2 Ⓐ Ⓑ Ⓒ Ⓓ	2 Ⓐ Ⓑ Ⓒ Ⓓ	2 Ⓐ Ⓑ Ⓒ Ⓓ
3 Ⓐ Ⓑ Ⓒ Ⓓ	3 Ⓐ Ⓑ Ⓒ Ⓓ	3 Ⓐ Ⓑ Ⓒ Ⓓ	3 Ⓐ Ⓑ Ⓒ Ⓓ
4 Ⓐ Ⓑ Ⓒ Ⓓ	4 Ⓐ Ⓑ Ⓒ Ⓓ	4 Ⓐ Ⓑ Ⓒ Ⓓ	4 Ⓐ Ⓑ Ⓒ Ⓓ

Part C—Mini Talks

EXERCISE 18: Announcements and Advertisements

Mini Talk One	Mini Talk Two	Mini Talk Three	Mini Talk Four
1 Ⓐ Ⓑ Ⓒ Ⓓ	1 Ⓐ Ⓑ Ⓒ Ⓓ	1 Ⓐ Ⓑ Ⓒ Ⓓ	1 Ⓐ Ⓑ Ⓒ Ⓓ
2 Ⓐ Ⓑ Ⓒ Ⓓ	2 Ⓐ Ⓑ Ⓒ Ⓓ	2 Ⓐ Ⓑ Ⓒ Ⓓ	2 Ⓐ Ⓑ Ⓒ Ⓓ
3 Ⓐ Ⓑ Ⓒ Ⓓ	3 Ⓐ Ⓑ Ⓒ Ⓓ	3 Ⓐ Ⓑ Ⓒ Ⓓ	3 Ⓐ Ⓑ Ⓒ Ⓓ
4 Ⓐ Ⓑ Ⓒ Ⓓ	4 Ⓐ Ⓑ Ⓒ Ⓓ	4 Ⓐ Ⓑ Ⓒ Ⓓ	4 Ⓐ Ⓑ Ⓒ Ⓓ
5 Ⓐ Ⓑ Ⓒ Ⓓ	5 Ⓐ Ⓑ Ⓒ Ⓓ	5 Ⓐ Ⓑ Ⓒ Ⓓ	5 Ⓐ Ⓑ Ⓒ Ⓓ

EXERCISE 19: News and Weather Reports

Mini Talk One	Mini Talk Two	Mini Talk Three	Mini Talk Four
1 Ⓐ Ⓑ Ⓒ Ⓓ	1 Ⓐ Ⓑ Ⓒ Ⓓ	1 Ⓐ Ⓑ Ⓒ Ⓓ	1 Ⓐ Ⓑ Ⓒ Ⓓ
2 Ⓐ Ⓑ Ⓒ Ⓓ	2 Ⓐ Ⓑ Ⓒ Ⓓ	2 Ⓐ Ⓑ Ⓒ Ⓓ	2 Ⓐ Ⓑ Ⓒ Ⓓ
3 Ⓐ Ⓑ Ⓒ Ⓓ	3 Ⓐ Ⓑ Ⓒ Ⓓ	3 Ⓐ Ⓑ Ⓒ Ⓓ	3 Ⓐ Ⓑ Ⓒ Ⓓ
4 Ⓐ Ⓑ Ⓒ Ⓓ	4 Ⓐ Ⓑ Ⓒ Ⓓ	4 Ⓐ Ⓑ Ⓒ Ⓓ	4 Ⓐ Ⓑ Ⓒ Ⓓ
5 Ⓐ Ⓑ Ⓒ Ⓓ	5 Ⓐ Ⓑ Ⓒ Ⓓ	5 Ⓐ Ⓑ Ⓒ Ⓓ	5 Ⓐ Ⓑ Ⓒ Ⓓ

EXERCISE 20: Informative Speeches

Mini Talk One	Mini Talk Two	Mini Talk Three	Mini Talk Four
1 Ⓐ Ⓑ Ⓒ Ⓓ	1 Ⓐ Ⓑ Ⓒ Ⓓ	1 Ⓐ Ⓑ Ⓒ Ⓓ	1 Ⓐ Ⓑ Ⓒ Ⓓ
2 Ⓐ Ⓑ Ⓒ Ⓓ	2 Ⓐ Ⓑ Ⓒ Ⓓ	2 Ⓐ Ⓑ Ⓒ Ⓓ	2 Ⓐ Ⓑ Ⓒ Ⓓ
3 Ⓐ Ⓑ Ⓒ Ⓓ	3 Ⓐ Ⓑ Ⓒ Ⓓ	3 Ⓐ Ⓑ Ⓒ Ⓓ	3 Ⓐ Ⓑ Ⓒ Ⓓ
4 Ⓐ Ⓑ Ⓒ Ⓓ	4 Ⓐ Ⓑ Ⓒ Ⓓ	4 Ⓐ Ⓑ Ⓒ Ⓓ	4 Ⓐ Ⓑ Ⓒ Ⓓ
5 Ⓐ Ⓑ Ⓒ Ⓓ	5 Ⓐ Ⓑ Ⓒ Ⓓ	5 Ⓐ Ⓑ Ⓒ Ⓓ	5 Ⓐ Ⓑ Ⓒ Ⓓ

EXERCISE 21: General Interest Statements

Mini Talk One	Mini Talk Two	Mini Talk Three	Mini Talk Four
1 Ⓐ Ⓑ Ⓒ Ⓓ	1 Ⓐ Ⓑ Ⓒ Ⓓ	1 Ⓐ Ⓑ Ⓒ Ⓓ	1 Ⓐ Ⓑ Ⓒ Ⓓ
2 Ⓐ Ⓑ Ⓒ Ⓓ	2 Ⓐ Ⓑ Ⓒ Ⓓ	2 Ⓐ Ⓑ Ⓒ Ⓓ	2 Ⓐ Ⓑ Ⓒ Ⓓ
3 Ⓐ Ⓑ Ⓒ Ⓓ	3 Ⓐ Ⓑ Ⓒ Ⓓ	3 Ⓐ Ⓑ Ⓒ Ⓓ	3 Ⓐ Ⓑ Ⓒ Ⓓ
4 Ⓐ Ⓑ Ⓒ Ⓓ	4 Ⓐ Ⓑ Ⓒ Ⓓ	4 Ⓐ Ⓑ Ⓒ Ⓓ	4 Ⓐ Ⓑ Ⓒ Ⓓ
5 Ⓐ Ⓑ Ⓒ Ⓓ	5 Ⓐ Ⓑ Ⓒ Ⓓ	5 Ⓐ Ⓑ Ⓒ Ⓓ	5 Ⓐ Ⓑ Ⓒ Ⓓ

EXERCISE 22: Informal Academic Statements

Mini Talk One	Mini Talk Two	Mini Talk Three	Mini Talk Four
1 Ⓐ Ⓑ Ⓒ Ⓓ	1 Ⓐ Ⓑ Ⓒ Ⓓ	1 Ⓐ Ⓑ Ⓒ Ⓓ	1 Ⓐ Ⓑ Ⓒ Ⓓ
2 Ⓐ Ⓑ Ⓒ Ⓓ	2 Ⓐ Ⓑ Ⓒ Ⓓ	2 Ⓐ Ⓑ Ⓒ Ⓓ	2 Ⓐ Ⓑ Ⓒ Ⓓ
3 Ⓐ Ⓑ Ⓒ Ⓓ	3 Ⓐ Ⓑ Ⓒ Ⓓ	3 Ⓐ Ⓑ Ⓒ Ⓓ	3 Ⓐ Ⓑ Ⓒ Ⓓ
4 Ⓐ Ⓑ Ⓒ Ⓓ	4 Ⓐ Ⓑ Ⓒ Ⓓ	4 Ⓐ Ⓑ Ⓒ Ⓓ	4 Ⓐ Ⓑ Ⓒ Ⓓ
5 Ⓐ Ⓑ Ⓒ Ⓓ	5 Ⓐ Ⓑ Ⓒ Ⓓ	5 Ⓐ Ⓑ Ⓒ Ⓓ	5 Ⓐ Ⓑ Ⓒ Ⓓ

EXERCISE 23: Formal Academic Statements

Mini Talk One	Mini Talk Two	Mini Talk Three	Mini Talk Four
1 Ⓐ Ⓑ Ⓒ Ⓓ	1 Ⓐ Ⓑ Ⓒ Ⓓ	1 Ⓐ Ⓑ Ⓒ Ⓓ	1 Ⓐ Ⓑ Ⓒ Ⓓ
2 Ⓐ Ⓑ Ⓒ Ⓓ	2 Ⓐ Ⓑ Ⓒ Ⓓ	2 Ⓐ Ⓑ Ⓒ Ⓓ	2 Ⓐ Ⓑ Ⓒ Ⓓ
3 Ⓐ Ⓑ Ⓒ Ⓓ	3 Ⓐ Ⓑ Ⓒ Ⓓ	3 Ⓐ Ⓑ Ⓒ Ⓓ	3 Ⓐ Ⓑ Ⓒ Ⓓ
4 Ⓐ Ⓑ Ⓒ Ⓓ	4 Ⓐ Ⓑ Ⓒ Ⓓ	4 Ⓐ Ⓑ Ⓒ Ⓓ	4 Ⓐ Ⓑ Ⓒ Ⓓ
5 Ⓐ Ⓑ Ⓒ Ⓓ	5 Ⓐ Ⓑ Ⓒ Ⓓ	5 Ⓐ Ⓑ Ⓒ Ⓓ	5 Ⓐ Ⓑ Ⓒ Ⓓ

EXERCISE 24: Cumulative Review (Part 1)

Mini Talk One	Mini Talk Two	Mini Talk Three	Mini Talk Four
1 Ⓐ Ⓑ Ⓒ Ⓓ	1 Ⓐ Ⓑ Ⓒ Ⓓ	1 Ⓐ Ⓑ Ⓒ Ⓓ	1 Ⓐ Ⓑ Ⓒ Ⓓ
2 Ⓐ Ⓑ Ⓒ Ⓓ	2 Ⓐ Ⓑ Ⓒ Ⓓ	2 Ⓐ Ⓑ Ⓒ Ⓓ	2 Ⓐ Ⓑ Ⓒ Ⓓ
3 Ⓐ Ⓑ Ⓒ Ⓓ	3 Ⓐ Ⓑ Ⓒ Ⓓ	3 Ⓐ Ⓑ Ⓒ Ⓓ	3 Ⓐ Ⓑ Ⓒ Ⓓ
4 Ⓐ Ⓑ Ⓒ Ⓓ	4 Ⓐ Ⓑ Ⓒ Ⓓ	4 Ⓐ Ⓑ Ⓒ Ⓓ	4 Ⓐ Ⓑ Ⓒ Ⓓ
5 Ⓐ Ⓑ Ⓒ Ⓓ	5 Ⓐ Ⓑ Ⓒ Ⓓ	5 Ⓐ Ⓑ Ⓒ Ⓓ	5 Ⓐ Ⓑ Ⓒ Ⓓ

Answer Sheet for Chapter 4

Part A—Structure Problems

EXERCISE 1: Verbs (Part 1)

1 Ⓐ Ⓑ Ⓒ Ⓓ	4 Ⓐ Ⓑ Ⓒ Ⓓ	7 Ⓐ Ⓑ Ⓒ Ⓓ	10 Ⓐ Ⓑ Ⓒ Ⓓ	13 Ⓐ Ⓑ Ⓒ Ⓓ
2 Ⓐ Ⓑ Ⓒ Ⓓ	5 Ⓐ Ⓑ Ⓒ Ⓓ	8 Ⓐ Ⓑ Ⓒ Ⓓ	11 Ⓐ Ⓑ Ⓒ Ⓓ	14 Ⓐ Ⓑ Ⓒ Ⓓ
3 Ⓐ Ⓑ Ⓒ Ⓓ	6 Ⓐ Ⓑ Ⓒ Ⓓ	9 Ⓐ Ⓑ Ⓒ Ⓓ	12 Ⓐ Ⓑ Ⓒ Ⓓ	15 Ⓐ Ⓑ Ⓒ Ⓓ

EXERCISE 2: Verbs (Part 2)

1 Ⓐ Ⓑ Ⓒ Ⓓ	4 Ⓐ Ⓑ Ⓒ Ⓓ	7 Ⓐ Ⓑ Ⓒ Ⓓ	10 Ⓐ Ⓑ Ⓒ Ⓓ	13 Ⓐ Ⓑ Ⓒ Ⓓ
2 Ⓐ Ⓑ Ⓒ Ⓓ	5 Ⓐ Ⓑ Ⓒ Ⓓ	8 Ⓐ Ⓑ Ⓒ Ⓓ	11 Ⓐ Ⓑ Ⓒ Ⓓ	14 Ⓐ Ⓑ Ⓒ Ⓓ
3 Ⓐ Ⓑ Ⓒ Ⓓ	6 Ⓐ Ⓑ Ⓒ Ⓓ	9 Ⓐ Ⓑ Ⓒ Ⓓ	12 Ⓐ Ⓑ Ⓒ Ⓓ	15 Ⓐ Ⓑ Ⓒ Ⓓ

EXERCISE 3: Verbs (Part 3)

1 Ⓐ Ⓑ Ⓒ Ⓓ	4 Ⓐ Ⓑ Ⓒ Ⓓ	7 Ⓐ Ⓑ Ⓒ Ⓓ	10 Ⓐ Ⓑ Ⓒ Ⓓ	13 Ⓐ Ⓑ Ⓒ Ⓓ
2 Ⓐ Ⓑ Ⓒ Ⓓ	5 Ⓐ Ⓑ Ⓒ Ⓓ	8 Ⓐ Ⓑ Ⓒ Ⓓ	11 Ⓐ Ⓑ Ⓒ Ⓓ	14 Ⓐ Ⓑ Ⓒ Ⓓ
3 Ⓐ Ⓑ Ⓒ Ⓓ	6 Ⓐ Ⓑ Ⓒ Ⓓ	9 Ⓐ Ⓑ Ⓒ Ⓓ	12 Ⓐ Ⓑ Ⓒ Ⓓ	15 Ⓐ Ⓑ Ⓒ Ⓓ

EXERCISE 4: Pronouns

1 Ⓐ Ⓑ Ⓒ Ⓓ	4 Ⓐ Ⓑ Ⓒ Ⓓ	7 Ⓐ Ⓑ Ⓒ Ⓓ	10 Ⓐ Ⓑ Ⓒ Ⓓ	13 Ⓐ Ⓑ Ⓒ Ⓓ
2 Ⓐ Ⓑ Ⓒ Ⓓ	5 Ⓐ Ⓑ Ⓒ Ⓓ	8 Ⓐ Ⓑ Ⓒ Ⓓ	11 Ⓐ Ⓑ Ⓒ Ⓓ	14 Ⓐ Ⓑ Ⓒ Ⓓ
3 Ⓐ Ⓑ Ⓒ Ⓓ	6 Ⓐ Ⓑ Ⓒ Ⓓ	9 Ⓐ Ⓑ Ⓒ Ⓓ	12 Ⓐ Ⓑ Ⓒ Ⓓ	15 Ⓐ Ⓑ Ⓒ Ⓓ

EXERCISE 5: Nouns

1 Ⓐ Ⓑ Ⓒ Ⓓ	4 Ⓐ Ⓑ Ⓒ Ⓓ	7 Ⓐ Ⓑ Ⓒ Ⓓ	10 Ⓐ Ⓑ Ⓒ Ⓓ	13 Ⓐ Ⓑ Ⓒ Ⓓ
2 Ⓐ Ⓑ Ⓒ Ⓓ	5 Ⓐ Ⓑ Ⓒ Ⓓ	8 Ⓐ Ⓑ Ⓒ Ⓓ	11 Ⓐ Ⓑ Ⓒ Ⓓ	14 Ⓐ Ⓑ Ⓒ Ⓓ
3 Ⓐ Ⓑ Ⓒ Ⓓ	6 Ⓐ Ⓑ Ⓒ Ⓓ	9 Ⓐ Ⓑ Ⓒ Ⓓ	12 Ⓐ Ⓑ Ⓒ Ⓓ	15 Ⓐ Ⓑ Ⓒ Ⓓ

EXERCISE 6: Modifiers (Part 1)

1 Ⓐ Ⓑ Ⓒ Ⓓ	4 Ⓐ Ⓑ Ⓒ Ⓓ	7 Ⓐ Ⓑ Ⓒ Ⓓ	10 Ⓐ Ⓑ Ⓒ Ⓓ	13 Ⓐ Ⓑ Ⓒ Ⓓ
2 Ⓐ Ⓑ Ⓒ Ⓓ	5 Ⓐ Ⓑ Ⓒ Ⓓ	8 Ⓐ Ⓑ Ⓒ Ⓓ	11 Ⓐ Ⓑ Ⓒ Ⓓ	14 Ⓐ Ⓑ Ⓒ Ⓓ
3 Ⓐ Ⓑ Ⓒ Ⓓ	6 Ⓐ Ⓑ Ⓒ Ⓓ	9 Ⓐ Ⓑ Ⓒ Ⓓ	12 Ⓐ Ⓑ Ⓒ Ⓓ	15 Ⓐ Ⓑ Ⓒ Ⓓ

EXERCISE 7: Modifiers (Part 2)

1 Ⓐ Ⓑ Ⓒ Ⓓ	4 Ⓐ Ⓑ Ⓒ Ⓓ	7 Ⓐ Ⓑ Ⓒ Ⓓ	10 Ⓐ Ⓑ Ⓒ Ⓓ	13 Ⓐ Ⓑ Ⓒ Ⓓ
2 Ⓐ Ⓑ Ⓒ Ⓓ	5 Ⓐ Ⓑ Ⓒ Ⓓ	8 Ⓐ Ⓑ Ⓒ Ⓓ	11 Ⓐ Ⓑ Ⓒ Ⓓ	14 Ⓐ Ⓑ Ⓒ Ⓓ
3 Ⓐ Ⓑ Ⓒ Ⓓ	6 Ⓐ Ⓑ Ⓒ Ⓓ	9 Ⓐ Ⓑ Ⓒ Ⓓ	12 Ⓐ Ⓑ Ⓒ Ⓓ	15 Ⓐ Ⓑ Ⓒ Ⓓ

EXERCISE 8: Comparatives

1 (A) (B) (C) (D)   4 (A) (B) (C) (D)   7 (A) (B) (C) (D)   10 (A) (B) (C) (D)   13 (A) (B) (C) (D)
2 (A) (B) (C) (D)   5 (A) (B) (C) (D)   8 (A) (B) (C) (D)   11 (A) (B) (C) (D)   14 (A) (B) (C) (D)
3 (A) (B) (C) (D)   6 (A) (B) (C) (D)   9 (A) (B) (C) (D)   12 (A) (B) (C) (D)   15 (A) (B) (C) (D)

EXERCISE 9: Connectors

1 (A) (B) (C) (D)   4 (A) (B) (C) (D)   7 (A) (B) (C) (D)   10 (A) (B) (C) (D)   13 (A) (B) (C) (D)
2 (A) (B) (C) (D)   5 (A) (B) (C) (D)   8 (A) (B) (C) (D)   11 (A) (B) (C) (D)   14 (A) (B) (C) (D)
3 (A) (B) (C) (D)   6 (A) (B) (C) (D)   9 (A) (B) (C) (D)   12 (A) (B) (C) (D)   15 (A) (B) (C) (D)

EXERCISE 10: Cumulative Review (Part 1)

1 (A) (B) (C) (D)   4 (A) (B) (C) (D)   7 (A) (B) (C) (D)   10 (A) (B) (C) (D)   13 (A) (B) (C) (D)
2 (A) (B) (C) (D)   5 (A) (B) (C) (D)   8 (A) (B) (C) (D)   11 (A) (B) (C) (D)   14 (A) (B) (C) (D)
3 (A) (B) (C) (D)   6 (A) (B) (C) (D)   9 (A) (B) (C) (D)   12 (A) (B) (C) (D)   15 (A) (B) (C) (D)

EXERCISE 11: Cumulative Review (Part 2)

1 (A) (B) (C) (D)   4 (A) (B) (C) (D)   7 (A) (B) (C) (D)   10 (A) (B) (C) (D)   13 (A) (B) (C) (D)
2 (A) (B) (C) (D)   5 (A) (B) (C) (D)   8 (A) (B) (C) (D)   11 (A) (B) (C) (D)   14 (A) (B) (C) (D)
3 (A) (B) (C) (D)   6 (A) (B) (C) (D)   9 (A) (B) (C) (D)   12 (A) (B) (C) (D)   15 (A) (B) (C) (D)

Part B—Written Expression

EXERCISE 12: Point of View

1 (A) (B) (C) (D)   6 (A) (B) (C) (D)   11 (A) (B) (C) (D)   16 (A) (B) (C) (D)   21 (A) (B) (C) (D)
2 (A) (B) (C) (D)   7 (A) (B) (C) (D)   12 (A) (B) (C) (D)   17 (A) (B) (C) (D)   22 (A) (B) (C) (D)
3 (A) (B) (C) (D)   8 (A) (B) (C) (D)   13 (A) (B) (C) (D)   18 (A) (B) (C) (D)   23 (A) (B) (C) (D)
4 (A) (B) (C) (D)   9 (A) (B) (C) (D)   14 (A) (B) (C) (D)   19 (A) (B) (C) (D)   24 (A) (B) (C) (D)
5 (A) (B) (C) (D)   10 (A) (B) (C) (D)   15 (A) (B) (C) (D)   20 (A) (B) (C) (D)   25 (A) (B) (C) (D)

EXERCISE 13: Agreement

1 (A) (B) (C) (D)   6 (A) (B) (C) (D)   11 (A) (B) (C) (D)   16 (A) (B) (C) (D)   21 (A) (B) (C) (D)
2 (A) (B) (C) (D)   7 (A) (B) (C) (D)   12 (A) (B) (C) (D)   17 (A) (B) (C) (D)   22 (A) (B) (C) (D)
3 (A) (B) (C) (D)   8 (A) (B) (C) (D)   13 (A) (B) (C) (D)   18 (A) (B) (C) (D)   23 (A) (B) (C) (D)
4 (A) (B) (C) (D)   9 (A) (B) (C) (D)   14 (A) (B) (C) (D)   19 (A) (B) (C) (D)   24 (A) (B) (C) (D)
5 (A) (B) (C) (D)   10 (A) (B) (C) (D)   15 (A) (B) (C) (D)   20 (A) (B) (C) (D)   25 (A) (B) (C) (D)

EXERCISE 14: Introductory Verbal Modifiers

1 (A) (B) (C) (D)   6 (A) (B) (C) (D)   11 (A) (B) (C) (D)   16 (A) (B) (C) (D)   21 (A) (B) (C) (D)
2 (A) (B) (C) (D)   7 (A) (B) (C) (D)   12 (A) (B) (C) (D)   17 (A) (B) (C) (D)   22 (A) (B) (C) (D)
3 (A) (B) (C) (D)   8 (A) (B) (C) (D)   13 (A) (B) (C) (D)   18 (A) (B) (C) (D)   23 (A) (B) (C) (D)
4 (A) (B) (C) (D)   9 (A) (B) (C) (D)   14 (A) (B) (C) (D)   19 (A) (B) (C) (D)   24 (A) (B) (C) (D)
5 (A) (B) (C) (D)   10 (A) (B) (C) (D)   15 (A) (B) (C) (D)   20 (A) (B) (C) (D)   25 (A) (B) (C) (D)

EXERCISE 15: Parallel Structure

1 Ⓐ Ⓑ Ⓒ Ⓓ	6 Ⓐ Ⓑ Ⓒ Ⓓ	11 Ⓐ Ⓑ Ⓒ Ⓓ	16 Ⓐ Ⓑ Ⓒ Ⓓ	21 Ⓐ Ⓑ Ⓒ Ⓓ
2 Ⓐ Ⓑ Ⓒ Ⓓ	7 Ⓐ Ⓑ Ⓒ Ⓓ	12 Ⓐ Ⓑ Ⓒ Ⓓ	17 Ⓐ Ⓑ Ⓒ Ⓓ	22 Ⓐ Ⓑ Ⓒ Ⓓ
3 Ⓐ Ⓑ Ⓒ Ⓓ	8 Ⓐ Ⓑ Ⓒ Ⓓ	13 Ⓐ Ⓑ Ⓒ Ⓓ	18 Ⓐ Ⓑ Ⓒ Ⓓ	23 Ⓐ Ⓑ Ⓒ Ⓓ
4 Ⓐ Ⓑ Ⓒ Ⓓ	9 Ⓐ Ⓑ Ⓒ Ⓓ	14 Ⓐ Ⓑ Ⓒ Ⓓ	19 Ⓐ Ⓑ Ⓒ Ⓓ	24 Ⓐ Ⓑ Ⓒ Ⓓ
5 Ⓐ Ⓑ Ⓒ Ⓓ	10 Ⓐ Ⓑ Ⓒ Ⓓ	15 Ⓐ Ⓑ Ⓒ Ⓓ	20 Ⓐ Ⓑ Ⓒ Ⓓ	25 Ⓐ Ⓑ Ⓒ Ⓓ

EXERCISE 16: Redundancy

1 Ⓐ Ⓑ Ⓒ Ⓓ	6 Ⓐ Ⓑ Ⓒ Ⓓ	11 Ⓐ Ⓑ Ⓒ Ⓓ	16 Ⓐ Ⓑ Ⓒ Ⓓ	21 Ⓐ Ⓑ Ⓒ Ⓓ
2 Ⓐ Ⓑ Ⓒ Ⓓ	7 Ⓐ Ⓑ Ⓒ Ⓓ	12 Ⓐ Ⓑ Ⓒ Ⓓ	17 Ⓐ Ⓑ Ⓒ Ⓓ	22 Ⓐ Ⓑ Ⓒ Ⓓ
3 Ⓐ Ⓑ Ⓒ Ⓓ	8 Ⓐ Ⓑ Ⓒ Ⓓ	13 Ⓐ Ⓑ Ⓒ Ⓓ	18 Ⓐ Ⓑ Ⓒ Ⓓ	23 Ⓐ Ⓑ Ⓒ Ⓓ
4 Ⓐ Ⓑ Ⓒ Ⓓ	9 Ⓐ Ⓑ Ⓒ Ⓓ	14 Ⓐ Ⓑ Ⓒ Ⓓ	19 Ⓐ Ⓑ Ⓒ Ⓓ	24 Ⓐ Ⓑ Ⓒ Ⓓ
5 Ⓐ Ⓑ Ⓒ Ⓓ	10 Ⓐ Ⓑ Ⓒ Ⓓ	15 Ⓐ Ⓑ Ⓒ Ⓓ	20 Ⓐ Ⓑ Ⓒ Ⓓ	25 Ⓐ Ⓑ Ⓒ Ⓓ

EXERCISE 17: Word Choice

1 Ⓐ Ⓑ Ⓒ Ⓓ	6 Ⓐ Ⓑ Ⓒ Ⓓ	11 Ⓐ Ⓑ Ⓒ Ⓓ	16 Ⓐ Ⓑ Ⓒ Ⓓ	21 Ⓐ Ⓑ Ⓒ Ⓓ
2 Ⓐ Ⓑ Ⓒ Ⓓ	7 Ⓐ Ⓑ Ⓒ Ⓓ	12 Ⓐ Ⓑ Ⓒ Ⓓ	17 Ⓐ Ⓑ Ⓒ Ⓓ	22 Ⓐ Ⓑ Ⓒ Ⓓ
3 Ⓐ Ⓑ Ⓒ Ⓓ	8 Ⓐ Ⓑ Ⓒ Ⓓ	13 Ⓐ Ⓑ Ⓒ Ⓓ	18 Ⓐ Ⓑ Ⓒ Ⓓ	23 Ⓐ Ⓑ Ⓒ Ⓓ
4 Ⓐ Ⓑ Ⓒ Ⓓ	9 Ⓐ Ⓑ Ⓒ Ⓓ	14 Ⓐ Ⓑ Ⓒ Ⓓ	19 Ⓐ Ⓑ Ⓒ Ⓓ	24 Ⓐ Ⓑ Ⓒ Ⓓ
5 Ⓐ Ⓑ Ⓒ Ⓓ	10 Ⓐ Ⓑ Ⓒ Ⓓ	15 Ⓐ Ⓑ Ⓒ Ⓓ	20 Ⓐ Ⓑ Ⓒ Ⓓ	25 Ⓐ Ⓑ Ⓒ Ⓓ

EXERCISE 18: Structure

1 Ⓐ Ⓑ Ⓒ Ⓓ	6 Ⓐ Ⓑ Ⓒ Ⓓ	11 Ⓐ Ⓑ Ⓒ Ⓓ	16 Ⓐ Ⓑ Ⓒ Ⓓ	21 Ⓐ Ⓑ Ⓒ Ⓓ
2 Ⓐ Ⓑ Ⓒ Ⓓ	7 Ⓐ Ⓑ Ⓒ Ⓓ	12 Ⓐ Ⓑ Ⓒ Ⓓ	17 Ⓐ Ⓑ Ⓒ Ⓓ	22 Ⓐ Ⓑ Ⓒ Ⓓ
3 Ⓐ Ⓑ Ⓒ Ⓓ	8 Ⓐ Ⓑ Ⓒ Ⓓ	13 Ⓐ Ⓑ Ⓒ Ⓓ	18 Ⓐ Ⓑ Ⓒ Ⓓ	23 Ⓐ Ⓑ Ⓒ Ⓓ
4 Ⓐ Ⓑ Ⓒ Ⓓ	9 Ⓐ Ⓑ Ⓒ Ⓓ	14 Ⓐ Ⓑ Ⓒ Ⓓ	19 Ⓐ Ⓑ Ⓒ Ⓓ	24 Ⓐ Ⓑ Ⓒ Ⓓ
5 Ⓐ Ⓑ Ⓒ Ⓓ	10 Ⓐ Ⓑ Ⓒ Ⓓ	15 Ⓐ Ⓑ Ⓒ Ⓓ	20 Ⓐ Ⓑ Ⓒ Ⓓ	25 Ⓐ Ⓑ Ⓒ Ⓓ

EXERCISE 19: Cumulative Review (Part 1)

1 Ⓐ Ⓑ Ⓒ Ⓓ	6 Ⓐ Ⓑ Ⓒ Ⓓ	11 Ⓐ Ⓑ Ⓒ Ⓓ	16 Ⓐ Ⓑ Ⓒ Ⓓ	21 Ⓐ Ⓑ Ⓒ Ⓓ
2 Ⓐ Ⓑ Ⓒ Ⓓ	7 Ⓐ Ⓑ Ⓒ Ⓓ	12 Ⓐ Ⓑ Ⓒ Ⓓ	17 Ⓐ Ⓑ Ⓒ Ⓓ	22 Ⓐ Ⓑ Ⓒ Ⓓ
3 Ⓐ Ⓑ Ⓒ Ⓓ	8 Ⓐ Ⓑ Ⓒ Ⓓ	13 Ⓐ Ⓑ Ⓒ Ⓓ	18 Ⓐ Ⓑ Ⓒ Ⓓ	23 Ⓐ Ⓑ Ⓒ Ⓓ
4 Ⓐ Ⓑ Ⓒ Ⓓ	9 Ⓐ Ⓑ Ⓒ Ⓓ	14 Ⓐ Ⓑ Ⓒ Ⓓ	19 Ⓐ Ⓑ Ⓒ Ⓓ	24 Ⓐ Ⓑ Ⓒ Ⓓ
5 Ⓐ Ⓑ Ⓒ Ⓓ	10 Ⓐ Ⓑ Ⓒ Ⓓ	15 Ⓐ Ⓑ Ⓒ Ⓓ	20 Ⓐ Ⓑ Ⓒ Ⓓ	25 Ⓐ Ⓑ Ⓒ Ⓓ

EXERCISE 20: Cumulative Review (Part 2)

1 Ⓐ Ⓑ Ⓒ Ⓓ	6 Ⓐ Ⓑ Ⓒ Ⓓ	11 Ⓐ Ⓑ Ⓒ Ⓓ	16 Ⓐ Ⓑ Ⓒ Ⓓ	21 Ⓐ Ⓑ Ⓒ Ⓓ
2 Ⓐ Ⓑ Ⓒ Ⓓ	7 Ⓐ Ⓑ Ⓒ Ⓓ	12 Ⓐ Ⓑ Ⓒ Ⓓ	17 Ⓐ Ⓑ Ⓒ Ⓓ	22 Ⓐ Ⓑ Ⓒ Ⓓ
3 Ⓐ Ⓑ Ⓒ Ⓓ	8 Ⓐ Ⓑ Ⓒ Ⓓ	13 Ⓐ Ⓑ Ⓒ Ⓓ	18 Ⓐ Ⓑ Ⓒ Ⓓ	23 Ⓐ Ⓑ Ⓒ Ⓓ
4 Ⓐ Ⓑ Ⓒ Ⓓ	9 Ⓐ Ⓑ Ⓒ Ⓓ	14 Ⓐ Ⓑ Ⓒ Ⓓ	19 Ⓐ Ⓑ Ⓒ Ⓓ	24 Ⓐ Ⓑ Ⓒ Ⓓ
5 Ⓐ Ⓑ Ⓒ Ⓓ	10 Ⓐ Ⓑ Ⓒ Ⓓ	15 Ⓐ Ⓑ Ⓒ Ⓓ	20 Ⓐ Ⓑ Ⓒ Ⓓ	25 Ⓐ Ⓑ Ⓒ Ⓓ

Answer Sheet for Chapter 5

EXERCISE 1: General Interest Passages

Passage One	Passage Two	Passage Three	Passage Four	Passage Five
1 Ⓐ Ⓑ Ⓒ Ⓓ	1 Ⓐ Ⓑ Ⓒ Ⓓ	1 Ⓐ Ⓑ Ⓒ Ⓓ	1 Ⓐ Ⓑ Ⓒ Ⓓ	1 Ⓐ Ⓑ Ⓒ Ⓓ
2 Ⓐ Ⓑ Ⓒ Ⓓ	2 Ⓐ Ⓑ Ⓒ Ⓓ	2 Ⓐ Ⓑ Ⓒ Ⓓ	2 Ⓐ Ⓑ Ⓒ Ⓓ	2 Ⓐ Ⓑ Ⓒ Ⓓ
3 Ⓐ Ⓑ Ⓒ Ⓓ	3 Ⓐ Ⓑ Ⓒ Ⓓ	3 Ⓐ Ⓑ Ⓒ Ⓓ	3 Ⓐ Ⓑ Ⓒ Ⓓ	3 Ⓐ Ⓑ Ⓒ Ⓓ
4 Ⓐ Ⓑ Ⓒ Ⓓ	4 Ⓐ Ⓑ Ⓒ Ⓓ	4 Ⓐ Ⓑ Ⓒ Ⓓ	4 Ⓐ Ⓑ Ⓒ Ⓓ	4 Ⓐ Ⓑ Ⓒ Ⓓ
5 Ⓐ Ⓑ Ⓒ Ⓓ	5 Ⓐ Ⓑ Ⓒ Ⓓ	5 Ⓐ Ⓑ Ⓒ Ⓓ	5 Ⓐ Ⓑ Ⓒ Ⓓ	5 Ⓐ Ⓑ Ⓒ Ⓓ
6 Ⓐ Ⓑ Ⓒ Ⓓ	6 Ⓐ Ⓑ Ⓒ Ⓓ	6 Ⓐ Ⓑ Ⓒ Ⓓ	6 Ⓐ Ⓑ Ⓒ Ⓓ	6 Ⓐ Ⓑ Ⓒ Ⓓ

EXERCISE 2: Academic Information

Passage One	Passage Two	Passage Three	Passage Four	Passage Five
1 Ⓐ Ⓑ Ⓒ Ⓓ	1 Ⓐ Ⓑ Ⓒ Ⓓ	1 Ⓐ Ⓑ Ⓒ Ⓓ	1 Ⓐ Ⓑ Ⓒ Ⓓ	1 Ⓐ Ⓑ Ⓒ Ⓓ
2 Ⓐ Ⓑ Ⓒ Ⓓ	2 Ⓐ Ⓑ Ⓒ Ⓓ	2 Ⓐ Ⓑ Ⓒ Ⓓ	2 Ⓐ Ⓑ Ⓒ Ⓓ	2 Ⓐ Ⓑ Ⓒ Ⓓ
3 Ⓐ Ⓑ Ⓒ Ⓓ	3 Ⓐ Ⓑ Ⓒ Ⓓ	3 Ⓐ Ⓑ Ⓒ Ⓓ	3 Ⓐ Ⓑ Ⓒ Ⓓ	3 Ⓐ Ⓑ Ⓒ Ⓓ
4 Ⓐ Ⓑ Ⓒ Ⓓ	4 Ⓐ Ⓑ Ⓒ Ⓓ	4 Ⓐ Ⓑ Ⓒ Ⓓ	4 Ⓐ Ⓑ Ⓒ Ⓓ	4 Ⓐ Ⓑ Ⓒ Ⓓ
5 Ⓐ Ⓑ Ⓒ Ⓓ	5 Ⓐ Ⓑ Ⓒ Ⓓ	5 Ⓐ Ⓑ Ⓒ Ⓓ	5 Ⓐ Ⓑ Ⓒ Ⓓ	5 Ⓐ Ⓑ Ⓒ Ⓓ
6 Ⓐ Ⓑ Ⓒ Ⓓ	6 Ⓐ Ⓑ Ⓒ Ⓓ	6 Ⓐ Ⓑ Ⓒ Ⓓ	6 Ⓐ Ⓑ Ⓒ Ⓓ	6 Ⓐ Ⓑ Ⓒ Ⓓ

EXERCISE 3: Textbooks/Biography

Passage One	Passage Two	Passage Three	Passage Four	Passage Five
1 Ⓐ Ⓑ Ⓒ Ⓓ	1 Ⓐ Ⓑ Ⓒ Ⓓ	1 Ⓐ Ⓑ Ⓒ Ⓓ	1 Ⓐ Ⓑ Ⓒ Ⓓ	1 Ⓐ Ⓑ Ⓒ Ⓓ
2 Ⓐ Ⓑ Ⓒ Ⓓ	2 Ⓐ Ⓑ Ⓒ Ⓓ	2 Ⓐ Ⓑ Ⓒ Ⓓ	2 Ⓐ Ⓑ Ⓒ Ⓓ	2 Ⓐ Ⓑ Ⓒ Ⓓ
3 Ⓐ Ⓑ Ⓒ Ⓓ	3 Ⓐ Ⓑ Ⓒ Ⓓ	3 Ⓐ Ⓑ Ⓒ Ⓓ	3 Ⓐ Ⓑ Ⓒ Ⓓ	3 Ⓐ Ⓑ Ⓒ Ⓓ
4 Ⓐ Ⓑ Ⓒ Ⓓ	4 Ⓐ Ⓑ Ⓒ Ⓓ	4 Ⓐ Ⓑ Ⓒ Ⓓ	4 Ⓐ Ⓑ Ⓒ Ⓓ	4 Ⓐ Ⓑ Ⓒ Ⓓ
5 Ⓐ Ⓑ Ⓒ Ⓓ	5 Ⓐ Ⓑ Ⓒ Ⓓ	5 Ⓐ Ⓑ Ⓒ Ⓓ	5 Ⓐ Ⓑ Ⓒ Ⓓ	5 Ⓐ Ⓑ Ⓒ Ⓓ
6 Ⓐ Ⓑ Ⓒ Ⓓ	6 Ⓐ Ⓑ Ⓒ Ⓓ	6 Ⓐ Ⓑ Ⓒ Ⓓ	6 Ⓐ Ⓑ Ⓒ Ⓓ	6 Ⓐ Ⓑ Ⓒ Ⓓ

EXERCISE 4: Textbooks/History and Civics

Passage One	Passage Two	Passage Three	Passage Four	Passage Five
1 Ⓐ Ⓑ Ⓒ Ⓓ	1 Ⓐ Ⓑ Ⓒ Ⓓ	1 Ⓐ Ⓑ Ⓒ Ⓓ	1 Ⓐ Ⓑ Ⓒ Ⓓ	1 Ⓐ Ⓑ Ⓒ Ⓓ
2 Ⓐ Ⓑ Ⓒ Ⓓ	2 Ⓐ Ⓑ Ⓒ Ⓓ	2 Ⓐ Ⓑ Ⓒ Ⓓ	2 Ⓐ Ⓑ Ⓒ Ⓓ	2 Ⓐ Ⓑ Ⓒ Ⓓ
3 Ⓐ Ⓑ Ⓒ Ⓓ	3 Ⓐ Ⓑ Ⓒ Ⓓ	3 Ⓐ Ⓑ Ⓒ Ⓓ	3 Ⓐ Ⓑ Ⓒ Ⓓ	3 Ⓐ Ⓑ Ⓒ Ⓓ
4 Ⓐ Ⓑ Ⓒ Ⓓ	4 Ⓐ Ⓑ Ⓒ Ⓓ	4 Ⓐ Ⓑ Ⓒ Ⓓ	4 Ⓐ Ⓑ Ⓒ Ⓓ	4 Ⓐ Ⓑ Ⓒ Ⓓ
5 Ⓐ Ⓑ Ⓒ Ⓓ	5 Ⓐ Ⓑ Ⓒ Ⓓ	5 Ⓐ Ⓑ Ⓒ Ⓓ	5 Ⓐ Ⓑ Ⓒ Ⓓ	5 Ⓐ Ⓑ Ⓒ Ⓓ
6 Ⓐ Ⓑ Ⓒ Ⓓ	6 Ⓐ Ⓑ Ⓒ Ⓓ	6 Ⓐ Ⓑ Ⓒ Ⓓ	6 Ⓐ Ⓑ Ⓒ Ⓓ	6 Ⓐ Ⓑ Ⓒ Ⓓ

EXERCISE 5: Textbooks/Social Sciences

Passage One	Passage Two	Passage Three	Passage Four	Passage Five
1 Ⓐ Ⓑ Ⓒ Ⓓ	1 Ⓐ Ⓑ Ⓒ Ⓓ	1 Ⓐ Ⓑ Ⓒ Ⓓ	1 Ⓐ Ⓑ Ⓒ Ⓓ	1 Ⓐ Ⓑ Ⓒ Ⓓ
2 Ⓐ Ⓑ Ⓒ Ⓓ	2 Ⓐ Ⓑ Ⓒ Ⓓ	2 Ⓐ Ⓑ Ⓒ Ⓓ	2 Ⓐ Ⓑ Ⓒ Ⓓ	2 Ⓐ Ⓑ Ⓒ Ⓓ
3 Ⓐ Ⓑ Ⓒ Ⓓ	3 Ⓐ Ⓑ Ⓒ Ⓓ	3 Ⓐ Ⓑ Ⓒ Ⓓ	3 Ⓐ Ⓑ Ⓒ Ⓓ	3 Ⓐ Ⓑ Ⓒ Ⓓ
4 Ⓐ Ⓑ Ⓒ Ⓓ	4 Ⓐ Ⓑ Ⓒ Ⓓ	4 Ⓐ Ⓑ Ⓒ Ⓓ	4 Ⓐ Ⓑ Ⓒ Ⓓ	4 Ⓐ Ⓑ Ⓒ Ⓓ
5 Ⓐ Ⓑ Ⓒ Ⓓ	5 Ⓐ Ⓑ Ⓒ Ⓓ	5 Ⓐ Ⓑ Ⓒ Ⓓ	5 Ⓐ Ⓑ Ⓒ Ⓓ	5 Ⓐ Ⓑ Ⓒ Ⓓ
6 Ⓐ Ⓑ Ⓒ Ⓓ	6 Ⓐ Ⓑ Ⓒ Ⓓ	6 Ⓐ Ⓑ Ⓒ Ⓓ	6 Ⓐ Ⓑ Ⓒ Ⓓ	6 Ⓐ Ⓑ Ⓒ Ⓓ

EXERCISE 6: Textbooks/Literature

Passage One	Passage Two	Passage Three	Passage Four	Passage Five
1 Ⓐ Ⓑ Ⓒ Ⓓ	1 Ⓐ Ⓑ Ⓒ Ⓓ	1 Ⓐ Ⓑ Ⓒ Ⓓ	1 Ⓐ Ⓑ Ⓒ Ⓓ	1 Ⓐ Ⓑ Ⓒ Ⓓ
2 Ⓐ Ⓑ Ⓒ Ⓓ	2 Ⓐ Ⓑ Ⓒ Ⓓ	2 Ⓐ Ⓑ Ⓒ Ⓓ	2 Ⓐ Ⓑ Ⓒ Ⓓ	2 Ⓐ Ⓑ Ⓒ Ⓓ
3 Ⓐ Ⓑ Ⓒ Ⓓ	3 Ⓐ Ⓑ Ⓒ Ⓓ	3 Ⓐ Ⓑ Ⓒ Ⓓ	3 Ⓐ Ⓑ Ⓒ Ⓓ	3 Ⓐ Ⓑ Ⓒ Ⓓ
4 Ⓐ Ⓑ Ⓒ Ⓓ	4 Ⓐ Ⓑ Ⓒ Ⓓ	4 Ⓐ Ⓑ Ⓒ Ⓓ	4 Ⓐ Ⓑ Ⓒ Ⓓ	4 Ⓐ Ⓑ Ⓒ Ⓓ
5 Ⓐ Ⓑ Ⓒ Ⓓ	5 Ⓐ Ⓑ Ⓒ Ⓓ	5 Ⓐ Ⓑ Ⓒ Ⓓ	5 Ⓐ Ⓑ Ⓒ Ⓓ	5 Ⓐ Ⓑ Ⓒ Ⓓ
6 Ⓐ Ⓑ Ⓒ Ⓓ	6 Ⓐ Ⓑ Ⓒ Ⓓ	6 Ⓐ Ⓑ Ⓒ Ⓓ	6 Ⓐ Ⓑ Ⓒ Ⓓ	6 Ⓐ Ⓑ Ⓒ Ⓓ

EXERCISE 7: Textbooks/Arts and Entertainment

Passage One	Passage Two	Passage Three	Passage Four	Passage Five
1 Ⓐ Ⓑ Ⓒ Ⓓ	1 Ⓐ Ⓑ Ⓒ Ⓓ	1 Ⓐ Ⓑ Ⓒ Ⓓ	1 Ⓐ Ⓑ Ⓒ Ⓓ	1 Ⓐ Ⓑ Ⓒ Ⓓ
2 Ⓐ Ⓑ Ⓒ Ⓓ	2 Ⓐ Ⓑ Ⓒ Ⓓ	2 Ⓐ Ⓑ Ⓒ Ⓓ	2 Ⓐ Ⓑ Ⓒ Ⓓ	2 Ⓐ Ⓑ Ⓒ Ⓓ
3 Ⓐ Ⓑ Ⓒ Ⓓ	3 Ⓐ Ⓑ Ⓒ Ⓓ	3 Ⓐ Ⓑ Ⓒ Ⓓ	3 Ⓐ Ⓑ Ⓒ Ⓓ	3 Ⓐ Ⓑ Ⓒ Ⓓ
4 Ⓐ Ⓑ Ⓒ Ⓓ	4 Ⓐ Ⓑ Ⓒ Ⓓ	4 Ⓐ Ⓑ Ⓒ Ⓓ	4 Ⓐ Ⓑ Ⓒ Ⓓ	4 Ⓐ Ⓑ Ⓒ Ⓓ
5 Ⓐ Ⓑ Ⓒ Ⓓ	5 Ⓐ Ⓑ Ⓒ Ⓓ	5 Ⓐ Ⓑ Ⓒ Ⓓ	5 Ⓐ Ⓑ Ⓒ Ⓓ	5 Ⓐ Ⓑ Ⓒ Ⓓ
6 Ⓐ Ⓑ Ⓒ Ⓓ	6 Ⓐ Ⓑ Ⓒ Ⓓ	6 Ⓐ Ⓑ Ⓒ Ⓓ	6 Ⓐ Ⓑ Ⓒ Ⓓ	6 Ⓐ Ⓑ Ⓒ Ⓓ

EXERCISE 8: Textbooks/Popular Culture

Passage One	Passage Two	Passage Three	Passage Four	Passage Five
1 Ⓐ Ⓑ Ⓒ Ⓓ	1 Ⓐ Ⓑ Ⓒ Ⓓ	1 Ⓐ Ⓑ Ⓒ Ⓓ	1 Ⓐ Ⓑ Ⓒ Ⓓ	1 Ⓐ Ⓑ Ⓒ Ⓓ
2 Ⓐ Ⓑ Ⓒ Ⓓ	2 Ⓐ Ⓑ Ⓒ Ⓓ	2 Ⓐ Ⓑ Ⓒ Ⓓ	2 Ⓐ Ⓑ Ⓒ Ⓓ	2 Ⓐ Ⓑ Ⓒ Ⓓ
3 Ⓐ Ⓑ Ⓒ Ⓓ	3 Ⓐ Ⓑ Ⓒ Ⓓ	3 Ⓐ Ⓑ Ⓒ Ⓓ	3 Ⓐ Ⓑ Ⓒ Ⓓ	3 Ⓐ Ⓑ Ⓒ Ⓓ
4 Ⓐ Ⓑ Ⓒ Ⓓ	4 Ⓐ Ⓑ Ⓒ Ⓓ	4 Ⓐ Ⓑ Ⓒ Ⓓ	4 Ⓐ Ⓑ Ⓒ Ⓓ	4 Ⓐ Ⓑ Ⓒ Ⓓ
5 Ⓐ Ⓑ Ⓒ Ⓓ	5 Ⓐ Ⓑ Ⓒ Ⓓ	5 Ⓐ Ⓑ Ⓒ Ⓓ	5 Ⓐ Ⓑ Ⓒ Ⓓ	5 Ⓐ Ⓑ Ⓒ Ⓓ
6 Ⓐ Ⓑ Ⓒ Ⓓ	6 Ⓐ Ⓑ Ⓒ Ⓓ	6 Ⓐ Ⓑ Ⓒ Ⓓ	6 Ⓐ Ⓑ Ⓒ Ⓓ	6 Ⓐ Ⓑ Ⓒ Ⓓ

EXERCISE 9: Textbooks/Business

Passage One	Passage Two	Passage Three	Passage Four	Passage Five
1 Ⓐ Ⓑ Ⓒ Ⓓ	1 Ⓐ Ⓑ Ⓒ Ⓓ	1 Ⓐ Ⓑ Ⓒ Ⓓ	1 Ⓐ Ⓑ Ⓒ Ⓓ	1 Ⓐ Ⓑ Ⓒ Ⓓ
2 Ⓐ Ⓑ Ⓒ Ⓓ	2 Ⓐ Ⓑ Ⓒ Ⓓ	2 Ⓐ Ⓑ Ⓒ Ⓓ	2 Ⓐ Ⓑ Ⓒ Ⓓ	2 Ⓐ Ⓑ Ⓒ Ⓓ
3 Ⓐ Ⓑ Ⓒ Ⓓ	3 Ⓐ Ⓑ Ⓒ Ⓓ	3 Ⓐ Ⓑ Ⓒ Ⓓ	3 Ⓐ Ⓑ Ⓒ Ⓓ	3 Ⓐ Ⓑ Ⓒ Ⓓ
4 Ⓐ Ⓑ Ⓒ Ⓓ	4 Ⓐ Ⓑ Ⓒ Ⓓ	4 Ⓐ Ⓑ Ⓒ Ⓓ	4 Ⓐ Ⓑ Ⓒ Ⓓ	4 Ⓐ Ⓑ Ⓒ Ⓓ
5 Ⓐ Ⓑ Ⓒ Ⓓ	5 Ⓐ Ⓑ Ⓒ Ⓓ	5 Ⓐ Ⓑ Ⓒ Ⓓ	5 Ⓐ Ⓑ Ⓒ Ⓓ	5 Ⓐ Ⓑ Ⓒ Ⓓ
6 Ⓐ Ⓑ Ⓒ Ⓓ	6 Ⓐ Ⓑ Ⓒ Ⓓ	6 Ⓐ Ⓑ Ⓒ Ⓓ	6 Ⓐ Ⓑ Ⓒ Ⓓ	6 Ⓐ Ⓑ Ⓒ Ⓓ

EXERCISE 10: Textbooks/Natural Sciences

Passage One	Passage Two	Passage Three	Passage Four	Passage Five
1 Ⓐ Ⓑ Ⓒ Ⓓ	1 Ⓐ Ⓑ Ⓒ Ⓓ	1 Ⓐ Ⓑ Ⓒ Ⓓ	1 Ⓐ Ⓑ Ⓒ Ⓓ	1 Ⓐ Ⓑ Ⓒ Ⓓ
2 Ⓐ Ⓑ Ⓒ Ⓓ	2 Ⓐ Ⓑ Ⓒ Ⓓ	2 Ⓐ Ⓑ Ⓒ Ⓓ	2 Ⓐ Ⓑ Ⓒ Ⓓ	2 Ⓐ Ⓑ Ⓒ Ⓓ
3 Ⓐ Ⓑ Ⓒ Ⓓ	3 Ⓐ Ⓑ Ⓒ Ⓓ	3 Ⓐ Ⓑ Ⓒ Ⓓ	3 Ⓐ Ⓑ Ⓒ Ⓓ	3 Ⓐ Ⓑ Ⓒ Ⓓ
4 Ⓐ Ⓑ Ⓒ Ⓓ	4 Ⓐ Ⓑ Ⓒ Ⓓ	4 Ⓐ Ⓑ Ⓒ Ⓓ	4 Ⓐ Ⓑ Ⓒ Ⓓ	4 Ⓐ Ⓑ Ⓒ Ⓓ
5 Ⓐ Ⓑ Ⓒ Ⓓ	5 Ⓐ Ⓑ Ⓒ Ⓓ	5 Ⓐ Ⓑ Ⓒ Ⓓ	5 Ⓐ Ⓑ Ⓒ Ⓓ	5 Ⓐ Ⓑ Ⓒ Ⓓ
6 Ⓐ Ⓑ Ⓒ Ⓓ	6 Ⓐ Ⓑ Ⓒ Ⓓ	6 Ⓐ Ⓑ Ⓒ Ⓓ	6 Ⓐ Ⓑ Ⓒ Ⓓ	6 Ⓐ Ⓑ Ⓒ Ⓓ

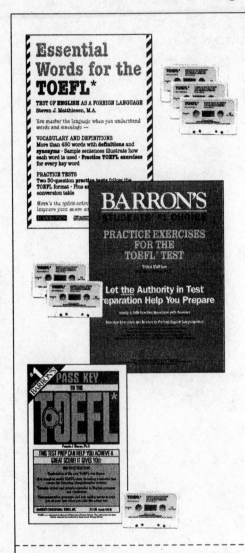

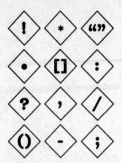

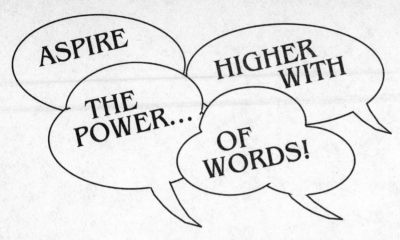

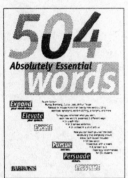

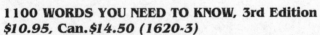
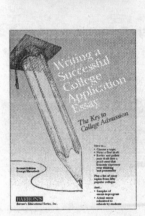
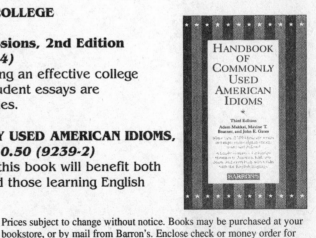

No One Can Build
Your Writing Skills Better
Than We Can...

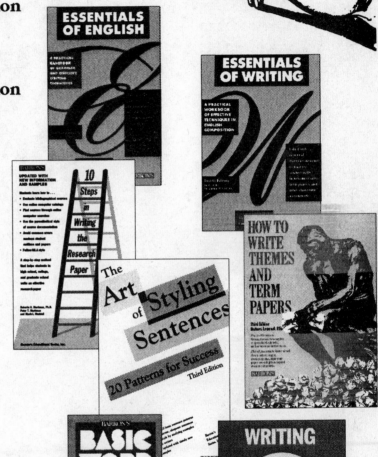